Everyman, I wi...
and be thy guide

D0924224

H. G. Wells

KIPPS

The Story of a Simple Soul

Edited by
PETER VANSITTART

EVERYMAN
J. M. DENT · LONDON
CHARLES E. TUTTLE
VERMONT

Introduction and other critical apparatus
© J. M. Dent 1993

First published in Everyman by J. M. Dent 1993

Made in Great Britain by
The Guernsey Press Co. Ltd,
Guernsey, C. I.

for
J. M. Dent
Orion Publishing Group
Orion House
5 Upper St Martin's Lane, London WC2H 9EA

and
Charles E. Tuttle Co. Inc
28 South Main Street, Rutland, Vermont
05071, USA

British Library Cataloguing in Publication Data is available
upon request

ISBN 0 460 87277 X

Everyman's Library
Reg. US Patent Office

CONTENTS

NOTE ON THE AUTHOR AND EDITOR

H. G. WELLS was born in Bromley, Kent in 1866. After work-ing as a draper's apprentice and pupil-teacher, he won a scholarship to the Normal School of Science, South Kensington, in 1884, studying under T. H. Huxley. He was awarded a first-class honours degree in biology and resumed teaching, but had to retire after a kick from an ill-natured pupil, at football, afflicted his kidneys. He worked in poverty in London as a crammer while experimenting in journalism and stories, and published textbooks on biology and physiography (1893), but it was *The Time Machine* (1895) that launched his literary career. Many scientific romances and short stories began to be paral-leled with sociological and political books and tracts, notably *Anticipations* (1901), *Mankind in the Making* (1903), *A Modern Utopia* (1905). His full-length, largely autobiographical novels began with *Love and Mr Lewisham* (1900), *Kipps* (1905), *Tono-Bungay* and *Ann Veronica* (1909), the last promoting the outspoken, socially and sexually liberated 'New Woman'. He married his cousin Isabel in 1891, but later eloped with, and subsequently married, Catherine Robbins, 'Jane'. A constant philanderer, he invited scandal by including his lightly concealed private affairs in *Ann Veronica* and *The New Machiavelli* (1911). Shaw and the Webbs had invited him into the Fabian Society and soon regretted it. Wells increasingly used fiction as a platform for the ideas and visions of a world-state which preoccupied him, but he foresaw that the Novel itself would decline, to be replaced by candid autobiography. After about 1920, critical attention was turning towards his natural succes-sor Aldous Huxley and the 'pure' non-journalistic novels of Joyce and Virginia Woolf. His mass public dwindled, though it welcomed *The Outline of History*, of that year, and long continued to do so. The Second World War and the cataclysm of Hiroshima confirmed the pessimism which had throughout accompanied his exuberant hopes and visions. His last book was titled, with some personal significance, *Mind at the End of its Tether* (1945), but his vigour continued almost to his death in 1946. In his last two decades he had produced some forty books.

PETER VANSITTART, born in 1920, is the author of twenty-five novels and many works of non-fiction, including an autobiography, *Paths from a White Horse* (1985) and an account of English history for children, *Green Knights, Black Angels: the Mosaic of History* (1969), as well as *Worlds and Underworlds:Anglo-European History Through the Centuries* (1974); *London:A Literary Companion* (1992), and *The Ancient Mariner and the Old Sailor: Delights and Uses of the English Language* (1985). He has also compiled several anthologies, including *Voices from the Great War* (1981) and *Voices from the Revolution* (1989), and edited John Masefield's *Letters from the Front:1915–1917* (1984) and John Buchan's posthumous *These for Remembrance* (1987).

NOTE ON THE TEXT

Kipps developed from an earlier story, *The Wealth of Mr Waddy*, which was left incomplete and then abandoned, but published posthumously by Wilson, Harris, at Carbondale, Illinois.

The text of *Kipps* used here is that of the first edition, published by Macmillan in 1905, which carried the prefatory note:

Kipps is essentially a novel, and is designed to present a typical member of the English lower middle-class in all its limitations and feebleness. Beneath a treatment deliberately kindly and genial, the book provides a sustained and exhaustive criticism of the ideals and ways of life of the great mass of middle-class English people.

CHRONOLOGY OF WELLS'S LIFE

Year	Age	Life
1865		
1866		Born 21 September, Bromley, Kent, to a working class family: father a gardener, shopkeeper and cricketer; mother a maid and housekeeper
1867		
1868		
1869		
1870		
1871		
1872		
1873	7	Entered Thomas Morley's Bromley Academy
1874		
1875		
1876		

CHRONOLOGY OF HIS TIMES

Year	Arts & Science	History & Politics
1865	Mendel's *Law of Heredity*	End of American Civil War; Lincoln assassinated
1866	Dostoevsky's *Crime and Punishment*	Russia defeated Austria at Sadowa
1867	Ibsen's *Peer Gynt*; Lister experiments with sterile surgery	Dominion of Canada founded
1868	Browning's *The Ring and the Book*; typewriter first patented	Gladstone Prime Minister
1869	Jules Verne's *20,000 Leagues Under the Sea*; Flaubert's *Education Sentimentale*; John Stuart Mill's *On the Subjection of Women*	Suez Canal opened
1870	Charles Dickens dies; T. H. Huxley's *Theory of Biogenesis*	Franco-Prussian War; Prussia defeats France at Sedan; fall of Napoleon III; Education Act, introducing elementary education for 5–13 year olds
1871	Lewis Carroll's *Alice Through the Looking Glass*; George Eliot's *Middlemarch*; Charles Darwin's *The Descent of Man*	Paris Commune suppressed; the Chicago Fire; unification of Germany
1872	Edison's duplex telegraph	The Secret Ballot Act
1873	Tolstoy's *Anna Karenina*; James Clarke Maxwell's *Electricity and Magnetism*	Napoleon III dies in exile in Kent; David Livingstone dies in what is now Zambia
1874	Thomas Hardy's *Far from the Madding Crowd*; First Impressionist exhibition in Paris	Disraeli Prime Minister; Factory Act introduces fifty-six and a half hour week
1875	Bizet's *Carmen*	London Medical School for Women founded
1876	Alexander Graham Bell's telephone; Twain's *Tom Sawyer*	Battle of Little Bighorn; death of General Custer; Queen Victoria becomes Empress of India

Year	Age	Life
1877		
1879		
1880	14	Apprenticed to Rodgers and Benyer, Drapers, at Windsor
1881	15	Pupil-teacher at Alfred Williams' school at Wookey, Somerset; pupil at Midhurst Grammar School; apprenticed to Southsea Drapery Emporium
1882		
1883–4		Under-master at Midhurst Grammar School; wins scholarship and bursary at Normal School of Science, South Kensington
1884–7		Studies under T. H. Huxley at the Normal School of Science; begins to write; first published work appears in May 1887 in the *Science Schools Journal* – *A Tale of the Twentieth Century*
1887	20	Teacher at Holt Academy, Wrexham
1888	22	Returns to London after illness, working as a teacher; *The Chronic Argonauts* published in *Science Schools Journal*
1889		
1890	24	B.Sci degree
1891	25	Tutor for University Correspondence College; marries his cousin, Isabel Wells; *The Rediscovery of the Unique* published in the *Fortnightly Review*

Year	Arts & Science	History & Politics
1877	Thomas Edison's phonograph	Britain annexes the Transvaal
1879	Dostoevsky's *The Brothers Karamazov*	Zulu Wars, South Africa
1880	Electric light devised by T. A. Edison (USA) and by J. W. Swan (Scotland)	Boer uprising in the Transvaal
1881	Henry James's *Portrait of a Lady*	President Garfield murdered, USA
1882	R. L. Stevenson's *Treasure Island*	Married Woman's Property Act
1883	Death of Karl Marx; William Thomson (later, Lord Kelvin) publishes *On the Size of Atoms*; first skyscraper in Chicago	Fabian Society founded
1884	Twain's *Huckleberry Finn*; invention of Maxim machine gun	Berlin Conference on division of Africa; Gladstone's Reform Act extends vote to country householders
1885	Zola's *Germinal*; Pasteur's vaccine to cure hydrophobia; Karl Benz's automobile	Battle of Khartoum; Death of General Gordon
1886	R. L. Stevenson's *Dr Jekyll and Mr Hyde*; Rimbaud's *Les Illuminations*	Lord Salisbury Prime Minister
1887	H. W. Goodwin's celluloid film invented; speed of light measured	Queen Victoria's Golden Jubilee
1888	Kipling's *Plain Tales from the Hills*; Eastman's box camera; Dunlop's pneumatic tyre; Hertz discovers electromagnetic waves	Kaiser Frederick III dies after only three months as Emperor of Germany; accession of Wilhelm II
1889	Death of Robert Browning; T. H. Huxley's *Agnosticism*; Eiffel Tower built	Archduke Rudolf, heir to the Emperor, commits suicide at Mayerling, Austria
1890	Emily Dickinson's *Poems*; discovery of tetanus and diptheria viruses	Bismarck dismissed by the Kaiser; the 'O'Shea' scandal; Charles Parnell resigns as leader of Irish party
1891	Wilde's *The Picture of Dorian Grey*; Hardy's *Tess of the D'Urbervilles*	

Year	Age	Life
1892	26	Meets Amy Catherine Robbins – 'Jane'
1893	27	Elopes with Jane; in poor health; first published book, *A Text Book of Biology*; lives by writing for the rest of his life
1894		
1895	29	Marries Jane; they settle in Woking; meets George Bernard Shaw; *The Time Machine*; *Select Conversations with an Uncle*; *The Wonderful Visit*; *The Stolen Bacillus*
1896	30	*The Island of Doctor Moreau*; *The Wheels of Chance*; meets George Gissing
1897	31	*The Invisible Man*; *The Plattner Story and Others*; *Thirty Strange Stories*; *The Star*
1898	32	In poor health again; travels to Italy; meets Edmund Gosse, Henry James, Joseph Conrad, J. M. Barrie; *The War of the Worlds*
1899	33	*When the Sleeper Awakes*; *Tales of Space and Time*
1900	34	Now rich enough to have house built at Sandgate, Kent; *Love and Mr Lewisham*
1901	35	*Anticipations*; *The First Men in the Moon*; birth of first son 'Gip', G. P. Wells

Year	Arts & Science	History & Politics
1892	Kipling's *Barrack Room Ballads*; Diesel's internal combustion engine	Keir Hardie wins first seat in Parliament for Labour (ILP)
1893	Henry Ford's first automobile	Gladstone's Irish Home Rule Bill defeated
1894	Shaw's *Arms and the Man*; Edison's Kinetoscope Parlour, New York; Emile Berliner's gramophone disc	Death of Alexander III, Tsar of Russia; accession of Nicholas II
1895	Conrad's *Almayer's Folly*; Freud's *Studies in Hysteria*; Wilhelm Rontgen introduces X-rays; Gillette's safety razor.	Hispano–Cuban war; London School of Economics founded; Jameson Raid, South Africa
1896	Chekhov's *The Sea Gull*; Nobel Prizes instituted; William Ramsay discovers helium. Rutherford publishes researches into magnetic detection of electrical waves; Becquerel determines radioactivity of Uranium	Cecil Rhodes resigns as PM of Cape Colony
1897	Shaw's *Candida*; The Webbs's *Industrial Democracy*; Havelock Ellis's *Studies in the Psychology of Sex*; Robert Ross discovers the cause of malaria; Marconi's first radio transmission	Queen Victoria's Diamond Jubilee; Indian revolt on North West Frontier
1898	Zola's *J'Accuse*; Wilde's *The Ballad of Reading Gaol*; Henry James's *The Turn of the Screw*; the Curies discover radium	Cuban–American War; death of Bismarck; Battle of Omdurman, Sudan; General Kitchener retakes Khartoum
1899	Wilde's *The Importance of Being Earnest*	Dreyfus pardoned; Boer War begins
1900	Conrad's *Lord Jim*; Chekhov's *Uncle Vanya*; Freud's *The Interpretation of Dreams*; Planck's Quantum Theory; deaths of Ruskin and Wilde	Boxer Rebellion in China
1901	Kipling's *Kim*; Thomas Mann's *Buddenbrooks*; Marconi transmits radio communication across the Atlantic	Assassination of President McKinley, USA; Theodore Roosevelt succeeds; Queen Victoria dies; accession of Edward VII

Year	Age	Life
1902	36	*The Sea Lady*; *The Discovery of the Future*
1903	37	Joins Fabian Society, the Coefficients, and the Reform Club; birth of second son, Frank; *Twelve Stories and a Dream*; *Mankind in the Making*
1904	38	*The Food of the Gods*
1905	39	*Kipps*; *A Modern Utopia*
1906	40	Affairs with Amber Reeves and Rosamund Bland; meets Gorky in New York; *In the Days of the Comet*; *Socialism and the Family*; *The Future in America*; *This Misery of Boots*; *The So-called Science of Sociology*
1907		
1908	42	Resigns from the Fabians; *First and Last Things*; *The War in the Air*; *New Worlds for Old*
1909	43	Birth of Wells's daughter, Anna, to Amber Reeves; Wells and Jane move to Hampstead; *Tono-Bungay*; *Ann Veronica*
1910	44	*The History of Mr Polly*

Year	Arts & Science	History & Politics
1902	Conrad's *Heart of Darkness*; Bennett's *Anna of the Five Towns*; William James's *The Varieties of Religious Experience*; Caruso's first record	End of the Boer War
1903	The Wright Brothers succeed in powered flight; Henry Ford starts Ford Motors; Samuel Butler's *The Way of All Flesh*; Shaw's *Man & Superman*	Bolshevik–Menshevik split in Russian socialists; Lenin becomes Bolshevik leader
1904	Picasso's *The Two Sisters*; Freud's *The Psychopathology of Everyday Life*; Chekhov's *The Cherry Orchard*	Russo–Japanese War begins; Theodore Roosevelt re-elected
1905	Einstein's Special Theory of Relativity; Debussy's *La Mer* Cezanne's *Les Grandes; Baigneuses*; Edith Wharton's *House of Mirth*; Shaw's *Major Barbara* forbidden by New York police	Russia defeated by Japan; riots in St Petersburg, 'the Potemkin' mutinies
1906	J. J. Thompson wins Nobel Prize for Physics	American occupation of Cuba; Liberal victory in General Election – maj. 218; Labour win 54 seats
1907	First Cubist exhibition in Paris; Kipling's Nobel Prize for Literature; Conrad's *The Secret Agent*	Defeat of Labour bill to give votes to women; arrest of fifty-seven suffragettes in London
1908	Arnold Bennett's *The Old Wives' Tale*; E. M. Forster's *A Room with a View*; Rutherford wins Nobel Prize for Physics; Wright Brothers tour Europe	Asquith Prime Minister; Mrs Pankhurst imprisoned
1909	Diaghilev's Russian Ballet in Paris; Peary Expedition at North Pole; Bleriot flies the Channel	Murderer Dr Crippen arrested
1910	Marie Curie's *Treatise on Radiography*; Stravinsky's *Firebird*; Roger Fry's Post–Impressionist Exhibition in London; E. M. Forster's *Howard's End*; Tolstoy dies	Death of Edward VII; accession of George V

Year	Arts & Science	History & Politics
1911	Amundsen at South Pole; Rutherford's *Theory of Atomic Structure*; D. H. Lawrence's *The White Peacock*; Ezra Pound's *Cantos*; Rupert Brooke's *Poems*	Lords Reform Bill passed in Lords after intervention of the King; Liberals announce first measures for National Insurance
1912	Schoenberg's *Pierrot Lunaire*; Jung's *The Theory of Psychoanalysis*	The *Titanic* disaster; Woodrow Wilson elected US President
1913	Vitamin A isolated at Yale, by Elmer McCollum; Lawrence's *Sons and Lovers*	Panama Canal opened; hunger strikes by Suffragettes in prison
1914	J. H. Jean's *Radiation and the Quantum Theory*; James Joyce's *Dubliners*	Assassination of Archduke Franz Ferdinand of Austria in Sarajevo; the Great War starts
1915	D. W. Griffith's film *Birth of a Nation*; Somerset Maugham's *Of Human Bondage*; Lawrence's *The Rainbow* banned; Joseph Conrad's *Victory*	The Allied failure at Gallipoli; Zeppelins attack London; The *Lusitania* sinking; Coalition Government formed in Britain
1916	Death of Henry James; James Joyce's *Portrait of the Artist as a Young Man*; Dadaism in Zurich	The battle of Verdun; the Easter Rising, Dublin; Battle of Jutland; President Wilson's plea for peace; Lloyd George Prime Minister
1917	Freud's *Introduction to Psychoanalysis*; T. S. Eliot's *Prufrock*	America enters the war; Russian Revolution; Lenin in power; Woodrow Wilson re-elected
1918	Matisse's *Odalisques*; Joyce's *Ulysses*	Collapse of the Central Powers ends the Great War; Versailles Peace Conference; vote given to women over thirty and men over twenty-one; first woman elected to Parliament – Countess Markiewicz (Sinn Fein)
1919	Thomas H. Morgan's *The Physical Basis of Heredity*; Thomas Hardy's *Collected Poems*; Maugham's *The Moon and Sixpence*; J. M. Keynes's *The Economic Consequences of the Peace*; Bauhaus founded; Alcock and Brown fly the Atlantic	Herbert Hoover takes control of European Relief; Prohibition in America; Versailles Treaty signed; President Wilson awarded Nobel Peace Prize; socialist uprising in Berlin crushed by troops; murder of Rosa Luxembourg

Year	Age	Life
1920	54	Visits Russia; meets Lenin and Moura Budberg; *The Outline of History*; *Russia in the Shadows*
1921	55	Visits USA; *The Salvaging of Civilization*
1922	56	*A Short History of the World*; *The Secret Places of the Heart*; unsuccessful as a Labour Parliamentary candidate for London University
1923	57	*Men Like Gods*; *The Story of a Great Schoolmaster*; *The Dream*; stands for Parliament again but defeated
1924	58	Begins affair with Odette Keun
1925	59	*Christina Alberta's Father*
1926	60	*The World of William Clissold*
1927	61	Death of Jane Wells; *Meanwhile*; *Collected Short Stories*; *Democracy Under Revision*; collected H. G. Wells (Atlantic edition) completed in USA
1928	62	*The Open Conspiracy: Blue Prints for a World Revolution*; *Mr Blettsworthy on Rampole Island*; introduction to *The Book of Catherine Wells*

Year	Arts & Science	History & Politics
1920	Eddington's *Space, Time and Gravitation*; F. Scott Fitzgerald's *This Side of Paradise*; Sinclair Lewis's *Main Street*; Edith Wharton's *The Age of Innocence*	America rejects the League of Nations; National Socialist Workers party (NAZI) publishes manifesto, Germany
1921	Einstein wins Nobel Prize for Physics	Victory of Red Army in Russian Civil War
1922	T. S. Eliot's *The Waste Land*; first transmissions by BBC	Mussolini establishes dictatorship in Italy; Irish Free State established
1923	Gershwin's *Rhapsody in Blue*; E. N. da C. Andrade's *The Structure of the Atom*; Freud's *The Ego and the Id*; W. B. Yeats awarded Nobel Prize for Literature	Hitler's NAZI coup fails in Munich; Stanley Baldwin Prime Minister; Matrimonial Bill passed, allowing wives to divorce husbands; British Mandate in Palestine
1924	E. M. Forster's *A Passage to India*; Thomas Mann's *Magic Mountain*	Lenin dies; Minority Labour government; Ramsay MacDonald Prime Minister
1925	John Logie Baird's successful television experiments; Einstein's film *Battleship Potemkin*; Chaplin's *The Gold Rush*; Fitzgerald's *The Great Gatsby*	Hitler publishes *Mein Kampf*
1926	Fritz Lang's film *Metropolis*; William Faulkner's *Soldier's Pay*; Kafka's *The Castle*; Hemingway's *The Sun also Rises*; R. H. Tawney's *Religion and the Rise of Capitalism*	British troops withdraw from the Rhineland; British Commonwealth instituted; General Strike
1927	Lindbergh's flight from New York to Paris; Abel Gance's film *Napoleon*; Virginia Woolf's *The Lighthouse*; *The Jazz Singer* (first talkie); completion of Proust's *A la Recherche du Temps Perdu*	Trotsky expelled from Russian Communist Party
1928	J. L. Baird demonstrates colour TV; Eisenstein's film *October*	Vote given to women over twenty-one – equal rights; Chiang Kai-shek President of China

Year	Age	Life
1929	63	First broadcasts on BBC; *The Autocracy Of Mr Parham*; *The Adventures of Tommy* (for children); film script of *The King Who Was a King*
1930	64	Moves back to London
1931	65	*The Science of Life* (A Summary of Contemporary Knowledge about Life and its Possibilities with Julian Huxley and G. P. Wells); diagnosed as diabetic; *What Are We To Do With Our Lives?*
1932	66	*The Bulpington of Bulp*; *The Work, Wealth and Happiness of Mankind*
1933	67	Begins affair with Moura Budberg; *The Shape of Things to Come*
1934	68	Talks with Stalin and with F. D. Roosevelt; *Experiment in Autobiography*
1935	69	Works with Alexander Korda on film version of *The Shape of Things to Come*; *The New America*

Year	Arts & Science	History & Politics
1929	Robert Graves's *Goodbye to All That*; Hemingway's *A Farewell to Arms*; Thomas Mann wins Nobel Prize for Literature	Crash of New York Stock Exchange, Wall Street; Second Minority Labour Government; thirteen women elected to Parliament; NAZI victory in Bavarian elections
1930	Freud's *Civilization and its Discontents*; W. H. Auden's *Poems*; Robert Frost's *Collected Poems*; Sinclair Lewis wins Nobel Prize for Literature; Amy Johnson's flight from London to Australia; death of DH Lawrence	Haile Selassie (Ras Tafari) becomes Emperor of Ethiopia; Gandhi's Salt March, India; NAZI party becomes second largest in Germany
1931	Death of Edison; Empire State Building completed; Chaplin's *City Lights*; Schweitzer's *My Life and Thoughts*; Faulkner's *Sanctuary*	World slump begins with the collapse of the Credit Anstadt bank, Vienna; first woman elected to the American Senate; National Government, Britain
1932	James Chadwick discovers the neutron; Fritz Lang's film of Huxley's *Brave New World*; Galsworthy's Nobel Prize for Literature	Franklin D. Roosevelt wins US Presidential election; New Deal initiated; Stalin purges begin, Russia
1933	A. N. Whitehead's *Adventures of Ideas*; Jung's *Psychology and Religion*; Orwell's *Down and Out in Paris and London*	Hitler becomes Chancellor; start of anti-Jewish measures in Germany; first concentration camps; Germany leaves League of Nations
1934	Gershwin's *Porgy and Bess*; Graves's *I Claudius*	'Night of the Long Knives' massacre in Germany; Hitler assumes title of 'Führer', after plebiscite
1935	The Curies awarded Nobel Prize for Chemistry, having synthesized radioactive elements; The Webbs's *Soviet Communism; A New Civilization*; Graham Greene's *England Made Me*; T. S. Eliot's *Murder in the Cathedral*	Hitler denounces Versailles Treaty, forms Air Force and imposes conscription; Russian Show Trials; Italy invades Abyssinia

Year	Age	Life
1936	70	Awarded Hon.D.Litt by London University; *The Anatomy of Frustration*; *The Croquet Player*; *The Man Who Could Work Miracles*; *The Idea of a World Encyclopaedia*
1937	71	*Brynhild*; *Star Begotten*; *The Camford Visitation*
1938	72	*Apropos of Dolores*; *World Brain*; *The Brothers*
1939	73	Visits Sweden; *The Fate Of Homo Sapiens*; *Travels of a Republican Radical In Search of Hot Water*; *The Holy Terror*
1940	74	In London during Blitz; speaking tour of USA; *The Commonsense of War and Peace* (originally given as address to German Reichstag in 1929); *Babes in the Darkling Wood*; *All Aboard for Ararat*
1941	75	*Guide to the New World*; *You Can't be Too Careful*
1942	76	*Phoenix*; *Science and the World Mind*; The Conquest of Time (final revision of *First and Last Things*)
1943	77	*Crux Ansata*

Year	Arts & Science	History & Politics
1936	Chaplin's *Modern Times*; Alexander Korda's film *Things to Come*; Dylan Thomas's *Twenty Five Poems*; Kipling, Houseman and Chesterton die; A. J. Ayer's *Language, Truth and Logic*	Hitler reoccupies the Rhineland; Spanish Civil War begins; Rome–Berlin Axis announced; death of George V; Edward VIII accedes in January, abdicates in December; 'Battle of Cable St' in London's East End
1937	Picasso's *Guernica*; Steinbeck's *Of Mice and Men*; Orwell's *The Road to Wigan Pier*; Sartre's *La Nausée*; Wallace Carothers invents Nylon	Stalin purges high Party and military officials; Japanese Imperialism in China, Peking and Shanghai captured
1938	Orson Welles's radio feature of H. G. Wells's *The War of the Worlds* terrifies America	Austria falls to Hitler; Munich Conference over Czecho-Slovakia; Appeasement Policy confirmed; Franco's victories in Spain; Roosevelt appeals to the dictators for peace
1939	Death of Freud; Jolie-Curie shows the potential of nuclear fission. Henry Moore's *Reclining Figure*; Joyce's *Finnegan's Wake*; Steinbeck's *The Grapes of Wrath*; death of Yeats, and of Ford Madox Ford	Germany invades Poland; Second World War begins; Hitler-Stalin Pact; Russia invades Finland and Poland; fall of Madrid to Franco
1940	Koestler's *Darkness at Noon*	Churchill Prime Minister; Dunkirk and collapse of France; Battle of Britain; start of Blitz on London; murder of Trotsky
1941	Welles's *Citizen Kane*; Carrol Reed's film *Kipps*	Hitler invades Russia; Japan bombs Pearl Harbor; America enters the War
1942	Evelyn Waugh's *Put Out More Flags*	Japan invades Burma, Malaya, Dutch East Indies; Singapore surrenders; Americans bomb Tokyo; Stalingrad siege begins; Montgomery wins El Alamein; start of Hitler's 'Final Solution'
1943	Henry Moore's sculpture *Madonna and Child*	Russian victory at Stalingrad; Warsaw Ghetto killings; Allies finally conquer North Africa; fall of Mussolini, Italy surrenders

Year	Age	Life
1944	78	'42 to '44: A Contemporary Memoir; thesis for Doctorate of Science (On the Quality of Illusion in the Continuity of the Individual Life in the Higher Metazoa with Particular Reference to the Species Homo Sapiens); in London during rocket attacks
1945	79	Mind at the End of Its Tether; The Happy Turning
1946		Dies in London, 13 August
1947		
1948		
1949		
1950		

Year	Arts & Science	History & Politics
1944	T. S. Eliot's *Four Quartets*	Leningrad relieved; Allies capture Rome and land in Normandy; de Gaulle enters Paris; V1 and V2 rocket raids on London
1945	Orwell's *Animal Farm*; Nobel Prize for medicine to Alexander Fleming, E. B. Chain and Howard Florey, for discovery of penicillin	Yalta Conference; Russians capture Warsaw and Berlin; Mussolini executed, Hitler's suicide; United Nations Charter; end of the Second World War in Europe; death of President Roosevelt; atomic bombs dropped on Hiroshima and Nagasaki; Japan surrenders; Labour win General Election; Attlee Prime Minister
1946	Electronic Brain constructed at Pennsylvania University; Cocteau's film *La Belle et La Bête*; Eugene O'Neill's *The Iceman Cometh*	First General Assembly of the United Nations; nationalization of Civil Aviation, coal and the Bank of England; Churchill's 'Iron Curtain' speech
1947	Transistor invented	GATT established
1948	Norman Mailer's *The Naked and the Dead*	National Health Service; Israel founded; East German blockade of Berlin; Allied airlift into Berlin
1949	Orwell's *1984*	West Germany established, confirming division of Europe
1950	Death of Orwell	Start of Korean War

INTRODUCTION

When Wells was born, in 1866, Abraham Lincoln had been dead since the previous year, Napoleon III ruled France, Gladstone and Disraeli dominated English politics, Dickens, George Eliot, Tennyson, Browning and Trollope were writing. Wells said of himself that he 'came up from the poor in a state of flaming rebellion, mostly blasphemous and unsaintly'. His father, Joseph, seems an amiable, somewhat feckless and unsuccessful character. A gardener and shopkeeper, he was also a professional cricketer who played for Kent, 1862–3, and is embalmed in *Wisden* for taking four wickets in four successive balls. Some of his son's tireless love of games, indoor and outdoor, his irresponsibility and mischievousness, his disrespect for 'the Quality', must have derived from Joe, who had something of Dickens' Joe Gargery about him; 'There has been larks,' while, like Mrs Joe, Mrs Wells was 'given to government'. There is plenty of Joe Wells in *Mr Polly*, both parents appear in *The New Machiavelli*, and their son said later: 'They were both economic innocents made by and for a social order ... that was falling to pieces all around them.'

Mrs Wells, alternating between the small Bromley shop and domestic service at Up Park, where once the future Lady Hamilton had performed her own services, was pious, narrow, subservient to the gentry, and unimaginative – all that H.G. most hated. His view of the Great House, from below stairs, is graphically reproduced in *Tono-Bungay*. His mother instructed him to 'know his place', its safety, routine, docility. H.G. certainly knew his place, but it was far from servants' halls, drapers' shops, and bowing his head. His place, he found, was amongst the stars; it was at the feet of T.H.Huxley the great rationalist; it was with the community of world writers and the glorious company of thinkers. In his bones he loathed whatever cramped, stifled, wasted human potential, whatever stuffily obstructed the clean flow of life and imagination: the Family, the semi-feudalism of the Great House, the class system of snobbery and privilege, the Monarchy, the Vatican, nationalism. To him tradition, at best, represented picturesque ways of sitting on what ancestors had looted.

'The life then offered me was a hideous insult to my possibilities.' He was soon to realize that, faced with competition from younger, fiercer nations, Britain under-used young talents at her peril. Meanwhile, his schooling was rudimentary, his body unhealthy and, like his voice, unimpressive. He had, however, an obstinate element of self-assertion. His contemporary, the composer Ethel Smythe, who wrote a march for her fellow suffragettes from prison, reflected at fifteen: 'I am the most interesting person I know, and I don't care if no one else knows it.' Wells must have felt the same, save that he would make sure that everyone else should know it. Young Kipps too, reflects: 'I don't suppose there was ever a chap like me before.' In this is the essence of the novel and, for many, the justification for almost all novels, the voice of individualism. Wells was untroubled by notions of a fluid, unidentifiable ego in constant flux: personality develops from chaos yet remains permanent. Very swiftly he was H.G., incessantly combative, taking on all comers, perky, a bit of a 'card', the Cheeky Chappie of the New Literature. Vincent Brome was to call him 'brilliantly ordinary'.

Gifted women loved him – Amber Reeve, Rebecca West, Moura Budberg, Odette Keun ... though he often plundered more than he gave. His love affairs were public knowledge and in such novels as *Ann Veronica*, *The New Machiavelli*, *Apropos of Dolores*, he made them more so, while pioneering sexual candour and freedom. 'To love is to go living radiantly through the world,' and he did not mean Christian benevolence or Buddhist *ahimsa*.

Reassessing Wells after half a century, Brome credited him with nine lives. He did not name them all, but this is easy. Scientific Romancer, Novelist, Socialist Propagandist, Lecturer, Journalist, Philanderer, Traveller, Prophet, World Celebrity. He was always craving a tenth ... partner of the Perfect Woman, Citizen of the Perfect Society ... but it was always just out of reach.

His literary yearnings began early. At thirteen he had written a small book, *The Desert Daisy*. It was not published but, never convicted of false modesty, he wrote of it: 'Beats *Paradise Lost* into eternal smash.' From Huxley, who popularized 'agnostic', he apprehended truths awaiting formal discovery; scientific, philosophical, ethical, many of them far beyond crude utilitariansim. A writer may write in order to define and understand himself and the world; Wells thought the world only too easily understandable and wanted to change it. His early book, *Anticipations*, full of his darting ideas and lightning, often arrogant and harsh opinions, his personal indignations and contempts, showed him as the original and by far the most convincing Angry Young Man and, unlike most of his successors, a constructive one, laying out the future as if with paving stones designed by himself alone.

> H.G.Wells
> Was made of cells
> He thought the Human Race
> A disgrace.

E.C.Bentley's amiable clerihew does catch another and pessimistic strain in Wells, often ignored by those who, ignorant of most of his work, credited him, as they did G.M.Trevelyan, with a shallow optimism about science, education and progress. Actually, his *When the Sleeper Awakes* (1899) anticipated Orwell's *1984*, depicting as it does a future and horrifying society, rigidly authoritarian, with the perfection of an ant-heap, and the lack of vision and purpose of a slave state. Such a picture corresponded with a mood already discernible in some sections of western culture, so often susceptible to irrational depression as a century nears its end, as though mankind might lose energy while completing its conquest of distance, ignorance and nature. Science itself might provoke a complex retribution, and nature also, indignant at man preferring conquest to co-operation. Later, in Hitler's Germany and Stalin's Russia charlatan scientific toadies like Lysenko, gifted conformists like Speer and von Braun, behaved as cravenly as anyone else. Science is fighting on the side of superstition, Orwell wrote in 1941. Wells's *The Island of Doctorr Moreau (1896)*, had already shown perverted science creating horror. Such works as *A Vision of Armageddon*, *The Empire of the Ants*, *In the Abyss*, *The Stolen Bacillus*, *A Slip under the Microscope*, suggested the incessant perils of modernity. *The Time Machine* was a sombre, even tragic, warning against assuming too much from material

advance. It depicted such advance as inducing passivity, under-
mining humanity's vital curiosity, its will to struggle and find
purpose. V. S. Pritchett has written that it 'will take its place
among the great stories of our language.' Wells also knew that
the Utopia for which he himself struggled could be endangered
by monotony, an ant-like perfection of routine that excluded
not only class warfare, sickness, hunger and cold, but rapture,
humour and debate. No more than Aldous Huxley, another
encyclopaedist, did he ever have unrestricted faith in progress
and technology.

The early scientific romances, only superficially recalling Jules
Verne, contained fantasies of disruptive angels and intrusive
mermaids, cosmic cataclysms and menacing comets. Reading
The War of the Worlds one could be scared and reassured
without leaving the armchair. Wells described, like matters of
course, moon landings, nuclear fission, tank and aerial warfare,
X-rays, television, motion pictures, electronic dishwashers.
'Man will step from star to star as we now step from stone to
stone across a stream.' He once lamented the absence of a
Professor of Foresight. His very titles were programmes, alarm-
ing or exciting, inducing new visions, a break out from time and
the world: *The Undying Fire, The Open Conspiracy, My First
Aeroplane, The Man who could Work Miracles, The Shape of
Things to Come, When the Sleeper Awakes, In the Days of the
Comet, Mankind in the Making, The Argonauts of the Air, The
Flying Man, The Land Ironclads, The Discovery of the Future,
The Invisible Man, The Research Magnificent, The First Men in
the Moon, The New Republic, A Modern Utopia, The New
Accelerator, First and Last Things.*

His rivals – Henry James, Conrad, Bennett, Moore, Stevenson, Galsworthy, ignored science, the world in time, evolution,
the universe. Seventy years before C. P. Snow and F. R. Leavis
quarrelled over The Two Cultures, Wells had observed the gap
between 'the superb and richly fruitful scientific investigations
that are going on, and the general thought of the educated
section of the community'. Shaw, in 1940, mentioned to Virginia
Woolf that the neglect of the aesthetic factor in science had
deprived it of its claim to be scientific.

Uninterested in the future, serious novelists were minutely
dissecting past and present with nostalgia, psychological penetration and historical acumen. For Wells, however, the past was

an unsavoury and imbecile muddle, uneducated and super-
stitious, occasionally illuminated 'by a gleam of enlightenment',
for which a Socrates or a Bruno were martyred, but more often
smudged by an Attila or Napoleon. He saw no evidence for a
benevolent and omnipotent Creator: at any instant, the caprice
of a new disease, a megalomaniac, a natural disaster, could
disrupt the marvellous future now at last made possibe not by
God but by man. At best, God was a clumsy experimenter
whose mistakes must be corrected, not least by H.G. Man
should forgive and transform God, not the reverse.

Always discontented, Wells, could not rest on his fame as a
romancer. He was profoundly aware of the claims of Henry
James, let alone of Dickens. He, too, wanted to submit such
claims. 'I want to write novels,' he wrote to Arnold Bennett,
'and before God I *will* write novels.' For some years he did,
fighting his instinctive journalistic powers and needs, in such
novels as *Kipps* and *The Adventures of Mr Polly*, which many
believe his most enduring work. Simultaneously he continued
his outflow of ideas. 'I write, like I walk, in order to get
somewhere.' He wanted to wake people up, not to cosset them
in Booklovers' Corner. He saw that rulers were ignorant and
obsolete, their subjects needed scolding. 'Adapt or perish.' They
must learn, act, co-operate. Always in a hurry, he left notebooks
scattered throughout the house to trap the flying ideas. He once
wrote nine books in two years. Exuberant as a child with a
secret, often slapdash, he wrote some hundred, and can be
imagined interrupting a solemn concert with 'Hey, just a
minute', scribbling furiously. He had something of the newsboy
or tavern confidant: 'Heard the latest?' He wrote on colonial
exploitation, industrialism, genetics, religion, high finance, children's games – hating uniforms, despising generals, he nevertheless loved playing toy soldiers – on sex, the New Woman,
eugenics; he invented, vainly, a device to overcome the appalling
Flanders mud during the Great War. He anticipated the World
Health Organisation, and pioneered – less on his own than he
sometimes maintained – the League of Nations. He wrote
incessantly on education and a world-state. Frank Swinnerton
called him a one-man arsenal of new and explosive ideas and
recalled the demonic energy with which he transformed a sedate
croquet contest into a 'mixture of golf and steeplechase'.
J.B.Priestley thought him a 'one-man Unesco'. For Christopher

Isherwood he seemed a war correspondent scribbling on a still-smoking battlefield.

Wells maintained that education should build up the imagination and in early writing was passionately assisting this, in visionary seas and skies, accounts of Neanderthal man, the Country of the Blind, the dream garden behind the Door in the Wall. Schools, he demanded, should replace ancient classics and parochial legends with universal history, philosophy and science. Kipps, at fifteen, having left school, never read a book or newspaper, 'except, occasionally, *Tit Bits* or a h'penny comic', and, 'by the nature of his training, he was indistinct in his speech, confused in his mind, and retreating in his manners.' Throughout England, schools were destroying curiosity, injecting dull, useless facts and pernicious ideology to overcome youthful eagerness. Children identified learning with the laborious and putrid, with capricious tyranny. Anthems for Doomed Youth were being written long before Wilfred Owen.

From his early experiences, Wells expected little from the ignorant and impoverished. 'I have never believed in the superiority of the inferior.' This was to make him enemies, particularly today. Meanwhile, he set himself to teach them, show them the way to fulfil their personal and biological purposes. Hugh Walpole alleged that Conrad told Wells, 'You don't care for humanity, but think they are to be improved. I love humanity, but know they are not.'

Part of Wells would have endorsed the fascistic Ezra Pound. 'Give a people almost perfect government, and in two generations they will let it run to rot through sheer laziness.' He disavowed the common man who insisted on remaining common, and asserted that people were but creatures of habit, custom and prejudice. In *Boon* is written: 'Men will go on in their ways though one rose from the dead to tell them that the Kingdom of Heaven was at hand, though the Kingdom itself and all its glory had become visible.'

He became, in the Enlightenment tradition, an encyclopaedist, collaborating with Julian Huxley and Professor G. P. Wells in *The Science of Life* and writing the massive *The Work, Wealth and Happiness of Mankind*. To remedy the ignorance of world history shared by all classes, he produced *The Outline of History*. It was not what he called 'drum and trumpet' history, but told the earth's story from an original cooling, from slime and Palaeozoic rocks to the Russian Revolution and the League of Nations. Like his science fiction, it opened vast horizons to a mass audience and is probably the most enduring of his non-fiction. Isherwood rated it a masterpiece, and Samuel Hynes (1991) roundly called it the most important history book, in English, of the twentieth century. This probably scandalized academics who, like the scientists, condescended to him as an amateur, the latter, to his chagrin, always rejecting his candidature for the Royal Society. Professional historians demurred at his inaccuracies and hasty generalizations, but he undertook the book only when most of them refused his plea to assist in writing it themselves. It showed people throughout the world that history was an enthralling and tragic progress, not a patriotic narrative of kings, generals and bishops. A.J.P. Taylor called it the 'most acceptable of universal histories'.

By 1900, *Wellsian* was a worldwide synonym for technological gadgetry, scientific blueprints for world orders, bizarre speculations and prophecy. It was an international catchword, more vividly clearcut than the *Shavian* of his more nimble-witted rival, whom Wells considered as incurably frivolous and posturing, and whom G. K. Chesterton described as a tree with its roots in the air. Wells himself, to friends, enemies, the world at large, was always 'H.G.', and, for many, still is. He had become clubman, travelling celebrity, international sage, largely ceasing to create worlds though never ceasing to report on the current world, with marked impatience, like an omniscient headmaster nagging a rowdy school. 'He trotted into the Kremlin,' Shaw said, in a phrase Wells never forgave. He talked with Lenin and later with Stalin. He briefly thought the latter 'kindly' but, in 1932, wrote, 'Stalin seems to possess all the vindictive romanticism of a typical Georgian.'

He was invited to address the Petrograd Soviet, the Weimar Reichstag, the Sorbonne. He met Theodore Roosevelt; he dined with F. D. R. His cockiness remained; he compared America to a burst haggis. Though he had entered the Establishment, he was never wholly accepted by it, nor did he cease to satirize and despise it. However, hedonistic and ambitious, he enjoyed clubs, salons, country houses and, an accomplished seducer, high-born ladies. He could never be ignored. Winston Churchill, a character in at least one Wells novel, wrote: 'Few first class men of letters

have more consistently crabbed and girded at the national
society and the social system in which they have had their being.'
Wells himself stood, vainly, as a Labour parliamentary candidate. Hilaire Belloc, himself an MP and admiring Parliament no
more than had Dickens, observed sardonically that in morals,
temperament, instruction and type of oratory, Wells was admirably suited to it.

After the Great War, while his many books still sold well
enough, they had small visible effect, though many teachers and
pupils must have been stirred. He had been disappointed with
the Fabians, the Labour Party, the League, the Russian Revolution, the New Deal, with publishers, his search for the ideal
woman, the ideal society, with humanity itself, so indifferent to
World Government, the rule of Platonic élites. He had piped; so
few had danced. Ancient titles, unearned privileges, colliding
national states still abounded. Science had culminated in Hiroshima, fulfilling his pessimism, souring his optimism.

Somerset Maugham had seen him in New York in 1940. 'He
was looking old, tired and shrivelled. He was as perky as he had
always been, but with something of an effort. His lectures were a
failure. People couldn't hear what he said and didn't want to listen
to what they could hear. They left in droves. He was hurt and
disappointed. He couldn't understand why they were impatient
with him for saying very much the same sort of thing as he had
been saying for the last thirty years. The river has flowed on and
left him high and dry on the bank. The writer has his little hour
(if he's lucky), but an hour is soon past. After all, he's had it and
he ought to be satisfied. It's only reasonable that others should
have their turn. One would have thought it would be enough
for H.G. to reflect on the great influence he had on a whole
generation and how much he did to alter the climate of opinion.
But he has always been too busy to be anything of a philosopher.'

Too old to rejoice in the Century of the Common Man, yet
still busy, H.G. at least died in possession of uncommon renown.
This would have comforted him not at all.

WELLS'S RELATION TO LITERARY GROUPS
AND MOVEMENTS

Arriving from nowhere, Wells knew all prominent writers: Conrad, James, Bennett, Chesterton, Belloc, Rolland, Gorky, Gissing, to whom he was constantly generous. Wells, however, was too independent and indeed too difficult to remain long in any permanent group. Popularly associated with Shaw, he actually had little in common, always deploring the Irishman's incessant witticisms, stylish self-promotion, love of 'larking'. He called himself a 'Republican in Search of Hot Water', a socialist, but very much on his own terms. His temperament rejected others' Politicial Correctness. He did join the Fabian Society, earlier called The Fellowship of the New Life, which contained Shaw, the Webbs and, at various times, Havelock Ellis, E. Nesbit, William Morris, Graham Wallas, Hubert Bland, Ramsay MacDonald, Clement Attlee and Leonard and Virginia Woolf. However, always impatient with prolonged discussion and always worsted by Shaw, of superior voice, style and presence, he soon withdrew interest when he lost all chance of assuming control.

Socialists, Beatrice Webb once said, should be respectable. H.G., who sometimes regarded himself as the only socialist, jibbed at respectability:

'Let us be clear about one thing: that socialism means revolution, and it means a change in the everyday texture of life. It may be a very gradual change but it will be a very complete one. You cannot change the world, and at the same time not change the world. You will find socialists about, or at any rate men calling themselves socialists, who will pretend that this is not so, and who will assure you that some little jobbing about municipal gas and water is Socialism, and backstreet intervention between Conservative and Liberal is the way to the millennium. You might as well call a gas jet in the lobby of a meeting-house the glory of God in heaven.'

One could claim that the Welfare State was a more practical objective and achievement than Wells's quest for the millennium. Yet his imagination was more exciting and comprehensible than the densities of Hegel and Marx, or the patient planning of Sidney Webb and MacDonald. The huge new reading public, people like J. B. Priestley's schoolmaster father, repeated such electrical remarks of Wells's, as that a postage stamp placed beneath Nelson's Column represented human history, and that the distance between this and Nelson's hat represented the human future. During the Second World War, George Orwell, who had serious democratic criticisms to make of Wells as prophet and sage, wrote:

'I doubt whether anyone who was writing books between 1900 and 1920, at any rate in the English language, influenced the young so much. The minds of all of us, and therefore the physical world, would be perceptibly different if Wells had never existed . . .

'Back in the nineteen hundreds it was a wonderful experience for a boy to discover H.G. Wells. There you were, in a world of pedants, clergymen and golfers, with your future employers exhorting you to 'get on or get out', your parents systemically warping your sexual life, and your dull-witted schoolmasters sniggering over their Latin tags; and here was this wonderful man who could tell you about the inhabitants of the planets and the bottom of the sea, and who knew that the future was not going to be what respectable people imagined.'

Wells found British reformers more concerned with minor pension, housing and health schemes than with his panoramic utopianism. He wanted the Perfect State; they preferred better government. Unlike Shaw, he had no zest or talent for local administration responsible to an ill-informed electorate. Again unlike Shaw, he could be quarrelsome, petty, petulant, tactless. A committee, a tea party, were opportunities for impetuous rejoinders, disruptive gibes and, in passing, he seduced two daughters of leading Fabians. He never quite shed early resentments and present envies. He mocked the Webbs in *The New Machiavelli* as he did the ageing Henry James in *Boon*, outraging 'the Master's' devotees by comparing his 'tales of nothingness' to the efforts of 'a magnificent but painful hippopotamus resolved at any cost, even at the cost of its dignity, upon picking up a pea which has got into the corner of its den'.

Yet his urchin ribaldry and bad-tempered outbursts were usually short. Despite his lonely path he never lacked friends, lovers, admiration – all but conversions to his own political correctness. Frank Swinnerton recalled (1935) weekends with H.G. and Jane: 'The pace was terrific. And through it all was Mr Wells, leader in every activity from lawn tennis, hockey, quoits, and dancing to bridge and a frightful pastime known as Demon Patience. Mr Wells, full of hospitality and the high spirits always engendered in him with society of the young, active, laughing people: Mr Wells, above all, the animated, unexhausted, and inexhaustible talker who, to the last moment of the day would receive with every word dropped by another person, and every small incident that occurred or was described, fresh inspiration.'

By 1912, however, Henry James was complaining that Wells had virtually rejected literature. 'He will still do a lot of writing, but it won't be that.' He would use fiction chiefly as extra space for his rapid-fire journalism, flinging out opinions, projects, taunts, denunciations: pungent, suggestive, challenging, yet unconcerned with the issues so valued by James and Conrad, Forster and Woolf, Joyce and Eliot. The Great War stirred him into writing the very considerable *Mr Britling Sees It Through*, and other flashes occurred: *Apropos of Dolores*, *The Passionate Friends*, *The Bulpington of Bulp*, but he was increasingly rejecting the Novel in favour of candid biography and autobiography. He did just this in *Experiment in Autobiography* (1934), while continuing loudly to demand the world-state without often acknowledging that, with Hitler and Stalin, this might be at hand and likely to fulfil the grisly forecasts in *When the Sleeper Awakes*. His plan for a League of Nations, 1917, envisaged Britain discarding Monarchy, Empire and the Navy. His antipathies remained unquelled. He still aroused outcries by his republicanism. In *Crux Ansata: An Indictment of the Roman Catholic Church* he paraded his conviction that the Vatican, 'an open ally of the Nazi-Fascist-Shinto alliance', was conniving at massacre, assisting the escape of war criminals, obstructing the Allied bombing of Rome' (1943). One passage was thought grossly offensive:

'Watch a priest in a public conveyance. He is fighting against disturbing suggestions. He must not look at women lest he think of sex. He must not look about him, for reality, that is to say the devil, waits to seduce him at every hand. You see him muttering his incantations, avoiding your eye. He is suppressing "sinful" thoughts.'

He had lost contact with those early, incredible visions and 'the stupid little tragedies of these clipped and limited lives', the lives of Mr Lewisham, Mr Polly, Artie and Ann Kipps. Like the later Aldous Huxley, but with less grace and wit, and with more monotony, he indulged in universal preaching.

Remaining aloof from organized groups, belonging to no literary côterie, he never ceased to be talked about, or from talking himself. Long ago, in 1904, Arnold Bennett had reflected: 'Nearly all Wells's conversation would make good table talk and one has a notion that it ought not to be wasted; it is so full of ideas and of intellectual radicalism. It seems a pity that it should not be gathered up. But after all there is a constant supply of it. You might as well be afraid of wasting water from a brook.'

By the 1930s the highbrows – a word that Robert Graves maintained that Wells had invented – no longer regarded him, and he thought little of them. Of T.S. Eliot, he told Virginia Woolf: 'Tee Ess has been the death of English literature.' He would not have applauded Eliot's dictum that modern poetry must be difficult; like Ruskin, Morris, G.M. Trevelyan, he wanted his works to be easily understandable, accessible, and to bear fruit. Art was not a privilege, but a birthright. Typically, he wanted the staid Frederick Macmillan to have *Kipps* advertised by London sandwich-men, a method unappealing to the sensibilities of Forster, Max Beerbohm, Woolf and Eliot. Wyndham Lewis scorned him. Lytton Strachey said: 'I stopped thinking about him when he became a thinker.' Lenin had called him an incurably bourgeois philistine. Hugh Walpole thought him a mere scribbler compared to Conrad. 'What an old bore he is,' he wrote in a tabloid, of *Babes in a Darkling Wood*. Virginia Woolf noted his cockney accent, as she would have Kipps', 'delivered in a little sparrow chirp'. She famously assaulted Wells, Bennett, Galsworthy, as 'materialists'.

'It is because they are concerned not with the spirit but with the body that they have disappointed us, and left us with the feeling that the sooner English fiction turns its back on them, as politely as possible, and marches, if only into the desert, the better for its soul. Naturally, no single word reaches the centre of three separate targets. In the case of Mr Wells it falls notably wide of the mark. And yet even with him it indicates to our way of thinking the fatal alloy in his genius, the great clod of clay that has got itself mixed up with the purity of his inspiration . . .

'It can scarcely be said of Mr Wells that he is a materialist in the sense that he takes too much delight in the solidity of his fabric. His mind is too generous in its sympathies to allow him to spend much time making things shipshape and substantial. He is a materialist from sheer goodness of heart, taking upon his shoulders the work that ought to have been discharged by Government officials, and in the plethora of his ideas and facts scarcely having to realize or forgetting to think important the crudity and coarseness of his human beings.'

Mrs Woolf was writing after the Great War. Of the Wells then writing, this is justified, though of *The Door in the Wall*, *The Pearl of Love*, *The Country of the Blind*, *The Time Machine*, *A Vision of Judgment*, it lacks perception. *Kipps* satirizes materialism, also the Higher Humbug with which its detractors associated Bloomsbury.

After a talk with H.G. (1937), Virginia Woolf wrote in her Diary: 'A humane man in some corner; also brutal; also entirely without poetry.'

There is poetry in the stories and also scattered about the early novels, only not Woolf's sort of poetry. In his autobiography, Stephen Spender recalled the stories 'in which H.G. Wells displays the feverish poetry of an inspired though literal minded man'. In *Kipps*, Artie and Ann are treated with a poetic sympathy, and some passages fall not so very far beneath the heightened atmosphere of *The Waves*.

'Out of the darkness beneath the shallow, weedy stream of his being, rose a question that looked up dimly and never reached the surface. It was the question of the wonder of the beauty, the purposeless, inconsecutive beauty that falls so strangely among the happenings and memories of life. It never reached the surface of his mind, it never took to itself substance and form; it looked up merely as the phantom of a face might look out, of deep waters, and sank again into nothingness.'

Isherwood, a writer of yet another literary set, related Wells to Chaplin, 'the comically cocky, the under-dog defiance'. One can add Dickens. The three shared social origins, talents singular to themselves, the energy and resolution necessary for survival, and the sharp blade of disrespect. As for the humane qualities, Wells was quite as friendly and helpful to younger writers as Virginia Woolf herself.

HISTORICAL AND LITERARY BACKROUND

The years of H.G.'s boyhood and adolescence, and the decades before 1914, were a ferment of new ideas, explosive theory, dramatic events. Wells's republicanism was wholly untruthful when he wrote: 'Queen Victoria was like a great paperweight that for half a century sat upon men's minds, and when she was removed their ideas began to blow all over the place haphazardly.' Long before 1901, Britain and Europe had been throbbing with ideas. Religious fundamentalism, political, social and sexual codes were challenged by new conceptions of human nature, of painting, music, dancing, women's rights, workers' rights, by dynamic theories of cultural relativity, the virtues of primitives, class war, state supremacy, natural selection and the survival of the fittest. Renan, Strauss, Schweitzer, demystified Christ; Comte and Zola, Lecky, Winwood Read, reinforced the rationalism of Marx and Darwin. Charles Lyell, a hero of H.G.'s, with his studies in geology and global surfaces, transformed ntions of the world's age from a few thousand years to hundreds of millions. Archeology, too, was redesigning the past. Havelock Ellis and Marie Stopes fought sexual ignorance, the latter's *Married Love* teaching thousands to know their own bodies and relieve emotional poverty. Freud was giving unexpected interpretations of dreams, motives, internal censorship, jokes, coincidences, at odds with traditional commandments, turning the world less upside down that inside out and, in literature, revealing novel and exciting suggestings in Greek drama, in Shakespeare, in Dostoevsky. Chitterlow, in *Kipps*, voices something of this: 'I believe in coincidences. People say they don't happen. *I* say they do. Everything's a coincidence. Seen properly.' This pervades the story. 'It's a rum go,' Kipps reflects. Awkward and shy, he is not one to make things happen; they happen to him. A house, servants, seem to emerge from the earth, money fall from the sky; love is encountered in what Wells called the stupendous Tomfoolery of Luck.

Faraday's electronic researches promised infinite possibilities; Edison was revolutionizing communications, abolishing distance. Women were slowly penetrating universities, entering public life, addressing serious audiences. The New Woman – Bennett's 'Hilda Lessways', Wells's 'Ann Veronica', from eighteenth-century beginnings, was striving to liberate herself from paternal tyranny, sexual and domestic slavery, through brains, ambition, courage and common sense.

Publicizing women's sexual needs and pleasures, accused of advocating free love, *Ann Veronica* and *The New Machiavelli*, like *Married Love*, were banned by many libraries and book-shops, while Wells complained, 'Our current civilization is a sexual lunatic.'

Ibsen, and his devotee, Bernard Shaw, were battering at the theatre, to strip it of middle-class gossip and melodrama, and aristocratic insouciance. Shaw sanitized hell, Wells transplanted heaven to a well-lit classroom crowded with attentive literates, adjoining a laboratory supervised by public-spirited savants. Morris, Ruskin, Blatchford, Hardie, proclaimed a socialism more humane than Marxism, rising from actual knowledge of the working man. Ruskin taught at the London Working Men's College as, it is said, did Lenin, and, later, D. H. Lawrence and G. M. Trevelyan. Carlyle, Dickens, Engels, savaged Economic Man and the Mammon of Unrighteousness. Such books as Ruskin's *Unto this Last*, which so affected Gandhi, Morris's *News from Nowhere*, and *The Earthly Paradise*, J. S. Mills's *On Liberty*, Grant Allen's *The Woman Who Did*, galvanized all levels of readers, as had *Capital*, *The Origin of Species*, *Thus Spake Zarathustra*. Winwood Read's epic of human cruelty, *The Martyrdom of Man*, profoundly moved Wells, Russell, Priestley, Orwell, A. J. Ayer.

Less attractive to H.G. were Ruskin, Joseph Chamberlain, Cecil Rhodes, extolling Anglo-Saxon virtues and the urgency for them to enrich the world through the rapidly expanding Empire. Kipling, whose hearty, brutal, mock-heroic *Stalky and Co* induced violent invective from Wells the educationalist, was depicting the virtues and vices of imperial India, shown through the proconsuls, magistrates, engineers, officers and, like Mase-field, giving due to the rankers, the failures, the toilers.

Despite constant social reform, the age also suffered mass prostitution, savage industrial unrest, hunger, anarchist, Fenian and suffragette violence, pogroms, anti-immigration angers. The American Civil War had initiated large-scale mechanized war-fare with scalding casualties. The blazing, prophetic and unnecessary nastiness of the Franco-Prussian War, 1870–1, led to Gothic horrors in Paris of massacres of Frenchmen by Frenchmen. Under the complacent eyes of the German conquerors, some 20,000 were shot in the City of Light reeking from arson. For Wells, almost all war was the ultimate degradation, further wastage engendered by stupid, selfish traditions, criminal rulers, greedy parasites. Like John Buchan, he loathed Napoleon; glory was the outcome of false teaching and moral turpitude. Of Louis XIV, synonym for *La Gloire*, he wrote in his 1927 *A Short History of the World* with relative restraint: 'He guided his country towards bankruptcy through the complications of a spirited foreign policy with an elaborate dignity that still extorts our admiration.'

All this quickened Wells's anger, impatience, imagination. Utopia was being obstructed by crowned charlatans, purblind capitalists, the rotting beliefs of a top-heavy system visibly blighting the youth of George Ponderevo, Mr Polly, Ann and Artie Kipps. Years later, in 1936, at seventy, he was still raging. 'Seven-eighths of the hideous killing going on in the world is being done by young people under thirty, youngsters fed on stale old dogmas or not fed at all.'

The 1870 Education Act reflected a growing demand for literacy, with unprecedented scope for writers with brains and energy. Wells possessed both, despite ill health. He surveyed the world, shook his head, took up his pen, never laid it down, eager not only to change the world but to share the fun. New libraries and shops, new publishers and periodicals – *Blackwoods, Strand, Cornhill, 19th Century* – catered for new readers, new authors: Anstey, Pett Ridge, Conan Doyle, Barrie, W. W. Jacobs, Jerome K. Jerome, Arthur Morrison, Belloc, the young Buchan and Maugham. A large public read Tennyson and Swinburne, then Kipling and Masefield. It welcomed popularized science, history, politics, sociology, religion, on all of which Wells had pronounced and accessible views.

He had early been impressed not only by Swift, but by Plato's *Republic*, an ideal society controlled and taught by an aloof, stern, self-sacrificing élite, as envisaged not only by Plato but by another Wells hero, Cromwell. *Kipps* contains several references, not to these but to Nietzsche. Wells and Shaw were fascinated by a concept of the Life Force, through dedication and effort, evolving superior human types, a loftier morality, in a world cleansed of primitive hankerings, astrological beliefs, and intellectual dross. Few today, however, would welcome Well's Modern Utopia, the New Republic, supervised by 'the

Samurai', that incorruptible band of technicians and idealists that suggests the Rule of the Saints, a Polit-Bureau, a Central Committee, a Committee of Public Safety dominated by a selfless but self-deceiving Robespierre, an intelligent, courageous but implacable Saint-Just and, beneath them, a swarming battalion of paternalist planners, eugenicists, genetic engineers. V. S. Pritchett, an admirer, has nevertheless acknowledged, 'Wells's optimism, whose other name, I fear, is ruthlessness'. Wells supported the savage Black and Tans in Ireland, asserting that they represented that higher culture necessary for the survival of the species. In the *New Statesman*, to which Wells had often contributed, John Gross reflected in 1969:

'The most disturbing aspect of Wells's work is his cult of power, the ruthlessness which was the other side of his bold social engineering. To his credit, he was a lifelong opponent of militarism in any of its traditional sabre-rattling guises; he was also one of the most aggressive writers of his time, his imagination teeming with catastrophes, bombardments, power-élites.'

Orwell, too, deplored Wells's over-reverence for power at a time when Mussolini was dragooning the Italians into supporting a power-regime whose showiness was balanced, at the critical test, by marked incompetence, a failure to admit any but the weakest elements of human nature.

Few European intellectuals had been unaffected by Darwinism, reduced to simplistic interpretations of the struggle for existence, and the slogans Natural Selection, the Survivial of the Fittest. The race-bragging Nazis did not come from nowhere. In human terms, the survival of the fittest is fallacious; in wars, virile youths often perish, weak veterans survive; without drugs and doctors, Nature would have early eliminated the puny, tubercular young H.G. himself. Yet he never quite relinquished a view of superior groups fulfilling their own potential and Nature's behests, at the expense of others. He too often made careless and callous dismissals of far-off and barely known peoples. In this context, like many of his contemporaries, he has been attacked for anti-Semitism by post-Holocaust critics, not least by Roman Catholics, whose priesthood had for centuries a disgraceful record of persecution, shrouded tribunals, genocide. Undeniably thoughtless, fitfully intolerant, always impatient, Wells, like Marx, Engels, Shaw, like Lenin and Mao, could recklessly castigate personal opponents as enemies of 'progress', and expel dissidents, misfits, eccentrics and the 'incorrect' from Utopia. All opposition he consigned to the dust. He was no friend of religion, but in his *Short History of the World* is a moving tribute to Jesus. G. K. Chesterton, himself a Roman Catholic, lampooner of South African millionaire Jews and cosmopolitan capitalists, once replied to Wells's hope that, if orthodox theology proved correct, he might, after all, be allowed into heaven as a friend of G.K.C. 'You will triumph, not for being a friend of mine but a friend of Man.' Norman and Jeanne Mackenzie, in their assiduously researched biography, admit that in *The Anatomy of Frustration*, Wells, always anti-nationalist, does assail the Jews as a special example of destructive nationalism, 'but the lashing they received was in essence no different from that which H.G. was to mete out to Catholics, monarchists, imperialists, and all who appeared to be frustrating the Wellsian plan for salvation.'

Wells always trumpeted his socialism, but the word is confusing. Louis Napoleon, Marx, Lenin, Bakunin, Stalin, Mao, Trotsky, MacDonald, Attlee, Eugene Debs, Shaw, Tito, Djilas, even Hitler, professed forms of socialism, though most would have disliked the rest, and some killed others. Wells's socialism was always one of patrician granting, not sharing. The rule of the proletariat, the Red Dawn, would have outraged him. His political tracts largely ignored the warm humanitarianism of Jaurès and Morris, Kropotkin and Ruskin, Patrick Geddes and Lewis Mumford. Here he can be more plausibly condemned. Also, despite Doctor Moreau and the Time Traveller, in his blue prints he underestimated the powers of the irrational, Man's lasting penchant for myths and idols, his distrust of concrete evidence, his hankering even for disaster and hysterical promises. A citizen, with the choice of rescuing a cat or an eminent surgeon, might, through mischief, perversity, an obsessive ideal, save the cat. Man can want his cake, then morosely destroy it. Well-endowed schools, benign homes, wise legislation, may produce scoundrels. Wells's romances had implied the beast lurking in man, a jungle insufficiently mapped, sadistic horror emerging from the laboratory. But, despite his cataclysmic forecasts, he failed to anticipate, not perhaps Mussolini, but a Hitler–Stalin Pact, and had actually denied the possibility of a ranting demagogue resuming power. He had conceived Lenin as one of his own Samurai, heading an austere and disciplined task force towards the Wellsian Republic. Finally, his belief in the world-state assumed that a vast, remote-controlled society is more reasonably governed, its bureaucracy more sensible and compassionate, its citizens more public-spirited and cheerful, than in a Norway, a Switzerland, or a New Zealand.

The intellectual worlds, pre-1914, were small enough to constantly overlap. Gerhard Masur, in his aptly named *Prophets of Yesterday* (1963) considered:

'It must have been a delight to live in this London where H.G.Wells, the Webbs, Somerset Maugham, Arthur Balfour and Winston Churchill might meet at the same dinner.' He continues, however: 'The optimism that filled the air of Bernard Shaw's London was as little justified as that of Croce's Naples or Bergson's Paris. It was the dusk of a civilization, which they mistook for the dawn of a new era.'

KIPPS: FORM AND CONTENT

Unlike James and Conrad, Wells was no perfectionist; he was always too hurried to linger like Flaubert, like Rilke, for the exact word, the most delicately precise phrase. Like Pasternak, he could find clichés handy. His language was lively, inventive, sometimes disfigured by the portentous or ugly. With the excitable range of the self-taught it can flourish a word like the raw and unpleasant 'renuclearation', in *Kipps*. His tone, though periodically eloquent, even passionate, is usually chirpy, conversational, now chatty, now wondering or abusing, prefering direct narrative to the oblique or symbolic or dispassionate.

'There were times when Kipps would like awake, all others in the dormitory asleep and snoring, and think dismally of the outlook Minton pictured. Dimly he perceived the thing that had happened to him, how the great stupid machine of retail trade had caught his life into its wheels, a vast irresistible force which he had neither strength of will or knowledge to escape. This was to be his life until his days should end. No adventures, no glory, no change, no freedom.'

Kipps, even at its saddest, bubbles with humour, the weapon of the non-violent poor, from an author once, like Artie, dependent on customers' good will, thus forced to be observant and knowing. Swinnerton noted that Wells perceived the significance of every gesture they made, every glance they cast. His humour is often casual:

'Once his aunt gave him a trumpet if he would promise faithfully not to blow it, and afterwards took it away again.'

and,

'"Your sister ain't a bad sort," he said off-handedly.

'"I clout her a lot," said Sidney modestly.'

Kipps's new house provokes period jocularity: it will be 'in the best Folkestone style, to include a Moorish gallery, a Tudor stained-glass window, crenellated battlements, an oriental dome.'

At the Drapery, the status of authors is diminished.

'"It's luck," said Buggins, "to a very large extent. They just happen to hit on something that catches on, and there you are!"

"Nice easy life they have of it, too," said Miss Mergle.

"Write, just an hour or so, and done for the day. Almost like gentlefolks."'

Buggins has his own sophistication. Kipps' dead mother's name was Euphemia.

'"It's giving girls names like that," said Buggins, "that nine times out of ten makes 'em go wrong. It unsettles them. If ever I was to have a girl, if ever I was to have a dozen girls, I'd call 'em all Jane. Every one of 'em. You couldn't have a better name than that. Euphemia indeed! What next?"'

P. G. Wodehouse's verbal comedy might have absorbed something of *Kipps*, where the social conformist, Chester Coote, has a cough, constantly used as reproach, disdain, warning. 'A sound more like a very, very old sheep a quarter of a mile away being blown to pieces by a small charge of gunpowder' recalls Wodehouse's 'that soft cough of his, the one that sounds like a sheep clearing its throat on a distant hillside'. Likewise, 'He found himself face to face with his uncle's advanced outpost of waistcoat buttons,' and '"You'll have a good time," he said abruptly, with a smile that would have interested a dentist.'

Wells himself loved Dickens, to whom he is often compared, though Pritchett, so often rejecting conventional judgments, finds more of Dickens in Joyce's *Ulysses* than in *Kipps* or *Tono-Bungay*.

Wells published *Kipps* in 1905, simultaneously issuing *A Modern Utopia* which was compared favourably to Plato and Thomas More. He was not yet tilted almost wholly to preaching and journalism, not yet complaining that Henry James was ignorant of the Novel as a guide to conduct. Of *Mr Lewisham*, *Kipps*, and *Mr Polly*, Frank Swinnerton wrote (1935): 'All these books belong to the same order. All are fairy stories, and all are about "simple souls". All are written, not merely as relaxations, but because one side of Wells's genius, the happiest side, has kinship with the comic genius of Dickens, his favourite author.' Drawing on his own experiences, with some bitterness, Wells also lets rip his own sense of comedy, with or without Dickens; fanciful, insolent, exuberant. Pritchett says further: 'No Frenchified or Russianized fiction this, but plain, cheerful, vulgar, stoic, stupid and hopelessly romantic English.'

After Kipps has inherited his fortune, he ruminates, as young H.G. must often have done. 'Suppose some day one met Royalty. By accident, say! He soared to that! After all – twelve hundred a year is a lift, a tremendous lift. How did one address Royalty? "Your Majesty's Goodness" it would be, no doubt, something like that – and on the knees. He became impersonal. Over a thousand a year made him an Esquire, didn't it? He thought that was it. In which case, wouldn't he have to be presented at court? Velvet breeches, like you wear cycling, and a sword! What a curious place a court must be; and what was it Miss Mergle used to talk about? Of course – ladies with long trains walking about backward. Everybody walked backward at court, he knew, when not actually on their knees. Perhaps, though, some people regular stood up to the King! Talked to him, just as one might talk to Buggins, say. Cheek, of course! Dukes, it might be, did that – by permission. Millionaires? . . .

'From such thoughts this free citizen of our Crowned Republic passed insensibly into dreams – turgid dreams of that vast ascent which constitutes a free-born Briton's social scheme, which terminates with retrogressive progression and a bending back.'

Behind the banter is Wells's lifelong anger with the flawed social scheme, though he still mainly wished to entertain. To adapt John Gross's phrase about *Mr Polly*, the objective was not Utopia but the Land of Cockaigne. 'It's a lark, our marrying,' Kipps says to Ann. Marriage with Helen, his earlier betrothed, would have been no lark, but prolonged examinations, initiation tests for the Higher Culture, Higher Humbug.

KIPPS', CRITICAL COMMENT

To complain of the improbable coincidences, miracles, the 'marvellous Tomfoolery of Luck' in *Kipps* is to mistake Wells's premises. Kipps is the honest simpleton of Romance, the Jack, the youngest son, with clumsy innocence and wholesale goodwill tempted towards the horizon, lured by wiles of the Distant Princess towards a false destiny. Throughout, he discovers vital secrets ands truths through tests that are often cruel and humiliating; he also tranforms failures to assets and eventually fulfils the quest, which is no Palace of Culture but simple happiness with the girl next door who will henceforth protect his vulnerability. A vulnerability that was to sink thousands of such youths into the Flanders mud for ever.

Bertie Wells, Artie Kipps. Expressing so much of his creator, Kipps is no cipher. Within an apparent dreamy passivity, he has, like Ann, a stubborn hold on life, a capacity to resist. He is not, of course, perfect. His imperfections produced the novel. Edward Shanks, introducing a 1928 edition, wrote: 'Simplicity invites pretence, which flourishes near it, like a reversal of nettle and dock, and this is a comedy of pretences. It is the story how Artie Kipps found his own simplicity, and clung to it as the most valuable thing in the world.'

The uncle and aunt had tried to shield their nephew from 'common' children; Helen and Coote resolved to rescue him from 'common' adults. They nearly succeed.

Like Dickens's Pip, he finds social ascent entails rejection of old friends. In the Drapery he conceals the handicap of his foster parents having been in service; to a cultured acquaintance he feigns literary ambitions. In Folkestone's high society he further rejects his better nature, feeling ashamed of the amiable but noisy Chitterlow, and of Ann. He accepts Helen's demand that he change his own name, poses as a 'swell', quarrels with Ann for refusing to conform to his assumed airs. She, and circumstances, contrive to make him lose this battle to shed the pretences and resume his true self.

The early Wells novels sermonized less than the later. In *Kipps*, Masterman, based somewhat on Gissing, was originally a major character, with long outbursts of socialist rhetoric. He was eventually fined down, lightening the novel, sensibly balancing Helen and the Cootery. The Wells tone remained. Society,

Masterman declares, is one body. 'This society we live in is ill. It's a fractious, feverish invalid, gouty, greedy, ill-nourished. You can't have a happy left leg with neuralgia, or a happy throat with a broken leg.'

For good measure he adds a flourish: 'You were starting a climb that doesn't lead anywhere. You would have clambered from one vulgarity to another, and never get to any satisfactory top. There isn't a top. It's a squirrel's cage, and the only top there is is a lot of blazing card-playing women and betting men, seasoned with archbishops and officials and all that sort of glossy pandering tosh.'

Masterman uses terms more acceptable to Edwardians than to ourselves, though a character in a Koestler novel did remark that one can judge the deficiencies of the Left by the ugliness of its women. Masterman lectures Kipps on the rich: 'They are ugly and cowardly and mean. Painted, dyed, and drugged, hiding their ugly shapes under a load of dress! There is not a woman at the present time who wouldn't sell herself body and soul, who wouldn't lick the boots of a Jew or marry a nigger, rather than live decently on a hundred a year.'

Such sentiments must enflame Wells's latter-day detractors, and he certainly, like Trevelyan, had a zest for cavalier generalizations, though Edwardians were apt to indulge these from snobbery rather than from reasoned or researched ideology. Himmler would have certainly been unacceptable to Jane and H.G.

Arnold Bennett, privately finding *Kipps* minor, compared to Zola's *L'Oeuvre*, an inappropriate comparison, objected to Wells's loathing for most of his characters. He exaggerated. The aunt and uncle are indeed preposterously genteel, fearing 'the low', despising 'the stuck-up', thus avoiding everyone, though Kipps himself is friendly to all. They are scarcely vicious, and the Pornicks, the Chitterlows, the Drapery employees, are sympathetically, if slightly patronizingly treated. Not so the swindling Mr Woodrow, with his high-sounding, fake degrees and wretched school where, 'in a glass cupboard in the passage were several shillingsworth of test tubes and chemicals, a tripod, a glass retort, and a damaged bunsen burner, manifesting that the "scientific laboratory" mentioned in the prospectus was no idle boast. This prospectus, which was in dignified but incorrect English . . .'

Not so Mr Shalford, with his vaunted system designed to bully his employees. Wells makes small attempt to get inside these butts, any more than the scornful yet toadying London flunkeys, and when he does it is indeed with scornful lack of sympathy. This matters little any more than it does in a Mystery or Morality play. Wells reserves his big guns for the pretentious Folkestone upper crust Helen Walshingham, who had matriculated, so can condescend to the Royal Academy and 'prod and worry honest pieces of wood into useless and unedifying patterns in relief'. Her cultural sensitivity and social breeding conceal a cold eye for the main chance.

'The sky was a vast splendour, and then, close to them, were the dark protecting trees, and the shining, smooth still water. He was an erect black outline to her; he plied his paddle with no unskillful gesture; the water broke to snaky silver and glittered far behind his strokes. Indeed, he did not seem so bad to her. Youth calls to youth the wide world through, and her soul rose in triumph over his subjection. And behind him was money and opportunity, freedom, and London, a great background of seductively indistinct thoughts.'

Kipps, her pupil, at first worships and fears her, neither sensation a recipe for genuine love, though acceptable to her. She has much to do before Mr Kipps, with his erratic hair, slipshod voice and average physique deplorably covered, rather than dressed, can be made to fulfil 'that pervading ambition of the British young man to be, if not a "gentleman", at least unmistakably like one'.

Wells is merciless to Helen. 'She told him things about his accent; she told him things about his bearing, about his costume and his way of looking at things. She thrust the blade of her intelligence into the tenderest corners of Kipps' secret vanity; she slashed his most intimate pride to bleeding tatters.'

Her voice is one which H.G. must often have heard: 'You mustn't be too-too dressy. It's possible to be over-conventional, over-elaborate. It makes you look like a shop . . . like a common well-off person. There's a sort of easiness that's better. A real gentleman looks right, without looking as though he had tried to be right.'

She inflicts him with Ruskin's *Sesame and Lilies*. To him, the world, the world and its doings are 'rum', but do not need exalted interpretations. The collision between her and the rowdy, theatrical Chitterlow, based upon Wells's boyhood friend Sidney Bowkett, is richly comic.

Helen is a leader of the Cootery, which has reduced life to etiquette, a set of rules: the 100 Best Books, the 100 Best Paintings. 'Of course, we can learn even from novels, nace novels, that is, but it isn't the same thing as serious reading.'

Chester Coote for awhile is Kipps' mentor: 'Coote sat back in the armchair smoking luxuriously and expanding pleasantly with the delightful sense of *savoir-faire*. Kipps sat forward, his elbows on his own armchair, alert, and his head a little on one side. You figure him as looking little and cheap, and feeling smaller and smaller amidst his new surroundings. But it was a most stimulating and interesting conversation. And it soon became less general, and more serious and intimate. Coote spoke of people who had got on ... and of people who hadn't; of people who seemed to be in everything, and people who seemed to be out of everything.'

Here is the quack Doctor of early comedy; proprietoral, grandiloquent, with a reptertoire of bogus texts and cure-alls.

Wells himself considered *Kipps* a complete study of life related to England's social condition, seen from an unusual vantage point. Like Orwell, he relished describing the incidentals of an England now faded, irretrievably lost, yet which can still be recalled. A world of small corner shops, genteel, seldom-used parlours, lamplighters, dim private schools preying on credulous widows and absentee fathers; stuffed animals, hurdy-gurdies, pianolas, music hall and tavern songs, paraffin lamps, golden sovereigns, penny dreadfuls, gobstoppers; cribs and swaps, cycling sprees, dog carts, wagonettes; the mashers, knuts, cards, fellers, toffs, bounders, cads, Burlington Berties; the ritual of church-going, grace before meals, afternoon tea, visiting cards; also the dreaded *faux-pas* and class-nervousness.

'He discovered that Miss Coote was asking him whether he took milk and sugar. "I don't mind," said Kipps, "Jest as you like."'

In a London grand hotel, Kipps worriedly tips everyone within sight, including a South African diamond tycoon.

Unusually for so swift a writer, Wells spent three years over *Kipps*. Some of the latter part seems, as Kipps might say, a bit scamped. Helen is disposed of too easily, and offstage, depriving the reader of an explosive or disdainful confrontation. Lovat

Dickson added: 'How the characters in his books got where they did was of little importance; what they saw, what they said, what they felt when they had arrived – that was the heart of the matter.'

The purist may find too much bluntly authorial comment, on what a modernist would leave to dialogue and the oblique. Masterman's explosions, by their crudities, must have made James and Conrad wince. Many of his adverbs are unncessary. With his thought rushing forward as if after a hockey ball, careless of all in his way, Wells too often has the tiresome habit of leaving paragraphs unfinished, with a row of dots. Astonishingly, he wrote the mammoth *Outline of History*, together with much else, in a year.

In his eagerness to be heard, to convince, to earn his rewards, H.G., though with a mass of original material, spent no time brooding over experimental fiction. He took the novel as he found it, the linear narrative flow which had served well enough Balzac, Zola, Dickens, Tolstoy. Beckett's pride in 'emancipating from identity' his characters would have meant little to him. The stream of consciousness, fragmentation of personality, complex, contradictory truths of any incident, however trivial, would have assisted neither his characters, his message, his vision. For him, untroubled by Freud and Jung, human motives, like social problems, were clear and accessible, not needing profound analysis. His modernity was not in form but in his quirky, radical content and comment, the articulation of a submerged class by one influenced by some of the most prominent political thinkers since Plato.

Finally, Kipps remains, almost but not quite, what he had always been, in keeping less with Wells's own disposition than with the spirit of romance. He and Ann have learnt more about themselves, about each other; their child will be reared with love outside the follies of the worldly wise, with parents still childlike, in vital conspiracy against adult busybodies, probably still trusting to cheerful improbabilities, envisaged by what Henry James called the easy impudence of genius.

Those individuals who have led secluded or isolated lives, or have hitherto moved in other spheres than those wherein well-bred people move, will gather all the information necessary from these pages to render them thoroughly conversant with the manners and amenities of society.

Manners and Rules of Good Society
By a Member of the Aristocracy

Book One

The Making of Kipps

Chapter One

The Little Shop at New Romney

I

Until he was nearly arrived at manhood, it did not become clear to Kipps how it was that he had come into the care of an aunt and uncle instead of having a father and mother like other little boys. He had vague memories of a somewhere else, a dim room, a window looking down on white buildings, and of a some one else who talked to forgotten people and who was his mother. He could not recall her features very distinctly, but he remembered with extreme definition a white dress she wore, with a pattern of little sprigs of flowers and little bows upon it, and a girdle of straight-ribbed white ribbon about the waist. Linked with this, he knew not how, were clouded, half-obliterated recollections of scenes in which there was weeping, weeping in which he was inscrutably moved to join. Some terrible tall man with a loud voice played a part in these scenes, and, either before or after them, there were impressions of looking for interminable periods out of the window of railway trains in the company of these two people.

He knew, though he could not remember that he had ever been told, that a certain faded wistful face that looked at him from a plush and gilt framed daguerreotype above the mantel of the 'sitting-room' was the face of his mother. But that knowledge did not touch his dim memories with any elucidation. In that photograph she was a girlish figure, leaning against a photographer's stile, and with all the self-conscious shrinking natural to that position. She had curly hair and a face far younger and prettier than any other mother in his experience. She swung a Dolly Varden hat* by the string, and looked with obedient respectful eyes on the photographer-gentleman who had commanded the pose. She was very slight and pretty. But the phantom mother that haunted his memory so elusively was not like that, though he could not remember how she differed.

Perhaps she was older or a little less shrinking, or, it may be, only dressed in a different way. . . .

It is clear she handed him over to his aunt and uncle at New Romney with explicit directions and a certain endowment. One gathers she had something of that fine sense of social distinctions that subsequently played so large a part in Kipps' career. He was not to go to a 'common' school, she provided, but to a certain seminary in Hastings, that was not only a 'middle-class academy' with mortar-boards and every evidence of a higher social tone, but also remarkably cheap. She seems to have been animated by the desire to do her best for Kipps even at a certain sacrifice of herself, as though Kipps were in some way a superior sort of person. She sent pocket-money to him from time to time for a year or more after Hastings had begun for him, but her face he never saw in the days of his lucid memory.

His aunt and uncle were already high on the hill of life when first he came to them. They had married for comfort in the evening or, at any rate, in the late afternoon of their days. They were at first no more than vague figures in the background of proximate realities, such realities as familiar chairs and tables, quiet to ride and drive, the newel of the staircase, kitchen furniture, pieces of firewood, the boiler tap, old newspapers, the cat, the High Street, the back yard, and the flat fields that are always so near in that little town. He knew all the stones in the yard individually, the creeper in the corner, the dustbin and the mossy wall, better than many men know the faces of their wives. There was a corner under the ironing-board which, by means of a shawl, could be made, under propitious gods, a very decent cubby-house, a corner that served him for several years as the indisputable hub of the world, and the stringy places in the carpet, the knots upon the dresser, and the several corners of the rag hearthrug his uncle had made, became essential parts of his mental foundations. The shop he did not know so thoroughly; it was a forbidden region to him, yet somehow he managed to know it very well.

His aunt and uncle were, as it were, the immediate gods of this world, and, like the gods of the world of old, occasionally descended right into it, with arbitrary injunctions and disproportionate punishments. And, unhappily, one rose to their Olympian level at meals. Then one had to say one's 'grace', hold one's spoon and fork in mad, unnatural ways called 'properly', and refrain from eating even nice sweet things 'too fast'. If he 'gobbled' there was trouble, and at the slightest *abandon* with knife, fork, and spoon his aunt rapped his knuckles, albeit his uncle always finished up his gravy with his knife. Sometimes, moreover, his uncle would come pipe in hand out of a sedentary remoteness in the most disconcerting way when a little boy was doing the most natural and attractive things, with 'Drat and drabbit that young rascal! What's he a-doing of now?' and his aunt would appear at door or window to interrupt interesting conversation with children who were upon unknown grounds considered 'low' and undesirable, and call him in. The pleasantest little noises, however softly you did them, drumming on tea-trays, trumpeting your fists, whistling on keys, ringing chimes with a couple of pails, or playing tunes on the window-panes, brought down the gods in anger. Yet what noise is fainter than your finger on the window – gently done? Sometimes, however, these gods gave him broken toys out of the shop, and then one loved them better – for the shop they kept was, among other things, a toy-shop. (The other things included books to read and books to give away, and local photographs; it had some pretensions to be a china-shop and the fascia spoke of glass; it was also a stationer's-shop with a touch of haberdashery about it, and in the windows and odd corners were mats and terra-cotta dishes and milking-stools for painting, and there was a hint of picture-frames, and fire-screens, and fishing-tackle, and air-guns, and bathing-suits, and tents – various things, indeed, but all cruelly attractive to a small boy's fingers.) Once his aunt gave him a trumpet if he would *promise* faithfully not to blow it, and afterwards took it away again. And his aunt made him say his catechism, and something she certainly called the 'Colic for the Day',* every Sunday in the year.

As the two grew old as he grew up, and as his impression of them modified insensibly from year to year, it seemed to him at last that they had always been as they were when in his adolescent days his impression of things grew fixed; his aunt he thought of as always lean, rather worried looking, and prone to a certain obliquity of cap, and his uncle massive, many chinned, and careless about his buttons. They neither visited nor received visitors. They were always very suspicious about their neighbours and other people generally; they feared the 'low' and they hated and despised the 'stuck up', and so they 'kept themselves *to* themselves', according to the English ideal. Consequently little Kipps had no playmates, except through the sin of disobedience. By inherent nature he had a sociable disposition. When he was in the High Street he made a point of saying 'Hello!' to passing cyclists, and he would put his tongue out at the Quodling children whenever their nursemaid was not looking. And he began a friendship with Sid Pornick, the son of the haberdasher next door, that, with wide intermissions, was destined to last his lifetime through.

Pornick the haberdasher, I may say at once, was, according to old Kipps, a 'blaring jackass'; he was a teetotaller, a 'nyar, nyar, 'im-singing Methodis', and altogether distasteful and detrimental, he and his together, to true Kipps ideals so far as little Kipps could gather them. This Pornick certainly possessed an enormous voice, and he annoyed old Kipps greatly by calling 'You — Arn' and 'Siddee' up and down his house. He annoyed old Kipps by private choral services on Sunday, all his family, 'nyar, nyar'-ing; and by mushroom culture, by behaving as though the pilaster between the two shops was common property, by making a noise of hammering in the afternoon when old Kipps wished to be quiet after his midday meal, by going up and down uncarpeted stairs in his boots, by having a black beard, by attempting to be friendly, and by — all that sort of thing. In fact, he annoyed old Kipps. He annoyed him especially with his shop-door mat. Old Kipps never beat his mat, preferring to let sleeping dust lie, and, seeking a motive for a foolish proceeding, he held that Pornick waited until there was a suitable wind in order that the dust disengaged in that operation might defile his neighbour's shop. These issues would frequently develop into loud and vehement quarrels, and on one occasion came so near to violence as to be subsequently described by Pornick (who read his newspaper) as a 'Disgraceful Frackass'. On that occasion he certainly went into his own shop with extreme celerity.

But it was through one of these quarrels that the friendship of little Kipps and Sid Pornick came about. The two small boys found themselves one day looking through the gate at the doctor's goats together; they exchanged a few contradictions about which goat could fight which, and then young Kipps was moved to remark that Sid's father was a 'blaring jackass'. Sid said he wasn't, and Kipps repeated that he was, and quoted his authority. Then Sid, flying off at a tangent rather alarmingly, said he could fight young Kipps with one hand, an assertion young Kipps with a secret want of confidence denied. There were some vain repetitions, and the incident might have ended there, but happily a sporting butcher boy chanced on the controversy at this stage, and insisted upon seeing fair play.

The two small boys, under his pressing encouragement, did at last button up their jackets, square, and fight an edifying drawn battle until it seemed good to the butcher boy to go on with Mrs Holyer's mutton. Then, according to his directions and under his experienced stage management, they shook hands and made it up. Subsequently, a little tear-stained perhaps, but flushed with the butcher boy's approval ('tough little kids'), and with cold stones down their necks as he advised, they sat side by side on the doctor's gate, projecting very much behind, staunching an honourable bloodshed, and expressing respect for one another. Each had a bloody nose and a black eye – three days later they matched to a shade – neither had given in, and, though this was tacit, neither wanted any more.

It was an excellent beginning. After this first encounter the attributes of their parents and their own relative value in battle never rose between them, and if anything was wanted to complete the warmth of their regard it was found in a joint dislike of the eldest Quodling. The eldest Quodling lisped, had a silly sort of straw hat and a large pink face (all covered over with self-satisfaction), and he went to the National school with a green-baize bag – a contemptible thing to do. They called him names and threw stones at him, and when he replied by threatenings ('Look 'ere, young Art Kipth, you better *thtoppit!*') they were moved to attack, and put him to flight.

And after that they broke the head of Ann Pornick's doll, so that she went home weeping loudly – a wicked and endearing proceeding. Sid was whacked, but, as he explained, he wore a newspaper tactically adjusted during the transaction, and really it didn't hurt him at all. . . . And Mrs Pornick put her head out of the shop door suddenly and threatened Kipps as he passed.

'Cavendish Academy', the school that had won the limited
choice of Kipps' vanished mother, was established in a battered
private house in the part of Hastings remotest from the sea; it
was called an Academy for Young Gentlemen, and many of the
young gentlemen had parents in 'India' and other unverifiable
places. Others were the sons of credulous widows anxious, as
Kipps' mother had been, to get something a little 'superior' to a
board school education as cheaply as possible, and others, again,
were sent to demonstrate the dignity of their parents and
guardians. And of course there were boys from France.

Its 'principal' was a lean long creature of indifferent digestion
and temper, who proclaimed himself on a gilt-lettered board in
his front area, George Garden Woodrow, F.S.Sc., letters indicating that he had paid certain guineas for a bogus diploma. A
bleak whitewashed outhouse constituted his schoolroom, and
the scholastic quality of its carved and worn desks and forms
was enhanced by a slippery blackboard and two large yellow
out-of-date maps – one of Africa and the other of Wiltshire –
that he had picked up cheap at a sale. There were other maps
and globes in his study, where he interviewed inquiring parents,
but these his pupils never saw. And in a glass cupboard in the
passage were several shillingsworth of test-tubes and chemicals,
a tripod, a glass retort, and a damaged Bunsen burner, manifesting that the 'Scientific laboratory' mentioned in the prospectus
was no idle boast.

This prospectus, which was in dignified but incorrect English,
laid particular stress on the sound preparation for a commercial
career given in the Academy, but the army, navy, and civil
service were glanced at in an ambiguous sentence. There was
something vague in the prospectus about 'examinational successes' – though Woodrow, of course, disapproved of 'cram' –
and a declaration that the curriculum included 'art', 'modern
foreign languages', and 'a sound technical and scientific training'. Then came insistence upon the 'moral well-being' of the
pupils, and an emphatic boast of the excellence of the religious
instruction, 'so often neglected nowadays even in schools of
wide repute'. 'That's bound to fetch 'em,' Mr Woodrow had
remarked when he drew up the prospectus. And in conjunction
with the mortar-boards it certainly did. Attention was directed

to the 'motherly' care of Mrs Woodrow, in reality a small partially effaced woman with a plaintive face and a mind above cookery, and the prospectus concluded with a phrase intentionally vague, 'Fare unrestricted, and our own milk and produce'.

The memories Kipps carried from that school into after-life were set in an atmosphere of stuffiness and mental muddle, and included countless pictures of sitting on creaking forms bored and idle; of blot licking and the taste of ink; of torn books with covers that set one's teeth on edge; of the slimy surface of the laboured slates; of furtive marble-playing, whispered story-telling, and of pinches, blows, and a thousand such petty annoyances being perpetually 'passed on' according to the custom of the place; of standing up in class and being hit suddenly and unreasonably for imaginary misbehaviour; of Mr Woodrow's raving days, when a scarcely sane injustice pre-vailed; of the cold vacuity of the hour of preparation before the bread-and-butter breakfast; and of horrible headaches and queer, unprecedented internal feelings, resulting from Mrs Woodrow's motherly rather than intelligent cookery. There were dreary walks when the boys marched two by two, all dressed in the mortar-board caps that so impressed the widowed mothers; there were dismal half-holidays when the weather was wet, and the spirit of evil temper and evil imagination had the pent boys to work its will on; there were unfair dishonourable fights, and miserable defeats and victories; there was bullying and being bullied. A coward boy Kipps particularly afflicted, until at last he was goaded to revolt by incessant persecution, and smote Kipps to tolerance with whirling fists. There were memories of sleeping three in a bed; of the dense leathery smell of the schoolroom when one returned thither after ten minutes' play; of a playground of mud and incidental sharp flints. And there was much furtive foul language.

'Our Sundays are our happiest days,' was one of Woodrow's formulae with the inquiring parent, but Kipps was not called in evidence. They were to him terrible gaps of inanity, no work, no play – a drear expanse of time with the mystery of church twice and plum-duff once in the middle. The afternoon was given up to furtive relaxations, among which 'Torture Chamber' games with the less agreeable weaker boys figured. It was from the difference between this day and common days that Kipps derived his first definite conceptions of the nature of God and heaven. His instinct was to evade any closer acquaintance as long as he could.

The solid work varied, according to the prevailing mood of Mr Woodrow. Sometimes that was a despondent lethargy, copy-books were distributed or sums were 'set', or the great mystery of book-keeping was declared in being, and beneath these superficial activities lengthy conversations and interminable guessing games with marbles went on, while Mr Woodrow sat inanimate at his desk heedless of school affairs, staring in front of him at unseen things. At times his face was utterly inane; at times it had an expression of stagnant amazement, as if he saw before his eyes with pitiless clearness the dishonour and mischief of his being. . . .

At other times the F.S.Sc. roused himself to action, and would stand up a wavering class and teach it, goading it with bitter mockery and blows through a chapter of Ahn's 'First French Course; or, France and the French', or a dialogue about a traveller's washing or the parts of an opera house. His own knowledge of French had been obtained years ago in another English private school, and he had refreshed it by occasional weeks of loafing and mean adventure in Dieppe. He would sometimes in their lessons hit upon some reminiscence of these brighter days, and then he would laugh inexplicably and repeat French phrases of an unfamiliar type.

Among the commoner exercises he prescribed the learning of long passages of poetry from a 'Potry Book', which he would delegate an elder boy to 'hear'; and there was reading aloud from the Holy Bible, verse by verse – it was none of your 'godless' schools! – so that you counted the verses up to your turn and then gave yourself to conversation; and sometimes one read from a cheap History of this land. They did, as Kipps reported, 'loads of catechism'. Also there was much learning of geographical names and lists, and sometimes Woodrow, in an outbreak of energy, would see these names were actually found in a map. And once, just once, there was a chemistry lesson – a lesson of indescribable excitement – glass things of the strangest shape, a smell like bad eggs, something bubbling in something, a smash and stench, and Mr Woodrow saying quite distinctly – they threshed it out in the dormitory afterwards – 'Damn!' Followed by the whole school being kept in, with extraordinary severities, for an hour. . . .

But interspersed with the memories of this grey routine were certain patches of brilliant colour, the Holidays, his holidays, which, in spite of the feud between their seniors, he spent as much as possible with Sid Pornick, the son of the irascible black-bearded haberdasher next door. They seemed to be memories of a different world. There were glorious days of 'mucking about' along the beach, the siege of unresisting Martello towers, the incessant interest of the mystery and motion of windmills, the windy excursions with boarded feet over the yielding shingle to Dungeness lighthouse – Sid Pornick and he far adrift from reality, smugglers and armed men from the moment they left Great Stone behind them – wanderings in the hedgeless reedy marsh, long excursions reaching even to Hythe where the machine guns of the Empire are for ever whirling and tapping, and to Rye and Winchelsea perched like dream-cities on their little hills. The sky in these memories was the blazing hemisphere of the marsh heavens in summer, or its wintry tumult of sky and sea; and there were wrecks, real wrecks, in it (near Dymchurch pitched high and blackened and rotting were the ribs of a fishing-smack, flung aside like an empty basket when the sea had devoured its crew), and there was bathing all naked in the sea, bathing to one's armpits, and even trying to swim in the warm sea-water (spite of his aunt's prohibition) and (with her indulgence) the rare eating of dinner from a paper parcel miles away from home. Toke and cold ground-rice puddin' with plums it used to be – there is no better food at all. And for the background, in the place of Woodrow's mean and fretting rule, were his aunt's spare but frequently quite amiable figure – for though she insisted on his repeating the English church cate-chism every Sunday, she had an easy way over dinners that one wanted to take abroad – and his uncle, corpulent and irascible, but sedentary and easily escaped. And freedom!

The holidays were indeed very different from school. They were free, they were spacious, and though he never knew it in these words – they had an element of beauty. In his memory of his boyhood they shone like strips of stained-glass window in a dreary waste of scholastic wall, they grew brighter and brighter as they grew remoter. There came a time at last and moods when he could look back to them with a feeling akin to tears.

The last of these windows was the brightest, and instead of the kaleidoscopic effects of its predecessors its glory was a single figure. For in the last of his holidays before the Moloch of Retail Trade got hold of him, Kipps made his first tentative essays at the mysterious shrine of Love. Very tentative they were, for he had become a boy of subdued passions, and potential rather than actual affectionateness.

And the object of these first stirrings of the great desire was no other than Ann Pornick, the head of whose doll he and Sid had broken long ago, and rejoiced over long ago, in the days when he had yet to learn the meaning of a heart.

III

Negotiations were already on foot to make Kipps into a draper before he discovered the lights that lurked in Ann Pornick's eyes. School was over, absolutely over, and it was chiefly present to him that he was never to go to school again. It was high summer. The 'breaking up' of school had been hilarious; and the excellent maxim, 'Last Day's Pay Day', had been observed by him with a scrupulous attention to his honour. He had punched the heads of all his enemies, wrung wrists and kicked shins; he had distributed all his unfinished copybooks, all his school books, his collection of marbles, and his mortar-board cap among such as loved him; and he had secretly written in obscure pages of their books 'remember Art Kipps'. He had also split the anaemic Woodrow's cane, carved his own name deeply in several places about the premises, and broken the scullery window. He had told everybody so often that he was to learn to be a sea captain, that he had come almost to believe the thing himself. And now he was home, and school was at an end for him for evermore.

He was up before six on the day of his return, and out in the hot sunlight of the yard. He set himself to whistle a peculiarly penetrating arrangement of three notes, supposed by the boys of the Hastings Academy and himself and Sid Pornick, for no earthly reason whatever, to be the original Huron* war-cry. As he did this he feigned not to be doing it, because of the hatred between his uncle and the Pornicks, but to be examining with respect and admiration a new wing of the dustbin recently erected by his uncle – a pretence that would not have deceived a nestling tomtit.

Presently there came a familiar echo from the Pornick hunting-ground. Then Kipps began to sing, 'Ar pars eight tra-la, in the lane be'ind the church.' To which an unseen person answered, 'Ar pars eight it is, in the lane be'ind the church.' The 'tra-la' was considered to render this statement incomprehensible to the uninitiated. In order to conceal their operations still more securely, both parties to this duet then gave vent to a vocalization of the Huron war-cry again, and after a lingering repetition of the last and shrillest note, dispersed severally, as became boys in the enjoyment of holidays, to light the house fires for the day.

Half-past eight found Kipps sitting on the sunlit gate at the top of the long lane that runs towards the sea, clashing his boots in a slow rhythm, and whistling with great violence all that he knew of an excruciatingly pathetic air. There appeared along by the churchyard wall a girl in a short frock, brown-haired, quick-coloured, and with dark blue eyes. She had grown so that she was a little taller than Kipps, and her colour had improved. He scarcely remembered her, so changed was she since last holidays – if, indeed, he had seen her during his last holidays, a thing he could not clearly recollect.

Some vague emotion arose at the sight of her. He stopped whistling and regarded her, oddly tongue-tied.

'He can't come,' said Ann, advancing boldly. 'Not yet.'

'What – not Sid?'

'No. Father's made him dust all his boxes again.'

'What for?'

'I dunno. Father's in a stew 's morning.'

'Oh!'

Pause. Kipps looked at her, and then was unable to look at her again. She regarded him with interest. 'You left school?' she remarked, after a pause.

'Yes.'

'So's Sid.'

The conversation languished. Ann put her hands on the top of the gate, and began a stationary hopping, a sort of ineffectual gymnastic experiment.

'Can you run?' she said presently.

'Run you any day,' said Kipps.

'Gimme a start?'

'Where for?' said Kipps.

Ann considered, and indicated a tree. She walked towards it and turned. 'Gimme to here?' she called. Kipps, standing now and touching the gate, smiled to express conscious superiority. 'Further!' he said.

'Here?'

'Bit more!' said Kipps; and then, repenting of his magnanimity, said 'Orf!' suddenly, and so recovered his lost concession.

They arrived abreast at the tree, flushed and out of breath. 'Tie!' said Ann, throwing her hair back from her face with her hand. 'I won,' panted Kipps. They disputed firmly, but quite politely. 'Run it again, then,' said Kipps. '*I* don't mind.'

They returned towards the gate.

'You don't run bad,' said Kipps, temperately, expressing sincere admiration. 'I'm pretty good, you know.'

Ann sent her hair back by an expert toss of the head. 'You give me a start,' she allowed.

They became aware of Sid approaching them. 'You better look out, young Ann,' said Sid, with that irreverent want of sympathy usual in brothers. 'You been out nearly 'arf-'our. Nothing ain't been done upstairs. Father said he didn't know where you was, but when he did he'd warm y'r young ear.'

Ann prepared to go.

'How about that race?' asked Kipps.

'Lor!' cried Sid, quite shocked. 'You ain't been racing *her*!'

Ann swung herself round the end of the gate with her eyes on Kipps, and then turned away suddenly and ran off down the lane. Kipps' eyes tried to go after her, and came back to Sid's.

'I give her a lot of start,' said Kipps, apologetically. 'It wasn't a proper race.' And so the subject was dismissed. But Kipps was *distrait* for some seconds perhaps, and the mischief had begun in him.

IV

They proceeded to the question of how two accomplished Hurons might most satisfactorily spend the morning. Manifestly their line lay straight along the lane to the sea. 'There's a new wreck,' said Sid, 'and my! – don't it stink just!'

'Stink?'

'Fair make you sick. It's rotten wheat.'

They fell to talking of wrecks, and so came to ironclads and wars and such-like manly matters. Halfway to the wreck Kipps made a casual irrelevant remark.

'Your sister ain't a bad sort,' he said off-handedly.

'I clout her a lot,' said Sidney, modestly; and, after a pause, the talk reverted to more suitable topics.

The new wreck was full of rotting grain, and stank abominably, even as Sid had said. This was excellent. They had it all to themselves. They took possession of it in force, at Sid's suggestion, and had speedily to defend it against enormous numbers of imaginary 'natives', who were at last driven off by loud shouts of *bang*, *bang*, and vigorous thrusting and shoving of sticks. Then, also at Sid's direction, they sailed with it into the midst of a combined French, German, and Russian fleet, demolishing the combination unassisted, and having descended to the beach, clambered up the side and cut out their own vessel in brilliant style, they underwent a magnificent shipwreck (with vocalized thunder) and floated 'water-logged' – so Sid insisted – upon an exhausted sea.

These things drove Ann out of mind for a time. But at last, as they drifted without food or water upon a stagnant ocean, haggard-eyed, chins between their hands, looking in vain for a sail, she came to mind again abruptly.

'It's rather nice 'aving sisters,' remarked one perishing mariner.

Sid turned round and regarded him thoughtfully.

'Not it!' he said.

'No?'

'Not a bit of it.'

He grinned confidentially. 'Know too much,' he said, and afterwards, 'get out of things.'

He resumed his gloomy scrutiny of the hopeless horizon. Presently he fell spitting jerkily between his teeth, as he had read was the way with such ripe manhood as chews its quid.

'Sisters,' he said, 'is rot. That's what sisters are. Girls if you like, but sisters – *No!*'

'But ain't sisters girls?'

'*N-eaow!*' said Sid, with unspeakable scorn; and Kipps answered, 'Of course. I didn't mean—I wasn't thinking of that.'

'You got a girl?' asked Sid, spitting very cleverly again.

Kipps admitted his deficiency. He felt compunction.

'You don't know who *my* girl is, Art Kipps, I bet.'

'Who *is*, then?' asked Kipps, still chiefly occupied by his own poverty.

'Ah!'

Kipps let a moment elapse before he did his duty. 'Tell us!'

Sid eyed him and hesitated.

'Secret?' he said.

'Secret.'

'Dying solemn?'

'Dying solemn!' Kipps' self-concentration passed into curiosity.

Sid administered a terrible oath.

Sid adhered lovingly to his facts. 'It begins with a Nem,' he said, doling it out parsimoniously.

'M-A-U-D,' he spelt, with a stern eye on Kipps. 'C-H-A-R-T-E-R-I-S.'

Now, Maud Charteris was a young person of eighteen and the daughter of the vicar of St Bavon's – besides which she had a bicycle – so that as her name unfolded the face of Kipps lengthened with respect. 'Get out,' he gasped incredulously. 'She ain't your girl, Sid Pornick.'

'She is!' answered Sid, stoutly.

'What – truth?'

'*Truth*.'

Kipps scrutinized his face. 'Reely?'

Sid touched wood, whistled, and repeated a binding doggerel with great solemnity.

Kipps still struggled with the amazing new light on the world about him. 'D'you mean – she knows?'

Sid flushed deeply, and his aspect became stern and gloomy. He resumed his wistful scrutiny of the sunlit sea. 'I'd die for that girl, Art Kipps,' he said presently; and Kipps did not press a question he felt to be ill-timed. 'I'd do anything she asked me to do,' said Sid; 'just anything. If she was to ask me to chuck myself into the sea.' He met Kipps' eye. 'I *would*,' he said.

They were pensive for a space, and then Sid began to discourse in fragments of Love, a theme upon which Kipps had already in a furtive way meditated a little, but which, apart from badinage, he had never yet heard talked about in the light of day. Of course, many and various aspects of life had come to light in the muffled exchange of knowledge that went on under the shadow of Woodrow, but this of Sentimental Love was not among them. Sid, who was a boy with an imagination, having once broached this topic, opened his heart, or, at any rate, a new chamber of his heart, to Kipps, and found no fault with Kipps for a lack of return. He produced a thumbed novelette that had played a part in his sentimental awakening; he proffered it to Kipps, and confessed there was a character in it, a baronet, singularly like himself. This baronet was a person of volcanic passions, which he concealed beneath a demeanour of 'icy cynicism'. The utmost expression he permitted himself was to grit his teeth, and, now his attention was called to it, Kipps remarked that Sid also had a habit of gritting his teeth, and, indeed, had had all the morning. They read for a time, and presently Sid talked again. The conception of love Sid made evident, was compact of devotion and much spirited fighting and a touch of mystery, but through all that cloud of talk there floated before Kipps a face that was flushed and hair that was tossed aside.

So they budded, sitting on the blackening old wreck in which men had lived and died, looking out to sea, talking of that other sea upon which they must presently embark. . . .

They ceased to talk, and Sid read; but Kipps, falling behind with the reading, and not wishing to admit that he read slowlier than Sid, whose education was of the inferior Elementary School brand, lapsed into meditation.

'I *would* like to 'ave a girl,' said Kipps.

'I mean just to talk to, and all that. . . .'

A floating sack distracted them at last from this obscure topic. They abandoned the wreck, and followed the new interest a mile along the beach, bombarding it with stones until it came to land. They had inclined to a view that it would contain romantic mysteries, but it was simply an ill-preserved kitten – too much even for them. And at last they were drawn dinnerward, and went home hungry and pensive side by side.

v

But Kipps' imagination had been warmed by that talk of love, and in the afternoon when he saw Ann Pornick in the High Street and said 'Hello!' it was a different 'hello' from that of their previous intercourse. And when they had passed they both looked back and caught each other doing so. Yes, he *did* want a girl badly. . . .

Afterwards he was distracted by a traction engine going through the town, and his aunt had got some sprats for supper. When he was in bed, however, sentiment came upon him again in a torrent quite abruptly and abundantly, and he put his head under the pillow and whispered very softly, 'I love Ann Pornick,' as a sort of supplementary devotion.

In his subsequent dreams he ran races with Ann, and they lived in a wreck together, and always her face was flushed and her hair about her face. They just lived in a wreck and ran races, and were very, very fond of one another. And their favourite food was rock chocolate, dates, such as one buys off barrows, and sprats – fried sprats. . . .

In the morning he could hear Ann singing in the scullery next door. He listened to her for some time, and it was clear to him that he must put things before her.

Towards dusk that evening they chanced on one another out by the gate by the church, but though there was much in his mind, it stopped there with a resolute shyness until he and Ann were out of breath catching cockchafers and were sitting on that gate of theirs again. Ann sat up upon the gate, dark against vast masses of flaming crimson and darkling purple, and her eyes looked at Kipps from a shadowed face. There came a stillness between them, and quite abruptly he was moved to tell his love.

'Ann,' he said, 'I *do* like you. I wish you was my girl. . . .'

'I say, Ann. Will you *be* my girl?'

Ann made no pretence of astonishment. She weighed the proposal for a moment with her eyes on Kipps. 'If you like, Artie,' she said lightly. '*I* don't mind if I am.'

'All right,' said Kipps, breathless with excitement, 'then you are.'

'All right,' said Ann.

Something seemed to fall between them, they no longer looked openly at one another. 'Lor!' cried Ann, suddenly, 'see that one!' and jumped down and darted after a cockchafer that had boomed within a yard of her face. And with that they were girl and boy again. . . .

They avoided their new relationship painfully.

They did not recur to it for several days, though they met twice. Both felt that there remained something before this great experience was to be regarded as complete; but there was an infinite diffidence about the next step. Kipps talked in fragments of all sorts of matters, telling particularly of the great things that were being done to make a man and a draper of him; how he had two new pairs of trousers and a black coat and four new shirts. And all the while his imagination was urging him to that unknown next step, and when he was alone and in the dark he became even an enterprising wooer. It became evident to him that it would be nice to take Ann by the hand; even the decorous novelettes Sid affected egged him on to that greater nearness of intimacy.

Then a great idea came to him, in a paragraph called 'Lover's Tokens' that he read in a torn fragment of *Tit Bits*.* It fell in to the measure of his courage – a divided sixpence! He secured his aunt's best scissors, fished a sixpence out of his jejune tin money-box, and jabbed his finger in a varied series of attempts to get it in half. When they met again the sixpence was still undivided. He had not intended to mention the matter to her at that stage, but it came up spontaneously. He endeavoured to explain the theory of broken sixpences and his unexpected failure to break one.

'But what you break it for?' said Ann. 'It's no good if it's broke.'

'It's a Token,' said Kipps.

'Like—?'

'Oh, you keep half and I keep half, and when we're sep'rated, you look at your half and I look at mine – see? Then we think of each other.'

'Oh!' said Ann, and appeared to assimilate this information.

'Only, *I* can't get it in 'arf nohow,' said Kipps.

They discussed this difficulty for some time without illumination. Then Ann had a happy thought.

'Tell you what,' she said, starting away from him abruptly and laying a hand on his arm, 'you let *me* 'ave it, Artie. I know where father keeps his file.'

Kipps handed her the sixpence, and they came upon a pause. 'I'll easy do it,' said Ann.

In considering the sixpence side by side, his head had come near her cheek. Quite abruptly he was moved to take his next step into the unknown mysteries of love.

'Ann,' he said, and gulped at his temerity, 'I *do* love you. Straight. I'd do anything for you, Ann. Reely – I would.'

He paused for breath. She answered nothing, but she was no doubt enjoying herself. He came yet closer to her, his shoulder touched hers. 'Ann, I wish you'd—'

He stopped.

'What?' said Ann.

'Ann – lemme kiss you.'

Things seemed to hang for a space; his tone, the drop of his courage made the thing incredible as he spoke. Kipps was not of that bold order of wooers who impose conditions.

Ann perceived that she was not prepared for kissing after all. Kissing, she said, was silly, and when Kipps would have displayed a belated enterprise she flung away from him. He essayed argument. He stood afar off as it were – the better part of a yard – and said she *might* let him kiss her, and then that he didn't see what good it was for her to be his girl if he couldn't kiss her. . . .

She repeated that kissing was silly. A certain estrangement took them homeward. They arrived in the dusky High Street not exactly together, and not exactly apart, but straggling. They had not kissed, but all the guilt of kissing was between them. When Kipps saw the portly contours of his uncle standing dimly in the shop doorway his footsteps faltered, and the space between our young couple increased. Above, the window over Pornick's shop was open, and Mrs Pornick was visible, taking the air. Kipps assumed an expression of extreme innocence. He found himself face to face with his uncle's advanced outposts of waistcoat buttons.

'Where ye bin, my boy?'

'Bin for a walk, uncle.'

'Not along of that brat of Pornick's?'

'Along of who?'

'That gell' – indicating Ann with his pipe.

'Oh no, uncle!' – very faintly.

'Run in, my boy.' Old Kipps stood aside, with an oblique glance upward, and his nephew brushed clumsily by him and vanished out of sight of the street into the vague obscurity of the little shop. The door closed behind old Kipps with a nervous jangle of its bell, and he set himself to light the single oil-lamp that illuminated the shop at nights. It was an operation requiring care and watching, or else it flared and 'smelt'. Often it smelt after all. Kipps, for some reason, found the dusky living-room with his aunt in it too populous for his feelings, and went upstairs.

'That brat of Pornick's!' It seemed to him that a horrible catastrophe had occurred. He felt he had identified himself inextricably with his uncle and cut himself off from her for ever by saying 'Oh no!' At supper he was so visibly depressed that his aunt asked him if he wasn't feeling well. Under this imminent threat of medicine he assumed an unnatural cheerfulness. . . .

He lay awake for nearly half an hour that night groaning because things had all gone wrong, because Ann wouldn't let him kiss her, and because his uncle had called her a brat. It seemed to Kipps almost as though he himself had called her a brat. . . .

There came an interval during which Ann was altogether inaccessible. One, two, three days passed and he did not see her. Sid he met several times; they went fishing, and twice they bathed, but though Sid lent and received back two further love stories, they talked no more of love. They kept themselves in accord however, agreeing that the most flagrantly sentimental story was 'proper'. Kipps was always wanting to speak of Ann, and never daring to do so. He saw her on Sunday evening going off to chapel. She was more beautiful than ever in her Sunday clothes, but she pretended not to see him because her mother was with her. But he thought she pretended not to see him because she had given him up for ever. Brat! – who could be expected ever to forgive that? He abandoned himself to despair, he ceased even to haunt the places where she might be found. . . .

With paralyzing unexpectedness came the end.

Mr Shalford, the draper at Folkestone to whom he was to be bound apprentice, had expressed a wish to 'shape the lad a bit' before the autumn sale. Kipps became aware that his box was being packed, and gathered the full truth of things on the evening before his departure. He became feverishly eager to see Ann just once more. He made silly and needless excuses to go out into the yard, he walked three times across the street without any excuse at all to look up at the Pornick windows. Still she was hidden. He grew desperate. It was within half an hour of his departure that he came on Sid.

'Hello!' he said, 'I'm orf!'

'Business?'

'Yes.'

Pause.

'I say, Sid. You going 'ome?'

'Straight now.'

'D'you mind—. Ask Ann about that.'

'About what?'

'She'll know.'

And Sid said he would. But even that, it seemed, failed to evoke Ann.

At last the Folkestone bus rumbled up, and he ascended. His aunt stood in the doorway to see him off. His uncle assisted with the box and portmanteau. Only furtively could he glance up at the Pornick windows, and still it seemed Ann hardened her heart against him. 'Get up!' said the driver, and the hoofs began to clatter. No – she would not come out even to see him off. The bus was in motion, and old Kipps was going back into his shop. Kipps stared in front of him, assuring himself that he did not care.

He heard a door slam, and instantly craned out his neck to look back. He knew that slam so well. Behold! out of the haberdasher's door a small untidy figure in homely pink print had shot resolutely into the road and was sprinting in pursuit. In a dozen seconds she was abreast of the bus. At the sight of her Kipps' heart began to beat very quickly, but he made no immediate motion of recognition.

'Artie!' she cried breathlessly. 'Artie! Artie! You know! I got *that*!'

The bus was already quickening its pace and leaving her behind again, when Kipps realized what 'that' meant. He became animated, he gasped, and gathered his courage together and mumbled an incoherent request to the driver to 'stop jest a jiff for sunthin''. The driver grunted, as the disparity of their years demanded, and then the bus had pulled up and Ann was below.

She leapt up upon the wheel. Kipps looked down into Ann's face, and it was foreshortened and resolute. He met her eyes just for one second as their hands touched. He was not a reader of eyes. Something passed quickly from hand to hand, something that the driver, alert at the corner of his eye, was not allowed to see. Kipps hadn't a word to say, and all she said was, 'I done it, smorning.' It was like a blank space in which something pregnant should have been written and wasn't. Then she dropped down, and the bus moved forward.

After the lapse of about ten seconds, it occurred to him to stand and wave his new bowler hat at her over the corner of the bus top, and to shout hoarsely, 'Goo'-bye, Ann! Don't forget me – while I'm away!'

She stood in the road looking after him, and presently she waved her hand.

He remained standing unstably, his bright flushed face looking back at her and his hair fluffing in the wind, and he waved his hat until at last the bend of the road hid her from his eyes. Then he turned about and sat down, and presently he began to put the half-sixpence he held clenched in his hand into his trouser-pocket. He looked sideways at the driver to judge how much he had seen.

Then he fell a thinking. He resolved that, come what might, when he came back to New Romney at Christmas, he would, by hook or by crook, kiss Ann.

Then everything would be perfect and right, and he would be perfectly happy.

Chapter Two

The Emporium

I

When Kipps left New Romney, with a small yellow tin box, a still smaller portmanteau, a new umbrella, and a keepsake half-sixpence, to become a draper, he was a youngster of fourteen, thin, with whimsical drakes'-tails at the pole of his head, smallish features, and eyes that were sometimes very light and sometimes very dark, gifts those of his birth; and by the nature of his training he was indistinct in his speech, confused in his mind, and retreating in his manners. Inexorable fate had appointed him to serve his country in commerce, and the same national bias towards private enterprise and leaving bad alone, which had left his general education to Mr Woodrow, now indentured him firmly into the hands of Mr Shalford of the Folkestone Drapery Bazaar. Apprenticeship is still the recognized English way to the distributing branch of the social service. If Mr Kipps had been so unfortunate as to have been born a German he might have been educated in an elaborate and costly special school ('over-educated – crammed up' – old Kipps) to fit him for his end – such being their pedagogic way. He might—. But why make unpatriotic reflections in a novel? There was nothing pedagogic about Mr Shalford.

He was an irascible, energetic little man with hairy hands, for the most part under his coat-tails, a long shiny bald head, a pointed aquiline nose a little askew, and a neatly trimmed beard. He walked lightly and with a confident jerk, and he was given to humming. He had added to exceptional business 'push', bankruptcy under the old dispensation, and judicious matrimony. His establishment was now one of the most considerable in Folkestone, and he insisted on marking every inch of frontage by alternate stripes of green and yellow down the houses over the shops. His shops were numbered 3, 5, and 7 on the street, and on his bill-heads 3 to 7. He encountered the abashed and awestricken Kipps with the praises of his System and himself.

He spread himself out behind his desk with a grip on the lapel of his coat and made Kipps a sort of speech. 'We expect y'r to work, y'r know, and we expect y'r to study our interests,' explained Mr Shalford, in the regal and commercial plural. 'Our System here is the best system y'r could have. I made it, and I ought to know. I began at the very bottom of the ladder when I was fourteen, and there isn't a step in it I don't know. Not a step. Mr Booch in the desk will give y'r the card of rules and fines. Jest wait a minute.' He pretended to be busy with some dusty memoranda under a paper-weight, while Kipps stood in a sort of paralysis of awe regarding his new master's oval baldness. 'Two thous'n three forty-seven pounds,' whispered Mr Shalford, audibly, feigning forgetfulness of Kipps. Clearly a place of great transactions!

Mr Shalford rose, and, handing Kipps a blotting-pad and an inkpot to carry, mere symbols of servitude, for he made no use of them, emerged into a counting-house where three clerks had been feverishly busy ever since his door-handle had turned. 'Booch,' said Mr Shalford, ''ave y'r copy of the Rules?' and a down-trodden, shabby little old man, with a ruler in one hand and a quill pen in his mouth, silently held out a small book with green and yellow covers, mainly devoted, as Kipps presently discovered, to a voracious system of Fines. He became acutely aware that his hands were full and that everybody was staring at him. He hesitated a moment before putting the inkpot down to free a hand.

'Mustn't fumble like *that*,' said Mr Shalford as Kipps pocketed the Rules. 'Won't do here. Come along, come along,' cocked his coat-tails high, as a lady might hold up her dress, and led the way into the shop.

A vast interminable place it seemed to Kipps, with unending shining counters and innumerable faultlessly dressed young men and, presently, Houri-like young women staring at him. Here there was a long vista of gloves dangling from overhead rods, there ribbons and baby linen. A short young lady in black mittens was making out the account of a customer, and was clearly confused in her addition by Shalford's eagle eye.

A thick-set young man with a bald head and a round, very wise face, who was profoundly absorbed in adjusting all the empty chairs down the counter to absolutely equal distances, awoke out of his preoccupation and answered respectfully to a

few Napoleonic and quite unnecessary remarks from his
employer. Kipps was told that this young man's name was Mr
Buggins, and that he was to do whatever Mr Buggins told him
to do.

They came round a corner into a new smell, which was
destined to be the smell of Kipps' life for many years, the vague
distinctive smell of Manchester goods. A fat man with a large
nose jumped – actually jumped – at their appearance, and began
to fold a pattern of damask in front of him exactly like an
automaton that is suddenly set going. 'Carshot, see to this boy
to-morrow,' said the master. 'See he don't fumble. Smart'n 'im
up.'

'Yussir,' said Carshot fatly, glanced at Kipps, and resumed his
pattern-folding with extreme zeal.

'Whatever Mr Carshot says y'r to do, ye *do*,' said Mr
Shalford, trotting onward; and Carshot blew out his face with
an appearance of relief.

They crossed a large room full of the strangest things Kipps
had ever seen. Lady-like figures, surmounted by black wooden
knobs in the place of the refined heads one might have reasonably expected, stood about with a lifelike air of conscious
fashion. 'Costume Room,' said Shalford. Two voices engaged in
some sort of argument – 'I can assure you, Miss Mergle, you are
entirely mistaken – entirely, in supposing I should do anything
so unwomanly,' – sank abruptly, and they discovered two young
ladies, taller and fairer than any of the other young ladies, and
with black trains to their dresses, who were engaged in writing
at a little table. Whatever they told him to do Kipps gathered he
was to do. He was also, he understood, to do whatever Carshot
and Booch told him to do. And there were also Buggins and Mr
Shalford. And not to forget or fumble!

They descended into a cellar called 'The Warehouse', and
Kipps had an optical illusion of errand-boys fighting. Some
aerial voice said 'Teddy!' and the illusion passed. He looked
again, and saw quite clearly that they were packing parcels, and
always would be, and that the last thing in the world that they
would or could possibly do was to fight. Yet he gathered from
the remarks Mr Shalford addressed to their busy backs that they
had been fighting – no doubt at some past period of their lives.

Emerging in the shop again among a litter of toys and what
are called 'fancy articles', Shalford withdrew a hand from

beneath his coat-tails to indicate an overhead change carrier. He entered into elaborate calculations to show how many minutes in one year were saved thereby, and lost himself among the figures. 'Seven tums eight seven nine – was it? Or seven eight nine? Now, *now*! Why, when I was a boy your age I c'd do a sum like that as soon as hear it. We'll soon get y'r into better shape than that. Make you Fishent. Well, y'r must take my word it comes to pounds and pounds saved in the year – pounds and pounds. System! System everywhere. Fishency.' He went on murmuring 'Fishency' and 'System' at intervals for some time. They passed into a yard, and Mr Shalford waved his hand to his three delivery vans, all striped green and yellow – 'uniform – green, yell'r – System'. All over the premises were pinned absurd little cards, 'This door locked after 7.30. By order, Edwin Shalford', and the like.

Mr Shalford always wrote 'By Order', though it conveyed no earthly meaning to him. He was one of those people who collect technicalities upon them as the Reduvius bug collects dirt. He was the sort of man who is not only ignorant but absolutely incapable of English. When he wanted to say he had a sixpenny-ha'penny longcloth to sell, he put it thus to startled customers: 'Can DO you one, six-half, if y' like.' He always omitted pronouns and articles and so forth; it seemed to him the very essence of the efficiently business-like. His only preposition was 'as' or the compound 'as per'. He abbreviated every word he could; he would have considered himself the laughing-stock of Wood Street if he had chanced to spell *socks* in any way but 'sox'. But, on the other hand, if he saved words here he wasted them there; he never acknowledged an order that was not an esteemed favour, nor sent a pattern without begging to submit it. He never stipulated for so many months' credit, but bought in November 'as Jan'. It was not only words he abbreviated in his London communications. In paying his wholesalers his 'System' admitted of a constant error in the discount of a penny or twopence, and it 'facilitated business', he alleged, to ignore odd pence in the cheques he wrote. His ledger clerk was so struck with the beauty of this part of the System that he started a private one on his own account with the stamp-box that never came to Shalford's knowledge.

This admirable British merchant would glow with a particular pride of intellect when writing his London orders.

'Ah! do y'r think *you'll* ever be able to write London orders?' he would say with honest pride to Kipps, waiting impatiently long after closing-time to take these triumphs of commercial efficiency to post, and so end the interminable day.

Kipps shook his head, anxious for Mr Shalford to get on.

'Now, here, f'example, I've written – see? "1 piece 1 in. cott blk elas 1 / or"; what do I mean by that *or* – eh? d'ye know?'

Kipps promptly hadn't the faintest idea.

'And then, "2 ea silk net as per patts herewith"; *ea* – eh?'

'Dunno, sir.'

It was not Mr Shalford's way to explain things. 'Dear, dear! Pity you couldn't get some c'mercial education at your school. 'Stid of all this lit'ry stuff. Well, my boy, if y'r not a bit sharper, y'll never write London orders, *that's* pretty plain. Jest stick stamps on all those letters, and mind y'r stick 'em right way up, and try and profit a little more by the opportunities your aunt and uncle have provided ye. Can't say *what'll* happen t'ye if ye don't.'

And Kipps, tired, hungry, and belated, set about stamping with vigour and despatch.

'Lick the *envelope*,' said Mr Shalford, 'lick the *envelope*,' as though he grudged the youngster the postage-stamp gum. 'It's the little things mount up,' he would say; and indeed that was his philosophy of life – to hustle and save, always to hustle and save. His political creed linked Reform, which meant nothing, with Peace and Economy, which meant a sweated expenditure, and his conception of a satisfactory municipal life was to 'keep down the rates'. Even his religion was to save his soul, and to preach a similar cheeseparing to the world.

II

The indentures that bound Kipps to Mr Shalford were antique and complex; they insisted on the latter gentleman's parental privileges, they forbade Kipps to dice and game, they made him over, body and soul, to Mr Shalford for seven long years, the crucial years of his life. In return there were vague stipulations about teaching the whole art and mystery of the trade to him, but as there was no penalty attached to negligence, Mr Shalford, being a sound practical business man, considered this a mere rhetorical flourish, and set himself assiduously to get as much out of Kipps and to put as little into him as he could in the seven years of their intercourse.

What he put into Kipps was chiefly bread and margarine, infusions of chicory and tea-dust, colonial meat by contract at threepence a pound, potatoes by the sack, and watered beer. If, however, Kipps chose to buy any supplementary material for growth, Mr Shalford had the generosity to place his kitchen resources at his disposal free – if the fire chanced to be going. He was also allowed to share a bedroom with eight other young men, and to sleep in a bed which, except in very severe weather, could be made, with the help of his overcoat and private underlinen, not to mention newspapers, quite sufficiently warm for any reasonable soul. In addition, Kipps was taught the list of fines, and how to tie up parcels, to know where goods were kept in Mr Shalford's systematized shop, to hold his hands extended upon the counter, and to repeat such phrases as 'What can I have the pleasure—?' 'No trouble, I 'ssure you,' and the like; to block, fold, and measure materials of all sorts, to lift his hat from his head when he passed Mr Shalford abroad, and to practise a servile obedience to a large number of people. But he was not, of course, taught the 'cost' mark of the goods he sold, nor anything of the method of buying such goods. Nor was his attention directed to the unfamiliar social habits and fashions to which his trade ministered. The use of half the goods he saw sold and was presently to assist in selling he did not understand; materials for hangings, cretonnes, chintzes, and the like; serviettes, and all the bright hard whitewear of a well-ordered house; pleasant dress materials, linings, stiffenings; they were to him from first to last no more than things, heavy and difficult to handle in bulk, that one folded up, unfolded, cut into lengths, and saw dwindle and pass away out into that mysterious happy world in which the Customer dwells. Kipps hurried from piling linen table-cloths, that were, collectively, as heavy as lead, to eat off oil-cloth in a gas-lit dining-room underground, and he dreamt of combing endless blankets beneath his overcoat, spare undershirt, and three newspapers. So he had at least the chance of learning the beginnings of philosophy.

In return for these benefits he worked so that he commonly went to bed exhausted and footsore. His round began at half-past six in the morning, when he would descend, unwashed and shirtless, in old clothes and a scarf, and dust boxes and yawn, and take down wrappers and clean the windows until eight. Then in half an hour he would complete his toilet, and take an austere breakfast of bread and margarine and what only an Imperial Englishman would admit to be coffee, after which refreshment he ascended to the shop for the labours of the day. Commonly these began with a mighty running to and fro with planks and boxes and goods for Carshot the window-dresser, who, whether he worked well or ill, nagged persistently, by reason of a chronic indigestion, until the window was done. Sometimes the costume window had to be dressed, and then Kipps staggered down the whole length of the shop from the costume-room with one after another of those ladylike shapes grasped firmly but shamefully each about her single ankle of wood. Such days as there was no window-dressing there was a mighty carrying and lifting of blocks and bales of goods into piles and stacks. After this there were terrible exercises, at first almost despairfully difficult; certain sorts of goods that came in folded had to be rolled upon rollers, and for the most part refused absolutely to be rolled, at any rate by Kipps; certain other sorts of goods that came from the wholesalers rolled had to be measured and folded, and folding makes young apprentices wish they were dead. All of it, too, quite avoidable trouble, you know, that is not avoided because of the cheapness of the genteeler sorts of labour and the dearness of forethought in the world. And then consignments of new goods had to be marked off and packed into paper parcels, and Carshot packed like conjuring tricks, and Kipps packed like a boy with tastes in some other direction – not ascertained. And always Carshot nagged—.

He had a curious formula of appeal to his visceral oeconomy that the refinement of our times and the earnest entreaties of my friends oblige me to render by an etiolated paraphrase.

'My Heart and Liver! I never see such a boy,' so I will present Carshot's refrain; and even when he was within a foot or so of the customer's face, the disciplined ear of Kipps would still at times develop a featureless intercalary murmur into – well, 'My Heart and Liver!'

There came a blessed interval when Kipps was sent abroad 'matching'. This consisted chiefly in supplying unexpected defects in buttons, ribbon, lining, and so forth in the dressmaking department. He was given a written paper of orders with patterns pinned thereto and discharged into the sunshine and interest of the street. Then until he thought it wise to return and stand the racket of his delay, he was a free man, clear of all reproach.

He made remarkable discoveries in topography, as, for example, that the most convenient way from the establishment of Mr Adolphus Davis to the establishment of Messrs Plummer, Roddis and Tyrrell, two of his principal places of call, is not, as is generally supposed, down the Sandgate road but up the Sandgate road, round by West Terrace and along the Leas to the lift, watch the lift up and down *twice*, but not longer, because that wouldn't do, back along the Leas, watch the Harbour for a short time, and then round by the churchyard, and so (hurrying) into Church Street and Rendezvous Street. But on some exceptionally fine days the route lay through Radnor Park to the pond where little boys sail ships and there are interesting swans.

He would return to find the shop settling down to the business of serving customers. And now he had to stand by to furnish any help that was necessary to the seniors who served, to carry parcels and bills about the shop, to clear away 'stuff' after each engagement, to hold up curtains until his arms ached, and, what was more difficult than all, to do nothing and not stare disconcertingly at customers when there was nothing for him to do. He plumbed an abyss of boredom, or stood a mere carcass with his mind far away, fighting the enemies of the empire, or steering a dream-ship perilously into unknown seas. To be recalled sharply to our higher civilization by some bustling senior's 'Nar then, Kipps. *Look* alive! Ketch 'old. (My Heart and Liver!)'

At half-past seven o'clock – except on late nights – a feverish activity of 'straightening up' began, and when the last shutter was up outside, Kipps, with the speed of an arrow leaving a bow, would start hanging wrappers over the fixtures and over the piles of wares upon the counters, preparatory to a vigorous scattering of wet sawdust and the sweeping out of the shop.

Sometimes people would stay long after the shop was closed. 'They don't mind a bit at Shalford's,' these ladies used to say, and while they loitered it was forbidden to touch a wrapper or take any measures to conclude the day until the doors closed behind them.

Mr Kipps would watch these later customers from the shadow of a stack of goods, and death and disfigurement was the least he wished for them. Rarely much later than nine, a supper of bread and cheese and watered beer awaited him downstairs, and, that consumed, the rest of the day was entirely at his disposal for reading, recreation, and the improvement of his mind. . . .

The front door was locked at half-past ten, and the gas in the dormitory extinguished at eleven.

III

On Sundays he was obliged to go to church once, and commonly he went twice, for there was nothing else to do. He sat in the free seats at the back; he was too shy to sing, and not always clever enough to keep his place in the Prayer-book, and he rarely listened to the sermon. But he had developed a sort of idea that going to church had a tendency to alleviate life. His aunt wanted to have him confirmed, but he evaded this ceremony for some years.

In the intervals between services he walked about Folkestone with an air of looking for something. Folkestone was not so interesting on Sundays as on week-days, because the shops were shut; but, on the other hand, there was a sort of confusing brilliance along the front of the Leas in the afternoon. Sometimes the apprentice next above him would condescend to go with him; but when the apprentice next but one above him condescended to go with the apprentice next above him, then Kipps, being habited as yet in ready-made clothes without tails, and unsuitable, therefore, to appear in such company, went alone.

Sometimes he would strike out into the country – still as if looking for something he missed – but the rope of meal-times haled him home again, and sometimes he would invest the major portion of the weekly allowance of a shilling that old Booch handed out to him, in a sacred concert on the pier. He would sometimes walk up and down the Leas between twenty and thirty times after supper, desiring much the courage to speak to some other person in the multitude similarly employed. Almost invariably he ended his Sunday footsore.

He never read a book, there were none for him to read, and besides, in spite of Mr Woodrow's guidance through a cheap and cheaply annotated edition of the *Tempest* (English Literature), he had no taste that way; he never read any newspapers except, occasionally, *Tit-Bits* or a ha'penny 'comic'. His chief intellectual stimulus was an occasional argey-bargey that sprang up between Carshot and Buggins at dinner. Kipps listened as if to unparalleled wisdom and wit, and treasured all the gems of repartee in his heart against the time when he too should be a Buggins and have the chance of courage for speech.

At times there came breaks in this routine – sale-times, darkened by extra toil and work past midnight, but brightened by a sprat supper and some shillings in the way of 'premiums'. And every year – not now and then, but every year – Mr Shalford, with parenthetic admiration of his own generosity and glancing comparisons with the austerer days when *he* was apprenticed, conceded Kipps no less than ten days holiday – ten whole days every year! Many a poor soul at Portland might well envy the fortunate Kipps. Insatiable heart of man! but how those days were grudged and counted as they snatched themselves away from him one after another!

Once a year came stock-taking, and at intervals gusts of 'marking off' goods newly arrived. Then the splendours of Mr Shalford's being shone with oppressive brilliancy. 'System!' he would say, 'system! Come! '*ussel*!' and issue sharp, confusing, contradictory orders very quickly. Carshot trotted about, confused, perspiring, his big nose up in the air, his little eye on Mr Shalford, his forehead crinkled, his lips always going to the formula, 'Oh, my Heart and Liver!' The smart junior and the second apprentice vied with one another in obsequious alacrity. The smart junior aspired to Carshot's position, and that made him almost violently subservient to Shalford. They all snapped at Kipps. Kipps held the blotting-pad and the safety inkpot and a box of tickets, and ran and fetched things. If he put the ink down before he went to fetch things Mr Shalford usually knocked it over, and if he took it away Mr Shalford wanted it before he returned. 'You make my tooth ache, Kipps,' Mr Shalford would say. 'You gimme n'ralgia. You got no more System in you than a bad potato.' And at the times when Kipps

carried off the inkpot Mr Shalford would become purple in the
face, and jab round with his dry pen at imaginary inkpots and
swear, and Carshot would stand and vociferate, and the smart
junior would run to the corner of the department and vociferate,
and the second apprentice would pursue Kipps, vociferating,
'Look Alive, Kipps! Look Alive! Ink, Man! Ink!'

A vague self-disgust that shaped itself as an intense hate of
Shalford and all his fellow-creatures filled the soul of Kipps
during these periods of storm and stress. He felt that the whole
business was unjust and idiotic, but the why and the wherefore
was too much for his unfortunate brain. His mind was a welter.
One desire, the desire to dodge some at least of a pelting storm
of disagreeable comment, guided him through a fumbling performance of his duties. His disgust was infinite! It was not
decreased by the inflamed ankles and sore feet that form a
normal incident in the business of making an English draper,
and the senior apprentice, Minton, a gaunt sullen-faced youngster with close-cropped wiry black hair, a loose ugly mouth, and
a moustache like a smudge of ink, directed his attention to
deeper aspects of the question and sealed his misery.

'When you get too old to work they chuck you away,' said
Minton. 'Lor! you find old drapers everywhere – tramps,
beggars, dock labourers, bus conductors – Quod. Anywhere but
in a crib.'

'Don't they get shops of their own?'

'Lord! 'Ow are they to get shops of their own? The 'aven't
any Capital! How's a draper's shopman to save up five hundred
pounds even? I tell you it can't be done. You got to stick to
Cribs until it's over. I tell you we're in a blessed drain-pipe, and
we've got to crawl along it till we die.'

The idea that fermented perpetually in the mind of Minton
was to 'hit the little beggar slap in the eye' – the little beggar
being Mr Shalford – 'and see how his blessed System met that.'

This threat filled Kipps with splendid anticipations whenever
Shalford went marking off in Minton's department. He would
look at Minton and look at Shalford and decide where he would
best like Shalford hit. . . . But for reasons known to himself
Shalford never pished and tushed with Minton as he did at the
harmless Carshot, and this interesting experiment upon the
System was never attempted.

IV

There were times when Kipps would lie awake, all others in the dormitory asleep and snoring, and think dismally of the outlook Minton pictured. Dimly he perceived the thing that had happened to him, how the great stupid machine of retail trade had caught his life into its wheels, a vast, irresistible force which he had neither strength of will nor knowledge to escape. This was to be his life until his days should end. No adventures, no glory, no change, no freedom. Neither – though the force of that came home to him later – might he dream of effectual love and marriage. And there was a terrible something called the 'swap', or 'the key of the street', and 'crib hunting', of which the talk was scanty but sufficient. Night after night he would resolve to enlist, to run away to sea, to set fire to the warehouse or drown himself, and morning after morning he rose up and hurried downstairs in fear of a sixpenny fine. He would compare his dismal round of servile drudgery with those windy, sunlit days at Littlestone, those windows of happiness shining ever brighter as they receded. The little figure of Ann seemed in all these windows now.

She, too, had happened on evil things. When Kipps went home for the first Christmas after he was bound, that great suspended resolve of his to kiss her flared up to hot determination, and he hurried out and whistled in the yard. There was a silence, and then old Kipps appeared behind him.

'It's no good your whistling there, my boy,' said old Kipps in a loud clear tone, designed to be audible over the wall. 'They've cleared out all you 'ad any truck with. *She's* gone as help to Ashford, my boy. *Help*! Slavery is what we used to call 'em, but times are changed. Wonder they didn't say lady-'elp while they was about it. It 'ud be like 'em.'

And Sid—? Sid had gone too. 'Arrand boy or somethink,' said old Kipps. 'To one of these here brasted cicle shops.'

'*Has* 'e!' said Kipps, with a feeling that he had been gripped about the chest; and he turned quickly and went indoors.

Old Kipps, still supposing him present, went on to further observations of an anti-Pornick tendency. . . .

When Kipps got upstairs, safe in his own bedroom, he sat down on the bed and stared at nothing. They were caught – they were all caught. All life took on the hue of one perpetual dismal Monday morning. The Hurons were scattered, the wrecks and the beach had passed away from him, the sun of those warm evenings at Littlestone had set for evermore. . . .

The only pleasure left for the brief remainder of his holiday after that was to think he was not in the shop. Even that was transient. Two more days, one more day, half a day. When he went back there were one or two very dismal nights indeed. He went so far as to write home some vague intimation of his feelings about business and his prospects, quoting Minton, but Mrs Kipps answered him, 'Did he want the Pornicks to say he wasn't good enough to be a draper?' This dreadful possibility was of course conclusive in the matter. 'No'; he resolved they should not say he failed at that.

He derived much help from a 'manly' sermon delivered in an enormous voice by a large, fat, sun-red clergyman, just home from a colonial bishopric he had resigned on the plea of ill-health, exhorting him that whatever his hand found to do, he was to do with all his might, and the revision of his catechism preparatory to his confirmation reminded him that it behoved him to do his duty in that state of life into which it had pleased God to call him.

After a time the sorrows of Kipps grew less acute, and, save for a miracle, the brief tragedy of his life was over. He subdued himself to his position even as his church required of him, seeing, moreover, no way out of it.

The earliest mitigation of his lot was that his soles and ankles became indurated to the perpetual standing. The next was an unexpected weekly whiff of freedom that came every Thursday. Mr Shalford, after a brave stand for what he called 'Innyvishal lib'ty' and the 'Idea of my System', a stand which, he explained, he made chiefly on patriotic grounds, was at last, under pressure of certain of his customers, compelled to fall in line with the rest of the local Early Closing Association, and Mr Kipps could emerge in daylight and go where he listed for long, long hours. Moreover, Minton, the pessimist, reached the end of his appointed time and left – to enlist in a cavalry regiment, and go about this planet leading an insubordinate but interesting life that ended at last in an intimate, vivid, and really, you know, by no means painful or tragic night grapple in the Terah Valley. In a little while Kipps cleaned windows no longer; he was serving customers (of the less important sort) and taking goods out on

approval, and presently he was third apprentice, and his moustache was visible, and there were three apprentices whom he
might legally snub and cuff. But one was (most dishonestly) too
big to cuff, in spite of his greener years.

V

There came still other distractions, the natural distractions of
adolescence, to take his mind off the inevitable. His costume,
for example, began to interest him more; he began to realize
himself as a visible object, to find an interest in the costume-
room mirrors and the eyes of the girl-apprentices.

In this he was helped by counsel and example. Pearce, his
immediate senior, was by way of being what was called a
Masher, and preached his cult. During slack times grave discus-
sions about collars, ties, the cut of trouser-legs, and the proper
shape of a boot toe, were held in the Manchester department. In
due course Kipps went to a tailor, and his short jacket was
replaced by a morning coat with tails. Stirred by this, he
purchased at his own expense three stand-up collars to replace
his former turn-down ones. They were nearly three inches high,
higher than those Pearce wore, and they made his neck quite
sore, and left a red mark under his ears. . . . So equipped, he
found himself fit company even for this fashionable apprentice,
who had now succeeded Minton in his seniority.

Most potent help of all in the business of forgetting his cosmic
disaster was this, that so soon as he was in tail-coats, the young
ladies of the establishment began to discover that he was no
longer a 'horrid little boy'. Hitherto they had tossed heads at
him and kept him in his place. Now they discovered that he was
a 'nice boy', which is next door at least to being a 'feller', and in
some ways even preferable. It is painful to record that his fidelity
to Ann failed at their first onset. I am fully sensible how entirely
better this story would be, from a sentimental point of view, if
he had remained true to that early love. Only then it would have
been a different story altogether. And at least Kipps was thus
far true, that with none of these later loves was there any of that
particular quality that linked Ann's flushed face and warmth
and the inner things of life so inseparably together. Though they
were not without emotions of various sorts.

It was one of the young ladies in the costume-room who first showed by her manner that he was a visible object and capable of exciting interest. She talked to him, she encouraged him to talk to her, she lent him a book she possessed, and darned a sock for him and said she would be his elder sister. She allowed him to escort her to church with a great air of having induced him to go. Then she investigated his eternal welfare, overcame a certain affectation of virile indifference to religion, and extorted a promise that he would undergo 'confirmation'. This excited the other young lady in the costumes, her natural rival, and she set herself with great charm and subtlety to the capture of the ripening heart of Kipps. She took a more worldly line. She went for a walk with him to the pier on Sunday afternoon, and explained to him how a gentleman must always walk 'outside' a lady on a pavement, and how all gentlemen wore or, at least, carried gloves, and generally the broad beginnings of the British social ideal. Afterwards the ladies exchanged 'words' upon Sabbatical grounds. In this way was the *toga virilis* bestowed on Kipps, and he became recognized as a suitable object for that Platonic Eros whose blunted darts devastate even the very highest class establishments. In this way, too, did that pervading ambition of the British young man to be, if not a 'gentleman', at least mistakably like one, took root in his heart.

He took to these new interests with a quite natural and personal zest. He became initiated into the mysteries of 'flirting' and – at a slightly later stage and with some leading hints from Pearce, who was of a communicative disposition in these matters – of the milder forms of 'spooning'. Very soon he was engaged. Before two years were out he had been engaged six times, and was beginning to be rather a desperate fellow, so far as he could make out. Desperate, but quite gentlemanly, be it understood, and without let or hindrance to the fact that he was in four brief lessons 'prepared' by a distant-mannered and gloomy young curate, and 'confirmed' a member of the Established Church.

The engagements in drapery establishments do not necessarily involve a subsequent marriage. They are essentially more refined, less coarsely practical, and altogether less binding than the engagements of the vulgar rich. These young ladies do not like not to be engaged, it is so unnatural, and Mr Kipps was as easy to get engaged to as one could wish. There are, from the young lady's point of view, many conveniences in being engaged.

You get an escort for church and walks, and so forth. It is not quite the thing to walk abroad with a 'feller', much more to 'spoon' with him, when he is neither one's *fiancé* nor an adopted brother; it is considered either a little fast or else as savouring of the 'walking-out' habits of the servant girls. Now, such is the sweetness of human charity, that the shop young lady in England has just the same horror of doing anything that savours of the servant girl as the lady journalist, let us say, has of anything savouring of the shop-girl, or the really quite nice young lady has of anything savouring of any sort of girl who has gone down into the economic battlefield to earn herself a living. . . . But the very deepest of these affairs was still among the shallow places of love, at best it was paddling where it is decreed that men must sink or swim. Of the deep and dangerous places, and of the huge buoyant lift of its waves, he tasted nothing. Affairs of clothes and vanities they were, jealousies about a thing said, flatteries and mutual boastings, climaxes in the answering grasp of hands, the temerarious use of Christian names, culminations in a walk, or a near confidence, or a little pressure more or less. Close sitting on a seat after twilight with some little fondling was, indeed, the boldest of lover's adventures, the utmost limit of his enterprises in the service of that stark Great Lady who is daughter of Uranus and the sea.* The 'young ladies' who reigned in his heart came and went like people in an omnibus; there was the vehicle, so to speak, upon the road, and they entered and left it without any cataclysm of emotion. For all that, this development of the sex interest was continuously very interesting to Kipps, and kept him going as much as anything through all these servile years. . . .

IV

For a tailpiece to this chapter one may vignette a specimen minute.

It is a bright Sunday afternoon; the scene is a secluded little seat halfway down the front of the Leas, and Kipps is four years older than when he parted from Ann. There is a quite perceptible down upon his upper lip, and his costume is just as tremendous a 'mash' as lies within his means. His collar is so high that it scars his inaggressive jaw-bone, and his hat has a curly brim, his

tie shows taste, his trousers are modestly brilliant, and his boots
have light cloth uppers and button at the side. He jabs at the
gravel before him with a cheap cane and glances sideways at Flo
Bates, the young lady from the cash desk. She is wearing a
brilliant blouse and a gaily trimmed hat. There is an air of
fashion about her that might disappear under the analysis of a
woman of the world, but which is quite sufficient to make Kipps
very proud to be distinguished as her particular 'feller', and to
be allowed at temperate intervals to use her Christian name.

The conversation is light and gay in the modern style, and Flo
keeps on smiling, good temper being her special charm.

'Ye see, you done mean what *I* mean,' he is saying.

'Well, what do *you* mean?'

'Not what you mean!'

'Well, tell me.'

'*Ah*! That's another story.'

Pause. They look meaningly at one another.

'You *are* a one for being roundabout,' says the lady.

'Well, you're not so plain, you know.'

'Not plain?'

'No.'

'You don't mean to say I'm roundabout?'

'No. I mean to say—Though—' Pause.

'Well?'

'You're not a bit plain – you're' (his voice jumps up to a
squeak) 'pretty. See?'

'Oh, get *out*!' – her voice lifts also – with pleasure.

She strikes him with her glove, then glances suddenly at a ring
upon her finger. Her smile disappears momentarily. Another
pause. Eyes meet and the smile returns.

'I wish I knew—' says Kipps.

'Knew—?'

'Where you got that ring.'

She lifts the hand with the ring until her eyes just show (very
prettily) over it. 'You'd just *like* to know,' she says slowly, and
smiles still more brightly with the sense of successful effect.

'I dessay I could guess.'

'I dessay you couldn't.'

'Couldn't I?'

'No!'

'Guess it in three.'

'Not the name.'

'Ah!'

'*Ah*!'

'Well, anyhow, lemme look at it.'

He looks at it. Pause. Giggles, slight struggle, and a slap on Kipps' coat-sleeve. A passer-by appears down the path and she hastily withdraws her hand.

She glances at the face of the approaching man. They maintain a bashful silence until he has passed. . . .

Chapter Three

The Woodcarving Class

I

Though these services to Venus Epipontia, and these studies in the art of dress, did much to distract his thoughts and mitigate his earlier miseries, it would be mere optimism to present Kipps as altogether happy. A vague dissatisfaction with life drifted about him, and every now and again enveloped him like a sea-fog. During these periods it was greyly evident that there was something, something vital in life, lacking. For no earthly reason that Kipps could discover, he was haunted by a suspicion that life was going wrong, or had already gone wrong in some irrevocable way. The ripening self-consciousness of adolescence developed this into a clearly felt insufficiency. It was all very well to carry gloves, open doors, never say 'Miss' to a girl, and walk 'outside', but were there not other things, conceivably even deeper things, before the complete thing was attained? For example, certain matters of knowledge. He perceived great bogs of ignorance about him, fumbling traps, where other people, it was alleged, *real* gentlemen and ladies, for example, and the clergy, had knowledge and assurance, bogs which it was some-times difficult to elude. A girl arrived in the millinery department who could, she said, *speak* French and German. She snubbed certain advances, and a realization of inferiority blistered Kipps. But he tried to pass the thing off as a joke by saying 'Parlez-vous Francey' whenever he met her, and inducing the junior apprentice to say the same.

He even made some dim half-secret experiments towards remedying the deficiencies he suspected. He spent five shillings on five serial numbers of a Home Educator, and bought (and even thought of reading) a Shakespeare and a Bacon's *Advancement of Learning*, and the poems of Herrick from a chap who was hard up. He battled with Shakespeare all one Sunday afternoon, and found the 'English Literature', with which Mr Woodrow had equipped him, had vanished down some crack in his mind. He had no doubt it was very splendid stuff, but he couldn't quite make out what it was all about. There was an occult meaning, he knew, in literature, and he had forgotten it. Moreover, he discovered one day, while taunting the junior apprentice with ignorance, that his 'rivers of England' had also slipped his memory, and he laboriously restored that fabric of rote learning: 'Ty Wear Tees 'Umber—'

I suppose some such phase of discontent is a normal thing in every adolescence. The ripening mind seeks something upon which its will may crystallize, upon which its discursive emotions, growing more abundant with each year of life, may concentrate. For many, though not for all, it takes a religious direction; but in those particular years the mental atmosphere of Folkestone was exceptionally free from any revivalistic disturbance that might have reached Kipps' mental being. Sometimes they fall in love. I have known this uneasiness end in different cases in a vow to read one book (not a novel) every week, to read the Bible through in a year, to pass in the Honours division of the London Matriculation examination, to become an accomplished chemist, and never more to tell a lie. It led Kipps finally into Technical Education, as we understand it in the south of England.

It was in the last year of his apprenticeship that he had pursued his researches after that missing qualification into the Folkestone Young Men's Association, where Mr Chester Coote prevailed. Mr Chester Coote was a young man of semi-independent means, who inherited a share in a house agency, read Mrs Humphrey Ward, and took an interest in social work. He was a whitish-faced young man, with a prominent nose, pale blue eyes, and a quivering quality in his voice. He was very active upon committees; he was very prominent and useful on all social occasions, in evidence upon platforms, and upon all those semi-public occasions when the Great descend. He lived with an only sister. To Kipps and his kind in the Young Men's Association he read a stimulating paper on 'Self-Help'. He said it was the noblest of all our distinctive English characteristics, and he was very much down upon the 'over-educated' Germans. At the close a young German hairdresser made a few commendatory remarks which developed somehow into an oration on Hanoverian politics. As he became excited he became guttural and obscure; the meeting sniggered cheerfully at such ridiculous

English, and Kipps was so much amused that he forgot a private project to ask this Chester Coote how he might set about a little Self-Help on his own private account in such narrow margins of time as the System of Mr Shalford spared him. But afterwards in the night-time it came to him again.

It was a few months later, and after his apprenticeship was over, and Mr Shalford had with depreciatory observations taken him on as an Improver at twenty pounds a year, that this question was revived by a casual article on Technical Education in a morning paper that a commercial traveller left behind him. It played the *rôle* of the word in season. Something in the nature of conversion, a faint sort of concentration of purpose, really occurred in him then. The article was written with penetrating vehemence, and it stimulated him to the pitch of inquiring about the local Science and Art Classes; and after he had told everybody in the shop about it, and taken the advice of all who supported his desperate resolution, he joined. At first he attended the class in Freehand, that being the subject taught on early closing night, and he had already made some progress in that extraordinary routine of reproducing freehand 'copies', which for two generations has passed with English people for instruction in art, when the dates of the classes were changed. Thereby, just as the March winds were blowing, he was precipitated into the Woodcarving class, and his mind diverted first to this useful and broadening pursuit, and then to its teacher.

II

The class in woodcarving was an extremely select class, conducted at that time by a young lady named Walshingham; and as this young lady was destined by Fortune to teach Kipps a great deal more than woodcarving, it will be well if the reader gets the picture of her correctly in mind. She was only a year or so older than he was, she had a pale intellectual face, dark grey eyes and black hair, which she wore over her forehead in an original and striking way that she had adapted from a picture by Rossetti in the South Kensington Museum. She was slender so that without ungainliness she had an effect of being tall, and her hands were shapely and white when they came into contrast with hands much exercised in rolling and blocking. She dressed in those loose and pleasant forms and those soft and tempered shades that arose in England in the socialistic-aesthetic epoch, and remain to this day among us as the badge of those who read Turgenev's novels, scorn current fiction, and think on higher planes. I think she was as beautiful as most beautiful people, and to Kipps she was altogether beautiful. She had, Kipps learnt, matriculated at London University, an astounding feat to his imagination, and the masterly way in which she demonstrated how to prod and worry honest pieces of wood into useless and unedifying patterns in relief, extorted his utmost admiration.

At first when Kipps had learnt he was to be taught by a 'girl' he was inclined to resent it, the more so as Buggins had recently been very strong on the gross injustice of feminine employment. 'We have to keep wives,' said Buggins (though, as a matter of fact, he did not keep even one), 'and how are we to do it with a lot of girls coming in to take the work out of our mouths?' Afterwards Kipps, in conjunction with Pearce, looked at it from another point of view, and thought it would be rather a 'lark'. Finally, when he saw her, and saw her teaching and coming nearer to him with an impressive deliberation, he was breathless with awe and the quality of her dark slender femininity.

The class consisted of two girls and a maiden lady of riper years, friends of Miss Walshingham's, and anxious rather to support her in an interesting experiment rather than to become really expert woodcarvers; an elderly, oldish young man with spectacles and a black beard, who never spoke to any one, and who was evidently too short-sighted to see his work as a whole; a small boy, who was understood to have a 'gift' for woodcarving; and a lodging-house keeper, who 'took classes' every winter, she told Mr Kipps, as though they were a tonic, and 'found they did her good'. And occasionally Mr Chester Coote – refined and gentlemanly – would come into the class, with or without papers, ostensibly on committee business, but in reality to talk to the less attractive of the two girl-students, and sometimes a brother of Miss Walshingham's, a slender dark young man with a pale face and fluctuating resemblances to the young Napoleon, would arrive just at the end of the class-time to see his sister home.

All these personages impressed Kipps with a sense of inferiority that in the case of Miss Walshingham became positively abysmal. The ideas and knowledge they appeared to have, their personal capacity and freedom, opened a new world to his imagination. These people came and went with a sense of absolute assurance, against an overwhelming background of plaster casts, diagrams and tables, benches and a blackboard, a background that seemed to him to be saturated with recondite knowledge and the occult and jealously guarded tips and secrets that constitute Art and the Higher Life. They went home, he imagined, to homes where the piano was played with distinction and freedom, and books littered the tables and foreign languages were habitually used. They had complicated meals no doubt. They 'knew etiquette', and how to avoid all the errors for which Kipps bought penny manuals – *What to Avoid*, *Common Errors in Speaking*, and the like. He knew nothing about it all, nothing whatever; he was a creature of the outer darkness blinking in an unsuspected light.

He heard them speak easily and freely to one another of examinations, of books and paintings, of 'last year's Academy' – a little contemptuously – and once just at the end of the class-time Mr Chester Coote and young Walshingham and the two girls argued about something or other called, he fancied, 'Vagner', or 'Vargner' – they seemed to say it both ways – and which presently shaped itself more definitely as the name of a man who made up music. (Carshot and Buggins weren't in it with them.) Young Walshingham, it appeared, said something or other that was an 'epigram', and they all applauded him. Kipps, I say, felt himself a creature of outer darkness, an inexcusable intruder in an altitudinous world. When the epigram happened he first of all smiled to pretend he understood, and instantly suppressed the smile to show he did not listen. Then he became extremely hot and uncomfortable, though nobody had noticed either phase.

It was clear his only chance of concealing his bottomless baseness was to hold his tongue, and meanwhile he chipped with earnest care and abased his soul before the very shadow of Miss Walshingham. She used to come and direct and advise him, with, he felt, an effort to conceal the scorn she had for him, and indeed it is true that at first she thought of him chiefly as the clumsy young man with the red ears.

And as soon as he emerged from the first effect of pure awe-stricken humility – he was greatly helped to emerge by the need the lodging-house keeper was under to talk while she worked, and as she didn't like Miss Walshingham and her friends very much, and the young man with spectacles was deaf, she naturally talked to Kipps – he perceived that he was in a state of adoration for Miss Walshingham that it seemed almost a blasphemous familiarity to speak of as being in love.

This state, you must understand, had nothing to do with 'flirting' or 'spooning' and that superficial passion that flashes from eye to eye upon the Leas and Pier – absolutely nothing. That he knew from the first. Her rather pallid, intellectual young face beneath those sombre clouds of hair put her in a class apart; towards her the thought of 'attentions' paled and vanished. To approach such a being, to perform sacrifices and to perish obviously for her, seemed the limit he might aspire to, he or any man. For if his love was abasement, at any rate it had this much of manliness that it covered all his sex. It had not yet come to Kipps to acknowledge any man as his better in his heart of hearts. When one does that the game is played, and one grows old indeed.

The rest of his sentimental interests vanished altogether in this great illumination. He meditated about her when he was blocking cretonne, her image was before his eyes at teatime, and blotted out the more immediate faces and made him silent and preoccupied and so careless in his bearing that the junior apprentice, sitting beside him, mocked at and parodied his enormous bites of bread and butter unreproved. He became conspicuously less popular on the 'fancy' side, the 'costumes' was chilly with him and the 'millinery' cutting. But he did not care. An intermittent correspondence with Flo Bates, that had gone on since she left Mr Shalford's desk for a position at Tunbridge, 'nearer home', and which had roused Kipps in its earlier stages to unparalleled heights of epistolary effort, died out altogether by reason of his neglect. He heard with scarcely a pang that, as a consequence perhaps of his neglect, Flo was 'carrying on with a chap who managed a farm'.

Every Thursday he jabbed and gouged at his wood, jabbing and gouging intersecting circles and diamond traceries, and that laboured inane which our mad world calls ornament, and he watched Miss Walshingham furtively whenever she turned away. The circles, in consequence, were jabbed crooked, and his panels, losing their symmetry, became comparatively pleasing to the untrained eye – and once he jabbed his finger. He would cheerfully have jabbed all his fingers if he could have found some means of using the opening to express himself of the vague emotions that possessed him. But he shirked conversation just as earnestly as he desired it; he feared that profound general ignorance of his might appear.

III

There came a time when she could not open one of the classroom windows. The man with the black beard pored over his chipping heedlessly. . . .

It did not take Kipps a moment to grasp his opportunity. He dropped his gouge and stepped forward. 'Lem *me*,' he said. . . .

He could not open the window either!

'Oh, please don't trouble,' she said.

'S'no trouble,' he gasped.

Still the sash stuck. He felt his manhood was at stake. He gathered himself together for a tremendous effort, and the pane broke with a snap, and he thrust his hand into the void beyond.

'*There*!' said Miss Walshingham, and the glass fell ringing into the courtyard below.

Then Kipps made to bring his hand back and felt the keen touch of the edge of the broken glass at his wrist. He turned dolefully. 'I'm tremendously sorry,' he said, in answer to the accusation in Miss Walshingham's eyes. 'I didn't think it would break like that' – as if he had expected it to break in some quite different and entirely more satisfactory manner. The boy with the gift for woodcarving, having stared at Kipps' face for a moment, became involved in a Laocoon struggle with a giggle.

'You've cut your wrist,' said one of the girl friends, standing up and pointing. She was a pleasant-faced, greatly freckled girl, with a helpful disposition, and she said, 'You've cut your wrist,' as brightly as if she had been a trained nurse.

Kipps looked down and saw a swift line of scarlet rush down his hand. He perceived the other man-student regarding this with magnified eyes. 'You *have* cut your wrist,' said Miss Walshingham; and Kipps regarded his damage with greater interest.

'He's cut his wrist,' said the maiden lady to the lodging-house keeper, and seemed in doubt what a lady should do. 'It's—' she hesitated at the word 'bleeding', and nodded to the lodging-house keeper instead.

'Dreadfully,' said the maiden lady, and tried to look and tried not to look at the same time.

'Of *course* he's cut his wrist,' said the lodging-house keeper, momentarily quite annoyed at Kipps; and the other young lady, who thought Kipps rather common, went on quietly with her wood-cutting with an air of its being the proper thing to do – though nobody else seemed to know it.

'You must tie it up,' said Miss Walshingham.

'We must tie it up,' said the freckled girl.

'I 'adn't the slightest idea that window was going to break like that,' said Kipps, with candour. 'Nort the slightest.'

He glanced again at the blood on his wrist, and it seemed to him that it was on the very point of dropping on the floor of that cultured class-room. So he very neatly licked it off, feeling at the same time for his handkerchief. 'Oh, *don't!*' said Miss Walshingham as he did so, and the girl with the freckles made a movement of horror. The giggle got the better of the boy with the gift, and celebrated its triumph by unseemly noises, in spite of which it seemed to Kipps at the moment that the act that had made Miss Walshingham say 'Oh, *don't!*' was rather a desperate and manly treatment of what was, after all, a creditable injury.

'It ought to be tied up,' said the lodging-house keeper, holding her chisel upright in her hand. 'It's a bad cut to bleed like that.'

'We must tie it up,' said the freckled girl, and hesitated in front of Kipps. 'Have you got a handkerchief?' she said.

'I dunno 'ow I managed *not* to bring one,' said Kipps. 'I—. Not 'aving a cold, I suppose some 'ow I didn't think—!'

He checked a further flow of blood.

The girl with the freckles caught Miss Walshingham's eye and held it for a moment. Both glanced at Kipps' injury. The boy with the gift, who had reappeared with a chastened expression from some noisy pursuit beneath his desk, made the neglected motions of one who proffers shyly. Miss Walshingham, under the spell of the freckled girl's eye, produced a handkerchief. The voice of the maiden lady could be heard in the background: 'I've been through all the technical education ambulance classes twice, and I know you go *so* if it's a vein, and *so* if it's an artery – at least you go *so* for one, and *so* for the other, whichever it may be – but. . . .'

'If you will give me your hand,' said the freckled girl; and proceeded, with Miss Walshingham's assistance, to bandage Kipps in a most businesslike way. Yes, they actually bandaged Kipps. They pulled up his cuffs – happily they were not a very frayed pair – and held his wrist and wrapped the soft handkerchief round it, and tightened the knot together. And Miss Walshingham's face, the face of that almost divine Over-human, came close to the face of Kipps.

'We're not hurting you, are we?' she said.

'Not a bit,' said Kipps, as he would have said if they had been sawing his arm off.

'We're not experts, you know,' said the freckled girl.

'I'm sure it's a dreadful cut,' said Miss Walshingham.

'It ain't much, reely,' said Kipps; 'and you're taking a lot of trouble. I'm sorry I broke that window. I can't think what I could have been doing.'

'It isn't so much the cut at the time, it's the poisoning afterwards,' came the voice of the maiden lady.

'Of course, I'm quite willing to pay for the window,' panted Kipps, opulently.

'We must make it just as tight as possible to stop the bleeding,' said the freckled girl.

'I don't think it's much, reely,' said Kipps. 'I'm awful sorry I broke that window, though.'

'Put your finger on the knot, dear,' said the freckled girl.

'Eh?' said Kipps. 'I mean—'

Both the young ladies became very intent on the knot, and Mr Kipps was very red and very intent upon the two young ladies.

'Mortified, and had to be sawn off,' said the maiden lady.

'Sawn off,' said the lodging-house keeper.

'Sawn *right* off,' said the maiden lady, and jabbed at her mangled design.

'*There*,' said the freckled girl, 'I think that ought to do. You're sure it's not too tight?'

'Not a bit,' said Kipps.

He met Miss Walshingham's eyes and smiled to show how little he cared for wounds and pain. 'It's only a little cut,' he added.

The maiden lady appeared as an addition to their group. 'You should have washed the wound, dear,' she said. 'I was just telling Miss Collis—' She peered through her glasses at the bandage. 'That doesn't look *quite* right,' she remarked critically. 'You should have taken the ambulance classes. But I suppose it will have to do. Are you hurting?'

'Not a bit,' said Kipps; and smiled at them all with the air of a brave soldier in hospital.

'I'm sure it *must* hurt,' said Miss Walshingham.

'Anyhow, you're a very good patient,' said the girl with the freckles.

Mr Kipps became bright pink. 'I'm only sorry I broke the window – that's all,' he said. 'But who would have thought it was going to break like that?'

Pause.

'I'm afraid you won't be able to go on carving to-night,' said Miss Walshingham.

'I'll try,' said Kipps. 'It reely doesn't hurt – not anything to matter.'

Presently Miss Walshingham came to him, as he carved heroically with his hand bandaged in her handkerchief. There was a touch of novel interest in her eyes. 'I'm afraid you're not getting on very fast,' she said.

The freckled girl looked up and regarded Miss Walshingham.

'I'm doing a little, anyhow,' said Kipps. 'I don't want to waste any time. A feller like me hasn't much time to spare.'

It struck the girls that there was a quality of modest disavowal about that 'feller like me'. It gave them a light into this obscure person, and Miss Walshingham ventured to commend his work as 'promising' and to ask whether he meant to follow it up. Kipps didn't 'altogether know' – 'things depended on so much', but if he was in Folkestone next winter he certainly should. It did not occur to Miss Walshingham at the time to ask why his progress in art depended upon his presence in Folkestone. There were some more questions and answers – they continued to talk to him for a little time even when Mr Chester Coote had come into the room – and when at last the conversation had died out, it dawned upon Kipps just how much his cut wrist had done for him. . . .

He went to sleep that night revisiting that conversation for the twentieth time, treasuring this and expanding that, and inserting things he might have said to Miss Walshingham – things he might still say about himself – in relation, more or less explicit, to her. He wasn't quite sure if he wouldn't like his arm to mortify a bit, which would make him interesting, or to heal up absolutely, which would show the exceptional purity of his blood. . . .

IV

The affair of the broken window happened late in April, and the class came to an end in May. In that interval there were several small incidents and great developments of emotion. I have done Kipps no justice if I have made it seem that his face was unsightly. It was, as the freckled girl pointed out to Helen Walshingham, an 'interesting' face, and that aspect of him which presented chiefly erratic hair and glowing ears ceased to prevail.

They talked him over, and the freckled girl discovered there was something 'wistful' in his manner. They detected a 'natural delicacy', and the freckled girl set herself to draw him out from that time forth. The freckled girl was nineteen, and very wise and motherly and benevolent, and really she greatly preferred drawing out Kipps to woodcarving. It was quite evident to her that Kipps was in love with Helen Walshingham, and it struck her as a queer and romantic and pathetic and extremely interesting phenomenon. And as at that time she regarded Helen as 'simply lovely', it seemed only right and proper that she should assist Kipps in his modest efforts to place himself in a state of absolute abandon upon her altar.

Under her sympathetic management the position of Kipps was presently defined quite clearly. He was unhappy in his position – misunderstood. He told her he 'didn't seem to get on like' with customers, and she translated this for him as 'too sensitive'. The discontent with his fate in life, the dreadful feeling that Education was slipping by him, troubles that time and usage were glazing over a little, revived to their old acuteness but not to their old hopelessness. As a basis for sympathy, indeed, they were even a source of pleasure.

And one day at dinner it happened that Carshot and Buggins fell talking of 'these here writers', and how Dickens had been a labeller of blacking, and Thackeray 'an artis' who couldn't sell a drawing', and how Samuel Johnson had walked to London without any boots, having thrown away his only pair 'out of pride'. 'It's Luck,' said Buggins, 'to a very large extent. They just happen to hit on something that catches on, and there you are!'

'Nice easy life they have of it, too,' said Miss Mergle. 'Write just an hour or so, and done for the day! Almost like gentlefolks.'

'There's more work in it than you'd think,' said Carshot, stooping to a mouthful.

'I wouldn't mind changing for all that,' said Buggins. 'I'd like to see one of these here authors marking off with Jimmy.'

'I think they copy from each other a good deal,' said Miss Mergle.

'Even then (chup, chup, chup)' said Carshot, 'there's writing it out in their own hands.'

They proceeded to enlarge upon the literary life, on its ease and dignity, on the social recognition accorded to those who led it, and on the ample gratifications their vanity achieved. 'Pictures everywhere – never get a new suit without being photographed – almost like Royalty,' said Miss Mergle. And all this talk impressed the imagination of Kipps very greatly. Here was a class that seemed to bridge the gulf. On the one hand essentially Low, but by factitious circumstances capable of entering upon these levels of social superiority to which all true Englishmen aspire, these levels from which one may tip a butler, scorn a tailor, and even commune with those who lead 'men' into battle. 'Almost like gentlefolks' – that was it! He brooded over these things in the afternoon, until they blossomed into daydreams. Suppose, for example, he had chanced to write a book, a well-known book, under an assumed name, and yet kept on being a draper all the time. . . . Impossible, of course; but *suppose*—It made quite a long dream.

And at the next woodcarving class he let it be drawn from him that his real choice in life was to be a Nawther – 'only one doesn't get a chance.'

After this there were times when Kipps had that pleasant sense that comes of attracting interest. He was a mute inglorious Dickens, or at any rate something of the sort, and they were all taking him at that. The discovery of this indefinable 'something in' him, the development of which was now painfully restricted and impossible, did much to bridge the gulf between himself and Miss Walshingham. He was unfortunate, he was futile, but he was not 'common'. Even now with help—? The two girls, and the freckled girl in particular, tried to 'stir him up' to some effort to do his imputed potentialities justice. They were still young enough to believe that to nice and niceish members of the male sex – more especially when under the stimulus of feminine encouragement – nothing is finally impossible.

The freckled girl was, I say, the stage manager of this affair, but Miss Walshingham was the presiding divinity. A touch of proprietorship came in her eyes at times when she looked at him. He was hers – unconditionally – and she knew it.

To her directly, Kipps scarcely ever made a speech. The enterprising things that he was continually devising to say to her, he usually did not say, or said, with a suitable modification, to the girl with the freckles. And one day the girl with the freckles smote him to the heart. She said to him, looking across the class-room to where her friend reached a cast from the shelf, 'I do think Helen Walshingham is sometimes the most lovely person in the world. Look at her now!'

Kipps gasped for a moment. The moment lengthened and she regarded him as an intelligent young surgeon might regard an operation without anaesthetics. 'You're right,' he said, and then looked at her with an entire abandonment of visage.

She coloured under his glare of silent avowal, and he blushed brightly. 'I think so too,' he said hoarsely, cleared his throat, and, after a meditative moment, proceeded sacramentally with his woodcarving.

'You *are* wonderful,' said the freckled girl to Miss Walshingham, *apropos* of nothing as they went on their way home together. 'He simply adores you.'

'But, my dear, what have I done?' said Helen.

'That's just it,' said the freckled girl. 'What *have* you done?'

And then with a terrible swiftness came the last class of the course to terminate this relationship altogether. Kipps was careless of dates, and the thing came upon him with an effect of abrupt surprise. Just as his petals were expanding so hopefully, 'Finis', and the thing was at an end. But Kipps did not fully appreciate that the end was indeed and really and truly the end until he was back in the Emporium after the end was over.

The end began practically in the middle of the last class, when the freckled girl broached the topic of terminations. She developed the question of just how he was going on after the class ended. She hoped he would stick to certain resolutions of self-improvement he had breathed. She said quite honestly that he owed it to himself to develop his possibilities. He expressed firm resolve, but dwelt on difficulties. He had no books. She instructed him how to get books from the public library. He was to get a form of application for a ticket signed by a ratepayer, and he said 'of course' when she said Mr Shalford would do that, though all the time he knew perfectly well it would 'never do' to ask Mr Shalford for anything of the sort. She explained that she was going to North Wales for the summer, information he received without immediate regret. At intervals he expressed his intention of going on with woodcarving when the summer was over, and once he added, 'if—'

She considered herself extremely delicate not to press for the completion of that 'if—'

After that talk there was an interval of languid woodcarving and watching Miss Walshingham.

Then presently there came a bustle of packing, a great ceremony of handshaking all round by Miss Collis and the maiden lady of ripe years, and then Kipps found himself outside the class-room, on the landing with his two friends. It seemed to him he had only just learnt that this was the last class of all. There came a little pause, and the freckled girl suddenly went back into the class-room, and left Kipps and Miss Walshingham alone together for the first time. Kipps was instantly breathless. She looked at his face with a glance that mingled sympathy and curiosity, and held out her white hand.

'Well, good-bye, Mr Kipps,' she said.

He took her hand and held it.

'I'd do anything,' said Kipps, and had not the temerity to add 'for you.' He stopped awkwardly.

He shook her hand and said 'Good-bye.'

There was a little pause. 'I hope you will have a pleasant holiday,' she said.

'I shall come back to the class next year, anyhow,' said Kipps, valiantly, and turned abruptly to the stairs.

'I hope you will,' said Miss Walshingham.

He turned back towards her.

'Really?' he said.

'I hope everybody will come back.'

'I will – anyhow,' said Kipps. 'You may count on that;' and he tried to make his tones significant.

They looked at one another through a little pause.

'Good-bye,' she said.

Kipps lifted his hat.

She turned towards the class-room.

'Well?' said the freckled girl, coming back towards her.

'Nothing,' said Helen. 'At least – presently.'

And she became very energetic about some scattered tools on a desk. The freckled girl went out and stood for a moment at the head of the stairs. When she came back she looked very hard at her friend. The incident struck her as important – wonderfully important. It was unassimilable, of course, and absurd, but there it was, the thing that is so cardinal to a girl, the emotion, the subservience, the crowning triumph of her sex. She could not help feeling that Helen took it on the whole a little too hardly.

Chapter Four

Chitterlow

I

The hour of the class on the following Thursday found Kipps in a state of nearly incredible despondency. He was sitting with his eyes on the reading-room clock, his chin resting on his fists, and his elbows on the accumulated comic papers, that were comic, alas! in vain. He paid no heed to the little man in spectacles glaring opposite to him, famishing for *Fun*. In this place it was he had sat night after night, each night more blissful than the last, waiting until it should be time to go to Her! And then – bliss! And now the hour had come and there was no class! There would be no class now until next October. It might be there would never be a class, so far as he was concerned, again.

It might be there would never be a class again, for Shalford, taking exception at a certain absent-mindedness that led to mistakes, and more particularly to the ticketing of several articles in Kipps' Manchester window upside down, had been 'on to' him for the past few days in an exceedingly onerous manner. . . .

He sighed profoundly, pushed the comic papers back – they were rent away from him instantly by the little man in spectacles – and tried the old engravings of Folkestone in the past that hung about the room. But these, too, failed to minister to his bruised heart. He wandered about the corridors for a time and watched the Library Indicator for a while. Wonderful thing that! But it did not hold him for long. People came and laughed near him, and that jarred with him dreadfully. He went out of the building, and a beastly cheerful barrel-organ mocked him in the street. He was moved to a desperate resolve to go down to the beach. There, it might be, he would be alone. The sea might be rough – and attuned to him. It would certainly be dark.

'If I 'ad a penny I'm blest if I wouldn't go and chuck myself off the end of the pier. . . . *She'd* never miss me. . . .'

He followed a deepening vein of thought.

'Penny, though! It's tuppence,' he said, after a space.

He went down Dover Street in a state of profound melancholia – at the pace and mood as it were of his own funeral procession – and he crossed at the corner of Tontine Street, heedless of all mundane things. And there it was that Fortune came upon him, in disguise and with a loud shout, the shout of a person endowed with an unusually rich, full voice, followed immediately by a violent blow in the back.

His hat was over his eyes, and an enormous weight rested on his shoulders, and something kicked him in the back of his calf.

Then he was on all fours in some mud that Fortune, in conjunction with the Folkestone corporation and in the pursuit of equally mysterious ends, had heaped together even lavishly for his reception.

He remained in that position for some seconds, awaiting further developments, and believing almost anything broken before his heart. Gathering at last that this temporary violence of things in general was over, and being perhaps assisted by a clutching hand, he arose, and found himself confronting a figure holding a bicycle and thrusting forward a dark face in anxious scrutiny.

'You aren't hurt, Matey?' gasped the figure.

'Was that *you* 'it me?' said Kipps.

'It's these handles, you know,' said the figure, with an air of being a fellow-sufferer. 'They're too *low*. And when I go to turn, if I don't remember, Bif! – and I'm *in* to something.'

'Well – you give me a oner in the back – anyhow,' said Kipps, taking stock of his damages.

'I was coming downhill, you know,' explained the bicyclist. 'These little Folkestone hills are a Fair Treat. It isn't as though I'd been on the level. I came rather a whop.'

'You did *that*,' said Kipps.

'I was back-pedalling for all I was worth, anyhow,' said the bicyclist. 'Not that I *am* worth much back-pedalling.'

He glanced round and made a sudden movement almost as if to mount his machine. Then he turned as rapidly to Kipps again, who was now stooping down, pursuing the tale of his injuries.

'Here's the back of my trouser-leg all tore down,' said Kipps, 'and I believe I'm bleeding. You reely ought to be more careful—'

The stranger investigated the damage with a rapid movement.

'Holy Smoke, so you are!' He laid a friendly hand on Kipps' arm. 'I say – look here! Come up to my diggings and sew it up. I'm—Of course I'm to blame, and I say—' His voice sank to a confidential friendliness. 'Here's a slop. Don't let on I ran you down. Haven't a lamp, you know. Might be a bit awkward, for *me*.'

Kipps looked up towards the advancing policeman. The appeal to his generosity was not misplaced. He immediately took sides with his assailant. He stood as the representative of the law drew nearer. He assumed an air which he considered highly suggestive of an accident not having happened.

'All right,' he said, 'go on!'

'Right you are,' said the cyclist, promptly, and led the way; and then, apparently with some idea of deception, called over his shoulder, 'I'm tremendous glad to have met you, old chap.

'It really isn't a hundred yards,' he said, after they had passed the policeman; 'it's just round the corner.'

'Of course,' said Kipps, limping slightly. 'I don't want to get a chap into trouble. Accidents *will* happen. Still—'

'Oh, *rather*! I believe you. Accidents *will* happen. Especially when you get *me* on a bicycle.' He laughed. 'You aren't the first I've run down, not by any manner of means! I don't think you can be hurt much either. It isn't as though I was scorching. You didn't see me coming. I was back-pedalling like anything. Only naturally it seems to you I must have been coming fast. And I did all I could to ease off the bump as I hit you. It was just the treadle, I think, came against your calf. But it was All Right of you about that policeman, you know. That was a Fair Bit of All Right. Under the Circs., if you'd told him I was riding, it might have been forty bob! Forty bob! I'd have had to tell 'em Time is Money just now for Mr H. C.

'I shouldn't have blamed you either, you know. Most men, after a bump like that, might have been spiteful. The least I can do is to stand you a needle and thread. And a clothes' brush. It isn't every one who'd have taken it like you.

'Scorching! Why, if I'd been scorching you'd have – coming as we did – you'd have been knocked silly.

'But I tell you, the way you caught on about that slop was something worth seeing. When I asked you – I didn't half expect it. Bif! Right off. Cool as a cucumber. Had your line at once. I tell you that there isn't many men would have acted as you have done, I *will* say that. You acted like a gentleman over that slop.'

Kipps' first sense of injury disappeared. He limped along a pace or so behind, making depreciatory noises in response to these flattering remarks, and taking stock of the very appreciative person who uttered them.

As they passed the lamps he was visible as a figure with a slight anterior plumpness, progressing buoyantly on knicker-bockered legs, with quite enormous calves, legs that, contrasting with Kipps' own narrow practice, were even exuberantly turned out at the knees and toes. A cycling cap was worn very much on one side, and from beneath it protruded carelessly straight wisps of dark-red hair, and ever and again an ample nose came into momentary view round the corner. The muscular cheeks of this person and a certain generosity of chin he possessed were blue shaven, and he had no moustache. His carriage was spacious and confident, his gestures up and down the narrow, deserted back street they traversed were irresistibly suggestive of owner-ship; a succession of broadly gesticulating shadows were born squatting on his feet, and grew and took possession of the road and reunited at last with the shadows of the infinite, as lamp after lamp was passed. Kipps saw by the flickering light of one of them that they were in Little Fenchurch Street, and then they came round a corner sharply into a dark court and stopped at the door of a particularly ramshackle-looking little house, held up between two larger ones, like a drunken man between policemen.

The cyclist propped his machine carefully against the window, produced a key and blew down it sharply. 'The lock's a bit tricky,' he said, and devoted himself for some moments to the task of opening the door. Some mechanical catastrophe ensued, and the door was open.

'You'd better wait here a bit while I get the lamp,' he remarked to Kipps; 'very likely it isn't filled,' and vanished into the blackness of the passage. 'Thank God for matches!' he said; and Kipps had an impression of a passage in the transitory pink flare and the bicyclist disappearing into a further room. Kipps was so much interested by these things that for the time he forgot his injuries altogether.

An interval, and Kipps was dazzled by a pink-shaded kerosene lamp. 'You go in,' said the red-haired man, 'and I'll bring in the bike,' and for a moment Kipps was alone in the lamp-lit room. He took in rather vaguely the shabby ensemble of the little apartment, the round table covered with a torn, red, glass-stained cover on which the lamp stood, a mottled looking-glass over the fireplace reflecting this, a disused gas-bracket, an extinct fire, a number of dusty postcards and memoranda stuck round the glass, a dusty, crowded paper-rack on the mantel with a number of cabinet photographs, a table littered with papers and cigarette ash, and a siphon of soda-water. Then the cyclist reappeared, and Kipps saw his blue-shaved, rather animated face, and bright, reddish-brown eyes for the first time. He was a man perhaps ten years older than Kipps, but his beardless face made them in a way contemporary.

'You behaved all right about that policeman, anyhow,' he repeated as he came forward.

'I don't see 'ow else I could 'ave done,' said Kipps, quite modestly. The cyclist scanned his guest for the first time, and decided upon hospitable details.

'We'd better let that mud dry a bit before we brush it. Whisky there is, good old Methusaleh, Canadian Rye; and there's some brandy that's all right. Which'll you have?'

'I dunno,' said Kipps, taken by surprise; and then seeing no other course but acceptance, 'Well, whisky, then.'

'Right you are, old boy; and if you'll take my advice you'll take it neat. I may not be a particular judge of this sort of thing, but I do know old Methusaleh pretty well. Old Methusaleh — four stars. That's me! Good old Harry Chitterlow, and good old Methusaleh. Leave 'em together. Bif! He's gone!'

He laughed loudly, looked about him, hesitated, and retired, leaving Kipps in possession of the room, and free to make a more precise examination of its contents.

II

He particularly remarked the photographs that adorned the apartment. They were chiefly photographs of ladies, in one case in tights, which Kipps thought a 'bit 'ot'; but one represented the bicyclist in the costume of some remote epoch. It did not take Kipps long to infer that the others were probably actresses and that his host was an actor, and the presence of the half of a large coloured playbill seemed to confirm this. A note in an Oxford frame that was a little too large for it he presently demeaned himself to read. 'Dear Mr Chitterlow,' it ran its brief course, 'if, after all, you will send the play you spoke of, I will endeavour to read it,' followed by a stylish but absolutely illegible signature, and across this was written in pencil, 'What price Harry now?' And in the shadow by the window was a rough and rather able sketch of the bicyclist in chalk on brown paper, calling particular attention to the curvature of the forward lines of his hull and calves and the jaunty carriage of his nose, and labelled unmistakably 'Chitterlow'. Kipps thought it 'rather a take-off'. The papers on the table by the siphon were in manuscript, Kipps observed, manuscript of a particularly convulsive and blottesque sort, and running obliquely across the page.

Presently he heard the metallic clamour as if of a series of irreparable breakages with which the lock of the front door discharged its function, and then Chitterlow reappeared, a little out of breath, and with a starry-labelled bottle in his large freckled hand.

'Sit down, old chap,' he said, 'sit down. I had to go out for it, after all. Wasn't a solitary bottle left. However, it's all right now we're here. No, don't sit on that chair, there's sheets of my play on that. That's the one – with the broken arm. I think this glass is clean, but, anyhow, wash it out with a squizz of siphon and shy it in the fireplace. Here, I'll do it! Lend it here!'

As he spoke Mr Chitterlow produced a corkscrew from a table drawer, attacked and overcame good old Methusaleh's cork in a style a bar-tender might envy, washed out two tumblers in his simple, effectual manner, and poured a couple of inches of the ancient fluid into each. Kipps took his tumbler, said 'Thenks' in an offhand way, and, after a momentary hesitation whether he should say 'Here's to you!' or not, put it to his lips without that ceremony. For a space fire in his throat occupied his attention to the exclusion of other matters, and then he discovered Mr Chitterlow with an intensely bulldog pipe alight, seated on the opposite side of the empty fireplace, and pouring himself out a second dose of whisky.

'After all,' said Mr Chitterlow, with his eye on the bottle and a little smile wandering to hide amidst his larger features, 'this accident might have been worse. I wanted some one to talk to a bit, and I didn't want to go to a pub, leastways not a Folkestone pub, because, as a matter of fact, I'd promised Mrs Chitterlow, who's away, not to, for various reasons, though of course if I'd wanted to, I'm just that sort, I should have all the same – and here we are! It's curious how one runs up against people out bicycling!'

'Isn't it!' said Kipps, feeling that the time had come for him to say something.

'Here we are, sitting and talking like old friends, and half an hour ago we didn't know we existed. Leastways we didn't know each other existed. I might have passed you in the street perhaps, and you might have passed me, and how was I to tell that, put to the test, you would have behaved as decently as you have behaved. Only it happened otherwise, that's all. You're not smoking!' he said. 'Have a cigarette?'

Kipps made a confused reply that took the form of not minding if he did, and drank another sip of old Methusaleh in his confusion. He was able to follow the subsequent course of that sip for quite a long way. It was as though the old gentleman was brandishing a burning torch through his vitals, lighting him here and lighting him there, until at last his whole being was in a glow. Chitterlow produced a tobacco-pouch and cigarette-papers, and, with an interesting parenthesis that was a little difficult to follow about some lady, named Kitty something or other, who had taught him the art when he was as yet only what you might call a nice boy, made Kipps a cigarette, and, with a consideration that won Kipps' gratitude, suggested that, after all, he might find a little soda-water an improvement with the whisky. 'Some people like it that way,' said Chitterlow; and then with voluminous emphasis, '*I* don't.'

Emboldened by the weakened state of his enemy, Kipps promptly swallowed the rest of him, and had his glass at once hospitably replenished. He began to feel he was of a firmer consistency than he commonly believed, and turned his mind to what Chitterlow was saying with the resolve to play a larger part in the conversation than he had hitherto done. Also he smoked through his nose quite successfully, an art he had only very recently acquired.

Meanwhile, Chitterlow explained that he was a playwright, and the tongue of Kipps was unloosened to respond that he knew a chap, or rather one of their fellows knew a chap, or at

least, to be perfectly correct, this fellow's brother did, who had
written a play. In response to Chitterlow's inquiries, he could
not recall the title of the play, nor where it had appeared, nor
the name of the manager who produced it, though he thought
the title was something about 'Love's Ransom', or something
like that.

'He made five 'undred pounds by it, though,' said Kipps. 'I
know that.'

'That's nothing,' said Chitterlow, with an air of experience
that was extremely convincing. 'Noth-ing. May seem a big sum
to *you* but *I* can assure you it's just what one gets any day.
There's any amount of money, an-y amount, in a good play.'

'I dessay,' said Kipps, drinking.

'Any amount of money!'

Chitterlow began a series of illustrative instances. He was
clearly a person of quite unequalled gift for monologue. It was
as though some conversational dam had burst upon Kipps, and
in a little while he was drifting along upon a copious rapid of
talk about all sorts of theatrical things by one who knew all
about them, and quite incapable of anticipating whither that
rapid meant to carry him. Presently, somehow, they had got to
anecdotes about well-known theatrical managers – little Teddy
Bletherskite, artful old Chumps, and the magnificent Behemoth,* 'petted to death, you know, fair sickened, by all these
society women'. Chitterlow described various personal encounters with these personages, always with modest self-deprecia-
tion, and gave Kipps a very amusing imitation of old Chumps in
a state of intoxication. Then he took two more stiff doses of old
Methusaleh in rapid succession.

Kipps reduced the hither end of his cigarette to a pulp as he
sat 'dessaying' and 'quite believing' Chitterlow in the sagest
manner, and admiring the easy way in which he was getting on
with this very novel and entertaining personage. He had another
cigarette made for him, and then Chitterlow, assuming by
insensible degrees more and more of the manner of a rich and
successful playwright being interviewed by a young admirer, set
himself to answer questions which sometimes Kipps asked, and
sometimes Chitterlow, about the particulars and methods of his
career. He undertook this self-imposed task with great earnestness and vigour, treating the matter, indeed, with such fulness
that at times it seemed lost altogether under a thicket of

parentheses, footnotes, and episodes that branched and budded from its stem. But it always emerged again, usually by way of illustration, to its own digressions. Practically it was a mass of material for the biography of a man who had been everywhere and done everything (including the Hon. Thomas Norgate, which was a Record), and in particular had acted with great distinction and profit (he dated various anecdotes, 'when I was getting thirty, or forty, or fifty dollars a week') throughout America and the entire civilized world.

And as he talked on and on in that full, rich, satisfying voice he had, and as old Methusaleh, indisputably a most drunken old reprobate of a whisky, busied himself throughout Kipps, lighting lamp after lamp until the entire framework of the little draper was illuminated and glowing like some public building on a festival, behold Chitterlow, and Kipps with him, and the room in which they sat were transfigured! Chitterlow became in very truth that ripe full man of infinite experience and humour and genius, fellow of Shakespeare and Ibsen and Maeterlinck (three names he placed together quite modestly far above his own), and no longer ambiguously dressed in a sort of yachting costume with cycling knickerbockers, but elegantly if unconventionally attired, and the room ceased to be a small and shabby room in a Folkestone slum, and grew larger and more richly furnished, and the flyblown photographs were curious old pictures, and the rubbish on the walls the most rare and costly bric-à-brac, and the indisputable paraffin lamp a soft and splendid light. A certain youthful heat that to many minds might have weakened old Methusaleh's starry claim to a ripe antiquity vanished in that glamour; two burnt holes and a claimant darn in the table-cloth, moreover, became no more than the pleasing contradictions natural in the house of genius; and as for Kipps – Kipps was a bright young man of promise, distinguished by recent quick, courageous proceedings not too definitely insisted upon, and he had been rewarded by admission to a sanctum and confidences, for which the common prosperous, for which 'society women' even, were notoriously sighing in vain. 'Don't *want* them, my boy; they'd simply play old Harry with the Work, you know! Chaps outside, bank clerks and university fellows, think the life's all *that* sort of thing. Don't you believe 'em! Don't you believe 'em.'

And then—!

'Boom . . . Boom . . . Boom . . . Boom . . .' right in the middle
of a most entertaining digression on flats who join touring
companies under the impression that they are actors, Kipps
much amused at their flatness as exposed by Chitterlow.

'Lor!' said Kipps, like one who awakens, 'that's not eleven!'

'Must be,' said Chitterlow. 'It was nearly ten when I got that
whisky. It's early yet—'

'All the same, I must be going,' said Kipps, and stood up.
'Even now – may be. Fact is – I 'ad *no* idea. The 'ouse door
shuts at 'arf-past ten, you know. I ought to 'ave thought before.'

'Well, if you *must* go—! I tell you what. I'll come too. . . .
Why! There's your leg, old man! Clean forgot it! You can't go
through the streets like that. I'll sew up the tear. And meanwhile
have another whisky.'

'I ought to be getting on *now*,' protested Kipps, feebly; and
then Chitterlow was showing him how to kneel on a chair in
order that the rent trouser leg should be attainable, and old
Methusaleh on his third round was busy repairing the temporary
eclipse of Kipps' arterial glow. Then suddenly Chitterlow was
seized with laughter, and had to leave off sewing to tell Kipps
that the scene wouldn't make a bad bit of business in a farcical
comedy, and then he began to sketch out the farcical comedy,
and that led him to a digression about another farcical comedy
of which he had written a ripping opening scene which wouldn't
take ten minutes to read. It had something in it that had never
been done on the stage before, and was yet perfectly legitimate,
namely, a man with a live beetle down the back of his neck
trying to seem at his ease in a roomful of people. . . .

'*They* won't lock you out,' he said, in a singularly reassuring
tone, and began to read and act what he explained to be (not
because he had written it, but simply because he knew it was so
on account of his exceptional experience of the stage), and what
Kipps also quite clearly saw to be, one of the best opening scenes
that had ever been written.

When it was over, Kipps, who rarely swore, was inspired to
say the scene was 'damned fine' about six times over, whereupon, as if by way of recognition, Chitterlow took a simply
enormous portion of the inspired antediluvian, declaring at the
same time that he had rarely met a '*finer*' intelligence than
Kipps' (stronger there might be, *that* he couldn't say with
certainty as yet, seeing how little, after all, they had seen of each

other, but a finer *never*), that it was a shame such a gallant and discriminating intelligence should be nightly either locked up or locked out at ten – well, ten-thirty, then – and that he had half a mind to recommend old somebody or other (apparently the editor of a London daily paper) to put on Kipps forthwith as a dramatic critic in the place of the current incapable.

'I don't think I've ever made up anything for print,' said Kipps, 'ever. I'd have a thundering good try, though, if ever I got a chance. I would that! I've written window tickets orfen enough. Made 'em up and everything. But that's different.'

'You'd come to it all the fresher for not having done it before. And the way you picked up every point in that scene, my boy, was a Fair Treat! I tell you, you'd knock William Archer* into fits. Not so literary, of course, you'd be, but I don't believe in literary critics any more than in literary playwrights. Plays *aren't* literature – that's just the point they miss. Plays are plays. No! That won't hamper you, anyhow. You're wasted down here, I tell you. Just as I was, before I took to acting. I'm hanged if I wouldn't like your opinion on these first two acts of that tragedy I'm on to. I haven't told you about that. It wouldn't take me more than an hour to read.'

III

Then, so far as he could subsequently remember, Kipps had 'another', and then it would seem that, suddenly regardless of the tragedy, he insisted that he 'really *must* be getting on', and from that point his memory became irregular. Certain things remained quite clearly, and as it is a matter of common knowledge that intoxicated people forget what happens to them, it follows that he was not intoxicated. Chitterlow came with him, partly to see him home and partly for a freshener before turning in. Kipps recalled afterwards very distinctly how in Little Fenchurch Street he discovered that he could not walk straight, and also that Chitterlow's needle and thread in his still unmended trouser leg was making an annoying little noise on the pavement behind him. He tried to pick up the needle suddenly by surprise, and somehow tripped and fell, and then Chitterlow, laughing uproariously, helped him up. 'It wasn't a bicycle this time, old boy,' said Chitterlow, and that appeared to them both at the time as being a quite extraordinarily good joke indeed. They punched each other about on the strength of it.

For a time after that Kipps certainly pretended to be quite desperately drunk and unable to walk, and Chitterlow entered into the pretence and supported him. After that Kipps remembered being struck with the extremely laughable absurdity of going downhill to Tontine Street in order to go uphill again to the Emporium, and trying to get that idea into Chitterlow's head and being unable to do so on account of his own merriment and Chitterlow's evident intoxication; and his next memory after that was of the exterior of the Emporium, shut and darkened, and, as it were, frowning at him with all its stripes of yellow and green. The chilly way in which 'SHALFORD' glittered in the moonlight printed itself with particular vividness on his mind. It appeared to Kipps that that establishment was closed to him for evermore. Those gilded letters, in spite of appearances, spelt FINIS for him and exile from Folkestone. He would never do woodcarving, never see Miss Walshingham again. Not that he had ever hoped to see her again. But this was the knife, this was final. He had stayed out, he had got drunk, there had been that row about the Manchester window dressing only three days ago. . . . In the retrospect he was quite sure that he was perfectly sober then and at bottom extremely unhappy, but he kept a brave face on the matter nevertheless, and declared stoutly he didn't care if he *was* locked out.

Whereupon Chitterlow slapped him on the back very hard and told him that was a 'Bit of All Right', and assured him that when he himself had been a clerk in Sheffield before he took to acting he had been locked out sometimes for six nights running.

'What's the result?' said Chitterlow. 'I could go back to that place now, and they'd be glad to have me. . . . Glad to have me,' he repeated, and then added, 'That is to say, if they remember me – which isn't very likely.'

Kipps asked a little weakly, 'What am I to do?'

'Keep out,' said Chitterlow. 'You can't knock 'em up now – that would give you Right away. You'd better try and sneak in in the morning with the Cat. That'll do you. You'll probably get in all right in the morning if nobody gives you away.'

Then for a time – perhaps as the result of that slap on the back – Kipps felt decidedly queer, and, acting on Chitterlow's advice, went for a bit of a freshener upon the Leas. After a time he threw off the temporary queerness, and found Chitterlow patting him on the shoulder and telling him that he'd be all right now in a minute and all the better for it – which he was. And the wind having dropped and the night being now a really very beautiful moonlight night indeed, and all before Kipps to spend as he liked, and with only a very little tendency to spin round now and again to mar its splendour, they set out to walk the whole length of the Leas to the Sandgate lift and back, and as they walked Chitterlow spoke first of moonlight transfiguring the sea and then of moonlight transfiguring faces, and so at last he came to the topic of Love, and upon that he dwelt a great while, and with a wealth of experience and illustrative anecdote that seemed remarkably pungent and material to Kipps. He forgot his lost Miss Walshingham and his outraged employer again. He became, as it were, a desperado by reflection.

Chitterlow had had adventures, a quite astonishing variety of adventures, in this direction; he was a man with a past, a really opulent past, and he certainly seemed to like to look back and see himself amidst its opulence.

He made no consecutive history, but he gave Kipps vivid momentary pictures of relations and entanglements. One moment he was in flight – only too worthily in flight – before the husband of a Malay woman in Cape Town. At the next he was having passionate complications with the daughter of a clergyman in York. Then he passed to a remarkable grouping at Seaford.

'They say you can't love two women at once,' said Chitterlow. 'But I tell you—' He gesticulated and raised his ample voice. 'It's *Rot*! *Rot*!'

'*I* know that,' said Kipps.

'Why, when I was in the smalls with Bessie Hopper's company there were Three.' He laughed, and decided to add, 'not counting Bessie, that is.'

He set out to reveal Life as it is lived in touring companies, a quite amazing jungle of interwoven 'affairs' it appeared to be, a mere amorous winepress for the crushing of hearts.

'People say this sort of thing's a nuisance and interferes with Work. I tell you it isn't. The Work couldn't go on without it. They *must* do it. They haven't the Temperament if they don't. If they hadn't the Temperament they wouldn't want to act; if they have — Bif!'

'You're right,' said Kipps. 'I see that.'

Chitterlow proceeded to a close criticism of certain historical indiscretions of Mr Clement Scott* respecting the morals of the stage. Speaking in confidence, and not as one who addresses the public, he admitted regretfully the general truth of these comments. He proceeded to examine various typical instances that had almost forced themselves upon him personally, and with especial regard to the contrast between his own character towards women and that of the Hon. Thomas Norgate, with whom it appeared he had once been on terms of great intimacy. . . .

Kipps listened with emotion to these extraordinary recollections. They were wonderful to him, they were incredibly credible. This tumultuous passionate irregular course was the way life ran — except in high-class establishments! Such things happened in novels, in plays — only he had been fool enough not to understand they happened. His share in the conversation was now, indeed, no more than faint writing in the margin; Chitterlow was talking quite continuously. He expanded his magnificent voice into huge guffaws, he drew it together into a confidential intensity, it became drawlingly reminiscent, he was frank, frank with the effect of a revelation, reticent also with the effect of a revelation, a stupendously gesticulating moonlit black figure, wallowing in itself, preaching Adventure and the Flesh to Kipps. Yet withal shot with something of sentiment, with a sort of sentimental refinement very coarsely and egotistically done. The Times he had had! — even before he was as old as Kipps he had had innumerable Times.

Well, he said with a sudden transition, he had sown his wild oats — one had to somewhen — and now, he fancied he had mentioned it earlier in the evening, he was happily married. She was, he indicated, a 'born lady'. Her father was a prominent lawyer, a solicitor in Kentish Town, 'done a lot of public-house business'; her mother was second cousin to the wife of Abel Jones, the fashionable portrait painter — 'almost Society people in a way'. That didn't count with Chitterlow. He was no snob. What *did* count was that she possessed what he ventured to assert, without much fear of contradiction, was the very finest completely untrained contralto voice in all the world. ('But to hear it properly,' said Chitterlow, 'you want a Big Hall.') He became rather vague, and jerked his head about to indicate when and how he had entered matrimony. She was, it seemed, 'away with her people'. It was clear that Chitterlow did not get on with these people very well. It would seem they failed to appreciate his playwriting, regarding it as an unremunerative pursuit, whereas, as he and Kipps knew, wealth beyond the dreams of avarice would presently accrue. Only patience and persistence were needful.

He went off at a tangent to hospitality. Kipps must come down home with him. They couldn't wander about all night, with a bottle of the right sort pining at home for them. 'You can sleep on the sofa. You won't be worried by broken springs, anyhow, for I took 'em all out myself two or three weeks ago. I don't see what they ever put 'em in for. It's a point I know about. I took particular notice of it when I was with Bessie Hopper. Three months we were, and all over England, North Wales, and the Isle of Man, and I never struck a sofa in diggings anywhere that hadn't a broken spring. Not once – all the time.'

He added, almost absently, 'It happens like that at times.'

They descended the slant road towards Harbour Street and went on past the Pavilion Hotel.

IV

They came into the presence of old Methusaleh again, and that worthy, under Chitterlow's direction, at once resumed the illumination of Kipps' interior with the conscientious thoroughness that distinguished him. Chitterlow took a tall portion to himself with an air of asbestos, lit the bulldog pipe again, and lapsed for a space into meditation, from which Kipps roused him by remarking that he expected 'a nacter 'as a lot of ups and downs like, now and then.'

At which Chitterlow seemed to bestir himself. 'Ra-ther,' he said. 'And sometimes it's his own fault and sometimes it isn't. Usually it is. If it isn't one thing it's another. If it isn't the manager's wife it's bar-bragging. I tell you things happen at times. I'm a fatalist. The fact is, Character has you. You can't get away from it. You may think you do, but you don't.'

He reflected for a moment. 'It's that what makes tragedy.

Psychology really. It's the Greek irony – Ibsen and – all that. Up to date.'

He emitted this exhaustive summary of high-toned modern criticism as if he was repeating a lesson while thinking of something else; but it seemed to rouse him as it passed his lips, by including the name of Ibsen.

He became interested in telling Kipps, who was, indeed, open to any information whatever about this quite novel name, exactly where he thought Ibsen fell short, points where it happened that Ibsen was defective just where it chanced that he, Chitterlow, was strong. Of course, he had no desire to place himself in any way on an equality with Ibsen; still, the fact remained that his own experience in England and America and the colonies was altogether more extensive than Ibsen could have had. Ibsen had probably never seen 'one decent bar scrap' in his life. That, of course, was not Ibsen's fault, or his own merit, but there the thing was. Genius, he knew, was supposed to be able to do anything or to do without anything; still, he was now inclined to doubt that. He had a play in hand that might perhaps not please William Archer – whose opinion, after all, he did not value as he valued Kipps' opinion – but which, he thought, was, at any rate, as well constructed as anything Ibsen ever did.

So with infinite deviousness Chitterlow came at last to his play. He decided he would not read it to Kipps; but tell him about it. This was the simpler, because much of it was still unwritten. He began to explain his plot. It was a complicated plot, and all about a nobleman who had seen everything and done everything and knew practically all that Chitterlow knew about women, that is to say, 'all about women' and suchlike matters. It warmed and excited Chitterlow. Presently he stood up to act a situation, which could not be explained. It was an extremely vivid situation.

Kipps applauded the situation vehemently. 'Tha's dam fine,' said the new dramatic critic, quite familiar with his part now, striking the table with his fist and almost upsetting his third portion (in the second series) of old Methusaleh. 'Tha's *dam* fine, Chit'low!'

'You see it?' said Chitterlow, with the last vestiges of that incidental gloom disappearing. 'Good old boy! I thought you'd see it. But it's just the sort of thing the literary critic can't see. However, it's only a beginning—'

He replenished Kipps and proceeded with his exposition.

In a little while it was no longer necessary to give that over-advertised Ibsen the purely conventional precedence he had hitherto had. Kipps and Chitterlow were friends, and they could speak frankly and openly of things not usually admitted. 'Any'ow,' said Kipps, a little irrelevantly, and speaking over the brim of the replenishment, 'what you read jus' now was dam fine. Nothing can't alter that.'

He perceived a sort of faint buzzing vibration about things that was very nice and pleasant, and with a little care he had no difficulty whatever in putting his glass back on the table. Then he perceived Chitterlow was going on with the scenario, and then that old Methusaleh had almost entirely left his bottle. He was glad there was so little more Methusaleh to drink, because that would prevent his getting drunk. He knew that he was not now drunk, but he knew that he had had enough. He was one of those who always know when they have had enough. He tried to interrupt Chitterlow to tell him this, but he could not get a suitable opening. He doubted whether Chitterlow might not be one of those people who did not know when they had had enough. He discovered that he disapproved of Chitterlow. Highly. It seemed to him that Chitterlow went on and on like a river. For a time he was inexplicably and quite unjustly cross with Chitterlow, and wanted to say to him 'you got the gift of the gab', and then Chitterlow thanked him and said he was better than Archer any day. So he eyed Chitterlow with a baleful eye until it dawned upon him that a most extraordinary thing was taking place. Chitterlow kept mentioning some one named Kipps. This presently began to perplex Kipps very greatly. Dimly but decidedly he perceived this was wrong.

'Look 'ere,' he said suddenly, '*what* Kipps?'

'This chap Kipps I'm telling you about.'

'What chap Kipps you're telling which about?'

'I told you.'

Kipps struggled with a difficulty in silence for a space. Then he reiterated firmly, '*What* chap Kipps?'

'This chap in my play – man who kisses the girl.'

'Never kissed a girl,' said Kipps, 'leastways—' and subsided for a space. He could not remember whether he had kissed Ann or not – he knew he had meant to. Then suddenly, in a tone of great sadness, and addressing the hearth, he said, '*My* name's Kipps.'

'Eh?' said Chitterlow.

'Kipps,' said Kipps, smiling a little cynically.

'What about him?'

'He's me.' He tapped his breastbone with his middle finger to indicate his essential self.

He leant forward very gravely towards Chitterlow. 'Look 'ere, Chit'low,' he said. 'You haven't no business putting my name into play. You mustn't do things like that. You'd lose me my crib, right away.' And they had a little argument – so far as Kipps could remember. Chitterlow entered upon a general explanation of how he got his names. These he had, for the most part, got out of a newspaper that was still, he believed, 'lying about'. He even made to look for it, and while he was doing so Kipps went on with the argument, addressing himself more particularly to the photograph of the girl in tights. He said that at first her costume had not commended her to him, but now he perceived she had an extremely sensible face. He told her she would like Buggins if she met him, he could see she was just that sort. She would admit – all sensible people would admit – that using names in plays was wrong. You could, for example, have the law of him.

He became confidential. He explained that he was already in sufficient trouble for stopping out all night, without having his name put in plays. He was certain to be in the deuce of a row, the duece of a row. Why had he done it? Why hadn't he gone at ten? Because one thing leads to another. One thing, he generalized, always does lead to another. . . .

He was trying to tell her that he was utterly unworthy of Miss Walshingham, when Chitterlow gave up the search, and suddenly accused him of being drunk and talking 'Rot—'

Chapter Five

Swapped

I

He awoke on the thoroughly comfortable sofa that had had all its springs removed, and although he had certainly not been intoxicated, he awoke with what Chitterlow pronounced to be, quite indisputably, a Head and a Mouth. He had slept in his clothes, and he felt stiff and uncomfortable all over, but the head and mouth insisted that he must not bother over little things like that. In the head was one large angular idea that it was physically painful to have there. If he moved his head, the angular idea shifted about in the most agonizing way. This idea was that he had lost his situation and was utterly ruined, and that it really mattered very little. Shalford was certain to hear of his escapade, and that, coupled with that row about the Manchester window—!

He raised himself into a sitting position under Chitterlow's urgent encouragement.

He submitted apathetically to his host's attentions. Chitterlow, who admitted being a 'bit off it' himself and in need of an egg-cupful of brandy, just an egg-cupful neat, dealt with that Head and Mouth as a mother might deal with the fall of an only child. He compared it with other Heads and Mouths that he had met, and in particular to certain experienced by the Hon. Thomas Norgate. 'Right up to the last,' said Chitterlow, 'he couldn't stand his liquor. It happens like that at times.' And after Chitterlow had pumped on the young beginner's head and given him some anchovy paste piping hot on buttered toast, which he preferred to all the other remedies he had encountered, Kipps resumed his crumpled collar, brushed his clothes, tacked up his knee, and prepared to face Mr Shalford and the reckoning for this wild unprecedented night – the first 'night out' that ever he had taken.

Acting on Chitterlow's advice to have a bit of a freshener before returning to the Emporium, Kipps walked some way

along the Leas and back, and then went down to a shop near
the Harbour to get a cup of coffee. He found that extremely
reinvigorating, and he went on up the High Street to face the
inevitable terrors of the office, a faint touch of pride in his
depravity tempering his extreme self-abasement. After all, it was
not an unmanly headache; he had been out all night, and he had
been drinking, and his physical disorder was there to witness
the fact. If it wasn't for the thought of Shalford, he would have
been even a proud man to discover himself at last in such a
condition. But the thought of Shalford was very dreadful. He
met two of the apprentices snatching a walk before shop began.
At the sight of them he pulled his spirits together, put his hat
back from his pallid brow, thrust his hands into his trousers
pockets, and adopted an altogether more dissipated carriage; he
met their innocent faces with a wan smile. Just for a moment he
was glad that his patch at the knee was, after all, visible, and
that some at least of the mud on his clothes had refused to move
at Chitterlow's brushing. What wouldn't they think he had been
up to? He passed them without speaking. He could imagine how
they regarded his back. Then he recollected Mr Shalford. . . .

The deuce of a row certainly, and perhaps—! He tried to
think of plausible versions of the affair. He could explain he had
been run down by rather a wild sort of fellow who was riding a
bicycle, almost stunned for the moment (even now he felt the
effects of the concussion in his head), and had been given whisky
to restore him, and 'the fact is, Sir,' – with an upward inflection
of the voice, an upward inflection of the eyebrows, and an air of
its being the last thing one would have expected whisky to do,
the manifestation indeed of a practically unique physiological
weakness, – 'it got into my *'ed*!' . . .

Put like that it didn't look so bad.

He got to the Emporium a little before eight, and the
housekeeper, with whom he was something of a favourite
('There's no harm in Mr Kipps,' she used to say), seemed to like
him, if anything, better for having broken the rules, and gave
him a piece of dry toast and a good hot cup of tea.

'I suppose the G. V.—' began Kipps.

'He knows,' said the housekeeper.

'He went down to the shop a little before time, and presently
Booch summoned him to the presence.

He emerged from the private office after an interval of ten minutes.

The junior clerk scrutinized his visage. Buggins put the frank question.

Kipps answered with one word.

'Swapped!' said Kipps.

II

Kipps leant against the fixtures with his hands in his pockets and talked to the two apprentices under him.

'I don't care if I *am* swapped,' said Kipps. 'I been sick of Teddy and his System some time.

'I was a good mind to chuck it when my time was up,' said Kipps. 'Wish I 'ad now.'

Afterwards Pearce came round, and Kipps repeated this.

'What's it for?' said Pearce. 'That row about the window tickets?'

'No fear!' said Kipps, and sought to convey a perspective of splendid depravity. 'I wasn't in las' night,' he said, and made even Pearce, 'man about town' Pearce, open his eyes.

'Why, where did you get to?' asked Pearce.

He conveyed that he had been 'fair round the town'. 'With a Nactor chap I know.

'One can't *always* be living like a curit,' he said.

'No fear,' said Pearce, trying to play up to him.

But Kipps had the top place in that conversation.

'My lor!' said Kipps, when Pearce had gone, 'but wasn't my mouth and 'ed bad this morning before I 'ad a pick-me-up!'

'Whad jer 'ave?'

'Anchovy on 'ot buttered toast. It's the very best pick-me-up there is. You trust me, Rodgers. I never take no other, and I don't advise you to. See?'

And when pressed for further particulars, he said again he had been 'fair all *round* the town, with a Nactor chap' he knew. They asked curiously all he had done, and he said, 'Well, what do *you* think?' And when they pressed for still further details, he said there were things little boys ought not to know, and laughed darkly, and found them some huckaback to roll.

And in this manner for a space did Kipps fend off the

contemplation of the 'key of the street' that Shalford had presented him.

III

This sort of thing was all very well when junior apprentices were about, but when Kipps was alone with himself it served him not at all. He was uncomfortable inside, and his skin was uncomfortable, and the Head and Mouth, palliated perhaps, but certainly not cured, were still with him. He felt, to tell the truth, nasty and dirty, and extremely disgusted with himself. To work was dreadful, and to stand still and think still more dreadful. His patched knee reproached him. These were the second best of his three pairs of trousers, and they had cost him thirteen and sixpence. Practically ruined they were. His dusting pair was unfit for shop, and he would have to degrade his best. When he was under inspection he affected the slouch of a desperado, but directly he found himself alone, this passed insensibly into the droop.

The financial aspect of things grew large before him. His whole capital in the world was the sum of five pounds in the Post Office Savings Bank, and four and sixpence cash. Besides, there would be two months' 'screw'. His little tin box upstairs was no longer big enough for his belongings, he would have to buy another, let alone that it was not calculated to make a good impression in a new 'crib'. Then there would be paper and stamps needed in some abundance for answering advertisements and railway fares when he went 'crib hunting'. He would have to write letters, and he never wrote letters. There was spelling, for example, to consider. Probably if nothing turned up before his month was up, he would have to go home to his Uncle and Aunt.

How would they take it? . . .

For the present, at any rate, he resolved not to write to them.

Such disagreeable things as this it was that lurked below the fair surface of Kipps' assertion, 'I been wanting a change. If 'e 'adn't swapped me, I should very likely 'ave swapped '*im*.'

In the perplexed privacies of his own mind he could not understand how everything had happened. He had been the Victim of Fate, or at least of one as inexorable – Chitterlow. He tried to recall the successive steps that had culminated so disastrously. They were difficult to recall. . . .

Buggins that night abounded in counsel and reminiscence.

'Curious thing,' said Buggins, 'but every time I've had the swap I've never believed I should get another Crib – never. But I have,' said Buggins. 'Always. So don't lose heart, whatever you do.

'Whatever you do,' said Buggins, 'keep hold of your collars and cuffs – shirts if you can, but collars anyhow. Spout them last. And anyhow, it's summer! you won't want your coat. . . . You got a good umbrella. . . .

'You'll no more get a shop from New Romney than – anything. Go straight up to London, get the cheapest room you can find – and hang out. Don't eat too much. Many a chap's put his prospects in his stomach. Get a cup o' coffee and a slice – egg if you like – but remember you got to turn up at the Warehouse tidy. The best places *now*, I believe, are the old cabmen's eating houses. Keep your watch and chain as long as you can. . . .

'There's lots of shops going,' said Buggins. 'Lots!'

And added reflectively, 'But not this time of year perhaps.'

He began to recall his own researches. ''Stonishing lot of chaps you see,' he said. 'All sorts. Look like Dukes some of 'em. High hat. Patent boots. Frock-coat. All there. All right for a West End crib. Others – Lord! It's a caution, Kipps. Boots been inked in some reading-rooms – *I* used to write in a Reading Room in Fleet Street, regular penny club – hat been wetted, collar frayed, tail-coat buttoned up, black chest-plaster tie – spread out. Shirt, you know, gone—' Buggins pointed upward with a pious expression.

'No shirt, I expect?'

'Eat it,' said Buggins.

Kipps meditated. 'I wonder where old Minton is,' he said at last. 'I often wondered about 'im.'

IV

It was the morning following Kipps' notice of dismissal that Miss Walshingham came into the shop. She came in with a dark, slender lady, rather faded, rather tightly dressed, whom Kipps was to know some day as her mother. He discovered them in the main shop, at the counter of the ribbon department. He had come to the opposite glove counter with some goods enclosed in a parcel that he had unpacked in his own department. The two ladies were both bent over a box of black ribbon.

He had a moment of tumultuous hesitations. The etiquette of the situation was incomprehensible. He put down his goods very quietly and stood, hands on counter, staring at these two ladies. Then, as Miss Walshingham sat back, the instinct of flight seized him. . . .

He returned to his Manchester shop wildly agitated. Directly he was out of sight of her he wanted to see her. He fretted up and down the counter, and addressed some snappish remarks to the apprentice in the window. He fumbled for a moment with a parcel, untied it needlessly, began to tie it up again, and then bolted back again into the main shop. He could hear his own heart beating.

The two ladies were standing in the manner of those who have completed their purchases and are waiting for their change. Mrs Walshingham regarded some remnants with impersonal interest; Helen's eyes searched the shop. They distinctly lit up when they discovered Kipps.

He dropped his hands to the counter by habit, and stood for a moment regarding her awkwardly. What would she do? Would she cut him? She came across the shop to him.

'How are *you*, Mr Kipps?' she said, in her clear distinct tones, and she held out her hand.

'Very well, thank you,' said Kipps; 'how are you?'

She said she had been buying some ribbon.

He became aware of Mrs Walshingham very much surprised. This checked something allusive about the class, and he said instead that he supposed she was glad to be having her holidays now. She said she was, it gave her more time for reading and that sort of thing. He supposed that she would be going abroad, and she thought that perhaps they *would* go to Knocke or Bruges for a time.

Then came a pause, and Kipps' soul surged within him. He wanted to tell her he was leaving and would never see her again. He could find neither words nor voice to say it. The swift seconds passed. The girl in the ribbons was handing Mrs

Walshingham her change. 'Well,' said Miss Walshingham, 'good-bye,' and gave him her hand again.

Kipps bowed over her hand. His manners, his counter manners, were the easiest she had ever seen upon him. She turned to her mother. It was no good now, no good. Her mother! You couldn't say a thing like that before her mother! All was lost but politeness. Kipps rushed for the door. He stood at the door bowing with infinite gravity, and she smiled and nodded as she went out. She saw nothing of the struggle within him, nothing but a gratifying emotion. She smiled like a satisfied goddess as the incense ascends.

Mrs Walshingham bowed stiffly and a little awkwardly.

He remained holding the door open for some seconds after they had passed out, then rushed suddenly to the back of the 'costume' window to watch them go down the street. His hands tightened on the window-rack as he stared. Her mother appeared to be asking discreet questions. Helen's bearing suggested the offhand replies of a person who found the world a satisfactory place to live in. 'Really, Mumsie, you cannot expect me to cut my own students dead,' she was, in fact, saying. . . .

They vanished round Henderson's corner.

Gone! And he would never see her again – never!

It was as though some one had struck his heart with a whip. Never! Never! Never! And she didn't know! He turned back from the window, and the department, with its two apprentices, was impossible. The whole glaring world was insupportable.

He hesitated, and made a rush, head down, for the cellar that was his Manchester warehouse. Rogers asked him a question that he pretended not to hear.

The Manchester warehouse was a small cellar apart from the general basement of the building, and dimly lit by a small gas flare. He did not turn that up, but rushed for the darkest corner, where, on the lowest shelf, the Sale window-tickets were stored. He drew out the box of these with trembling hands and upset them on the floor, and so having made himself a justifiable excuse for being on the ground with his head well in the dark, he could let his poor bursting little heart have its way with him for a space.

And there he remained until the cry of 'Kipps! Forward!' summoned him once more to face the world.

Chapter Six

The Unexpected

I

Now in the slack of that same day, after the midday dinner and before the coming of the afternoon customers, this disastrous Chitterlow descended upon Kipps with the most amazing coincidence in the world. He did not call formally, entering and demanding Kipps, but privately, in a confidential and mysterious manner.

Kipps was first aware of him as a dark object bobbing about excitedly outside the hosiery window. He was stooping and craning and peering in the endeavour to see into the interior between and over the socks and stockings. Then he transferred his attention to the door, and after a hovering scrutiny, tried the baby-linen display. His movements and gestures suggested a suppressed excitement.

Seen by daylight, Chitterlow was not nearly such a magnificent figure as he had been by the subdued nocturnal lightings and beneath the glamour of his own interpretation. The lines were the same, indeed, but the texture was different. There was a quality about the yachting cap, an indefinable finality of dustiness, a shiny finish on all the salient surfaces of the reefer coat. The red hair and the profile, though still forcible and fine, were less in the quality of Michael Angelo and more in that of the merely picturesque. But it was a bright brown eye still that sought amidst the interstices of the baby-linen.

Kipps was by no means anxious to interview Chitterlow again. If he had felt sure that Chitterlow would not enter the shop, he would have hid in the warehouse until the danger was past, but he had no idea of Chitterlow's limitations. He decided to keep up the shop in the shadows until Chitterlow reached the side window of the Manchester department, and then to go outside as if to inspect the condition of the window and explain to him that things were unfavourable to immediate intercourse. He might tell him he had already lost his situation. . . .

'Ullo, Chit'low,' he said, emerging.

'Very man I want to see,' said Chitterlow, shaking with vigour. 'Very man I want to see.' He laid a hand on Kipps' arm. 'How *old* are you, Kipps?'

'One and twenty,' said Kipps. 'Why?'

'Talk about coincidences! And your name, now? Wait a minute.' He held out a finger. '*Is* it Arthur?'

'Yes,' said Kipps.

'You're the man,' said Chitterlow.

'What man?'

'It's about the thickest coincidence I ever struck,' said Chitterlow, plunging his extensive hand into his breast-coast pocket. 'Half a jiff and I'll tell you your mother's Christian name.' He laughed and struggled with his coat for a space, produced a washing-book and two pencils, which he deposited in his side pocket, then in one capacious handful, a bent but but no means finally disabled cigar, the rubber proboscis of a bicycle pump, some twine and a lady's purse, and finally a small pocket-book, and from this, after dropping and recovering several visiting-cards, he extracted a carelessly torn piece of newspaper. 'Euphemia,' he read, and brought his face close to Kipps'. 'Eh?' He laughed noisily. 'It's about as fair a Bit of All Right as any one *could* have – outside a coincidence play. Don't say her name wasn't Euphemia, Kipps, and spoil the whole blessed show.'

'Whose name – Euphemia?' asked Kipps.

'Your mother's.'

'Lemme see what it says on the paper.'

Chitterlow handed him the fragment and turned away. 'You may say what you like,' he said, addressing a vast deep laugh to the street generally.

Kipps attempted to read. 'WADDY or KIPPS. If Arthur Waddy or Arthur Kipps, the son of Margaret Euphemia Kipps, who—'

Chitterlow's finger swept over the print. 'I went down the column, and every blessed name that seemed to fit my play I took. I don't believe in made-up names. As I told you. I'm all with Zola in that. Documents whenever you can. I like 'em hot and real. See? Who was Waddy?'

'Never heard his name.'

'Not Waddy?'

'No!'

Kipps tried to read again, and abandoned the attempt. 'What does it mean?' he said. 'I don't understand.'

'It means,' said Chitterlow, with a momentary note of lucid exposition, 'so far as I can make out, that you're going to strike it Rich. Never mind about the Waddy – that's a detail. What does it usually mean? You'll hear of something to your advantage – very well. I took that newspaper up to get my names by the merest chance. Directly I saw it again and read that – I knew it was you. I believe in coincidences. People say they don't happen. *I* say they do. Everything's coincidence. Seen properly. Here you are. Here's one! Incredible? Not a bit of it! See? It's you! Kipps! Waddy be damned! It's a Mascot. There's luck in my play. Bif! You're there. *I'm* there. Fair *in* it! Snap!' And he discharged his fingers like a pistol. 'Never you mind about the "Waddy".'

'Eh?' said Kipps, with a nervous eye on Chitterlow's fingers.

'You're all right,' said Chitterlow, 'you may bet the seat of your only breeches on that! Don't you worry about the Waddy – that's as clear as day. You're about as right side up as a billiard ball . . . whatever you do. Don't stand there gaping, man! Read the paper if you don't believe me. Read it.'

He shook it under Kipps' nose.

Kipps became aware of the second apprentice watching them from the shop. His air of perplexity gave place to a more confident bearing.

'—"who was born at East Grinstead." I certainly was born there. I've 'eard my Aunt say—'

'I knew it,' said Chitterlow, taking hold of one edge of the paper and bringing his face close alongside Kipps'.

'—on September the first, eighteen hundred and seventy-eight—'

'*That's* all right,' said Chitterlow. 'It's all, all right, and all you have to do is to write to Watson and Bean and get it—'

'Get what?'

'Whatever it is.'

Kipps sought his moustache. 'You'd write?' he asked.

'Ra-ther.'

'But what d'you think it is?'

'That's the fun of it!' said Chitterlow, taking three steps in some as yet uninvented dance. 'That's where the joke comes in.

It may be anything – it may be a million. If so! Where does little Harry come in? Eh?'

Kipps was trembling slightly. 'But—' he said, and thought. 'If you was me—' he began. 'About that Waddy—?'

He glanced up and saw the second apprentice disappear with amazing swiftness from behind the goods in the window.

'*What*?' asked Chitterlow, but he never had an answer.

'Lor! There's the guv'nor!' said Kipps, and made a prompt dive for the door.

He dashed in, only to discover that Shalford, with the junior apprentice in attendance, had come to mark off remnants of Kipps' cotton dresses, and was demanding him. 'Hullo, Kipps,' he said, 'outside—?'

'Seein' if the window was straight, Sir,' said Kipps.

'Umph!' said Shalford.

For a space Kipps was too busily employed to think at all of Chitterlow or the crumpled bit of paper in his trouser pocket. He was, however, painfully aware of a suddenly disconnected excitement at large in the street. There came one awful moment when Chitterlow's nose loomed interrogatively over the ground glass of the department door, and his bright little red-brown eye sought for the reason of Kipps' disappearance, and then it became evident that he saw the high light of Shalford's baldness, and grasped the situation and went away. And then Kipps (with that advertisement in his pocket) was able to come back to the business in hand.

He became aware that Shalford had asked a question. 'Yessir, nosir, rightsir. I'm sorting up zephyrs to-morrow, Sir,' said Kipps.

Presently he had a moment to himself again, and, taking up a safe position behind a newly unpacked pile of summer lace curtains, he straightened out the piece of paper and re-perused it. It was a little perplexing. That 'Arthur Waddy or Arthur Kipps' – did that imply two persons or one? He would ask Pearce or Buggins. Only—

It had always been impressed upon him that there was something demanding secrecy about his mother.

'Don't you answer no questions about your mother,' his aunt had been wont to say. 'Tell them you don't know, whatever it is they ask you.'

'Now, this—?'

Kipps' face became portentously careful, and he tugged at his moustache, such as it was, hard.

He had always represented his father as being a 'gentleman farmer'. 'It didn't pay,' he used to say, with a picture in his own mind of a penny magazine aristocrat prematurely worn out by worry. 'I'm a Norfan, both sides,' he would explain, with the air of one who had seen trouble. He said he lived with his uncle and aunt, but he did not say that they kept a toy-shop, and to tell any one that his uncle had been a butler – *a servant*! – would have seemed the maddest of indiscretions. Almost all the assistants in the Emporium were equally reticent and vague, so great is their horror of 'Lowness' of any sort. To ask about this 'Waddy or Kipps' would upset all these little fictions. He was not, as a matter of fact, perfectly clear about his real status in the world (he was not, as a matter of fact, perfectly clear about anything), but he knew that there was a quality about his status that was – detrimental.

Under the circumstances—?

It occurred to him that it would save a lot of trouble to destroy the advertisement there and then.

In which case he would have to explain to Chitterlow!

'Eng!' said Mr Kipps.

'Kipps!' cried Carshot, who was shopwalking. 'Kipps Forward!'

He thrust back the crumpled paper into his pocket, and sallied forth to the customer.

'I want,' said the customer, looking vaguely about her through glasses, 'a little bit of something to cover a little stool I have. Anything would do – a remnant or anything.'

The matter of the advertisement remained in abeyance for half an hour, and at the end the little stool was still a candidate for covering, and Kipps had a thoroughly representative collection of the textile fabrics in his department to clear away. He was so angry about the little stool that the crumpled advertisement lay for a space in his pocket, absolutely forgotten.

II

Kipps sat on his tin box under the gas-bracket that evening, and looked up the name Euphemia, and learnt what it meant in the *Inquire Within About Everything* that constituted Buggins' reference library. He hoped Buggins, according to his habit, would ask him what he was looking for, but Buggins was busy turning out his week's washing. 'Two collars,' said Buggins, 'half pair socks, two dickeys. Shirt? . . . M'm. There ought to be another collar somewhere.'

'Euphemia,' said Kipps at last, unable altogether to keep to himself this suspicion of a high origin that floated so delightfully about him. 'Eu-phemia; it isn't a name *common* people would give to a girl is it?'

'It isn't the name any decent people would give to a girl,' said Buggins, 'common or not.'

'Lor!' said Kipps. 'Why?'

'It's giving girls names like that,' said Buggins, 'that nine times out of ten makes 'em go wrong. It unsettles 'em. If ever I was to have a girl, if ever I was to have a dozen girls, I'd call 'em all Jane. Every one of 'em. You couldn't have a better name than that. Euphemia indeed! What next? . . . Good Lord! . . . That isn't one of my collars there, is it, under your bed?'

Kipps got him the collar.

'I don't see no great 'arm in Euphemia,' he said as he did so.

After that he became restless. 'I'm a good mind to write that letter,' he said; and then, finding Buggins preoccupied wrapping his washing up in the '½ sox', added to himself, 'a thundering good mind'.

So he got his penny bottle of ink, borrowed the pen from Buggins, and with no very serious difficulty in spelling or composition, did as he had resolved.

He came back into the bedroom about an hour afterwards, a little out of breath and pale. 'Where you been?' said Buggins, who was now reading the *Daily World Manager*, which came to him in rotation from Carshot.

'Out to post some letters,' said Kipps, hanging up his hat.

'Crib hunting?'

'Mostly,' said Kipps.

'Rather,' he added with a nervous laugh; 'what else?'

Buggins went on reading. Kipps sat on his bed and regarded the back of the *Daily World Manager* thoughtfully.

'Buggins,' he said at last.

Buggins lowered his paper and looked.

'I say, Buggins, what do these here advertisements mean that say so-and-so will hear of something greatly to his advantage?'

'Missin' people,' said Buggins, making to resume reading.

'How d'yer mean?' asked Kipps. 'Money left, and that sort of thing?'

Buggins shook his head. 'Debts,' he said, 'more often than not.'

'But that ain't to his advantage.'

'They put that to get 'old of 'em,' said Buggins. 'Often it's wives.'

'What do you mean?'

'Deserted wives try and get their husbands back that way.'

'I suppose it *is* legacies sometimes, eh? Perhaps, if some one was left a hundred pounds by some one—'

'Hardly ever,' said Buggins.

'Well, 'ow—?' began Kipps, and hesitated.

Buggins resumed reading. He was very much excited by a leader on Indian affairs. 'By Jove!' he said, 'it won't do to give these here Blacks votes.'

'No fear,' said Kipps.

'They're different altogether,' said Buggins. 'They 'aven't the sound sense of Englishmen, and they 'aven't the character. There's a sort of tricky dishonesty about 'em – false witness and all that – of which an Englishman has no idea. Outside their courts of law – it's a pos'tive fact, Kipps – there's witnesses waitin' to be 'ired. Reg'lar trade. Touch their 'ats as you go in. Englishmen 'ave no idea, I tell you – not ord'nary Englishmen. It's in their blood. They're too timid to be honest. Too slavish. They aren't used to being free like we are, and if you gave 'em freedom they wouldn't make a proper use of it. Now, *we*—Oh, *Damn*!'

For the gas had suddenly gone out, and Buggins had the whole column of Society Club Chat still to read.

Buggins could talk of nothing after that but Shalford's meanness in turning off the gas, and after being extremely satirical about their employer, undressed in the dark, hit his bare toe against a box, and subsided, after unseemly ejaculations, into silent ill-temper.

Though Kipps tried to get to sleep before the affair of the letter he had just posted resumed possession of his mind, he could not do so. He went over the whole thing again, quite exhaustively.

Now that his first terror was abating, he couldn't quite determine whether he was glad or sorry that he had posted that letter. If it *should* happen to be a hundred pounds!

It *must* be a hundred pounds!

If it was he could hold out for a year, for a couple of years even, before he got a Crib.

Even if it was fifty pounds—!

Buggins was already breathing regularly when Kipps spoke again. '*Bug*-gins,' he said.

Buggins pretended to be asleep, and thickened his regular breathing (a little too hastily) to a snore.

'I say, Buggins,' said Kipps, after an interval.

'*What's* up now?' said Buggins, unamiably.

'S'pose *you* saw an advertisement in a paper, with your name in it, see, asking you to come and see some one, like, so as to hear of something very much to your—'

'Hide,' said Buggins, shortly.

'But—'

'I'd hide.'

'Er?'

'Goo'-night, o' man,' said Buggins, with convincing earnestness. Kipps lay still for a long time, then blew profoundly, turned over and stared at the other side of the dark.

He had been a fool to post that letter!

Lord! *Hadn't* he been a fool!

III

It was just five days and a half after the light had been turned out while Buggins was reading, that a young man with a white face, and eyes bright and wide open, emerged from a side road, upon the Leas front. He was dressed in his best clothes, and, although the weather was fine, he carried his umbrella, just as if he had been to church. He hesitated, and turned to the right. He

scanned each house narrowly as he passed it, and presently came
to an abrupt stop. 'Hughenden',* said the gateposts in firm
black letters, and the fanlight in gold repeated 'Hughenden'. It
was a stucco house, fit to take your breath away, and its balcony
was painted a beautiful sea green, enlivened with gilding. He
stood looking up at it.

'Gollys!' he said at last in an awe-stricken whisper.

It had rich-looking crimson curtains to all the lower windows,
and brass-railed blinds above. There was a splendid tropical
plant in a large artistic pot in the drawing-room window. There
was a splendid bronzed knocker (ring also) and two bells – one
marked 'servants'.

'Gollys! *Servants*, eh?'

He walked past away from it with his eyes regarding it, and
then turned and came back. He passed through a further
indecision, and finally drifted away to the sea front, and sat
down on a seat a little way along the Leas and put his arm over
the back and regarded 'Hughenden'. He whistled an air very
softly to himself, put his head first on one side and then on the
other. Then for a space he scowled fixedly at it.

A very stout old gentleman with a very red face and very
protuberant eyes sat down beside Kipps, removed a Panama hat
of the most abandoned desperado cut, and mopped his brow
and blew. Then he began mopping the inside of his hat. Kipps
watched him for a space, wondering how much he might have a
year, and where he bought his hat. Then 'Hughenden' reasserted
itself.

An impulse overwhelmed him. 'I say,' he said, leaning forward
to the old gentleman.

The old gentleman started and stared.

'*What* did you say?' he asked fiercely.

'You wouldn't think,' said Kipps, indicating with his fore-
finger, 'that that 'ouse there belongs to me.'

The old gentleman twisted his neck round to look at 'Hughenden'. Then he came back to Kipps, looked at his mean little
garments with apoplectic intensity, and blew at him by way of
reply.

'It does,' said Kipps, a little less confidently.

'Don't be a Fool,' said the old gentleman, and put his hat on
and wiped out the corners of his eyes. 'It's hot enough,' panted
the old gentleman, indignantly, 'without Fools.' Kipps looked

from the old gentleman to the house, and back to the old gentleman. The old gentleman looked at Kipps, and snorted and looked out to sea, and again, snorting very contemptuously, at Kipps.

'Mean to say it doesn't belong to me?' said Kipps.

The old gentleman just glanced over his shoulder at the house in dispute, and then fell to pretending Kipps didn't exist. 'It's been lef' me this very morning,' said Kipps. 'It ain't the only one that's been 'lef me, neither.'

'Aw!' said the old gentleman, like one who is sorely tried. He seemed to expect the passers-by presently to remove Kipps.

'It *as*,' said Kipps. He made no further remark to the old gentleman for a space, but looked with a little less certitude at the house. . . .

'I got—' he said, and stopped.

'It's no good telling you if you don't believe,' he said.

The old gentleman, after a struggle with himself, decided not to have a fit. 'Try that game on with me,' he panted. 'Give you in charge.'

'What game?'

'Wasn't born yesterday,' said the old gentleman, and blew. 'Besides,' he added, '*Look* at you!

'I know you,' said the old gentleman, and coughed shortly, and nodded to the horizon, and coughed again.

Kipps looked dubiously from the house to the old gentleman, and back to the house. Their conversation, he gathered, was over.

Presently he got up and went slowly across the grass to its stucco portal again. He stood, and his mouth shaped the precious word, 'Hughenden'. It was all *right*! He looked over his shoulder as if in appeal to the old gentleman, then turned and went his way. The old gentleman was so evidently past all reason!

He hung for a moment some distance along the parade, as though some invisible string was pulling him back. When he could no longer see the house from the pavement he went out into the road. Then with an effort he snapped the string.

He went on down a quiet side street, unbuttoned his coat furtively, took out three bank-notes in an envelope, looked at them, and replaced them. Then he fished up five new sovereigns from his trouser pocket and examined them. To such a confidence had his exact resemblance to his dead mother's portrait carried Messrs Watson and Bean.

It was right enough.

It really was *all* right.

He replaced the coins with grave precaution, and went his way with a sudden briskness. It was all right – he had it now – he was a rich man at large. He went up a street and round a corner and along another street, and started towards the Pavilion, and changed his mind and came round back, resolved to go straight to the Emporium and tell them all.

He was aware of some one crossing a road far off ahead of him, some one curiously relevant to his present extraordinary state of mind. It was Chitterlow. Of course, it was Chitterlow who had told him first of the whole thing! The playwright was marching buoyantly along a cross street. His nose was in the air, the yachting cap was on the back of his head, and the large freckled hand grasped two novels from the library, a morning newspaper, a new hat done up in paper, and a lady's net bag full of onions and tomatoes. . . .

He passed out of sight behind the wine-merchant's at the corner, as Kipps decided to hurry forward and tell him of the amazing change in the Order of the Universe that had just occurred.

Kipps uttered a feeble shout, arrested as it began and waved his umbrella. Then he set off at a smart pace in pursuit. He came round the corner, and Chitterlow had gone; he hurried to the next, and there was no Chitterlow; he turned back unavailingly, and his eyes sought some other possible corner. His hand fluttered to his mouth, and he stood for a space on the pavement edge, staring about him. No good!

But the sight of Chitterlow was a wholesome thing, it connected events together, joined him on again to the past at a new point, and that was what he so badly needed. . . .

It was all right – all right.

He became suddenly very anxious to tell everybody at the Emporium, absolutely everybody, all about it. That was what wanted doing. He felt that telling was the thing to make this business real. He gripped his umbrella about the middle, and walked very eagerly.

He entered the Emporium through the Manchester department. He flung open the door (over whose ground glass he had so recently, in infinite apprehension, watched the nose of Chitterlow), and discovered the second apprentice and Pearce in conversation. Pearce was prodding his hollow tooth with a pin and talking in fragments about the distinctive characteristics of Good Style.

Kipps came up in front of the counter.

'I say,' he said. 'What d'yer think?'

'What?' said Pearce over the pin.

'Guess.'

'You've slipped out because Teddy's in London.'

'Something more.'

'What?'

'Been left a fortune.'

'Garn!'

'I 'ave.'

'Get out!'

'Straight. I been lef' twelve 'undred pounds – twelve 'undred pounds a year!'

He moved towards the little door out of the department into the house, moving, as heralds say, *regardant passant*. Pearce stood with mouth wide open and pin poised in air. 'No!' he said at last.

'It's right,' said Kipps, 'and I'm going.'

And he fell over the doormat into the house.

IV

It happened that Mr Shalford was in London buying summer sale goods, and, no doubt, also interviewing aspirants to succeed Kipps.

So that there was positively nothing to hinder a wild rush of rumour from end to end of the Emporium. All the masculine members began their report with the same formula. 'Heard about Kipps?'

The new girl in the cash desk had had it from Pearce, and had dashed out into the fancy shop to be the first with the news on the fancy side. Kipps had been left a thousand pounds a year – twelve thousand pounds a year. Kipps had been left twelve hundred thousand pounds. The figures were uncertain, but the essential facts they had correct. Kipps had gone upstairs. Kipps was packing his box. He said he wouldn't stop another day in the old Emporium not for a thousand pounds! It was said that he was singing ribaldry about old Shalford.

He had come down! He was in the counting-house. There was a general movement thither. (Poor old Buggins had a customer, and couldn't make out what the deuce it was all about! Completely out of it, was Buggins.)

There was a sound of running to and fro, and voices saying this, that, and the other thing about Kipps. Ring-a-dinger, ring-a-dinger went the dinner-bell, all unheeded. The whole of the Emporium was suddenly bright-eyed, excited, hungry to tell somebody, to find at any cost somebody who didn't know, and be first to tell them, 'Kipps has been left thirty – forty – fifty thousand pounds!'

'*What*!' cried the senior porter, 'Him!' and ran up to the counting-house as eagerly as though Kipps had broken his neck.

'One of our chaps just been left sixty thousand pounds,' said the first apprentice, returning after a great absence, to his customer.

'Unexpectedly?' said the customer.

'Quite.' said the first apprentice. . . .

'I'm sure if Anyone deserves it, it's Mr Kipps,' said Miss Mergle; and her train rustled as she hurried to the counting-house.

There stood Kipps amidst a pelting shower of congratulations. His face was flushed, and his hair disordered. He still clutched his hat and best umbrella in his left hand. His right hand was any one's to shake rather than his own. ('Ring-a-dinger, ring-a-dinger ding, ding, ding, dang you!' went the neglected dinner-bell.)

'Good old Kipps!' said Pearce, shaking. 'Good old Kipps!'

Booch rubbed one anaemic hand upon the other. 'You're sure it's all right, Mr Kipps?' he said in the background.

'I'm sure we all congratulate him,' said Miss Mergle.

'Great Scott!' said the new young lady in the glove department. 'Twelve hundred a year! Great Scott! You aren't thinking of marrying any one, are you, Mr Kipps?'

'Three pounds five and ninepence a day,' said Mr Booch, working in his head almost miraculously. . . .

Every one, it seemed, was saying how glad they were it was Kipps, except the junior apprentice, upon whom – he being the only son of a widow, and used to having the best of everything as a right – an intolerable envy, a sense of unbearable wrong, had cast its gloomy shade. All the rest were quite honestly and simply glad – gladder, perhaps, at that time than Kipps, because they were not so overpowered. . . .

Kipps went downstairs to dinner, emitting fragmentary disconnected statements. 'Never expected anything of the sort. . . . When this here old Bean told me, you could have knocked me down with a feather. . . . He says, "You been lef' money." Even then I didn't expect it'd be mor'n a hundred pounds, perhaps. Something like that.'

With the sitting down to dinner and the handing of plates, the excitement assumed a more orderly quality. The housekeeper emitted congratulations as she carved, and the maidservant became dangerous to clothes with the plates – she held them anyhow; one expected to see one upside-down, even – she found Kipps so fascinating to look at. Every one was the brisker and hungrier for the news (except the junior apprentice), and the housekeeper carved with unusual liberality. It was High Old Times there under the gaslight, High Old Times. 'I'm sure if Anyone deserves it,' said Miss Mergle – 'pass the salt, please – it's Mr Kipps.'

The babble died away a little as Carshot began barking across the table at Kipps. 'You'll be a bit of a Swell, Kipps,' he said. 'You won't hardly know yourself.'

'Quite the gentleman,' said Miss Mergle.

'Many real gentlemen's families,' said the housekeeper, 'have to do with less.'

'See you on the Leas,' said Carshot. 'My—!' He met the housekeeper's eye. She had spoken about that expression before. 'My eye!' he said, tamely, lest words should mar the day.

'You'll go to London, I reckon,' said Pearce. 'You'll be a man about town. We shall see you mashing 'em, with violets in your button 'ole, down the Burlington Arcade.'

'One of these West End Flats. That'd be *my* style,' said Pearce. 'And a first class club.'

'Aren't these Clubs a bit 'ard to get into?' asked Kipps, open-eyed over a mouthful of potato.

'No fear. Not for Money,' said Pearce. And the girl in the laces, who had acquired a cynical view of Modern Society from the fearless exposures of Miss Marie Corelli,* said, 'Money goes everywhere nowadays, Mr Kipps.'

But Carshot showed the true British strain.

'If I was Kipps,' he said, pausing momentarily for a knifeful of gravy, 'I should go to the Rockies and shoot bears.'

'I'd certainly 'ave a run over to Boulogne,' said Pearce, 'and look about a bit. I'm going to do that next Easter myself, anyhow – see if I don't.'

'Go to Oireland, Mr Kipps,' came the soft insistence of Biddy Murphy, who managed the big work-room, flushed and shining in the Irish way as she spoke. 'Go to Oireland. Ut's the loveliest country in the world. Outside currs. Fishin', shootin', huntin'. An' pretty gals! Eh! You should see the Lakes of Killarney, Mr Kipps!' And she expressed ecstasy by a facial pantomime, and smacked her lips.

And presently they crowned the event.

It was Pearce who said, 'Kipps, you ought to stand Sham!'

And it was Carshot who found the more poetical word 'Champagne'.

'Rather!' said Kipps, hilariously; and the rest was a question of detail and willing emissaries. 'Here it comes!' they said, as the apprentice came down the staircase. 'How about the shop?' said some one. 'Oh, *hang* the shop!' said Carshot; and made gruntulous demands for a corkscrew with a thing to cut the wire. Pearce, the dog! had a wire-cutter in his pocket-knife. How Shalford would have stared at the gold-tipped bottles if he had chanced to take an early train! Bang went the corks, and bang! Gluck, gluck, gluck, and sizzle!

When Kipps found them all standing about him under the gas flare, saying almost solemnly 'Kipps!' with tumblers upheld, 'Have it in tumblers,' Carshot had said, 'have it in tumblers. It isn't a wine like you have in glasses. Not like port and sherry. It cheers you up, but you don't get drunk. It isn't hardly stronger than lemonade. They drink it at dinner, some of 'em, every day!'

'What! At three and six a bottle!' said the housekeeper, incredulously.

'*They* don't stick at *that*,' said Carshot. 'Not the champagne sort.'

The housekeeper pursed her lips and shook her head. . . .

When Kipps, I say, found them all standing up to toast him in that manner, there came such a feeling in his throat and face that for the life of him he scarcely knew for a moment whether he was not going to cry. 'Kipps!' they all said, with kindly eyes. It was very good of them, and hard there wasn't a stroke of luck for them all!

But the sight of upturned chins and glasses pulled him together again. . . .

They did him honour. Unenviously and freely they did him honour.

For example, Carshot, being subsequently engaged in serving cretonne, and desiring to push a number of rejected blocks up the counter in order to have space for measuring, swept them by a powerful and ill-calculated movement of the arm, with a noise like thunder, partly on to the floor, and partly on to the foot of the still gloomily preoccupied junior apprentice. And Buggins, whose place it was to shopwalk while Carshot served, shop-walked with quite unparalleled dignity, dangling a new season's sunshade with a crooked handle on one finger. He arrested each customer who came down the shop with a grave and penetrating look. 'Showing very tractive line new sheasons shunshade,' he would remark; and after a suitable pause, ''Markable thing, one our 'sistant leg'sy twelve 'undred a year. Very tractive. Nothing more to-day, mum? No!' And he would then go and hold the door open for them with perfect decorum, and with the sun-shade dangling elegantly from his left hand. . . .

And the second apprentice, serving a customer with cheap ticking, and being asked suddenly if it was strong, answered remarkably –

'Oo, *no*, mum! Strong! Why, it ain't 'ardly stronger than lemonade.' . . .

The head porter, moreover, was filled with a virtuous resolve to break the record as a lightning packer, and make up for lost time. Mr Swaffenham of the Sandgate Riviera, for example, who was going out to dinner that night at seven, received at half-past six, instead of the urgently needed dress shirt he expected, a corset specially adapted to the needs of persons inclined to embonpoint. A parcel of summer underclothing selected by the elder Miss Waldershawe was somehow distrib-uted in the form of gratis additions throughout a number of parcels of a less intimate nature, and a box of millinery on approval to Lady Pamshort (at Wampachs) was enriched by the addition of the junior porter's cap. . . .

These little things, slight in themselves, witness perhaps none the less eloquently to the unselfish exhilaration felt throughout the Emporium at the extraordinary and unexpected enrichment of Mr Kipps.

V

The bus that plies between New Romney and Folkestone is painted a British red, and inscribed on either side with the word 'Tip-Top' in gold amidst voluptuous scrolls. It is a slow and portly bus; even as a young bus it must have been slow and portly. Below it swings a sort of hold, hung by chains between the wheels, and in the summer time the top has garden seats. The front over those two dauntless unhurrying horses rises in tiers like a theatre; there is first a seat for the driver and his company, and above that a seat, and above that, unless my memory plays me false, a seat. You sit in a sort of composition by some Italian painter – a celestial group of you. There are days when this bus goes, and days when it doesn't go – you have to find out. And so you get to New Romney. So you will continue to get to New Romney for many years, for the light railway concession along the coast is happily in the South Eastern Railway Company's keeping, and the peace of the marsh is kept inviolate save for the bicycle bells of such as Kipps and I. This bus it was, this ruddy, venerable and, under God's mercy, immortal bus, that came down the Folkestone hill with unflinching deliberation, and trundled through Sandgate and Hythe, and out into the windy spaces of the Marsh, with Kipps and all his fortunes on its brow.

You figure him there. He sat on the highest seat diametrically above the driver, and his head was spinning and spinning with champagne and this stupendous Tomfoolery of Luck; and his heart was swelling, swelling indeed at times as though it would burst him, and his face towards the sunlight was transfigured. He said never a word, but ever and again, as he thought of this or that, he laughed. He seemed full of chuckles for a time, detached and independent chuckles, chuckles that rose and burst on him like bubbles in a wine. . . . He held a banjo sceptre-fashion and resting on his knee. He had always wanted a banjo, now he had got one at Melchior's, while he was waiting for the bus.

There sat beside him a young servant, who was sucking peppermint, and a little boy with a sniff whose flitting eyes showed him curious to know why ever and again Kipps laughed, and beside the driver were two young men in gaiters talking about 'tegs'. And there sat Kipps, all unsuspected, twelve hundred a year, as it were, except for the protrusion of the banjo, disguised as a common young man. And the young man in gaiters to the left of the driver eyed Kipps and his banjo, and especially his banjo, ever and again, as if he found it and him, with his rapt face, an insoluble enigma. And many a King has ridden into a conquered city with a lesser sense of splendour than Kipps.

Their shadows grew long behind them, and their faces were transfigured in gold as they rumbled on towards the splendid west. The sun set before they had passed Dymchurch, and as they came lumbering into New Romney past the windmill the dusk had come.

The driver handed down the banjo and the portmanteau, and Kipps having paid him, 'That's aw right,' he said to the change, as a gentleman should, turned about, and ran the portmanteau smartly into Old Kipps, whom the sound of the stopping of the bus had brought to the door of the shop in an aggressive mood and with his mouth full of supper.

''Ullo, Uncle; didn't see you,' said Kipps.

'Blunderin' ninny,' said Old Kipps. 'What's brought *you* here? Ain't early closing, is it? Not Toosday?'

'Got some news for you, Uncle,' said Kipps, dropping the portmanteau.

'Ain't lost your situation, 'ave you? What's that you got there? I'm blowed if it ain't a banjo. Goolord! Spendin' your money on banjoes! Don't put down your portmanty there – anyhow. Right in the way of everybody. I'm blowed if ever I saw such a boy as you've got lately. Here! Molly! And look here! What you got a portmanty for? Why! Goolord! You ain't *really* lost your place, 'ave you?'

'Somethin's happened,' said Kipps, slightly dashed. 'It's all right, Uncle. I'll tell you in a minute.'

Old Kipps took the banjo as his nephew picked up the portmanteau again.

The living-room door opened quickly, showing a table equipped with elaborate simplicity for supper, and Mrs Kipps appeared.

'If it ain't young Artie!' she said. 'Why, whatever's brought *you* 'ome?'

''Ullo, Aunt,' said Artie. 'I'm coming in. I got somethin' to tell you. I've 'ad a bit of luck.'

He wouldn't tell them all at once. He staggered with the portmanteau round the corner of the counter, set a bundle of children's tin pails into clattering oscillation, and entered the little room. He desposited his luggage in the corner beside the tall clock, and turned to his Aunt and Uncle again. His Aunt regarded him doubtfully; the yellow light from the little lamp on the table escaped above the shade, and lit her forehead and the tip of her nose. It would be all right in a minute. He wouldn't tell them all at once. Old Kipps stood in the shop door with the banjo in his hand, breathing noisily. 'The fact is, Aunt, I've 'ad a bit of Luck.'

'You ain't been backin' gordless 'orses, Artie?' she asked.

'No fear.'

'It's a draw he's been in,' said Old Kipps, still panting from the impact of the portmanteau, 'it's a dratted draw. Jest look here, Molly. He's won this 'ere trashy banjer and throwed up his situation on the strength of it – that's what he's done. Goin' about singing. Dash and plunge. Jest the very fault poor Pheamy always 'ad. Blunder right in, and no one mustn't stop 'er!'

'You ain't thrown up your place, Artie, 'ave you?' said Mrs Kipps.

Kipps perceived his opportunity. 'I 'ave,' he said; 'I've throwed it up.'

'What for?' said Old Kipps.

'So's to learn the banjo!'

'Goo *Lord*!' said Old Kipps, in horror to find himself verified.

'I'm going about playing,' said Kipps, with a giggle. 'Goin' to black my face, Aunt, and sing on the beach. I'm going to 'ave a most tremenjous lark and earn any amount of money – you see. Twenty six fousand pounds I'm going to earn just as easy as nothing!'

'Kipps,' said Mrs Kipps, 'he's been drinking!'

They regarded their nephew across the supper table with long faces. Kipps exploded with laughter, and broke out again when his aunt shook her head very sadly at him. Then suddenly he fell grave. He felt he could keep it up no longer. 'It's all right, Aunt. Reely. I ain't mad, and I ain't been drinking. I been lef' money. I been left twenty-six fousand pounds.'

Pause.

'And you thrown up your place?' said Old Kipps.

'Yes,' said Kipps, 'Rather!'

'And bort this banjer, put on your best noo trousers, and come right on 'ere?'

'Well,' said Mrs Kipps, 'I – never – did!'

'These ain't my noo trousers, Aunt,' said Kipps, regretfully. 'My noo trousers wasn't done.'

'I shouldn't ha' thought that *even you* could ha' been such a fool as that,' said Old Kipps.

Pause.

'It's *all* right,' said Kipps, a little disconcerted by their distrustful solemnity. 'It's all right – reely! Twenny-six thousan' pounds. And a 'ouse.'

Old Kipps pursed his lips and shook his head.

'A 'ouse on the Leas. I could have gone there. Only I didn't. I didn't care to. I didn't know what to say. I wanted to come and tell you.'

'How d'yer know the 'ouse—?'

'They told me.'

'Well,' said Old Kipps, and nodded his head portentously towards his nephew, with the corners of his mouth pulled down in a strikingly discouraging way. 'Well, you *are* a young Gaby.'

'I didn't *think* it of you, Artie!' said Mrs Kipps.

'Wadjer mean?' asked Kipps, faintly, looking from one to the other with a withered face.

Old Kipps closed the shop door. 'They been 'avin' a lark with you,' said Old Kipps, in a mournful undertone. 'That's what I mean, my boy. They jest been seein' what a Gaby like you 'ud do.'

'I dessay that young Quodling was in it,' said Mrs Kipps. ''E's jest that sort.'

(For Quodling of the green-baize bag had grown up to be a fearful dog, the terror of New Romney.)

'It's somebody after your place very likely,' said Old Kipps.

Kipps looked from one sceptical reproving face to the other, and round him at the familiar shabby little room, with his familiar cheap portmanteau on the mended chair, and that banjo amidst the supper-things like some irrevocable deed. Could he be rich indeed? Could it be that these things had really happened? Or had some insane fancy whirled him hither?

Still – perhaps a hundred pounds—

'But,' he said. 'It's all right, reely, Uncle. You don't think—? I 'ad a letter.'

'Got up,' said Old Kipps.

'But I answered it and went to a norfis.'

Old Kipps felt staggered for a moment, but he shook his head and chins sagely from side to side. As the memory of old Bean and Shalford's revived, the confidence of Kipps came back to him.

'I saw a nold gent, Uncle – perfect gentleman. And 'e told me all about it. Mos' respectable 'e was. Said 'is name was Watson and Bean – leastways 'e was Bean. Said it was lef' me' – Kipps suddenly dived into his breast pocket – 'by my Grandfather—'

The old people stared.

Old Kipps uttered an exclamation and wheeled round towards the mantel-shelf, above which the daguerreotype of his lost younger sister smiled its fading smile upon the world.

'Waddy, 'is name was,' said Kipps, with his hand still deep in his pocket. 'It was *is* son was my father—'

'Waddy!' said Old Kipps.

'Waddy!' said Mrs Kipps.

'She'd never say,' said Old Kipps.

There was a long silence.

Kipps fumbled with a letter, a crumpled advertisement and three bank-notes. He hesitated between these items.

'Why! That young chap what was arsting questions—' said Old Kipps, and regarded his wife with an eye of amazement.

'Must 'ave been,' said Mrs Kipps.

'Must 'ave been,' said Old Kipps.

'James,' said Mrs Kipps, in an awe-stricken voice. 'After all – perhaps—It's true!'

''*Ow* much did you say?' asked Old Kipps. ''Ow much did you, say e'd lef' you, me b'y?'

It was thrilling, though not quite in the way Kipps had expected. He answered almost meekly across the meagre supper-things, with his documentary evidence in his hand—

'Twelve 'undred pounds. Proximately, he said. Twelve

'undred pounds a year. 'E made 'is will jest before 'e died – not more'n a month ago. When 'e was dying, 'e seemed to change like, Mr Bean said. 'E'd never forgive 'is son, never – not till then. 'Is son 'ad died in Australia, years and years ago, and *then* 'e 'adn't forgiven 'im. You know – 'is son what was my father. But jest when 'e was ill and dying 'e seemed to get worried like, and longing for some one of 'is own. And 'e told Mr Bean it was 'im that had prevented them marrying. So 'e thought. That's 'ow it all come about. . . .'

VI

At last Kipps' flaring candle went up the narrow uncarpeted staircase to the little attic that had been his shelter and refuge during all the days of his childhood and youth. His head was whirling. He had been advised, he had been warned, he had been flattered and congratulated, he had been given whisky and hot water and lemon and sugar, and his health had been drunk in the same. He had also eaten two Welsh rarebits – an unusual supper. His Uncle was chiefly for his going into Parliament, his Aunt was consumed with a great anxiety. 'I'm afraid he'll go and marry beneath 'im.'

'Y'ought to 'ave a bit o' shootin' somewheer,' said Old Kipps.

'It's your *duty* to marry into a country family, Artie – remember that.'

'There's lots of young noblemen'll be glad to 'eng on to you,' said Old Kipps. 'You mark my words. And borry your money. And then good-day to ye.'

'I got to be precious careful,' said Kipps. 'Mr Bean said that.'

'And you got to be precious careful of this old Bean,' said Old Kipps. 'We may be out of the world in Noo Romney, but I've 'eard a bit about solicitors for all that. You keep your eye on old Bean, me b'y.'

''Ow do we know what 'e's up to, with your money, even now?' said Old Kipps, pursuing this uncomfortable topic.

''E *looked* very respectable,' said Kipps.

Kipps undressed with great deliberation and with vast gaps of pensive margin. Twenty-six thousand pounds!

His Aunt's solicitude had brought back certain matters into
the foreground that his 'Twelve 'undred a year!' had for a time
driven away altogether. His thoughts went back to the woodcarving class. Twelve Hundred a Year. He sat on the edge of the
bed in profound meditation, and his boots fell 'whop' and
'whop' upon the floor, with a long interval between each 'whop'.
Twenty-six thousand pounds. 'By Gum!' He dropped the
remainder of his costume about him on the floor, got into bed,
pulled the patchwork quilt over him, and put his head on the
pillow that had been first to hear of Ann Pornick's accession to
his heart. But he did not think of Ann Pornick now.

It was about everything in the world except Ann Pornick that
he seemed to be trying to think of – simultaneously. All the
vivid happenings of the day came and went in his overtaxed
brain – 'that old Bean' explaining and explaining, the fat man
who wouldn't believe, an overpowering smell of peppermint,
the banjo, Miss Mergle saying he deserved it, Chitterlow vanish-
ing round a corner, the wisdom and advice and warnings of his
Aunt and Uncle. She was afraid he would marry beneath him,
was she? She didn't know. . . .

His brain made an excursion into the woodcarving class and
presented Kipps with the picture of himself amazing that class
by a modest yet clearly audible remark, 'I been left twenty-six
thousand pounds.' Then he told them all quietly but firmly that
he had always loved Miss Walshingham – always, and so he
had brought all his twenty-six thousand pounds with him to
give to her there and then. He wanted nothing in return. . . .
Yes, he wanted nothing in return. He would give it to her all in
an envelope and go. Of course he would keep the banjo – and a
little present for his Aunt and Uncle – and a new suit perhaps –
and one or two other things she would not miss. He went off at
a tangent. He might buy a motor-car, he might buy one of these
here things that will play you a piano – that would make old
Buggins sit up! He could pretend he had learnt to play – he
might buy a bicycle and a cyclist suit. . . .

A terrific multitude of plans of what he might do, and in
particular of what he might buy, came crowding into his brain,
and he did not so much fall asleep as pass into a disorder of
dreams in which he was driving a four-horse Tip-Top coach
down Sandgate Hill ('I shall have to be precious careful'),
wearing innumerable suits of clothes, and through some terrible

accident wearing them all wrong. Consequently, he was being laughed at. The coach vanished in the interest of the costume. He was wearing golfing suits and a silk hat. This passed into a nightmare that he was promenading on the Leas in a Highland costume, with a kilt that kept shrinking, and Shalford was following him with three policemen. 'He's my assistant,' Shalford kept repeating; 'he's escaped. He's an escaped Improver. Keep by him, and in a minute you'll have to run him in. I know 'em. We say they wash, but they won't.' . . . He could feel the kilt creeping up his legs. He would have tugged at it to pull it down, only his arms were paralyzed. He had an impression of giddy crises. He uttered a shriek of despair. '*Now!*' said Shalford. He woke in horror, his quilt had slipped off the bed.

He had a fancy he had just been called, that he had somehow overslept himself and missed going down for dusting. Then he perceived it was still night, and light by reason of the moonlight, and that he was no longer in the Emporium. He wondered where he could be. He had a curious fancy that the world had been swept and rolled up like a carpet, and that he was nowhere. It occurred to him that perhaps he was mad. 'Buggins!' he said. There was no answer, not even the defensive snore. No room, no Buggins, nothing!

Then he remembered better. He sat on the edge of his bed for some time. Could any one have seen his face, they would have seen it white, and drawn with staring eyes. Then he groaned weakly. 'Twenty-six thousand pounds!' he whispered.

Just then it presented itself in an almost horribly overwhelming mass.

He remade his bed and returned to it. He was still dreadfully wakeful. It was suddenly clear to him that he need never trouble to get up punctually at seven again. That fact shone out upon him like a star through clouds. He was free to lie in bed as long as he liked, get up when he liked, go where he liked; have eggs every morning for breakfast, or rashers, or bloater-paste, or . . . Also he was going to astonish Miss Walshingham. . . .

Astonish her and astound her. . . .

He was awakened by a thrush singing in the fresh dawn. The whole room was flooded with warm golden sunshine. 'I say!' said the thrush. 'I say! I say! Twelve 'undred a year! Twelve 'Undred a Year! Twelve 'UNDRED a Year! I say! I say! I say!'

He sat up in bed and rubbed the sleep from his eyes with his knuckles. Then he jumped out of bed and began dressing very eagerly. He did not want to lose any time in beginning the new life.

Book Two

Mr Coote the Chaperon

Chapter One

The New Conditions

There comes a gentlemanly figure into these events, and for a space takes a leading part therein, a Good Influence, a refined and amiable figure, Mr Chester Coote. You must figure him as about to enter our story, walking with a curious rectitude of bearing through the evening dusk towards the Public Library, erect, large-headed – he had a great big head, full of the suggestion of a powerful mind well under control – with a large official-looking envelope in his white and knuckly hand. In the other he carries a gold-handled cane. He wears a silken grey jacket suit, buttoned up, and anon he coughs behind the official envelope. He has a prominent nose, slaty grey eyes, and a certain heaviness about the mouth. His mouth hangs breathing open, with a slight protusion of the lower jaw. His straw hat is pulled down a little in front, and he looks each person he passes in the eye, and, directly his look is answered, looks away.

Thus Mr Chester Coote, as he was on the evening when he came upon Kipps. He was a local house-agent, and a most active and gentlemanly person, a conscious gentleman, equally aware of society and the serious side of life. From amateur theatricals of a nice refined sort to science classes, few things were able to get along without him. He supplied a fine full bass, a little flat and quavery perhaps, but very abundant, to the St Stylites' choir. . . .

He goes on towards the Public Library, lifts the envelope in salutation to a passing curate, smiles and enters. . . .

It was in the Public Library that he came upon Kipps.

By that time Kipps had been rich a week or more, and the change in his circumstances was visible upon his person. He was wearing a new suit of drab flannels, a Panama hat, and a red tie for the first time, and he carried a silver-mounted stick with a tortoiseshell handle. He felt extraordinarily different, perhaps more different than he really was, from the meek Improver of a week ago. He felt as he felt Dukes must feel, yet at bottom he was still modest. He was leaning on his stick and regarding the indicator with a respect that never palled. He faced round to meet Mr Coote's overflowing smile.

'What are you doang hea?' asked Mr Chester Coote.

Kipps was momentarily abashed. 'Oh,' he said slowly, and then, 'Mooching round a bit.'

That Coote should address him with this easy familiarity was a fresh reminder of his enhanced social position. 'Jest mooching round,' he said. 'I been back in Folkestone free days now. At my 'ouse, you know.'

'Ah!' said Mr Coote. 'I haven't yet had an opportunity of congratulating you on your good fortune.'

Kipps held out his hand. 'It was the cleanest surprise that ever was,' he said. 'When Mr Bean told me of it – you could have knocked me down with a feather.'

'It must mean a tremendous change for you.'

'O-o. Rather. Change? Why, I'm like the chap in the song they sing, I don't 'ardly know where I are. *You* know.'

'An extraordinary change,' said Mr Coote. 'I can quite believe it. Are you stopping in Folkestone?'

'For a bit. I got a 'ouse, you know. What my gran'father 'ad. I'm stopping there. His housekeeper was kep' on. Fancy – being in the same town and everything!'

'Precisely,' said Mr Coote. 'That's it,' and coughed like a sheep behind four straight fingers.

'Mr Bean got me to come back to see to things. Else I was out in New Romney, where my Uncle and Aunt live. But it's a Lark coming back. In a way. . . .'

The conversation hung for a moment.

'Are you getting a book?' asked Coote.

'Well, I 'aven't got a ticket yet. But I shall get one all right, and have a go in at reading. I've often wanted to. Rather. I was just 'aving a look at this Indicator. First-class idea. Tells you all you want to know.'

'It's simple,' said Coote, and coughed again, keeping his eyes fixed on Kipps. For a moment they hung, evidently disinclined to part. Then Kipps jumped at an idea he had cherished for a day or more – not particularly in relation to Coote, but in relation to any one.

'You doing anything?' he asked.

'Just called with a papah about the classes.'

'Because – Would you care to come up and look at my 'ouse and 'ave a smoke and a chat – eh?' He made indicative back jerks of the head, and was smitten with a horrible doubt whether possibly this invitation might not be some hideous breach of etiquette. Was it, for example, the correct hour? 'I'd be awfully glad if you would,' he added.

Mr Coote begged for a moment while he handed the official-looking envelope to the librarian, and then declared himself at Kipps' service. They muddled a moment over precedence at each door they went through, and so emerged to the street.

'It feels awful rum to me at first, all this,' said Kipps. ''Aving a 'ouse of my own – and all that. It's strange, you know. 'Aving all day. Reely I don't 'ardly know what to do with my time.'

'D'ju smoke?' he said suddenly, proffering a magnificent gold-decorated, pigskin cigarette-case, which he produced from nothing, almost as though it was some sort of trick. Coote hesitated and declined, and then with great liberality, 'Don't let me hinder you. . . .'

They walked a little way in silence, Kipps being chiefly concerned to affect ease in his new clothes and keeping a wary eye on Coote. 'It's rather a big windfall,' said Coote, presently. 'It yields you an income—?'

'Twelve 'undred a year,' said Kipps. 'Bit over—if anything.'

'Do you think of living in Folkestone?'

'Don't know 'ardly yet. I *may*. Then again, I may not. I got a furnished 'ouse, but I may let it.'

'Your plans are undecided?'

'That's jest it,' said Kipps.

'Very beautiful sunset it was to-night,' said Coote, and Kipps said, 'Wasn't it?' and they began to talk of the merits of sunsets. Did Kipps paint? Not since he was a boy. He didn't believe he could now. Coote said his sister was a painter, and Kipps received this intimation with respect. Coote sometimes wished he could find time to paint himself, but one couldn't do everything, and Kipps said that was 'jest it'.

They came out presently upon the end of the Leas, and looked down to where the squat, dark masses of the harbour and harbour station, gemmed with pinpoint lights, crouched against the twilit grey of the sea. 'If one could do *that*,' said Coote; and Kipps was inspired to throw his head back, cock it on one side, regard the harbour with one eye shut and say that it would take some doing. Then Coote said something about 'Abend', which Kipps judged to be in a foreign language, and got over by lighting another cigarette from his by no means completed first one. 'You're right – *puff, puff*.'

He felt that so far he had held up his end of the conversation in a very creditable manner, but that extreme discretion was advisable.

They turned away, and Coote remarked that the sea was good for crossing, and asked Kipps if he had been over the water very much. Kipps said he hadn't been – 'much', but he thought very likely he'd have a run over to Boulogne soon; and Coote proceeded to talk of the charms of foreign travel, mentioning quite a number of unheard-of places by name. He had been to them! Kipps remained on the defensive, but behind his defences his heart sank. It was all very well to pretend, but presently it was bound to come out. *He* didn't know anything of all this. . . .

So they drew near the house. At his own gate Kipps became extremely nervous. It was a fine impressive door. He knocked neither a single knock nor a double, but about one and a half – an apologetic half. They were admitted by an irreproachable housemaid with a steady eye, before which Kipps cringed dreadfully. He hung up his hat and fell about over hall chairs and things. 'There's a fire in the study, Mary?' he had the audacity to ask, though evidently he knew, and led the way upstairs panting. He tried to shut the door, and discovered the housemaid behind him coming to light his lamp. This enfeebled him further. He said nothing until the door closed behind her. Meanwhile, to show his *sang-froid*, he hummed and flitted towards the window and here and there.

Coote went to the big hearthrug and turned and surveyed his host. His hand went to the back of his head and patted his occiput – a gesture frequent with him.

''Ere we are,' said Kipps, hands in his pockets, and glancing round him.

It was a gaunt, Victorian room, with a heavy, dirty cornice, and the ceiling enriched by the radiant plaster ornament of an obliterated gas chandelier. It held two large glass-fronted book-cases, one of which was surmounted by a stuffed terrier encased in glass. There was a mirror over the mantel, and hangings and curtains of magnificent crimson patternings. On the mantel were a huge black clock of classical design, vases in the Burslem Etruscan style, spills and toothpicks in large receptacles of carved rock, large lava ash-trays, and an exceptionally big box of matches. The fender was very great and brassy. In a favourable position under the window was a spacious rosewood writing-desk, and all the chairs and other furniture were of rosewood and well stuffed.

'This,' said Kipps, in something near an undertone, 'was the o' gentleman's study – my grandfather that was. 'E used to sit at that desk and write.'

'Books?'

'No. Letters to the *Times* and things like that. 'E's got 'em all cut out – stuck in a book.... Leastways he *'ad*. It's in that bookcase.... Won't you sit down?'

Coote did, blowing very slightly, and Kipps secured his vacated position on the extensive black-skin rug. He spread out his legs compass fashion, and tried to appear at his ease. The rug, the fender, the mantel and mirror, conspired with great success to make him look a trivial and intrusive little creature amidst their commonplace hauteur, and his own shadow on the opposite wall seemed to think everything a great lark, and mocked and made tremendous fun of him. ...

II

For a space Kipps played a defensive game, and Coote drew the lines of the conversation. They kept away from the theme of Kipps' change of fortune, and Coote made remarks upon local and social affairs. 'You must take an interest in these things now,' was as much as he said in the way of personalities. But it speedily became evident that he was a person of wide and commanding social relationships. He spoke of 'society' being mixed in the neighbourhood, and of the difficulty of getting people to work together and 'do' things; they were cliquish. Incidentally he alluded quite familiarly to men with military titles, and once even to some one with a title, a Lady Punnet. Not snobbishly, you understand, nor deliberately, but quite in passing. He had, it appeared, talked to Lady Punnet about private theatricals! In connection with the Hospitals. She had been unreasonable, and he had put her right – gently, of course, but firmly. 'If you stand up to these people,' said Coote, 'they like you all the better.' It was also very evident he was at his ease with the clergy; 'my friend Mr Densemore – a curate, you know, and rather curious, the Reverend *and* Honourable.' Coote grew visibly in Kipps' eyes as he said these things; he became, not only the exponent of 'Vagner or Vargner', the man whose sister had painted a picture to be exhibited at the Royal Academy, the type of the hidden thing called culture, but a delegate, as it were, or at least an intermediary from that great world 'up there', where there were men-servants, where there were titles, where people dressed for dinner, drank wine at meals, wine costing very often as much as three and sixpence the bottle, and followed through a maze of etiquette, the most stupendous practices. . . .

Coote sat back in the armchair smoking luxuriously and expanding pleasantly with the delightful sense of *savoir faire*; Kipps sat forward, his elbows on his chair arm, alert, and his head a little on one side., You figure him as looking little and cheap, and feeling smaller and cheaper amidst his new surroundings. But it was a most stimulating and interesting conversation. And soon it became less general, and more serious and intimate. Coote spoke of people who had got on, and of people who hadn't; of people who seemed to be in everything, and people who seemed to be out of everything; and then he came round to Kipps.

'You'll have a good time,' he said abruptly, with a smile that would have interested a dentist.

'I dunno,' said Kipps.

'There's mistakes, of course.'

'That's jest it.'

Coote lit a new cigarette. 'One can't help being interested in what you will do,' he remarked. 'Of course – for a young man of spirit, come suddenly into wealth – there's temptations.'

'I got to go careful,' said Kipps. 'O' Bean told me that at the very first.'

Coote went on to speak of pitfalls, of Betting, of Bad Companions. 'I know,' said Kipps, 'I know.' 'There's Doubt again,' said Coote. 'I know a young fellow – a solicitor – handsome, gifted. And yet, you know – utterly sceptical. Practically altogether a Sceptic.'

'Lor!' said Kipps, 'not a Natheist?'

'I fear so,' said Coote. 'Really, you know, an awfully fine

young fellow – Gifted! But full of this dreadful Modern Spirit – Cynical! All this Overman* stuff. Nietzsche and all that. . . . I wish I could do something for him.'

'Ah!' said Kipps, and knocked the ash off his cigarette. 'I know a chap – one of our apprentices he was – once. Always scoffing. . . . He lef'.'

He paused. 'Never wrote for his refs,' he said, in the deep tone proper to a moral tragedy; and then, after a pause, 'Enlisted!'

'Ah!' said Coote.

'And often,' he said, after a pause, 'it's just the most spirited chaps, just the chaps one likes best, who Go Wrong.'

'It's temptation,' Kipps remarked.

He glanced at Coote, leant forward, knocked the ash from his cigarette into the mighty fender. 'That's jest it,' he said, 'you get tempted. Before you know where you are.'

'Modern life,' said Coote, 'is so – complex. It isn't every one is Strong. Half the young fellows who go wrong aren't really bad.'

'That's jest it,' said Kipps.

'One gets a tone from one's surroundings—'

'That's exactly it,' said Kipps.

He meditated. '*I* picked up with a chap,' he said. 'A Nacter. Leastways, he writes plays. Clever feller. But—'

He implied extensive moral obloquy by a movement of his head. 'Of course it's seeing life,' he added.

Coote pretended to understand the full implication of Kipps' remark. 'Is it *worth* it?' he asked.

'That's jest it,' said Kipps.

He decided to give some more. 'One gets talking,' he said. 'Then it's "'ave a drink!" Old Methusaleh three stars – and where *are* you? *I* been drunk,' he said, in a tone of profound humility, and added, 'lots of times.'

'Tt – tt,' said Coote.

'Dozens of times,' said Kipps, smiling sadly; and added, 'Lately.'

His imagination became active and seductive. 'One thing leads to another. Cards, p'raps. Girls—'

'I know,' said Coote. 'I know.'

Kipps regarded the fire, and flushed slightly. He borrowed a sentence that Chitterlow had recently used. 'One can't tell tales out of school,' he said.

'I can imagine it,' said Coote.

Kipps looked with a confidential expression into Coote's face. 'It was bad enough when money was limited,' he remarked. 'But now' – he spoke with raised eyebrows – 'I got to steady down.'

'You *must*,' said Coote, protruding his lips into a sort of whistling concern for a moment.

'I must,' said Kipps, nodding his head slowly, with raised eyebrows. He looked at his cigarette end and threw it into the fender. He was beginning to think he was holding his own in this conversation rather well after all.

Kipps was never a good liar. He was the first to break silence. 'I don't mean to say I been reely bad or reely bad drunk. A 'eadache, perhaps – three or four times, say. But there it is!'

'I have never tasted alcohol in my life,' said Coote, with an immense frankness, 'never!'

'No?'

'Never. I don't feel *I* should be likely to get drunk at all, – it isn't that. And I don't go so far as to say even that in small quantities – at meals – it does one harm. But if I take it, some one else who doesn't know where to stop – you see?'

'That's jest it,' said Kipps, with admiring eyes.

'I smoke,' admitted Coote. 'One doesn't want to be a Pharisee.'

It struck Kipps what a tremendously Good chap this Coote was, not only tremendously clever and educated and a gentleman, and one knowing Lady Punnet, but Good. He seemed to be giving all his time and thought to doing good things to other people. A great desire to confide certain things to him arose. At first Kipps hesitated whether he should confide an equal desire for Benevolent activities or for further Depravity – either was in his mind. He rather affected the pose of the Good Intentioned Dog. Then suddenly his impulses took quite a different turn – fell, indeed, into what was a far more serious rut in his mind. It seemed to him Coote might be able to do for him something he very much wanted done.

'Companionship accounts for so much,' said Coote.

'That's jest it,' said Kipps. 'Of course, you know, in my new position— That's just the difficulty.'

He plunged boldly at his most secret trouble. He knew that

he wanted refinement – culture. It was all very well – but he knew. But how was one to get it? He knew no one, knew no people—He rested on the broken sentence. The shop chaps were all very well, very good chaps and all that, but not what one wanted. 'I feel be'ind,' said Kipps. 'I feel out of it. And consequently I feel it's no good. And then if temptation comes along—'

'Exactly,' said Coote.

Kipps spoke of his respect for Miss Walshingham and her freckled friend. He contrived not to look too self-conscious. 'You know, I'd like to talk to people like that, but I can't. A chap's afraid of giving himself away.'

'Of course,' said Coote, 'of course.'

'I went to a middle-class school, you know. You mustn't fancy I'm one of these here board-school chaps, but you know it reely wasn't a first-class affair. Leastways he didn't take pains with us. If you didn't want to learn you needn't – I don't believe it was *much* better than one of these here national schools. We wore mortar-boards o' course. But what's *that*?

'I'm a regular fish out of water with this money. When I got it – it's a week ago – reely I thought I'd got everything I wanted. But I dunno what to *do*.'

His voice went up into a squeak. 'Practically,' he said, 'it's no good shuttin' my eyes to things – I'm a gentleman.'

Coote indicated a serious assent.

'And there's the responsibilities of a gentleman,' he remarked.

'That's jest it,' said Kipps.

'There's calling on people,' said Kipps. 'If you want to go on knowing Someone you knew before, like. People that's refined.' He laughed nervously. 'I'm a regular fish out of water,' he said, with expectant eyes on Coote.

But Coote only nodded for him to go on.

'This actor chap,' he meditated, 'is a good sort of chap. But 'e isn't what *I* call a gentleman. I got to 'old myself in with 'im. 'E'd make me go it wild in no time. 'E's pretty near the on'y chap I know. Except the shop chaps. They've come round to 'ave supper once already and a bit of a sing-song afterwards. I sang. I got a banjo, you know, and I vamp a bit. Vamping – you know. Haven't got far in the book – 'Ow to Vamp – but still I'm getting on. Jolly, of course, in a way, but what does it *lead* to? . . . Besides that, there's my Aunt and Uncle. *They're* very

good old people – very – jest a bit interfering p'raps and
thinking one isn't grown up, but Right enough. Only—It isn't
what I *want*. I feel I've got be'ind with everything. I want to
make it up again. I want to get with educated people who know
'ow to do things – in the regular proper way.'

His beautiful modesty awakened nothing but benevolence in
the mind of Chester Coote.

'If I had some one like you,' said Kipps, 'that I knew regular
like—'

From that point their course ran swift and easy. 'If I *could* be
of any use to you,' said Coote. . . .

'But you're so busy, and all that.'

'Not *too* busy. You know, your case is a very interesting one.
It was partly that made me speak to you and draw you out.
Here you are with all this money and no experience, a spirited
young chap—'

'That's jest it,' said Kipps.

'I thought I'd see what you were made of, and I must confess
I've rarely talked to any one that I've found quite so interesting
as you have been—'

'I seem able to say things to you, like, somehow,' said Kipps.

'I'm glad. I'm tremendously glad.'

'I want a Friend. That's it – straight.'

"My dear chap, if I—'

'Yes; but—'

'*I* want a Friend too.'

'Reely?'

'Yes. You know, my dear Kipps – if I may call you that.'

'Go on,' said Kipps.

'I'm rather a lonely dog myself. *This* to-night—I've not had
any one I've spoken to so freely of my Work for months.'

'No?'

'Yes. And, my dear chap, if I can do anything to guide or help
you—'

Coote displayed all his teeth in a kindly tremulous smile, and
his eyes were shiny. 'Shake 'ands,' said Kipps, deeply moved;
and he and Coote rose and clasped with mutual emotion.

'It's reely too good of you,' said Kipps.

'Whatever I can do I will,' said Coote.

And so their compact was made. From that moment they
were Friends – intimate, confidential, high-thinking, *sotto-voce*

friends. All the rest of their talk (and it inclined to be interminable) was an expansion of that. For that night Kipps wallowed
in self-abandonment, and Coote behaved as one who had
received a great trust. That sinister passion for pedagogy to
which the Good-Intentioned are so fatally liable, that passion of
infinite presumption that permits one weak human being to
arrogate the direction of another weak human being's affairs,
had Coote in its grip. He was to be a sort of lay confessor and
director of Kipps; he was to help Kipps in a thousand ways; he
was, in fact, to chaperon Kipps into the higher and better sort
of English life. He was to tell him his faults, advise him about
the right thing to do—

'It's all these things I don't know,' said Kipps. 'I don't know,
for instance, what's the right sort of dress to wear – I don't even
know if I'm dressed right now—'

'All these things,' – Coote stuck out his lips and nodded
rapidly to show he understood – 'trust me for that,' he said;
'trust me.'

As the evening wore on Coote's manner changed, became
more and more the manner of a proprietor. He began to take up
his *rôle*, to survey Kipps with a new, with a critical affection. It
was evident the thing fell in with his ideas. 'It will be awfully
interesting,' he said. 'You know, Kipps, you're really good stuff.'
(Every sentence now he said 'Kipps' or 'my dear Kipps' with a
curiously authoritative intonation.)

'I know,' said Kipps, 'only there's such a lot of things I don't
seem to be up to some'ow. That's where the trouble comes in.'

They talked and talked, and now Kipps was talking freely.
They rambled over all sorts of things. Among others Kipps'
character was dealt with at length. Kipps gave valuable lights on
it. 'When I'm reely excited,' he said, 'I don't seem to care *what* I
do. I'm like that.' And again, 'I don't like to do anything
under'and. I *must* speak out. . . .'

He picked a piece of cotton from his knee, the fire grimaced
behind his back, and his shadow on the wall and ceiling was
disrespectfully convulsed.

III

Kipps went to bed at last with an impression of important things settled, and he lay awake for quite a long time. He felt he was lucky. He had known – in fact Buggins and Carshot and Pearce had made it very clear indeed – that his status in life had changed, and that stupendous adaptations had to be achieved; but how they were to be effected had driven that adaptation into the incredible. Here in the simplest, easiest way was the adapter. The thing had become possible. Not, of course, easy, but possible.

There was much to learn, sheer intellectual toil, methods of address, bowing, an enormous complexity of laws. One broken, you are an outcast. How, for example, would one encounter Lady Punnet? It was quite possible some day he might really have to do that. Coote might introduce him. 'Lord!' he said aloud to the darkness between grinning and dismay. He figured himself going into the Emporium, to buy a tie, for example, and there in the face of Buggins, Carshot, Pearce, and the rest of them, meeting 'my friend, Lady Punnet!' It might not end with Lady Punnet! His imagination plunged and bolted with him, galloped, took wings and soared to romantic, to poetical altitudes. . . .

Suppose some day one met Royalty. By accident, say! He soared to that! After all – twelve hundred a year is a lift, a tremendous lift. How did one address Royalty? 'Your Majesty's Goodness' it would be, no doubt – something like that – and on the knees. He became impersonal. Over a thousand a year made him an Esquire, didn't it? He thought that was it. In which case, wouldn't he have to be presented at court? Velvet breeches, like you wear cycling, and a sword! What a curious place a court must be! Kneeling and bowing; and what was it Miss Mergle used to talk about? Of course! – ladies with long trains walking about backward. Everybody walked about backward at court he knew, when not actually on their knees. Perhaps, though, some people regular stood up to the King! Talked to him, just as one might talk to Buggins, say. Cheek, of course! Dukes, it might be, did that – by permission? Millionaires? . . .

From such thoughts this free citizen of our Crowned Republic passed insensibly into dreams – turgid dreams of that vast ascent which constitutes the true-born Briton's social scheme, which terminates with retrogressive progression and a bending back.

IV

The next morning he came down to breakfast looking grave – a man with much before him in the world.

Kipps made a very special thing of his breakfast. Daily once hopeless dreams came true then. It had been customary in the Emporium to supplement Shalford's generous, indeed unlimited supply of bread and butter-substitute by private purchases, and this had given Kipps very broad artistic conceptions of what the meal might be. Now there would be a cutlet or so or a mutton chop – this splendour Buggins had reported from the great London clubs – haddock, kipper, whiting or fish-balls, eggs, boiled or scrambled, or eggs and bacon, kidney also frequently, and sometimes liver. Amidst a garland of such themes, sausages, black and white puddings, bubble-and-squeak, fried cabbage and scallops, came and went. Always as camp followers came potted meat in all varieties, cold bacon, German sausage, brawn, marmalade, and two sorts of jam; and when he had finished these he would sit among his plates and smoke a cigarette, and look at all these dishes crowded round him with beatific approval. It was his principal meal. He was sitting with his cigarette regarding his apartment with the complacency begotten of a generous plan of feeding successfully realized, when newspapers and post arrived.

There were several things by the post, tradesmen's circulars and cards, and two pathetic begging letters – his luck had got into the papers – and there was a letter from a literary man and a book to enforce his request for 10s to put down Socialism. The book made it very clear that prompt action on the part of property owners was becoming urgent, if property was to last out the year. Kipps dipped in it, and was seriously perturbed. And there was a letter from old Kipps, saying it was difficult to leave the shop and come over and see him again just yet, but that he had been to a sale at Lydd the previous day, and bought a few good old books and things it would be difficult to find the equal of in Folkestone. 'They don't know the value of these things out here,' wrote old Kipps, 'but you may depend upon it they are valuable,' and a brief financial statement followed. 'There is an engraving some one might come along and offer you a lot of money for one of these days. Depend upon it, these old things are about the best investment you could make. . . .'

Old Kipps had long been addicted to sales, and his nephew's good fortune had converted what had once been but a looking and a craving – he had rarely even bid for anything in the old days, except the garden tools or the kitchen gallipots or things like that, things one gets for sixpence and finds a use for – into a very active pleasure. Sage and penetrating inspection, a certain mystery of bearing, tactical bids and Purchase – Purchase! – the old man had had a good time.

While Kipps was re-reading the begging letters, and wishing he had the sound, clear common sense of Buggins to help him a little, the Parcels Post brought along the box from his uncle. It was a large, insecure-looking case, held together by a few still loyal nails, and by what the British War Office would have recognized as an Army Corps of string, – rags, and odds and ends tied together. Kipps unpacked it with a table knife, assisted at a critical point by the poker, and found a number of books and other objects of an antique type.

There were three bound volumes of early issues of *Chamber's Journal*, a copy of Punch's *Pocket Book* for 1875, Sturm's *Reflections*, an early version of Gill's Curvature, an early edition of Kirke's *Human Physiology*, *The Scottish Chiefs*, and a little volume on the Language of Flowers. There was a fine steel engraving, oak-framed, and with some rusty spots, done in the Colossal style and representing the Handwriting on the Wall. There was also a copper kettle, a pair of candle-snuffers, a brass shoe-horn, a tea-caddy to lock, two decanters (one stoppered), and what was probably a portion of an eighteenth-century child's rattle. Kipps examined these objects one by one, and wished he knew more about them. Turning over the pages of the *Physiology* again, he came upon a striking plate, in which a youth of agreeable profile displayed his interior in an unstinted manner to the startled eye. It was a new view of humanity altogether, for Kipps, and it arrested his mind. 'Chubes,' he whispered. 'Chubes!'

This anatomized figure made him forget for a space that he was 'practically a gentleman' altogether, and he was still survey-ing its extraordinary complications when another reminder of a world quite outside those spheres of ordered gentility into which his dreams had carried him overnight arrived (following the servant) in the person of Chitterlow.

V

'Ul-*lo*!' said Kipps, rising.

'Not busy?' said Chitterlow, enveloping Kipps' hand for a moment in one of his own, and tossing the yachting cap upon the monumental carved oak sideboard.

'Only a bit of reading,' said Kipps.

'Reading, eh?' Chitterlow cocked the red eye at the books and other properties for a moment, and then, 'I've been expecting you round again one night.'

'I been comming round,' said Kipps; 'on'y there's a chap 'ere—I was coming round last night, on'y I met 'im.'

He walked to the hearthrug. Chitterlow drifted round the room for a time, glancing at things as he talked. 'I've altered that play tremendously since I saw you,' he said. 'Pulled it all to pieces.'

'What play's that, Chit'low?'

'The one we were talking about. You know. You said something – I don't know if you meant it – about buying half of it. Not the tragedy. I wouldn't sell my own twin brother a share in that. That's my investment. That's my Serious Work. No! I mean that new farce I've been on to. Thing with the business about a beetle.'

'Oo yes,' said Kipps. '*I* remember.'

'I thought you would. Said you'd take a fourth share for a hundred pounds. *You* know.'

'I seem to remember something—'

'Well, it's all different. Every bit of it. I'll tell you. You remember what you said about a butterfly. You got confused, you know – Old Meth. Kept calling it quite different. Quite different. Instead of Popplewaddle – thundering good farce-name that, you know, for all that it came from a Visitors' List – instead of Popplewaddle getting a beetle down his neck and rushing about, I've made him a collector – collects butterflies, and this one you know's a rare one. Comes in at window, centre!' Chitterlow began to illustrate with appropriate gestures.

'Pop rushes about after it. Forget he mustn't let on he's in the house. After that—Tells 'em. Rare butterfly, worth lots of money. Some are, you know. Every one's on to it after that. Butterfly can't get out of room; every time it comes out to have a try, rush and scurry. Well, I've worked on that. Only—'

He came very close to Kipps. He held up one hand horizontally and tapped it in a striking and confidential manner with the fingers of the other. 'Something else,' he said. 'That's given me a Real Ibsenish Touch – like the Wild Duck. You know that woman – I've made her lighter – and she sees it. When they're chasing the butterfly the third time, she's on! She looks. "That's me!" she says. Bif! Pestered Butterfly. *She's* the Pestered Butterfly. It's legitimate. Much more legitimate than the Wild Duck – where there isn't a duck!

'Knock 'em! The very title ought to knock 'em. I've been working like a horse at it. . . . You'll have a gold-mine in that quarter share, Kipps – *I* don't mind. It's suited me to sell it, and suited you to buy. Bif!'

Chitterlow interrupted his discourse to ask, 'You haven't any brandy in the house, have you? Not to drink, you know. But I want just an egg-cupful to pull me steady. My liver's a bit queer. . . . It doesn't matter if you haven't. Not a bit. I'm like that. Yes, whisky'll do. Better!'

Kipps hesitated for a moment, then turned and fumbled in the cupboard of his sideboard. Presently he disinterred a bottle of whisky and placed it on the table. Then he put out first one bottle of soda-water, and, after the hesitation of a moment, another. Chitterlow picked up the bottle and read the label. 'Good old Methusaleh,' he said. Kipps handed him the corkscrew, and then his hand fluttered up to his mouth. 'I'll have to ring now,' he said, 'to get glasses.' He hesitated for a moment before doing so, leaning doubtfully, as it were, towards the bell.

When the housemaid appeared, he was standing on the hearthrug with his legs wide apart, with the bearing of a desperate fellow. And after they had both had whiskies, 'You know a decent whisky,' Chitterlow remarked, and took another, 'just to drink.' Kipps produced cigarettes, and the conversation flowed again.

Chitterlow paced the room. He was, he explained, taking a day off; that was why he had come round to see Kipps. Whenever he thought of any extensive change in a play he was writing, he always took a day off. In the end it saved time to do so. It prevented his starting rashly upon work that might have to be re-written. There was no good in doing work when you might have to do it over again, none whatever.

Presently they were descending the steps by the Parade *en route* for the Warren, with Chitterlow doing the talking and going with a dancing drop from step to step. . . .

They had a great walk, not a long one, but a great one. They went up by the Sanatorium, and over the East Cliff and into that queer little wilderness of slippery and tumbling clay and rock under the chalk cliffs – a wilderness of thorn and bramble, wild rose and wayfaring tree, that adds so greatly to Folkestone's charm. They traversed its intricacies and clambered up to the crest of the cliffs at last by a precipitous path that Chitterlow endowed in some mysterious way with suggestions of Alpine adventure. Every now and then he would glance aside at sea and cliffs with a fresh boyishness of imagination that brought back New Romney and the stranded wrecks to Kipps' memory; but mostly he talked of his great obsession of plays and playwriting, and that empty absurdity that is so serious to his kind, his Art. That was a thing that needed a monstrous lot of explaining. Along they went, sometimes abreast, sometimes in single file, up the little paths and down the little paths, and in among the bushes and out along the edge above the beach; and Kipps went along trying ever and again to get an insignificant word in edgeways, and the gestures of Chitterlow flew wide and far, and his great voice rose and fell, and he said this and he said that, and he biffed and banged into the circumambient Inane.

It was assumed that they were embarked upon no more trivial enterprise than the Reform of the British Stage, and Kipps found himself classed with many opulent and even royal and noble amateurs – the Honourable Thomas Norgate came in here – who had interested themselves in the practical realization of high ideals about the Drama. Only he had a finer understanding of these things, and instead of being preyed upon by the common professional – 'and they *are* a lot,' said Chitterlow; 'I haven't toured for nothing' – he would have Chitterlow. Kipps gathered few details. It was clear he had bought the quarter of a farcical comedy – practically a gold-mine – and it would appear it would be a good thing to buy the half. A suggestion, or the suggestion of a suggestion, floated out that he should buy the whole play and produce it forthwith. It seemed he was to produce the play upon a royalty system of a new sort, whatever a royalty system of any sort might be. Then there was some doubt, after all, whether that farcical comedy was in itself sufficient to revolutionize the present lamentable state of the British Drama. Better, perhaps, for such a purpose was that tragedy – as yet unfinished – which was to display all that Chitterlow knew about women, and which was to centre about a Russian nobleman embodying the fundamental Chitterlow personality. Then it became clearer that Kipps was to produce several plays. Kipps was to produce a great number of plays. Kipps was to found a National Theatre. . . .

It is probable that Kipps would have expressed some sort of disavowal, if he had known how to express it. Occasionally his face assumed an expression of whistling meditation, but that was as far as he got towards protest.

In the clutch of Chitterlow and the Incalculable, Kipps came round to the house in Fenchurch Street, and was there made to participate in the midday meal. He came to the house forgetting certain confidences, and was reminded of the existence of a Mrs Chitterlow (with the finest completely untrained contralto voice in England) by her appearance. She had an air of being older than Chitterlow, although probably she wasn't, and her hair was a reddish brown, streaked with gold. She was dressed in one of those complaisant garments that are dressing-gowns, or tea-gowns, or bathing wraps, or rather original evening robes, according to the exigencies of the moment – from the first Kipps was aware that she possessed a warm and rounded neck, and her well-moulded arms came and vanished from the sleeves – and she had large, expressive brown eyes, that he discovered ever and again fixed in an enigmatical manner upon his own.

A simple but sufficient meal had been distributed with careless spontaneity over the little round table in the room with the photographs and looking-glass, and when a plate had, by Chitterlow's direction, been taken from under the marmalade in the cupboard, and the kitchen fork and knife that was not loose in its handle had been found for Kipps, they began and made a tumultuous repast. Chitterlow ate with quiet enormity, but it did not interfere with the flow of his talk. He introduced Kipps to his wife very briefly; she had obviously heard of Kipps before, and he made it vaguely evident that the production of the comedy was the thing chiefly settled. His reach extended over the table, and he troubled nobody. When Mrs Chitterlow, who for a little while seemed socially self-conscious, reproved him for taking a potato with a jab of his fork, he answered, 'Well, you shouldn't have married a man of Genius,' and from a subsequent remark it was perfectly clear that Chitterlow's standing in this respect was made no secret of in his household.

They drank old Methusaleh and syphon soda, and there was no clearing away; they just sat among the plates and things, and Mrs Chitterlow took her husband's tobacco-pouch and made a cigarette and smoked, and blew smoke, and looked at Kipps with her large brown eyes. Kipps had seen cigarettes smoked by ladies before, 'for fun', but this was real smoking. It frightened him rather. He felt he must not encourage this lady – at any rate, in Chitterlow's presence.

They became very cheerful after the repast, and as there was now no waste to deplore, such as one experiences in the windy open air, Chitterlow gave his voice full vent. He fell to praising Kipps very highly and loudly. He said he had known Kipps was the right sort, he had seen it from the first, almost before he got up out of the mud on that memorable night. 'You can,' he said, 'sometimes. That was why—' He stopped, but he seemed on the verge of explaining that it was his certainty of Kipps being the right sort had led him to confer this great Fortune upon him. He left that impression. He threw out a number of long sentences and material for sentences of a highly philosophical and incoherent character about Coincidences. It became evident he considered dramatic criticism in a perilously low condition. . . .

About four Kipps found himself stranded, as it were, by a receding Chitterlow on a seat upon the Leas.

He was chiefly aware that Chitterlow was an overwhelming personality. He puffed his cheeks and blew.

No doubt this was seeing life, but had he particularly wanted to see life that day? In a way Chitterlow had interrupted him. The day he had designed for himself was altogether different from this. He had been going to read through a precious little volume called *Don't* that Coote had sent round for him – a book of invaluable hints, a summary of British deportment, that had only the one defect of being at points a little out of date.

That reminded him he had intended to perform a difficult exercise called an Afternoon Call upon the Cootes, as a preliminary to doing it in deadly earnest upon the Walshinghams. It was no good to-day, anyhow, now.

He came back to Chitterlow. He would have to explain to Chitterlow he was taking too much for granted – he would have to do that. It was so difficult to do in Chitterlow's presence, though; in his absence it was easy enough. This half-share, and taking a theatre and all of it, was going too far.

The quarter share was right enough, he supposed, but even that – ! A hundred pounds! What wealth is there left in the world after one has paid out a hundred pounds from it?

He had to recall that, in a sense, Chitterlow had indeed brought him his fortune before he could face even that.

You must not think too hardly of him. To Kipps, you see, there was as yet no such thing as proportion in these matters. A hundred pounds went to his horizon. A hundred pounds seemed to him just exactly as big as any other large sum of money.

Chapter Two

The Walshinghams

I

The Cootes lived in a little house in Bouverie Square, with a tangle of Virginia creeper up the verandah.

Kipps had been troubled in his mind about knocking double or single – it is these things show what a man is made of – but happily there was a bell.

A queer little maid with a big cap admitted Kipps, and took him through a bead curtain and a door into a little drawing-room, with a black and gold piano, a glazed bookcase, a Moorish cosy corner, and a draped looking-glass over-mantel, bright with Regent Street ornaments and photographs of various intellectual lights. A number of cards of invitation to meetings and the match list of a Band of Hope cricket club were stuck into the looking-glass frame, with Coote's name as a Vice-President. There was a bust of Beethoven over the bookcase, and the walls were thick with conscientiously executed but carelessly selected 'views' in oil and water colours and gilt frames. At the end of the room, facing the light, was a portrait that struck Kipps at first as being Coote in spectacles and feminine costume, and that he afterwards decided must be Coote's mother. Then the original appeared, and he discovered that it was Coote's elder and only sister, who kept house for him. She wore her hair in a knob behind, and the sight of the knob suggested to Kipps an explanation for a frequent gesture of Coote's, a patting exploratory movement to the back of his head. And then it occurred to him that this was quite an absurd idea altogether.

She said, 'Mr Kipps, I believe,' and Kipps laughed pleasantly, and said, 'That's it!' and then she told him that 'Chester' had gone down to the art school to see about sending off some drawing or other, and that he would be back soon. Then she asked Kipps if he painted, and showed him the pictures on the wall. Kipps asked her where each one was 'of', and when she

showed him some of the Leas slopes, he said he never would
have recognized them. He said it was funny how things looked
in a picture very often. 'But they're awfully *good*,' he said. 'Did
you do them?' He would look at them with his neck arched like
a swan's, his head back and on one side, and then suddenly peer
closely into them. 'They *are* good. I wish I could paint.' 'That's
what Chester says,' she answered. 'I tell him he has better things
to do.' Kipps seemed to get on very well with her.

Then Coote came in, and they left her and went upstairs
together, and had a good talk about reading and the Rules of
Life. Or rather Coote talked, and the praises of thought and
reading were in his mouth. . . .

You must figure Coote's study, a little bedroom put to
studious uses, and over the mantel an array of things he had
been led to believe indicative of culture and refinement – an
autotype of Rossetti's 'Annunciation', an autotype of Watts'
'Minotaur', a Swiss carved pipe with many joints and a photograph of Amiens Cathedral (these two the spoils of travel), a
phrenological bust, and some broken fossils from the Warren. A
rotating bookshelf carried the *Encyclopaedia Britannica* (tenth
edition), and on the top of it a large official-looking, age-grubby
envelope, bearing the mystic words, 'On His Majesty's Service',
a number or so of the *Bookman*, and a box of cigarettes were
lying. A table under the window bore a little microscope, some
dust in a saucer, some grimy glass slips, and broken cover
glasses, for Coote had 'gone in for' biology a little. The longer
side of the room was given over to bookshelves, neatly edged
with pinked American cloth, and with an array of books – no
worse an array of books than you find in any public library; an
almost haphazard accumulation of obsolete classics, contemporary successes, the Hundred Best Books (including Samuel Warren's *Ten Thousand a Year*), old school-books, directories, the
Times Atlas, Ruskin in bulk, Tennyson complete in one volume,
Longfellow, Charles Kingsley, Smiles,* a guide-book or so,
several medical pamphlets, odd magazine numbers, and much
indescribable rubbish – in fact, a compendium of the contemporary British mind. And in front of this array stood Kipps, ill-
taught and untrained, respectful, awe-stricken, and, for the
moment at any rate, willing to learn, while Coote, the exemplary
Coote, talked to him of reading and the virtue in books.

'Nothing enlarges the mind,' said Coote, 'like Travel and Books. . . . And they're both so easy nowadays, and so cheap!'

'I've often wanted to 'ave a good go in at reading,' Kipps replied.

'You'd hardly believe,' Coote said, 'how much you can get out of books. Provided you avoid trashy reading, that is. You ought to make a rule, Kipps, and read one Serious Book a week. Of course we can Learn even from Novels, Nace Novels that is, but it isn't the same thing as serious reading. I made a rule, One Serious Book and One Novel – no more. There's some of the Serious Books I've been reading lately – on that table: *Sartor Resartus*,* Mrs Twaddletome's *Pond Life*, *The Scottish Chiefs*, *Life and Letters of Dean Farrar**. . . .'

II

There came at last the sound of a gong, and Kipps descended to tea in that state of nervous apprehension at the difficulties of eating and drinking that his Aunt's knuckle rappings had implanted in him for ever. Over Coote's shoulder he became aware of a fourth person in the Moorish cosy corner, and he turned, leaving incomplete something incoherent he was saying to Miss Coote about his modest respect and desire for literature, to discover this fourth person was Miss Helen Walshingham, hatless, and looking very much at home.

She rose at once with an extended hand to meet his hesitation. 'You're stopping in Folkestone, Mr Kipps?'

''Ere on a bit of business,' said Kipps. 'I thought you was away in Bruges.'

'That's later,' said Miss Walshingham. 'We're stopping until my brother's holiday begins, and we're trying to let our house. Where are you staying in Folkestone?'

'I got a 'ouse of mine – on the Leas.'

'I've heard all about your good fortune – this afternoon.'

'Isn't it a Go!' said Kipps. 'I 'aven't nearly got to believe it's reely 'appened yet. When that – Mr Bean told me of it, you could 'ave knocked me down with a feather. . . . It's a tremenjous change for me.'

He discovered Miss Coote was asking him whether he took milk and sugar. '*I* don't mind,' said Kipps. 'Jest as you like.'

Coote became active, handing tea and bread-and-butter. It was thinly cut, and the bread was rather new, and the half of the slice that Kipps took fell upon the floor. He had been holding it by the edge, for he was not used to this migratory method of taking tea without plates or table. This little incident ruled him out of the conversation for a time, and when he came to attend to it again, they were talking about something or other prodigious – a performer of some sort – that was coming, called, it seemed, 'Padrooski!' So Kipps, who had dropped quietly into a chair, ate his bread-and-butter, said 'no, thank you' to any more, and by this discreet restraint got more freedom with his cup and saucer.

Apart from the confusion natural to tea, he was in a state of tremulous excitement on account of the presence of Miss Walshingham. He glanced from Miss Coote to her brother, and then at Helen. He regarded her over the top of his cup as he drank. Here she was, solid and real. It was wonderful. He remarked, as he had done at times before, the easy flow of the dark hair back from her brow over her ears, the shapeliness of the white hands that came out from her simple white cuffs, the delicate pencilling of her brow.

Presently she turned her face to him almost suddenly, and smiled with the easiest assurance of friendship.

'You will go, I suppose?' she said, and added, 'to the Recital.'

'If I'm in Folkestone I shall,' said Kipps, clearing away a little hoarseness. 'I don't *know* much about music, but what I do know I like.'

'I'm sure you'll like Paderewski,' she said.

'If you do,' he said, 'I dessay I shall.'

He found Coote very kindly taking his cup.

'Do you think of living in Folkestone?' asked Miss Coote, in a tone of proprietorship from the hearthrug.

'No,' said Kipps, 'that's jest it – I hardly know.' He also said that he wanted to look round a bit before doing anything. 'There's so much to consider,' said Coote, smoothing the back of his head.

'I may go back to New Romney for a bit,' said Kipps. 'I got an Uncle and Aunt there. I reely don't know.'

Helen regarded him thoughtfully for a moment.

'You must come and see us,' she said, 'before we go to Bruges.'

'Oo, rather!' said Kipps. 'If I may.'

'Yes, do,' she said, and suddenly stood up before Kipps could formulate an inquiry when he should call.

'You're sure you can spare that drawing-board?' she said to Miss Coote; and the conversation passed out of range.

And when he had said 'Good-bye' to Miss Walshingham, and she had repeated her invitation to call, he went upstairs again with Coote to look out certain initiatory books they had had under discussion. And then Kipps, blowing very resolutely, went back to his own place, bearing in his arm (1) *Sesame and Lilies*,* (2) *Sir George Tressady*, (3) an anonymous book on 'Vitality' that Coote particularly esteemed. And having got to his own sitting-room, he opened *Sesame and Lilies* and read with ruthless determination for some time.

III

Presently he leant back and gave himself up to the business of trying to imagine just exactly what Miss Walshingham could have thought of him when she saw him. Doubts about the precise effect of the grey flannel suit began to trouble him. He turned to the mirror over the mantel, and then got into a chair to study the hang of the trousers. It looked all right. Luckily she had not seen the Panama hat. He knew he had the brim turned up wrong, but he could not find out which way the brim was right. However, that she had not seen. He might, perhaps, ask at the shop where he bought it.

He meditated for a while on his reflected face – doubtful whether he liked it or not – and then got down again and flitted across to the sideboard where there lay two little books, one in a cheap magnificent cover of red and gold, and the other in green canvas. The former was called, as its cover witnessed, *Manners and Rules of Good Society, by a Member of the Aristocracy*, and after the cover had indulged in a band of gilded decoration, light-hearted, but natural under the circumstances, it added, 'TWENTY-FIRST EDITION'. The second was that admirable classic, *The Art of Conversing*. Kipps returned with these to his seat, placed the two before him, opened the latter with a sigh, and flattened it under his hand.

Then with knitted brows he began to read onward from a mark, his lips moving.

'Having thus acquired possession of an idea, the little ship should not be abruptly launched into deep waters, but should be first permitted to glide gently and smoothly into the shallows; that is to say, the conversation should not be commenced by broadly and roundly stating a fact, or didactically expressing an opinion, as the subject would be thus virtually or summarily disposed of, or perhaps be met with a "Really" or "Indeed", or some equally brief monosyllabic reply. If an opposite opinion were held by the person to whom the remark were addressed, he might not, if a stranger, care to express it in the form of a direct contradiction or actual dissent. To glide imperceptibly into conversation is the object to be attained—'

At this point Mr Kipps rubbed his fingers through his hair with an expression of some perplexity, and went back to the beginning.

IV

When Kipps made his call on the Walshinghams, it all happened so differently from the *Manners and Rules* prescription ('Paying Calls') that he was quite lost from the very outset. Instead of the footman or maidservant proper in these cases, Miss Walshingham opened the door to him herself. 'I'm so glad you've come,' she said, with one of her rare smiles.

She stood aside for him to enter the rather narrow passage.

'I thought I'd call,' he said, retaining his hat and stick.

She closed the door and led the way to a little drawing-room, which impressed Kipps as being smaller and less emphatically coloured than that of the Cootes, and in which, at first, only a copper bowl of white poppies upon the brown tablecloth caught his particular attention.

'You won't think it unconventional to come in, Mr Kipps, will you?' she remarked. 'Mother is out.'

'I don't mind,' he said, smiling amiably, 'if you don't.'

She walked round the table and stood regarding him across it, with that same look between speculative curiosity and appreciation that he remembered from the last of the art-class meetings.

'I wondered whether you would call or whether you wouldn't before you left Folkestone.'

'I'm not leaving Folkestone for a bit, and any'ow I should have called on you.'

'Mother will be sorry she was out. I've told her about you, and she wants, I know, to meet you.'

'I saw 'er – if that was 'er – in the shop,' said Kipps.

'Yes – you did, didn't you?. . . . She has gone out to make some duty calls, and I didn't go. I had something to write. I write a little, you know.'

'Reely!' said Kipps.

'It's nothing much,' she said, 'and it comes to nothing.' She glanced at a little desk near the window, on which there lay some paper. 'One must do something.' She broke off abruptly. 'Have you seen our outlook?' she asked, and walked to the window, and Kipps came and stood beside her. 'We look on the Square. It might be worse, you know. That out-porter's truck there is horrid – and the railings, but it's better than staring one's social replica in the face, isn't it? It's pleasant in early spring – bright green laid on with a dry brush – and it's pleasant in autumn.'

'I like it,' said Kipps. 'That laylock there is pretty, isn't it?'

'Children come and pick it at times,' she remarked.

'I dessay they do,' said Kipps.

He rested on his hat and stick and looked appreciatively out of the window, and she glanced at him for one swift moment. A suggestion that might have come from the *Art of Conversing* came into his head. 'Have you a garden?' he said.

She shrugged her shoulders. 'Only a little one,' she said, and then, 'Perhaps you would like to see it.'

'I like gardening,' said Kipps, with memories of a pennyworth of nasturtiums he had once trained over his uncle's dustbin.

She led the way with a certain relief.

They emerged through a four-seasons' coloured glass door to a little iron verandah, that led by iron steps to a minute walled garden. There was just room for a patch of turf and a flower-bed; one sturdy variegated Euonymus grew in the corner. But the early June flowers, the big narcissus, snow upon the mountains, and a fine show of yellow wallflowers, shone gay.

'That's our garden,' said Helen. 'It's not a very big one, is it?'

'I like it,' said Kipps.

'It's small,' she said, 'but this is the day of small things.'

Kipps didn't follow that.

'If you were writing when I came,' he remarked, 'I'm interrupting you.'

She turned round with her back to the railing and rested leaning on her hands. 'I had finished,' she said. 'I couldn't get on.'

'Were you making up something?' asked Kipps.

There was a little interval before she smiled. 'I try – quite vainly – to write stories,' she said. 'One must do something. I don't know whether I shall ever do any good – at that – anyhow. It seems so hopeless. And, of course – one must study the popular taste. But now my brother has gone to London – I get a lot of leisure.'

'I seen your brother, 'aven't I?'

'He came to the class once or twice. Very probably you have. He's gone to London to pass his examinations and become a solicitor. And then I suppose he'll have a chance. Not much, perhaps, even then. But he's luckier than I am.'

'You got your classes and things.'

'They ought to satisfy me. But they don't. I suppose I'm ambitious. We both are. And we hadn't much of a spring board.' She glanced over her shoulder at the cramped little garden with an air of reference in her gesture.

'I should think you could do anything if you wanted to?' said Kipps.

'As a matter of fact, I can't do anything I want to.'

'You done a good deal.'

'What?'

'Well, didn't you pass one these here University things?'

'Oh, I matriculated!'

'I should think I was no end of a swell if *I* did – I know that.'

'Mr Kipps, do you know how many people matriculate into London University every year?'

'How many, then?'

'Between two and three thousand.'

'Well, just think how many don't!'

Her smile came again and broke into a laugh. 'Oh, *they* don't count,' she said; and then realizing that might penetrate Kipps if he was left with it, she hurried on to, 'The fact is, I'm a discontented person, Mr Kipps. Folkestone, you know, is a Sea

Front, and it values people by sheer vulgar prosperity. We're not prosperous, and we live in a back street. We have to live here because this is our house. It's a mercy we haven't to "let". One feels one hasn't opportunities. If one had, I suppose one wouldn't use them. Still—'

Kipps felt he was being taken tremendously into her confidence. 'That's jest it,' he said.

He leant forward on his stick and said very earnestly, 'I believe you could do anything you wanted to, if you tried.'

She threw out her hands in disavowal.

'I *know*,' said he, very sagely, and nodding his head. 'I watched you once or twice when you were teaching that woodcarving class.'

For some reason this made her laugh – a rather pleasant laugh, and that made Kipps feel a very witty and successful person. 'It's very evident,' she said, 'that you're one of those rare people who believe in me, Mr Kipps,' to which he answered, 'Oo, I *do*!' and then suddenly they became aware of Mrs Walshingham coming along the passage. In another moment she appeared through the four-seasons' door, bonneted and ladylike and a little faded, exactly as Kipps had seen her in the shop. Kipps felt a certain apprehension at her appearance, in spite of the reassurances he had had from Coote.

'Mr Kipps has called on us,' said Helen; and Mrs Walshingham said it was very, very kind of him, and added that new people didn't call on them very much nowadays. There was nothing of the scandalized surprise Kipps had seen in the shop; she had heard, perhaps, he was a gentleman now. In the shop he had thought her rather jaded and haughty, but he had scarcely taken her hand, which responded to his touch with a friendly pressure, before he knew how mistaken he had been. She then told her daughter that some one called Mrs Wace had been out, and turned to Kipps again to ask him if he had had tea. Kipps said he had not, and Helen moved towards some mysterious interior. 'But *I* say,' said Kipps, 'don't you on my account—'

Helen vanished, and he found himself alone with Mrs Walshingham. Which, of course, made him breathless and Boreas-looking for a moment.

'You were one of Helen's pupils in the woodcarving class?' asked Mrs Walshingham, regarding him with the quiet watchfulness proper to her position.

'Yes,' said Kipps; 'that 'ow I 'ad the pleasure—'

'She took a great interest in her woodcarving class. She is so energetic, you know, and it gives her an Outlet.'

'I thought she taught something splendid.'

'Every one says she did very well. Helen, I think, would do anything well that she undertook to do. She's so very clever. And she throws herself into things so.'

She untied her bonnet-strings with a pleasant informality.

'She has told me all about her class. She used to be full of it. And about your cut hand.'

'Lor!' said Kipps; 'fancy telling that!'

'Oh yes. And how brave you were!'

(Though, indeed, Helen's chief detail had been his remarkable expedient for checking bloodshed.)

Kipps became bright pink. 'She said you didn't seem to feel it a bit.'

Kipps felt he would have to spend weeks over *The Art of Conversing*.

While he still hung fire, Helen returned with the apparatus for afternoon tea upon a tray.

'Do you mind pulling out the table?' asked Mrs Walshingham.

That again was very homelike. Kipps put down his hat and stick in the corner, and amidst an iron thunder pulled out a little rusty, green-painted, iron table, and then in the easiest manner followed Helen in to get chairs.

So soon as he had got rid of his teacup – he refused all food, of course, and they were merciful – he became wonderfully at his ease. Presently he was talking. He talked quite modestly and simply about his changed condition, and his difficulties and plans. He spread what indeed had an air of being all his simple little soul before their eyes. In a little while his clipped defective accent had become less perceptible to their ears, and they began to realize, as the girl with the freckles had long since realized, that there were passable aspects of Kipps. He confided, he submitted, and for both of them he had the realest, the most seductively flattering undertone of awe and reverence.

He remained about two hours, having forgotten how terribly incorrect it is to stay at such a length. They did not mind at all.

Chapter Three

Engaged

Within two months, within a matter of three-and-fifty days, Kipps had clambered to the battlements of Heart's Desire.

It all became possible by the Walshinghams – it would seem at Coote's instigation – deciding, after all, not to spend the holidays at Bruges. Instead they remained in Folkestone, and this happy chance gave Kipps just all those opportunities of which he stood in need.

His crowning day was at Lympne, and long before the summer warmth began to break, while, indeed, August still flamed on high. They had organized – no one seemed to know who suggested it first – a water party on the still reaches of the old military canal at Hythe, and they were to picnic by the brick bridge, and afterwards to clamber to Lympne Castle. The host of the gathering, it was understood very clearly, was Kipps.

They went a merry party. The canal was weedy, with only a few inches of water at the shallows, and so they went in three canoes. Kipps had learnt to paddle – it had been his first athletic accomplishment; and his second – with the last three or four of ten private lessons still to come – was to be cycling. But Kipps did not paddle at all badly; muscles hardened by lifting pieces of cretonne could cut a respectable figure by the side of Coote's exertions, and the girl with the freckles, the girl who understood him, came in his canoe. They raced the Walshinghams, brother and sister; and Coote, in a liquefying state and blowing mightily, but still persistent, and always quite polite and considerate, toiled behind with Mrs Walshingham. She could not be expected to paddle (though, of course, she 'offered'), and she reclined upon specially adjusted cushions under a black-and-white sunshade, and watched Kipps and her daughter, and feared at intervals that Coote was getting hot.

They were all more or less in holiday costume; the eyes of the girls looked out under the shade of wide-brimmed hats; even the freckled girl was unexpectedly pretty, and Helen, swinging sunlit to her paddle, gave Kipps, almost for the first time, the suggestion of a graceful body. Kipps was arrayed in the completest boating costume, and when his fashionable Panama was discarded and his hair blown into disorder, he became, in his white flannels, as sightly as most young men. His complexion was a notable asset.

Things favoured him, every one favoured him. Young Walshingham, the girl with the freckles, Coote, and Mrs Walshingham, were playing up to him in the most benevolent way, and between the landing-place and Lympne, Fortune, to crown their efforts, had placed a small convenient field entirely at the disposal of an adolescent bull. Not a big, real, resolute bull, but, on the other hand, no calf; a young bull, at the same stage of emotional development as Kipps, 'where the brook and river meet'. Detachedly our party drifted towards him.

When they landed, young Walshingham, with the simple directness of a brother, abandoned his sister to Kipps and secured the freckled girl, leaving Coote to carry Mrs Walshingham's light wool wrap. He started at once in order to put an effectual distance between himself and his companion on the one hand, and a certain pervasive chaperonage that went with Coote, on the other. Young Walshingham, I think I have said, was dark, with a Napoleonic profile, and it was natural for him therefore to be a bold thinker and an epigrammatic speaker, and he had long ago discovered great possibilities of appreciation in the freckled girl. He was in a very happy frame that day because he had just been intrusted with the management of Kipps' affairs (old Bean inexplicably dismissed), and that was not a bad beginning for a solicitor of only a few months' standing; and, moreover, he had been reading Nietzsche, and he thought that in all probability he was the Non-Moral Overman referred to by that writer. He wore fairly large-sized hats. He wanted to expand the theme of the Non-Moral Overman in the ear of the freckled girl, to say it over, so to speak, and in order to seclude his exposition they went aside from the direct path and trespassed through a coppice, avoiding the youthful bull. They escaped to these higher themes but narrowly, for Coote and Mrs Walshingham, subtle chaperones both, and each indisposed, for excellent reasons, to encumber Kipps and Helen, were hot upon their heels. These two kept the direct route to the stile of the bull's field, and the sight of the animal at once awakened Coote's innate aversion to brutality in any shape or form. He said the stiles were too high, and that they could do better by going round by the hedge, and Mrs Walshingham, nothing loth, agreed.

This left the way clear for Kipps and Helen, and they encountered the bull. Helen did not observe the bull; Kipps did; but that afternoon, at any rate, he was equal to facing a lion. And the bull really came at them. It was not an affair of the bull-ring exactly, no desperate rushes and gorings, but he came; he regarded them with a large, wicked, bluish eye, opened a mouth below his moistly glistening nose, and booed, at any rate, if he did not exactly bellow, and he shook his head wickedly, and showed that tossing was in his mind. Helen was frightened, without any loss of dignity, and Kipps went extremely white. But he was perfectly calm, and he seemed to her to have lost his last vestiges of his accent and his social shakiness. He directed her to walk quietly towards the stile and made an oblique advance towards the bull.

'You be orf!' he said. . . .

When Helen was well over the stile, Kipps withdrew in good order. He got over the stile under cover of a feint, and the thing was done – a small thing, no doubt, but just enough to remove from Helen's mind an incorrect deduction, that a man who was so terribly afraid of a teacup as Kipps must necessarily be abjectly afraid of everything else in the world. In her moment of reaction she went, perhaps, too far in the opposite direction. Hitherto Kipps had always had a certain flimsiness of effect for her. Now suddenly he was discovered solid. He was discovered possible in many new ways. Here, after all, was the sort of back a woman can get behind. . . .

As they went past the turf-crowned mass of Portus Lemanus, up the steep slopes towards the castle on the crest, the thing was almost manifest in her eyes.

II

Every one who stays in Folkestone goes sooner or later to Lympne. The castle became a farmhouse, and the farmhouse, itself now ripe and venerable, wears the walls of the castle as a little man wears a big man's coat. The kindliest of farm ladies entertains a perpetual stream of visitors, and shows you her vast mangle and her big kitchen, and takes you out upon the sunniest little terrace-garden in all the world, and you look down the sheep-dotted slopes, to where, beside the canal and under the trees, the crumbled memories of Rome sleep for ever. One climbs the Keep, up a tortuous spiral of stone, worn now to the pitch of perforation, and there one is lifted to the centre of far more than a hemisphere of view. Away below one's feet, almost at the bottom of the hill, the Marsh begins and spreads and spreads in a mighty crescent that sweeps about the sea, the Marsh dotted with the church towers of forgotten mediaeval towns, and breaking at last into the low blue hills by Winchelsea and Hastings; east hangs France between the sea and sky; and round the north, bounding the wide perspectives of farms and houses and woods, the Downs, with their hangers and chalk-pits, sustain the passing shadows of the sailing clouds.

And here it was, high out of the world of every day, and in the presence of spacious beauty, that Kipps and Helen found themselves agreeably alone. All six, it had seemed, had been coming for the Keep; but Mrs Walshingham had hesitated at the horrid little stairs, and then suddenly felt faint, and so she and the freckled girl had remained below, walking up and down in the shadow of the house; and Coote had remembered they were all out of cigarettes, and had taken off young Walshingham into the village. There had been shouting to explain between ground and parapet, and then Helen and Kipps turned again to the view and commended it, and fell silent.

Helen sat fearlessly in an embrasure, and Kipps stood beside her.

'I've always been fond of scenery,' Kipps repeated, after an interval.

Then he went off at a tangent. 'D'you reely think that was right what Coote was saying?'

She looked interrogation.

'About my name.'

'Being really C-U-Y-P-S? I have my doubts. I thought at first— What makes Mr Coote add an 'S' to Cuyp?'

'*I* dunno,' said Kipps, foiled. 'I was jest thinking'. . . .

She shot one wary glance at him, and then turned her eyes to the sea.

Kipps was out for a space. He had intended to lead from this question to the general question of surnames and change of names; it had seemed a light and witty way of saying something he had in mind, and suddenly he perceived that this was an unutterably vulgar and silly project. The hitch about that 'S' had saved him. He regarded her profile for a moment, framed in weather-beaten stone, and backed by the blue elements.

He dropped the question of his name out of existence, and spoke again of the view. 'When I see scenery – and things that – that are beautiful, it makes me feel—'

She looked at him suddenly, and saw him fumbling for his words.

'Silly like,' he said.

She took him in with her glance, the old look of proprietorship it was, touched with a certain warmth. She spoke in a voice as unambiguous as her eyes. 'You needn't,' she said. 'You know, Mr Kipps, you hold yourself too cheap.'

Her eyes and words smote him with amazement. He stared at her like a man who awakens. She looked down.

'You mean—' he said; and then, 'Don't you hold me cheap?'

She glanced up again and shook her head.

'But – for instance – you don't think of me – as an equal like.'

'Why not?'

'Oo! But, reely—'

His heart beat very fast.

'If I thought—' he said; and then, 'You know so much.'

'That's nothing,' she said.

Then, for a long time, as it seemed to them, both kept silence – a silence that said and accomplished many things.

'I know what I am,' he said at length. . . . 'If I thought it was possible – If I thought *you*. . . . I believe I could do anything—'

He stopped, and she sat downcast and strikingly still.

'Miss Walshingham,' he said, 'is it possible that you . . . could care for me enough to – to 'elp me? Miss Walshingham, do you care for me at all?'

It seemed she was never going to answer. She looked up at him. 'I think,' she said, 'you are the most generous – look at what you have done for my brother! – the most generous and the most modest of – men. And this afternoon – I thought you were the bravest.'

She turned her head, glanced down, waved her hand to some one on the terrace below, and stood up.

'Mother is signalling,' she said. 'We must go down.'

Kipps became polite and deferential by habit, but his mind was a tumult that had nothing to do with that.

He moved before her towards the little door that opened on the winding stairs – 'always precede a lady down or up stairs' – and then, on the second step, he turned resolutely. 'But—' he said, looking up out of the shadow, flannel clad and singularly like a man.

She looked down on him, with her hand upon the stone lintel.

He held out his hand as if to help her. 'Can you tell me?' he said. 'You must know—'

'What?'

'If you care for me?'

She did not answer for a long time. It was as if everything in the world was drawn to the breaking-point, and in a minute must certainly break.

'Yes,' she said at last, 'I know.'

Abruptly, by some impalpable sign, he knew what the answer would be, and he remained still.

She bent down over him and softened to her wonderful smile.

'Promise me,' she insisted.

He promised with his still face.

'If *I* do not hold you cheap, you will never hold yourself cheap.'

'If you do not hold me cheap! You mean—?'

She bent down quite close to him. 'I hold you,' she said, and then whispered, '*dear*.'

'Me?'

She laughed aloud.

He was astonished beyond measure. He stipulated lest there might be some misconception. 'You will marry me?'

She was laughing, inundated by the sense of bountiful power, of possession and success. He looked quite a nice little man to have. 'Yes,' she laughed. 'What else could I mean?' and, 'Yes.'

He felt as a praying hermit might have felt, snatched from the midst of his quiet devotions, his modest sackcloth and ashes, and hurled neck and crop over the glittering gates of Paradise, smack among the iridescent wings, the bright-eyed Cherubim.

He felt like some lowly and righteous man dynamited into Bliss. . . .

His hand tightened on the rope that steadies one upon the stairs of stone. He was for kissing her hand and did not.

He said not a word more. He turned about, and, with something very like a scared expression on his face, led the way into the obscurity of their descent. . . .

III

Every one seemed to understand. Nothing was said, nothing was explained; the merest touch of the eyes sufficed. As they clustered in the castle gateway, Coote, Kipps remembered afterwards, laid hold of his arm as if by chance, and pressed it. It was quite evident he knew. His eyes, his nose, shone with benevolent congratulation; shone, too, with the sense of a good thing conducted to its climax. Mrs Walshingham, who had seemed a little fatigued by the hill, recovered, and was even obviously stirred by affection for her daughter. There was in passing a motherly caress. She asked Kipps to give her his arm in walking down the steep. Kipps in a sort of dream obeyed. He found himself trying to attend to her, and soon he was attending.

She and Kipps talked like sober responsible people and went slowly, while the others drifted down the hill together a loose little group of four. He wondered momentarily what they would talk about, and then sank into his conversation with Mrs Walshingham. He conversed, as it were, out of his superficial personality, and his inner self lay stunned in unsuspected depths within. It had an air of being an interesting and friendly talk, almost their first long talk together. Hitherto he had had a sort of fear of Mrs Walshingham as of a person possibly satirical, but she proved a soul of sense and sentiment, and Kipps, for all his abstraction, got on with her unexpectedly well. They talked a little upon scenery and the inevitable melancholy attaching to old ruins and the thought of vanished generations.

'Perhaps they jousted here,' said Mrs Walshingham.

'They was up to all sorts of things,' said Kipps; and then the two came round to Helen. She spoke of her daughter's literary ambitions. 'She will do something, I feel sure. You know, Mr

Kipps, it's a great responsibility to a mother to feel her daughter is – exceptionally clever.'

'I dessay it is,' said Kipps. 'There's no mistake about that.'

She spoke, too, of her son – almost like Helen's twin – alike yet different. She made Kipps feel quite fatherly. 'They are so quick, so artistic,' she said, 'so full of ideas. Almost they frighten me. One feels they need opportunities – as other people need air.'

She spoke of Helen's writing. 'Even when she was quite a little dot she wrote verse.'

(Kipps, sensation.)

'Her father had just the same tastes—' Mrs Walshingham turned a little beam of half-pathetic reminiscence on the past. 'He was more artist than business man. That was the trouble. . . . He was misled by his partner, and when the crash came every one blamed him. . . . Well, it doesn't do to dwell on horrid things . . . especially to-day. There are bright days, Mr Kipps, and dark days. And mine have not always been bright.'

Kipps presented a face of Coote-like sympathy.

She diverged to talk of flowers, and Kipps' mind was filled with the picture of Helen bending down towards him in the Keep. . . .

They spread the tea under the trees before the little inn, and at a certain moment Kipps became aware that every one in the party was simultaneously and furtively glancing at him. There might have been a certain tension had it not been first of all for Coote and his tact, and afterwards for a number of wasps. Coote was resolved to make this memorable day pass off well, and displayed an almost boisterous sense of fun. Then young Walshingham began talking of the Roman remains below Lympne, intending to lead up to the Overman. 'These old Roman chaps—' he said; and then the wasps arrived. They killed three in the jam alone.

Kipps killed wasps, as it were, in a dream, and handed things to the wrong people, and maintained a thin surface of ordinary intelligence with the utmost difficulty. At times he became aware – aware with an extraordinary vividness – of Helen. Helen was carefully not looking at him, and behaving with amazing coolness and ease. But just for that one time there was the faintest suggestion of pink beneath the ivory of her cheeks. . . .

Tacitly the others conceded to Kipps the right to paddle back with Helen; he helped her into the canoe and took his paddle, and, paddling slowly, dropped behind the others. And now his inner self stirred again. He said nothing to her. How could he ever say anything to her again? She spoke to him at rare intervals about reflections and flowers and the trees, and he nodded in reply. But his mind moved very slowly forward now from the point at which it had fallen stunned in the Lympne Keep, moving forward to the beginnings of realization. As yet he did not say even in the recesses of his heart that she was his! But he perceived that the goddess had come from her altar, amazingly, and had taken him by the hand!

The sky was a vast splendour, and then close to them were the dark protecting trees, and the shining, smooth still water. He was an erect black outline to her; he plied his paddle with no unskilful gesture; the water broke to snaky silver and glittered far behind his strokes. Indeed, he did not seem so bad to her. Youth calls to youth the wide world through, and her soul rose in triumph over his subjection. And behind him was money and opportunity, freedom and London, a great background of seductively indistinct hopes. To him her face was a warm dimness. In truth he could not see her eyes, but it seemed to his love-witched brain he did, and that they shone out at him like dusky stars.

All the world that evening was no more than a shadowy frame of darkling sky and water and dipping boughs about Helen. He seemed to see through things with an extraordinary clearness; she was revealed to him certainly, as the cause and essence of it all.

He was, indeed, at his Heart's Desire. It was one of those times when there seems to be no future, when Time has stopped and we are at the end. Kipps that evening could not have imagined a to-morrow; all that his imagination had pointed towards was attained. His mind stood still, and took the moments as they came.

IV

About nine that night Coote came round to Kipps' new apartment in the Upper Sandgate Road – the house on the Leas had been let furnished – and Kipps made an effort towards realization. He was discovered sitting at the open window and without a lamp – quite still. Coote was deeply moved, and he pressed Kipps' palm and laid a knobbly white hand on his shoulder, and displayed the sort of tenderness becoming in a crisis. Kipps, too, was moved that night, and treated Coote like a very dear brother.

'She's splendid,' said Coote, coming to it abruptly.

'Isn't she?' said Kipps.

'I couldn't help noticing her face,' said Coote. . . . 'You know, my dear Kipps, this is better than a legacy.'

'I don't deserve it,' said Kipps.

'You can't say that.'

'I don't. I can't 'ardly believe it. I can't believe it at all. No!'

There followed an expressive stillness.

'It's wonderful,' said Kipps. 'It takes me like that.'

Coote made a faint blowing noise, and so again they came for a time on silence.

'And it began – before your money?'

'When I was in 'er class,' said Kipps, solemnly.

Coote, speaking out of a darkness which he was illuminating strangely with efforts to strike a match, said it was beautiful. He could not have *wished* Kipps a better fortune. . . .

He lit a cigarette, and Kipps was moved to do the same, with a sacramental expression.

Presently speech flowed more freely.

Coote began to praise Helen, and her mother and brother; he talked of when 'it' might be; he presented the thing as concrete and credible. 'It's a county family, you know,' he said. 'She is connected, you know, with the Beauprés family – you know Lord Beauprés.'

'No!' said Kipps, 'reely!'

'Distantly, of course,' said Coote. 'Still—'

He smiled a smile that glimmered in the twilight.

'It's too much,' said Kipps, overcome. 'It's so all like that.'

Coote exhaled. For a time Kipps listened to Helen's praises and matured a point of view.

'I say, Coote,' he said. 'What ought I to do now?'

'What do you mean?' said Coote.

'I mean about calling on 'er and all that.'

He reflected. 'Naturally I want to do it all right.'

'Of course,' said Coote.

'It would be awful to go and do something now – all wrong.'

Coote's cigarette glowed as he meditated. 'You must call, of course,' he decided. 'You'll have to speak to Mrs Walshingham.'

''Ow?' said Kipps.

'Tell her you mean to marry her daughter.'

'I dessay she knows,' said Kipps, with defensive penetration.

Coote's head was visible, shaking itself judicially.

'Then there's the ring,' said Kipps. 'What 'ave I to do about that?'

'What ring do you mean?'

''Ngagement Ring. There isn't anything at all about that in *Manners and Rules of Good Society* – not a word.'

'Of course you must get something – tasteful. Yes.'

'What sort of ring?'

'Something nace. They'll show you in the shop.'

'O' course. I s'pose I got to take it to 'er, eh? Put it on 'er finger.'

'Oh no! Send it. Much better.'

'Ah!' said Kipps for the first time with a note of relief.

'Then 'ow about this call? – on Mrs Walshingham I mean. 'Ow ought one to go?'

'Rather a ceremonial occasion,' reflected Coote.

'Wadyer mean? Frock-coat?'

'I *think* so,' said Coote, with discrimination.

'Light trousers, and all that?'

'Yes.'

'Rose?'

'I think it might run to a buttonhole.'

The curtain that hung over the future became less opaque to the eyes of Kipps. To-morrow, and then other days, became perceptible at least as existing. Frock-coat, silk hat, and a rose! With a certain solemnity he contemplated himself in the process of slow transformation into an Engish gentleman, Arthur Cuyps, frock-coated on occasions of ceremony, the familiar acquaintance of Lady Punnet, the recognized wooer of a distant connection of the Earl of Beauprés.

Something like awe at the magnitude of his own fortunes came upon him. He felt the world was opening out like a magic flower in a transformation scene at the touch of this wand of gold. And Helen, nestling beautiful in the red heart of the flower. Only ten weeks ago he had been no more than the shabbiest of improvers and shamefully dismissed for dissipation, the mere soil-buried seed, as it were, of these glories. He resolved the engagement ring should be of expressively excessive quality and appearance, in fact the very best they had.

'Ought I to send 'er flowers?' he speculated.

'Not necessarily,' said Coote. 'Though, of course, it's an attention'. . . .

Kipps meditated on flowers.

'When you see her,' said Coote, 'you'll have to ask her to name the day.'

Kipps started. 'That won't be just yet a bit, will it?'

'Don't know any reason for delay.'

'Oo, but – a year say.'

'Rather a long taime,' said Coote.

'Is it?' said Kipps, turning his head sharply. 'But—'

There was quite a long pause.

'I say!' he said at last, and in an altered voice, 'you'll 'ave to 'elp me about the wedding.'

'Only too happy!' said Coote.

'O' course,' said Kipps, 'I didn't think—' He changed his line of thought. 'Coote,' he asked, 'wot's a "tate-ch-tate"?'

'A "tate-ah-tay,"' said Coote, improvingly, 'is a conversation alone together.'

'Lor!' said Kipps, 'but I thought— It says *strictly* we oughtn't to enjoy a tater-tay, not sit together, walk together, ride together, or meet during any part of the day. That don't leave much time for meeting, does it?'

'The book says that?' asked Coote.

'I jest learnt it by 'eart before you came. I thought that was a bit rum, but I s'pose it's all right.'

'You won't find Mrs Walshingham so strict as all that,' said Coote. 'I think that's a bit extreme. They'd only do that now in very strict old aristocratic families. Besides, the Walshinghams are so modern – advanced you might say. I expect you'll get plenty of chances of talking together.'

'There's a tremendous lot to think about,' said Kipps, blowing a profound sigh. 'D'you mean – p'raps we might be married in a few months or so.'

'You'll *have* to be,' said Coote. 'Why not?'. . . .

Midnight found Kipps alone, looking a little tired, and turning over the leaves of the red-covered text-book with a studious

expression. He paused for a moment at page 233, his eye caught
by the words –

'FOR AN UNCLE OR AUNT BY MARRIAGE the period is
six weeks black with jet trimmings.'

'No,' said Kipps, after a vigorous mental effort. 'That's not
it.' The pages rustled again. He stopped and flattened out the
little book decisively at the beginning of the chapter on
'Weddings'.

He became pensive. He stared at the lamp-wick. 'I suppose I
ought to go over and tell them,' he said at last.

v

Kipps called on Mrs Walshingham attired in the proper costume
for Ceremonial Occasions in the Day. He carried a silk hat, and
he wore a deep-skirted frock-coat; his boots were patent leather,
and his trousers a dark grey. He had generous white cuffs with
gold links, and his grey gloves, one thumb of which had burst
when he put them on, he held loosely in his hand. He carried a
small umbrella, rolled to an exquisite tightness. A sense of
singular correctness pervaded his being and warred with the
enormity of the occasion for possession of his soul. Anon he
touched his silk cravat. The world smelt of his rosebud.

He seated himself on a newly re-covered chintz armchair, and
stuck out the elbow of the arm that held his hat.

'I know,' said Mrs Walshingham, 'I know everything,' and
helped him out most amazingly. She deepened the impression he
had already received of her sense and refinement. She displayed
an amount of tenderness that touched him.

'This is a great thing,' she said, 'to a mother,' and her hand
rested for a moment on his impeccable coat-sleeve.

'A daughter, Arthur,' she explained, 'is so much more than a
son.'

Marriage, she said, was a lottery, and without love and
toleration – there was much unhappiness. Her life had not
always been bright – there had been dark days and bright days.
She smiled rather sweetly. 'This is a bright one,' she said.

She said very kind and flattering things to Kipps, and she
thanked him for his goodness to her son. ('That wasn't anything,' said Kipps.) And then she expanded upon the theme of

her two children. 'Both so accomplished,' she said, 'so clever. I call them my Twin Jewels.'

She was repeating a remark she had made at Lympne, that she always said her children needed opportunities as other people needed air, when she was abruptly arrested by the entry of Helen. They hung on a pause, Helen perhaps surprised by Kipps' week-day magnificence. Then she advanced with outstretched hand.

Both the young people were shy. 'I jest called round,' began Kipps, and became uncertain how to end.

'Won't you have some tea?' asked Helen.

She walked to the window, looked at the familiar out-porter's barrow, turned, surveyed Kipps for a moment ambiguously, said, 'I will get some tea,' and so departed again.

Mrs Walshingham and Kipps looked at one another, and the lady smiled indulgently. 'You two young people mustn't be shy of each other,' said Mrs Walshingham, which damaged Kipps considerably.

She was explaining how sensitive Helen always had been, even about quite little things, when the servant appeared with the tea-things; and then Helen followed, and, taking up a secure position behind the little bamboo tea-table, broke the ice with officious teacup clattering. Then she introduced the topic of a forthcoming open-air performance of *As You Like It*, and steered past the worst of the awkwardness. They discussed stage illusions. 'I mus' say,' said Kipps, 'I don't quite like a play in a theayter. It seems sort of unreal some'ow.'

'But most plays are written for the stage,' said Helen, looking at the sugar.

'I know,' admitted Kipps.

'They got through tea. 'Well,' said Kipps, and rose.

'You mustn't go yet,' said Mrs Walshingham, rising and taking his hand. 'I'm sure you two must have heaps to say to each other;' and so she escaped towards the door.

VI

Among other projects that seemed almost equally correct to Kipps at that exalted moment was one of embracing Helen with ardour so soon as the door closed behind her mother, and one of headlong flight through the open window. Then he remembered he ought to hold the door open for Mrs Walshingham, and turned from that duty to find Helen still standing, beautifully inaccessible, behind the tea-things. He closed the door and advanced towards her with his arms akimbo and his hands upon his coat skirts. Then feeling angular, he moved his right hand to his moustache. Anyhow, he was dressed all right. Somewhere at the back of his mind, dim and mingled with doubt and surprise, appeard the perception that he felt now quite differently towards her, that something between them had been blown from Lympne Keep to the four winds of heaven. . . .

She regarded him with an eye of critical proprietorship.

'Mother has been making up to you,' she said, smiling slightly. She added, 'It was nice of you to come round to see her.'

They stood through a brief pause, as though each had expected something different in the other, and was a little perplexed at its not being there. Kipps found he was at the corner of the brown-covered table, and he picked up a little flexible book that lay upon it to occupy his mind.

'I bought you a ring to-day,' he said, bending the book and speaking for the sake of saying something, and then he moved to genuine speech. 'You know,' he said, 'I can't 'ardly believe it.'

Her face relaxed slightly again. 'No?' she said, and may have breathed, 'Nor I.'

'No,' he went on. 'It's as though everything 'ad changed. More even than when I got that money. 'Ere we are going to marry. It's like being some one else. What I feel is—'

He turned a flushed and earnest face to her. He seemed to come alive to her with one natural gesture. 'I don't *know* things. I'm not good enough. I'm not refined. The more you see of me, the more you'll find me out.'

'But I'm going to help you.'

'You'll 'ave to 'elp me a fearful lot.'

She walked to the window, glanced out of it, made up her mind, turned and came towards him, with her hands clasped behind her back.

'All these things that trouble you are very little things. If you don't mind – if you will let me tell you things—'

'I wish you would.'

'Then I will.'

'They're little things to you, but they aren't to me.'

'It all depends, if you don't mind being told.'

'By you?'

'I don't expect you to be told by strangers.'

'Oo!' said Kipps, expressing much.

'You know, there are just a few little things—For instance, you know, you are careless with your pronunciation. . . . You don't mind my telling you?'

'I like it,' said Kipps.

'There's aitches.'

'I know,' said Kipps, and then endorsingly, 'I been told. Fact is, I know a chap, a Nacter, *he's* told me. He's told me, and he's going to give me a lesson or so.'

'I'm glad of that. It only requires a little care.'

'Of course, on the stage they got to look out. They take regular lessons.'

'Of course,' said Helen, a little absently.

'I dessay I shall soon get into it,' said Kipps.

'And then there's dress,' said Helen, taking up her thread again.

Kipps became pink, but he remained respectfully attentive.

'You don't mind?' she said.

'Oo no.'

'You mustn't be too – too dressy. It's possible to be over conventional, over elaborate. It makes you look like a shop . . . like a common well-off person. There's a sort of easiness that is better. A real gentleman looks right, without looking as though he had tried to be right.'

'Jest as though 'e'd put on what came first?' said the pupil, in a faded voice.

'Not exactly that, but a sort of ease.'

Kipps nodded his head intelligently. In his heart he was kicking his silk hat about the room in an ecstasy of disappointment.

'And you must accustom yourself to be more at your ease when you are with people,' said Helen. 'You've only to forget yourself a little and not be anxious—'

'I'll try,' said Kipps, looking rather hard at the teapot. 'I'll do my best to try.'

'I know you will,' she said; and laid a hand for an instant upon his shoulder and withdrew it.

He did not perceive her caress. 'One has to learn,' he said. His attention was distracted by the strenuous efforts that were going on in the back of his head to translate 'I say, didn't you ought to name the day?' into easy as well as elegant English, a struggle that was still undecided when the time came for them to part. . . .

He sat for a long time at the open window of his sitting-room with an intent face, recapitulating that interview. His eyes rested at last almost reproachfully on the silk hat beside him. 'Ow *is* one to know?' he asked. His attention was caught by a rubbed place in the nap, and, still thoughtful, he rolled up his handkerchief skilfully into a soft ball and began to smooth this down.

His expression changed slowly.

''Ow the Juice is one to know?' he said, putting down the hat with some emphasis.

'He rose up, went across the room to the sideboard, and, standing there opened and began to read in *Manners and Rules*.

Chapter Four

The Bicycle Manufacturer

I

So Kipps embarked upon his engagement, steeled himself to the high enterprise of marrying above his breeding. The next morning found him dressing with a certain quiet severity of movement, and it seemed to his landlady's housemaid that he was unusually dignified at breakfast. He meditated profoundly over his kipper and his kidney and bacon. He was going to New Romney to tell the old people what had happened and where he stood. And the love of Helen had also given him courage to do what Buggins had once suggested to him as a thing he would do were in in Kipps' place, and that was to hire a motor-car for the afternoon. He had an early cold lunch, and then, with an air of quiet resolution, assumed a cap and coat he had purchased to this end, and, thus equipped, strolled round, blowing slightly, to the motor-shop. The transaction was unexpectedly easy, and within the hour, Kipps, spectacled and wrapped about, was tootling through Dymchurch.

They came to a stop smartly and neatly outside the little toy-shop. 'Make that thing 'oot a bit, will you?' said Kipps. 'Yes. That's it.' 'Whup,' said the motor-car. 'Whurrup.' Both his Aunt and Uncle came out on the pavement. 'Why, it's Artie!' cried his Aunt; and Kipps had a moment of triumph.

He descended to hand-claspings, removed wraps and spectacles, and the motor-driver retired to take 'an hour off'. Old Kipps surveyed the machinery and disconcerted Kipps for a moment by asking him, in a knowing tone, what they asked him for a thing like that. The two men stood inspecting the machine and impressing the neighbours for a time, and then they strolled through the shop into the little parlour for a drink.

'They ain't settled,' old Kipps had said at the neighbours. 'They ain't got no further than experiments. There's a bit of take-in about each. You take my advice and wait, me boy, even if it's a year or two before you buy one for your own use.'

(Though Kipps had said nothing of doing anything of the sort.)

"Ow d'you like that whisky I sent?' asked Kipps, dodging the old familiar bunch of children's pails.

Old Kipps became tactful. 'It's very good whisky, my boy,' said old Kipps. 'I 'aven't the slightest doubt it's a very good whisky, and cost you a tidy price. But – dashed if it soots me! They put this here Foozle Ile in it, my boy, and it ketches me jest 'ere.' He indicated his centre of figure. 'Gives me the heartburn,' he said, and shook his head rather sadly.

'It's a very good whisky,' said Kipps. 'It's what the actor-manager chaps drink in London, I 'appen to know.'

'I dessay they do, my boy,' said old Kipps, 'but then they've 'ad their livers burnt out – and I 'aven't. They ain't dellicat like me. My stummik always 'as been extry-dellicat. Sometimes it's almost been as though nothing would lay on it. But that's in passing. I liked those segars. You can send me some more of them segars. . . .'

You cannot lead a conversation straight from the gastric consequences of Foozle Ile to Love, and so Kipps, after a friendly inspection of a rare old engraving after Morland* (perfect except for a hole kicked through the centre) that his Uncle had recently purchased by private haggle, came to the topic of the old people's removal.

At the outset of Kipps' great fortunes there had been much talk of some permanent provision for them. It had been conceded they were to be provided for comfortably, and the phrase 'retire from business' had been very much in the air. Kipps had pictured an ideal cottage with a creeper always in exuberant flower about the door, where the sun shone for ever, and the wind never blew, and a perpetual welcome hovered in the doorway. It was an agreeable dream, but when it came to the point of deciding upon this particular cottage or that, and on this particular house or that, Kipps was surprised by an unexpected clinging to the little home, which he had always understood to be the worst of all possible houses.

'We don't want to move in a 'urry,' said Mrs Kipps.

'When we want to move, we want to move for life. I've had enough moving about in my time,' said old Kipps.

'We can do here a bit more now we done here so long,' said Mrs Kipps.

'You lemme look about a bit *fust*,' said old Kipps.

And in looking about old Kipps found perhaps a finer joy than any mere possession could have given. He would shut his shop more or less effectually against the intrusion of customers, and toddle abroad seeking new matter for his dream; no house was too small and none too large for his knowing inquiries. Occupied houses took his fancy more than vacant ones, and he would remark, 'You won't be a-livin' 'ere for ever, even if you think you will', when irate householders protested against the unsolicited examination of their more intimate premises. . . .

Remarkable difficulties arose, of a totally unexpected sort.

'If we 'ave a larger 'ouse,' said Mrs Kipps, with sudden bitterness, 'we shall want a servant, and I don't want no gells in the place larfin' at me, sniggering' and larfin' and prancin' and trapesin', lardy da!'

'If we 'ave a smaller 'ouse,' said Mrs Kipps, 'there won't be room to swing a cat.'

Room to swing a cat, it seemed, was absolutely essential. It was an infrequent but indispensable operation.

'When we *do* move,' said old Kipps, 'if we could get a bit of shootin'—'

'I don't want to sell off all this here stock for nothin',' said old Kipps. 'It's took years to 'cumulate. I put a ticket in the winder sayin' "sellin' orf", but it 'asn't brought nothing like a roosh. One of these 'ere dratted visitors, pretendin' to want an air-gun, was all we 'ad in yesterday. Jest an excuse for spyin' round, and then go away and larf at you. Nothanky to everything, it didn't matter what. . . . That's 'ow *I* look at it, Artie.'

They pursued meandering fancies about the topic of their future settlement for a space, and Kipps became more and more hopeless of any proper conversational opening that would lead to his great announcement, and more and more uncertain how such an opening should be taken. Once, indeed, old Kipps, anxious to get away from this dangerous subject of removals, began, 'And what are you a-doin' of in Folkestone? I shall have to come over and see you one of these days,' but before Kipps could get in upon that, his Uncle had passed into a general exposition of the proper treatment of landladies and their humbugging cheating ways, and so the opportunity vanished. It seemed to Kipps the only thing to do was to go out into the town for a stroll, compose an effectual opening at leisure, and then come back and discharge it at them in its consecutive completeness. And even out-of-doors and alone he found his mind distracted by irrelevant thoughts.

II

His steps led him out of the High Street towards the church, and he leant for a time over the gate that had once been the winning-post of his race with Ann Pornick, and presently found himself in a sitting position on the top rail. He had to get things smooth again, he knew; his mind was like the mirror of water after a breeze. The image of Helen and his great future was broken and mingled into fragmentary reflections of remoter things, of the good name of Old Methusaleh Three Stars, of long-dormant memories the High Street saw fit, by some trick of light and atmosphere, to arouse that afternoon. . . .

Abruptly a fine full voice from under his elbow shouted, 'What-o, Art!' and behold Sid Pornick was back in his world, leaning over the gate beside him, and holding out a friendly hand.

He was oddly changed, and yet oddly like the Sid that Kipps had known. He had the old broad face and mouth, abundantly freckled, the same short nose, and the same blunt chin, the same odd suggestion of his sister Ann without a touch of her beauty; but he had quite a new voice, loud, and a little hard, and his upper lip carried a stiff and very fair moustache.

Kipps shook hands. 'I was jest thinking of *you*, Sid,' he said, 'jest this very moment, and wondering if ever I should see you again – ever. And 'ere you are!'

'One likes a look round at times,' said Sid. 'How are *you*, old chap?'

'All right,' said Kipps. 'I just been lef'—'

'You aren't changed much,' interrupted Sid.

'Ent I?' said Kipps, foiled.

'I knew your back directly I came round the corner. Spite of that 'at you got on. Hang it, I said, that's Art Kipps or the devil. And so it was.'

Kipps made a movement of his neck as if he would look at his back and judge. Then he looked Sid in the face. 'You got a moustache, Sid,' he said.

'I s'pose you're having your holidays?' said Sid.

'Well, partly. But I just been lef'—'

'*I'm* taking a bit of a holiday,' Sid went on. 'But the fact is, I have to give *myself* holidays nowadays. I've set up for myself.'

'Not down here?'

'No fear! I'm not a turnip. I've started in Hammersmith, manufacturing.' Sid spoke offhand, as though there was no such thing as pride.

'Not drapery?'

'No fear! Engineer. Manufacture bicycles.' He clapped his hand to his breast pocket and produced a number of pink handbills. He handed one to Kipps, and prevented him reading it by explanations and explanatory dabs of a pointing finger. 'That's our make – my make, to be exact – the Red Flag – see? I got a transfer with my name – Pantocrat tyres, eight pounds – yes, *there* – Clinchers ten, Dunlops eleven, Ladies' one pound more – that's the lady's. Best machine at a democratic price in London. No guineas and no discounts – honest trade. I build 'em – to order. I've built,' he reflected, looking away seaward, 'seventeen. Counting orders in 'and. . . .

'Come down to look at the old place a bit,' said Sid. 'Mother likes it at times.'

'Thought you'd all gone away—'

'What! after my father's death? No! My mother's come back, and she's living at Muggett's cottages. The sea-air suits 'er. She likes the old place better than Hammersmith . . . and I can afford it. Got an old crony or so here. . . . Gossip . . . have tea. . . . S'pose *you* ain't married, Kipps?'

Kipps shook his head. 'I—' he began.

'*I* am,' said Sid. 'Married these two years, and got a nipper. Proper little chap.'

Kipps got his word in at last. 'I got engaged day before yesterday,' he said.

'Ah!' said Sid, airily. 'That's all right. Who's the fortunate lady?'

Kipps tried to speak in an offhand way. He stuck his hands in his pockets as he spoke. 'She's a solicitor's daughter,' he said, 'in Folkestone. Rather'r nice set. County family. Related to the Earl of Beauprés—'

'Steady on!' cried Sid.

'You see, I've 'ad a bit of luck, Sid. Been lef' money.'

Sid's eye travelled instinctively to mark Kipps' garments. 'How much?' he asked.

''Bout twelve 'undred a year,' said Kipps, more offhandedly than ever.

'Lord!' said Sid, with a note of positive dismay, and stepped back a pace or two.

'My granfaver it was,' said Kipps, trying hard to be calm and simple. ''Ardly knew I '*ad* a granfaver. And then – bang! When o' Bean, the solicitor, told me of it, you could 'ave knocked me down—'

''*Ow* much?' demanded Sid, with a sharp note in his voice.

'Twelve 'undred pound a year – proximately, that is.'. . . .

Sid's attempt at genial unenvious congratulation did not last a minute. He shook hands with an unreal heartiness, and said he was jolly glad. 'It's a blooming stroke of Luck,' he said.

'It's a bloomin' stroke of Luck,' he repeated, 'that's what it is,' with the smile fading from his face. 'Of course, better you 'ave it than me, o' chap. So I don't envy you, anyhow. *I* couldn't keep it if I did 'ave it.'

''Ow's that?' said Kipps, a little hipped by Sid's patent chagrin.

'I'm a Socialist, you see,' said Sid. 'I don't 'old with Wealth. What *is* Wealth? Labour robbed out of the poor. At most it's only yours in trust. Leastways, that's 'ow *I* should take it.'

He reflected. 'The Present distribution of Wealth,' he said, and stopped.

Then he let himself go, with unmasked bitterness. 'It's no sense at all. It's jest damn foolishness. Who's going to work and care in a muddle like this? Here first you do – something anyhow – of the world's work and it pays you hardly anything, and then it invites you to do nothing, nothing whatever, and pays you twelve hundred pounds a year. Who's going to respect laws and customs when they come to damn silliness like that?'

He repeated, 'Twelve hundred pounds a year!'

At the sight of Kipps's face he relented slightly.

'It's not you I'm thinking of, o' man; it's the system. Better you than most people. Still—'

He laid both hands on the gate and repeated to himself, 'Twelve 'undred a year. . . . Gee-whiz, Kipps! You'll be a swell!'

'I shan't,' said Kipps, with imperfect conviction. 'No fear.'

'You can't 'ave money like that and not swell out. You'll soon be too big to speak to – 'ow do they put it? – a mere mechanic like me.'

'No fear, Siddee,' said Kipps, with conviction. 'I ain't that sort.'

'Ah!' said Sid, with a sort of unwilling scepticism, 'money'll be too much for you. Besides – you're caught by a swell already.'

''Ow d'yer mean?'

'That girl you're going to marry. Masterman says—'

'Oo's Masterman?'

'Rare good chap, I know – takes my first-floor front room. Masterman says it's always the wife pitches the key. Always. There's no social differences – till women come in.'

'Ah!' said Kipps, profoundly. 'You don't know.'

Sid shook his head. 'Fancy!' he reflected. 'Art Kipps! ... Twelve 'Undred a Year!'

Kipps tried to bridge that opening gulf. 'Remember the Hurons, Sid?'

'Rather,' said Sid.

'Remember that wreck?'

'I can smell it now – sort of sour smell.'

Kipps was silent for a moment, with reminiscent eyes on Sid's still troubled face.

'I say, Sid, 'ow's Ann?'

'*She's* all right,' said Sid.

'Where is she now?'

'In a place. . . . Ashford.'

'Oh!'

Sid's face had become a shade sulkier than before.

'The fact is,' he said, 'we don't get on very well together. *I* don't hold with service. We're common people, I suppose, but I don't like it. I don't see why a sister of mine should wait at other people's tables. No. Not even if they got Twelve 'Undred a Year.'

Kipps tried to change the point of application. 'Remember 'ow you came out once when we were racing here? ... She didn't run bad for a girl.'

And his own words raised an image brighter than he could have suppressed, so bright it seemed to breathe before him, and did not fade altogether, even when he was back in Folkestone an hour or so later.

But Sid was not to be deflected from that other rankling theme by any reminiscences of Ann.

'I wonder what you will do with all that money,' he speculated. 'I wonder if you will do any good at all. I wonder what you *could* do. You should hear Masterman. He'd tell you things. Suppose it came to me; what should I do? It's no good giving it back to the State as things are. Start an Owenite profit-sharing factory perhaps. Or a new Socialist paper. We want a new Socialist paper.'

He tried to drown his personal chagrin in elaborate exemplary suggestions. . . .

III

'I must be gettin' on to my motor,' said Kipps at last, having to a large extent heard him out.

'What! Got a motor?'

'No!' said Kipps, apologetically. 'Only jobbed for the day.'

''Ow much?'

'Five pounds.'

'Keep five families for a week! Good Lord!' That seemed to crown Sid's disgust.

Yet drawn by a sort of fascination, he came with Kipps and assisted at the mounting of the motor. He was pleased to note it was not the most modern of motors, but that was the only grain of comfort. Kipps mounted at once, after one violent agitation of the little shop-door to set the bell ajangle and warn his Uncle and Aunt. Sid assisted with the great fur-lined overcoat and examined the spectacles.

'Good-bye, o' chap!' said Kipps.

'Good-bye, o' chap!' said Sid.

The old people came out to say good-bye.

Old Kipps was radiant with triumph. ''Pon my sammy, Artie! I'm a goo' mind to come with you,' he shouted; and then, 'I got something you might take with you!'

He dodged back into the shop and returned with the perforated engraving after Morland.

'You stick to this, my boy,' he said. 'You get it repaired by some one who knows. It's the most vallyble thing I got you so far – you take my word.'

'Warrup!' said the motor, and tuff, tuff, tuff, and backed and snorted, while old Kipps danced about on the pavement as if foreseeing complex catastrophes, and told the driver, 'That's all right.'

He waved his stout stick to his receding nephew. Then he turned to Sid. 'Now, if you could make something like that, young Pornick, you *might* blow a bit!'

'I'll make a doocid sight better than *that* before I done', said Sid, hands deep in his pockets.

'Not *you*,' said old Kipps.

The motor set up a prolonged sobbing moan and vanished round the corner. Sid stood motionless for a space, unheeding some further remark from old Kipps. The young mechanic had just discovered that to have manufactured seventeen bicycles, including orders in hand, is not so big a thing as he had supposed, and such discoveries try one's manhood. . . .

'Oh, well!' said Sid, at last, and turned his face towards his mother's cottage.

She had got a hot teacake for him, and she was a little hurt that he was dark and preoccupied as he consumed it. He had always been such a boy for teacake, and then when one went out specially and got him one—!

He did not tell her – he did not tell any one – he had seen young Kipps. He did not want to talk about Kipps for a bit to any one at all.

Chapter Five

The Pupil Lover

I

When Kipps came to reflect upon his afternoon's work, he had his first inkling of certain comprehensive incompatibilities lying about the course of true love in his particular case. He had felt without understanding the incongruity between the announcement he had failed to make and the circle of ideas of his Aunt and Uncle. It was this rather than the want of a specific intention that had silenced him, the perception that when he travelled from Folkestone to New Romney he travelled from an atmosphere where his engagement to Helen was sane and excellent to an atmosphere where it was only to be regarded with incredulous suspicion. Coupled and associated with this jar was his sense of the altered behaviour of Sid Pornick, the evident shock to that ancient alliance caused by the fact of his enrichment, the touch of hostility in his 'You'll soon be swelled too big to speak to a poor mechanic like me.' Kipps was unprepared for the unpleasant truth – that the path of social advancement is, and must be, strewn with broken friendships. This first protrusion of that fact caused a painful confusion in his mind. It was speedily to protrude in a far more serious fashion in relation to the 'hands' from the Emporium, and Chitterlow.

From the day at Lympne Castle his relations with Helen had entered upon a new footing. He had as little understanding of what it was he prayed for. And now that period of standing humbly in the shadows before the shrine was over, and the goddess, her veil of mystery flung aside, had come down to him and taken hold of him, a good strong firm hold, and walked by his side. . . . She liked him. What was singular was, that very soon she had kissed him thrice, whimsically upon the brow, and he had never kissed her at all. He could not analyze his feelings, only he knew the world was wonderfully changed about them; but the truth was that, though he still worshipped and feared her, though his pride in his engagement was ridiculously vast, he loved her now no more. That subtle something, woven of the most delicate strands of self-love and tenderness and desire, had vanished imperceptibly, and was gone now for ever. But that she did not suspect in him, nor, as a matter of fact, did he.

She took him in hand in perfect good faith. She told him things about his accent; she told him things about his bearing, about his costume and his way of looking at things. She thrust the blade of her intelligence into the tenderest corners of Kipps' secret vanity; she slashed his most intimate pride to bleeding tatters. He sought very diligently to anticipate some at least of these informing thrusts by making great use of Coote. But the unanticipated made a brave number. . . .

She found his simple willingness a very lovable thing.

Indeed, she liked him more and more. There was a touch of motherliness in her feelings towards him. But his upbringing and his associations had been, she diagnosed, 'awful'. At New Romney she glanced but little – that was remote. But in her inventory – she went over him as one might go over a newly taken house, with impartial thoroughness – she discovered more proximate influences, surprising intimations of nocturnal 'sing-songs' – she pictured it as almost shocking that Kipps should sing to the banjo – much low-grade wisdom treasured from a person called Buggins – 'Who *is* Buggins?' said Helen – vague figures of indisputable vulgarity – Pearce and Carshot – and more particularly a very terrible social phenomenon – Chitterlow.

Chitterlow blazed upon them with unheralded oppressive brilliance, the first time they were abroad together.

They were going along the front of the Leas to see a school-play in Sandgate – at the last moment Mrs Walshingham had been unable to come with them – when Chitterlow loomed up into the new world. He was wearing the suit of striped flannel and the straw hat that had followed Kipps' payment in advance for his course in elocution, his hand were deep in his side-pockets and animated the corners of his jacket, and his attentive gaze at the passing loungers, the faint smile under his boldly drawn nose, showed him engaged in studying character – no doubt for some forthcoming play.

'What HO!' said he, at the sight of Kipps, and swept off the straw hat with so ample a clutch of his great flat hand that it suggested to Helen's startled mind a conjuror about to palm a halfpenny.

''Ello, Chitt'low,' said Kipps, a little awkwardly, and not saluting.

Chitterlow hesitated. 'Half a mo', my boy,' he said, and arrested Kipps by extending a large hand over his chest. 'Excuse me, my dear, he said, bowing like his Russian count by way of apology to Helen, and with a smile that would have killed at a hundred yards. He effected a semi-confidential grouping of himself and Kipps, while Helen stood in white amazement.

'About that play,' he said.

''Ow about it?' asked Kipps, acutely aware of Helen.

'It's all right,' said Chitterlow. 'There's a strong smell of syndicate in the air, I may tell you. Strong.'

'That's aw right,' said Kipps.

'You needn't tell everybody,' said Chitterlow, with a transitory confidential hand to his mouth, which pointed the application of the 'everybody' just a trifle too strongly. 'But I think it's coming off. However—I mustn't detain you now. So long. You'll come round, eh?'

'Right you are,' said Kipps.

'To-night?'

'At eight.'

And then, and more in the manner of a Russian prince than any common count, Chitterlow bowed and withdrew. Just for a moment he allowed a conquering eye to challenge Helen's, and noted her a girl of quality. . . .

There was a silence between our lovers for a space.

'That,' said Kipps, with an allusive movement of the head, 'was Chitt'low.'

'Is he – a friend of yours?'

'In a way. . . . You see, I met 'im. Leastways 'e met me. Run into me with a bicycle, 'e did, and so we got talking together.'

He tried to appear at his ease. The young lady scrutinized his profile.

'What is he?'

''E's a Nacter chap,' said Kipps. 'Leastways 'e writes plays.'

'And sells them?'

'Partly.'

'Whom to?'

'Different people. Shares he sells. . . . It's all right, reely – I meant to tell you about him before.'

Helen looked over her shoulder to catch a view of Chitterlow's retreating aspect. It did not compel her complete confidence.

She turned to her lover, and said in a tone of quiet authority, 'You must tell me all about Chitterlow. Now.'

The explanation began. . . .

The School Play came almost as a relief to Kipps. In the flusterment of going in he could almost forget, for a time, his Laocoon* struggle to explain, and in the intervals he did his best to keep forgetting. But Helen, with a gentle insistence, resumed the explanation of Chitterlow as they returned towards Folkestone.

Chitterlow was confoundedly difficult to explain. You could hardly imagine!

There was an almost motherly anxiety in Helen's manner, blended with the resolution of a schoolmistress to get to the bottom of the affair. Kipps' ears were soon quite brightly red.

'Have you seen one of his plays?'

''E's tole me about one.'

'But on the stage.'

'No. He 'asn't 'ad any on the stage yet. That's all coming. . . .'

'Promise me,' she said in conclusion, 'you won't do anything without consulting me.'

And, of course, Kipps promised. 'Oo no!'

They went on their way in silence.

'One can't know everybody,' said Helen in general.

'Of course,' said Kipps, 'in a sort of way it was him that helped me to my money.' And he indicated in a confused manner the story of the advertisement. 'I don't like to drop 'im all at once,' he added.

Helen was silent for a space, and when she spoke she went off at a tangent. 'We shall live in London – soon,' she remarked. 'It's only while we are here.'

It was the first intimation she gave him of their post-nuptial prospects.

'We shall have a nice little flat somewhere, not too far west, and there we shall build up a circle of our own.'

II

All that declining summer Kipps was the pupil lover. He made an extraordinarily open secret of his desire for self-improvement; indeed Helen had to hint once or twice that his modest frankness was excessive, and all this new circle of friends did, each after his or her manner, everything that was possible to supplement Helen's efforts and help him to ease and skill in the more cultivated circles to which he had come. Coote was still the chief teacher, the tutor – there are so many little difficulties that a man may take to another man that he would not care to propound to the woman he loves – but they were all, so to speak, upon the staff. Even the freckled girl said to him once in a pleasant way, 'You mustn't say "contre temps", you must say "contraytom", when he borrowed that expression from *Manners and Rules*, and she tried, at his own suggestion, to give him clear ideas upon the subject of 'as' and 'has'. A certain confusion between these words was becoming evident, the first fruits of a lesson from Chitterlow on the aspirate. Hitherto he had discarded that dangerous letter almost altogether, but now he would pull up at words beginning with 'h' and draw a sawing breath – rather like a startled kitten – and then aspirate with vigour.

Said Kipps one say, '*As* 'e?' – I should say, ah – Has 'e? Ye know I got a lot of difficulty over them two words, which is which?'

'Well, "as" is a conjunction, and "has" is a verb.'

'I know,' said Kipps, 'but when is "has" a conjunction and when is "as" a verb?'

'Well,' said the freckled girl, preparing to be very lucid. 'It's *has* when it means one has, meaning having, but if it isn't it's *as*. As, for instance, one says 'e – I mean *he* – He has. But one says "as he has."'

'I see,' said Kipps. 'So I ought to say "as 'e"?'

'No, if you are asking a question you say *has* 'e – I mean he – 'as he?' She blushed quite brightly, but still clung to her air of lucidity.

'I see,' said Kipps. He was about to say something further, but he desisted. 'I got it much clearer now. *Has* 'e? *Has* 'e as. Yes.'

'If you remember about having.'

'Oo, I will, said Kipps. . . .

Miss Coote specialized in Kipps' artistic development. She had early formed an opinion that he had considerable artistic sensibility; his remarks on her work had struck her as decidedly intelligent, and whenever he called round to see them she would show him some work of art – now an illustrated book, now perhaps a colour print of a Botticelli, now the Hundred Best Paintings, now *Academy Pictures*, now a German art handbook, and now some magazine of furniture and design. 'I know you like these things,' she used to say, and Kipps said, 'Oo I *do*.' He soon acquired a little armoury of appreciative sayings. When presently the Walshinghams took him up to the Arts and Crafts, his deportment was intelligent in the extreme. For a time he kept a wary silence and suddenly pitched upon a colour print. 'That's rather nace,' he said to Mrs Walshingham. 'That lill' thing. There.' He always said things like that by preference to the mother rather than the daughter unless he was perfectly sure.

He quite took to Mrs Walshingham. He was impressed by her conspicuous tact and refinement; it seemed to him that the ladylike could go no further. She was always dressed with a delicate fussiness that was never disarranged, and even a sort of faded quality about her hair, and face, and bearing, and emotions, contributed to her effect. Kipps was not a big man, and commonly he did not feel a big man, but with Mrs Walshingham he always felt enormous and distended, as though he was a navvy who had taken some disagreeable poison which puffed him up inside his skin as a preliminary to bursting. He felt, too, as though he had been rolled in clay and his hair dressed with gum. And he felt that his voice was strident and his accent like somebody swinging a crowded pig's-pail in a free and careless manner. All this increased and enforced his respect for her. Her hand, which flitted often and again to his hand and arm, was singularly well shaped and cool. 'Arthur' she called him from the very beginning.

She did not so much positively teach and tell him as tactfully guide and infect him. Her conversation was not so much didactic as exemplary. She would tell him anecdotes of nice things done, of gentlemanly feats of graceful consideration; she would record her neat observations of people in trains and omnibuses, how, for example, a man had passed her change to the conductor, 'quite a common man he looked', but he had lifted his hat. She stamped Kipps so deeply with the hat-raising habit that he would uncover if he found himself in the same railway-ticket office with a lady, and so stand ceremoniously until the difficulties of change drove him to an apologetic provisional oblique resumption of his headgear. . . . And robbing these things of any air of personal application, she threw about them an abundant talk about her two children – she called them her Twin Jewels quite frequently – about their gifts, their temperaments, their ambition, their need of opportunity. They needed opportunity, she would say, as other people needed air. . . .

In his conversations with her Kipps always assumed – and she seemed to assume – that she was to join that home in London Helen foreshadowed; but he was surprised one day to gather that this was not to be the case. 'It wouldn't do,' said Helen, with decision. 'We want to make a circle of our own.'

'But won't she be a bit lonely down here?' asked Kipps.

'There's the Waces, and Mrs Prebble, and Mrs Bindon Botting, and – lots of people she knows.' And Helen dismissed this possibility. . . .

Young Walshingham's share in the educational syndicate was smaller. But he shone out when they went to London on that Arts and Crafts expedition. Then this rising man of affairs showed Kipps how to buy the more theatrical weeklies for consumption in the train, how to buy and what to buy in the way of cigarettes with gold tips and shilling cigars, and how to order hock for lunch and sparkling Moselle for dinner, how to calculate the fare of a hansom cab – penny a minute while he goes – how to look intelligently at an hotel tape, and how to sit still in a train like a thoughtful man instead of talking like a fool and giving yourself away. And he, too, would glance at the good time coming when they were to be in London for good and all.

That prospect expanded and developed particulars. It presently took up a large part of Helen's conversation. Her conversations with Kipps were never of a grossly sentimental sort; there was a shyness of speech in that matter with both of them; but these new adumbrations were at least as interesting, and not so directly disagreeable, as the clear-cut intimations of personal defect that for a time had so greatly chastened Kipps' delight in her presence. The future presented itself with an almost perfect frankness as a joint campaign of Mrs Walshingham's Twin Jewels upon the Great World, with Kipps in the capacity of baggage and supply. They would still be dreadfully poor, of course – this amazed Kipps, but he said nothing – until 'Brudderkins' began to succeed; but if they were clever and lucky they might do a great deal.

When Helen spoke of London a brooding look, as of one who contemplates a distant country, came into her eyes. Already it seemed they had the nucleus of a set. Brudderkins was a member of the Theatrical Judges, an excellent and influential little club of journalists and literary people, and he knew Shimer and Stargate and Whiffle of the 'Red Dragons', and besides these were the Revels. They knew the Revels quite well. Sidney Revel, before his rapid rise to prominence as a writer of epigrammatic essays that were quite above the ordinary public, had been an assistant master at one of the best Folkestone schools. Brudderkins had brought him home to tea several times, and it was he had first suggested Helen should try and write. 'It's perfectly easy,' Sidney had said. He had been writing occasional things for the evening papers and for the weekly reviews even at that time. Then he had gone up to London, and had almost unavoidably become a dramatic critic. Those brilliant essays had followed, and then *Red Hearts a Beating*, the romance that had made him. It was a tale of spirited adventure, full of youth and beauty and naïve passion and generous devotion, bold, as the *Bookman* said, and frank in places, but never in the slightest degree morbid. He had met and married an American widow with quite a lot of money, and they had made a very distinct place for themselves, Kipps learnt, in the literary and artistic society of London. Helen seemed to dwell on the Revels a great deal; it was her exemplary story, and when she spoke of Sidney – she often called him Sidney – she would become thoughtful. She spoke most of him, naturally, because she had still to meet Mrs Revel. . . . Certainly they would be in the world in no time, even if the distant connection with the Beauprés family came to nothing.

Kipps gathered that with his marriage and the movement to London they were to undergo that subtle change of name Coote had first adumbrated. They were to become 'Cuyps', Mr and Mrs Cuyps. Or was it Cuyp?

'It'll be rum at first,' said Kipps.

'I dessay I shall soon get into it,' he said. . . .

So in their several ways they all contributed to enlarge and refine and exercise the intelligence of Kipps. And behind all these other influences, and as it were presiding over and correcting these influences, was Kipps' nearest friend, Coote, a sort of master of the ceremonies. You figure his face, blowing slightly with solicitude, his slate-coloured, projecting, but not unkindly eye intent upon our hero. The thing, he thought, was going off admirably. He studied Kipps' character immensely. He would discuss him with his sister, with Mrs Walshingham, with the freckled girl, with any one who would stand it. 'He is an interesting character,' he would say, 'likeable – a sort of gentleman by instinct. He takes to all these things. He improves every day. He'll soon get Sang Froid. We took him up just in time. He wants now—Well—Next year, perhaps, if there is a good Extention Literature course he might go in for it. He wants to go in for something like that.'

'He's going in for his bicycle now,' said Mrs Walshingham.

'That's all right for summer,' said Coote, 'but he wants to go in for some serious intellectual interest, something to take him out of himself a little more. Savoir Faire and self-forgetfulness is more than half the secret of Sang Froid.'

III

The world, as Coote presented it, was in part an endorsement, in part an amplification, and in part a rectification of the world of Kipps – the world that derived from the old couple in New Romney and had been developed in the Emporium; the world, in fact, of common British life. There was the same subtle sense of social gradation that had moved Mrs Kipps to prohibit intercourse with labourers' children, and the same dread of anything 'common' that had kept the personal quality of Mr Shalford's establishment so high. But now a certain disagreeable doubt about Kipps' own position was removed, and he stood with Coote inside the sphere of gentlemen assured. Within the sphere of gentlemen there are distinctions of rank indeed, but none of class; there are the Big People, and the modest, refined, gentlemanly little people, like Coote, who may even dabble in the professions and counterless trades; there are lords and magnificences, and there are gentle-folk who have to manage – but they can all call on one another, they preserve a general equality of deportment throughout, they constitute that great state within the state – Society.

'But reely,' said the Pupil, 'not what you call being in Society?'

'Yes,' said Coote. 'Of course, down here, one doesn't see much of it, but there's local society. It has the same rules.'

'Calling and all that?'

'Precisely,' said Coote.

Kipps thought, whistled a bar, and suddenly broached a question of conscience. 'I often wonder,' he said, 'whether I oughtn't to dress for dinner – when I'm alone 'ere.'

Coote protruded his lips and reflected. 'Not full dress,' he adjudicated; 'that would be a little excessive. But you should *change*, you know. Put on a mess jacket, and that sort of thing – easy dress. That is what *I* should do, certainly, if I wasn't in harness – and poor.'

He coughed modestly, and patted his hair behind.

And after that the washing-bill of Kipps quadrupled, and he was to be seen at times by the bandstand with his light summer overcoat unbuttoned, to give a glimpse of his nice white tie. He and Coote would be smoking the gold-tipped cigarettes young Walshingham had prescribed as 'chic', and appreciating the music highly. 'That's – puff – a very nice bit,' Kipps would say; or better, 'That's nace'. And at the first grunts of the loyal anthem up they stood with religiously uplifted hats. Whatever else you might call them, you could never call them disloyal.

The boundary of Society was admittedly very close to Coote and Kipps, and a leading solicitude of the true gentleman was to detect clearly those 'beneath' him, and to behave towards them in a proper spirit. 'It's jest there it's so 'ard for me,' said Kipps. He had to cultivate a certain 'distance' to acquire altogether the art of checking the presumption of bounders and old friends. It was difficult, Coote admitted.

'I got mixed up with this lot 'ere,' said Kipps. 'That's what's so harkward – I mean awkward.'

'You could give them a hint,' said Coote.

"Ow?"

'Oh – the occasion will suggest something.'

The occasion came one early-closing night, when Kipps was sitting in a canopy chair near the bandstand with his summer overcoat fully open, and a new Gibus pulled slightly forward over his brow, waiting for Coote. They were to hear the band for an hour, and then go down to assist Miss Coote and the freckled girl in trying over some Beethoven duets, if they remembered them, that is, sufficiently well. And as Kipps lounged back in his chair and occupied his mind with his favourite amusement on such evenings, which consisted chiefly in supposing that every one about him was wondering who he was, came a rude rap at the canvas back and the voice of Pearce.

'It's nice to be a gentleman,' said Pearce, and swung a penny chair into position, while Buggins appeared smiling agreeably on the other side, and leant upon his stick. *He was smoking a common briar pipe*!

Two real ladies, very fashionably dressed, and sitting close at hand, glanced quickly at Pearce, and then away again, and it was evident *their* wonder was at an end.

'*He's* all right,' said Buggins, removing his pipe and surveying Kipps.

''Ello, Buggins!' said Kipps, not too cordially. ''Ow goes it?'

'All right. Holidays next week. If you don't look out, Kipps, I shall be on the Continong before you. Eh?'

'You going t'Boologne?'

'Ra-ther. Parley vous Francey. You bet.'

'*I* shall 'ave a bit of a run over there one of these days,' said Kipps.

There came a pause. Pearce applied the top of his stick to his mouth for a space, and regarded Kipps. Then he glanced at the people about them.

'I say, Kipps,' he said in a distinct loud voice, 'see 'er Ladyship lately?'

Kipps perceived the audience was to be impressed, but he responded half-heartedly. 'No, I 'aven't,' he said.

'She was along of Sir William the other night,' said Pearce, still loud and clear, 'and she asked to be remembered to you.'

It seemed to Kipps that one of the two ladies smiled faintly, and said something to the other, and then certainly they glanced at Pearce. Kipps flushed scarlet. '*Did* she?' he answered.

Buggins laughed good-humouredly over his pipe.

'Sir William suffers a lot from his gout,' Pearce continued unabashed.

(Buggins much amused with his pipe between his teeth.)

Kipps became aware of Coote at hand.

Coote nodded rather distantly to Pearce. 'Hope I haven't kept you waiting, Kipps,' he said.

'I kep' a chair for you,' said Kipps, and removed a guardian foot.

'But you've got your friends,' said Coote.

'Oh, *we* don't mind,' said Pearce, cordially, 'the more the merrier;' and, 'Why don't you get a chair, Buggins?' Buggins shook his head in a sort of aside to Pearce, and Coote coughed behind his hand.

'Been kep' late at business?' asked Pearce.

Coote turned quite pale, and pretended not to hear. His eyes sought in space for a time, and with a convulsive movement he recognized a distant acquaintance and raised his hat.

Pearce had also become a little pale. He addressed himself to Kipps in an undertone.

'Mr Coote, isn't he?' he asked.

Coote addressed himself to Kipps directly and exclusively. His manner had the calm of extreme tension.

'I'm rather late,' he said. 'I think we ought almost to be going on *now*.'

Kipps stood up. 'That's all right,' he said.

'Which way are you going?' said Pearce, standing also, and brushing some crumbs of cigarette ash from his sleeve.

For a moment Coote was breathless. 'Thank you,' he said, and gasped. Then he delivered the necessary blow, 'I don't think we're in need of your society, you know,' and turned away.

Kipps found himself falling over chairs and things in the wake of Coote, and then they were clear of the crowd.

For a space Coote said nothing; then he remarked abruptly, and quite angrily for him, 'I think that was *awful* Cheek!'

Kipps made no reply. . . .

The whole thing was an interesting little object-lesson in 'distance', and it stuck in the front of Kipps' mind for a long time. He had particularly vivid the face of Pearce with an expression between astonishment and anger. He felt as though he had struck Pearce in the face under circumstances that gave Pearce no power to reply. He did not attend very much to the duets, and even forgot at the end of one of them to say how perfectly lovely it was.

IV

But you must not imagine that the national ideal of a gentleman, as Coote developed it, was all a matter of deportment and selectness, a mere isolation from debasing associations. There is a Serious Side, a deeper aspect of the true True Gentleman. But it is not vocal. The True Gentleman does not wear his heart on his sleeve. For example, he is deeply religious, as Coote was, as Mrs Walshingham was; but outside the walls of a church it never appears, except perhaps now and then in a pause, in a profound look, in a sudden avoidance. In quite a little while Kipps also had learnt the pause, the profound look, the sudden avoidance, that final refinement of spirituality, impressionistic piety.

And the True Gentleman is patriotic also. When one saw Coote lifting his hat to the National Anthem, then perhaps one got a glimpse of what patriotic emotions, what worship, the polish of a gentleman may hide. Or singing out his deep notes against the Hosts of Midian, in the St Stylites' choir; then indeed you plumbed his spiritual side.

> Christian, dost thou heed them
>   On the holy ground,
> How the hosts of Mid-i-an
>   Prowl and prowl around?
> Christian, up and smai-it them. . . .*

But these were but gleams. For the rest, Religion, Nationality, Passion, Finance, Politics, much more so those cardinal issues Birth and Death, the True Gentleman skirted about, and became facially rigid towards, and ceased to speak, and panted and blew.

'One doesn't talk of that sort of thing,' Coote would say, with a gesture of the knuckly hand.

'O' course,' Kipps would reply, with an equal significance.

Profundities. Deep, as it were, blowing to deep.

One does not talk, but on the other hand one is punctilious to do. Action speaks. Kipps – in spite of the fact that the Walshinghams were more than a little lax – Kipps, who had formerly flitted Sunday after Sunday from one Folkestone church to another, had now a sitting of his own, paid for duly, at Saint Stylites. There he was to be seen, always at the surplice evening service, and sometimes of a morning, dressed with a sober precision, and with an eye on Coote in the chancel. No difficulties now about finding the place in his book. He became a communicant again – he had lapsed soon after his confirmation when the young lady in the costume-room who was his adopted sister left the Emporium – and he would sometimes go round to the Vestry for Coote, after the service. One evening he was introduced to the Hon. and Rev. Densmore. He was much too confused to say anything, and the noble cleric had nothing to say, but they were introduced. . . .

No! You must not imagine that the national ideal of a gentleman is without its 'serious side', without even its stern and uncompromising side. The imagination, no doubt, refuses to see Coote displaying extraordinary refinements of courage upon the stricken field, but in the walks of peace there is sometimes sore need of sternness. Charitable as one may be, one must admit there are people who *do* things – impossible things; people who place themselves 'out of it' in countless ways; people, moreover, who are by a sort of predestination out of it from the beginning; and against these Society has invented a terrible protection for its Cootery – the Cut. The cut is no joke for any one. It is excommunication. You may be cut by an individual, you may be cut by a set, or you may be – and this is so tragic that beautiful romances have been written about it – 'Cut by the County'. One figures Coote discharging this last duty and cutting somebody – Coote, erect and pale, never speaking, going past with eyes of pitiless slate, lower jaw protruding a little, face pursed up and cold and stiff. . . .

It never dawned upon Kipps that he would one day have to face this terrible front, to be to Coote not only as one dead, but as one gone more than a stage or so in decay, cut and passed, banned and outcast for ever. It never dawned upon either of them.

Yet so it was to be!

One cannot hide any longer that all this fine progress of Kipps is doomed to end in collapse. So far, indeed, you have seen him ascend. You have seen him becoming more refined and careful day by day, more carefully dressed, less clumsy in the uses of social life. You have seen the gulf widening between himself and his former low associates. I have brought you at last to the vision of him, faultlessly dressed and posed, in an atmosphere of candlelight and chanting, in his own sitting, his own sitting! in one of the most fashionable churches in Folkestone.... I have refrained from the lightest touch upon the tragic note that must now creep into my tale. Yet the net of his low connections has been about his feet, and, moreover, there was something interwoven in his being. . . .

Chapter Six

Discords

One day Kipps set out upon his newly mastered bicycle to New Romney, to break the news of his engagement to his Uncle and Aunt – positively. He was now a finished cyclist, but as yet an unseasoned one; the south-west wind, even in its summer guise, as one meets it in the Marsh, is the equivalent of a reasonable hill, and ever and again he got off and refreshed himself by a spell of walking. He was walking just outside New Romney, preparatory to his triumphal entry (one hand off), when abruptly he came upon Ann Pornick.

It chanced he was thinking about her at the time. He had been thinking curious things; whether, after all, the atmosphere of New Romney and the Marsh had not some difference, some faint impalpable quality that was missing in the great and fashionable world of Folkestone behind there on the hill. Here there was a homeliness, a familiarity. He had noted as he passed that old Mr Cliffordown's gate had been mended with a fresh piece of string. In Folkestone he didn't take notice, and he didn't care if they built three hundred houses. Come to think of it, that was odd. It was fine and grand to have twelve hundred a year; it was fine to go about on trams and omnibuses and think not a person abroad was as rich as one's self; it was fine to buy and order this and that and never have any work to do, and to be engaged to a girl distantly related to the Earl of Beauprés; but yet there had been a zest in the old time out here, a rare zest in the holidays, in sunlight, on the sea beach, and in the High Street, that failed from these new things. He thought of those bright windows of holiday that had seemed to glorious to him in the retrospect from his apprentice days. It was strange that now, amidst his present splendours, they were glorious still!

All those things were over now – perhaps that was it! Something had happened to the world, and the old light had been turned out. He himself was changed, and Sid was changed, terribly changed, and Ann, no doubt, was changed.

He thought of her with the hair blown about her flushed cheeks as they stood together after their race. . . .

Certainly she must be changed, and all the magic she had been fraught with to the very hem of her short petticoats gone, no doubt, for ever. And as he thought that, or before and while he thought it – for he came to all these things in his own vague and stumbling way – he looked up, and there was Ann!

She was seven years older, and greatly altered; yet for the moment it seemed to him that she had not changed at all. 'Ann!' he said; and she, with a lifting note, 'It's Art Kipps!'

Then he became aware of changes – improvements. She was as pretty as she had promised to be, her blue eyes as dark as his memory of them, and with a quick, high colour; but now Kipps by several inches was the taller again. She was dressed in a simple grey dress, that showed her very clearly as a straight and healthy little woman, and her hat was Sundayfied, with pink flowers. She looked soft and warm and welcoming. Her face was alight to Kipps with her artless gladness at their encounter.

'It's Art Kipps!' she said.

'Rather,' said Kipps.

'You got your holidays?'

It flashed upon Kipps that Sid had not told her of his great fortune. Much regretful meditation upon Sid's behaviour had convinced him that he himself was to blame for exasperating boastfulness in that affair, and this time he took care not to err in that direction. So he erred in the other.

'I'm taking a bit of a 'oliday,' he said.

'So'm I,' said Ann.

'You been for a walk?' asked Kipps.

Ann showed him a bunch of wayside flowers.

'It's a long time since I seen you, Ann. Why, 'ow long must it be? Seven – eight years nearly.'

'It don't do to count,' said Ann.

'It don't look like it,' said Kipps, with the slightest emphasis.

'You got a moustache,' said Ann, smelling her flowers and looking at him over them, not without admiration.

Kipps blushed. . . .

Presently they came to the bifurcation of the roads.

'I'm going down this way to mother's cottage,' said Ann.

'I'll come a bit your way, if I may.'

In New Romney social distinctions that are primary realities in Folkestone are absolutely non-existent, and it seemed quite permissible for him to walk with Ann, for all that she was no more than a servant. They talked with remarkable ease to one another, they slipped into a vein of intimate reminiscence in the easiest manner. In a little while Kipps was amazed to find Ann and himself at this –

'You r'member that half-sixpence? What we cut togevver?'

'Yes?'

'I got it still.'

She hesitated. 'Funny, wasn't it?' she said, and then, 'You got yours, Artie?'

'Rather,' said Kipps. 'What do *you* think?' and wondered in his heart of hearts why he had never looked at that sixpence for so long.

Ann smiled at him frankly.

'I didn't expect you'd keep it,' she said. 'I thought often – it was silly to keep mine.'

'Besides,' she reflected, 'it didn't mean anything really.'

She glanced at him as she spoke and met his eye.

'Oh, didn't it!' said Kipps, a little late with his response, and realizing his infidelity to Helen even as he spoke.

'It didn't mean much anyhow,' said Ann. 'You still in the drapery?'

'I'm living at Folkestone,' began Kipps, and decided that that sufficed. 'Didn't Sid tell you he met me?'

'No! Here?'

'Yes. The other day. 'Bout a week or more ago.'

'That was before I came.'

'Ah, that was it,' said Kipps.

''E's got on,' said Ann. 'Got 'is own shop now, Artie.'

''E tole me.'

They found themselves outside Muggett's cottages. 'You going in?' said Kipps.

'I s'pose so,' said Ann.

They both hung upon the pause. Ann took a plunge.

'D'you often come to New Romney?' she asked.

'I ride over a bit at times,' said Kipps.

Another pause. Ann held out her hand.

'I'm glad I seen you,' she said.

Extraordinary impulses arose in neglected parts of Kipps' being. 'Ann,' he said, and stopped.

'Yes,' said she, and was bright to him.

They looked at one another.

All, and more than all, of those first emotions of his adolescence had come back to him. Her presence banished a multitude of countervailing considerations. It was Ann more than ever. She stood breathing close to him with her soft-looking lips a little apart and gladness in her eyes.

'I'm awful glad to see you again,' he said; 'it brings back old times.'

'Doesn't it?'

Another pause. He would have liked to have had a long talk to her, to have gone for a walk with her or something, to have drawn nearer to her in any conceivable way, and above all to have had some more of the appreciation that shone in her eyes, but a vestige of Folkestone, still clinging to him, told him it 'wouldn't do'. 'Well,' he said, 'I must be getting on,' and turned away reluctantly, with a will under compulsion. . . .

When he looked back from the corner she was still at the gate. She was perhaps a little disconcerted by his retreat. He felt that. He hesitated for a moment, half turned, stood, and suddenly did great things with his hat. That hat! The wonderful hat of our civilization! . . .

In another minute he was engaged in a singularly absent-minded conversation with his Uncle about the usual topics.

His Uncle was very anxious to buy him a few upright clocks as an investment for subsequent sale. And there were also some very nice globes, one terrestrial and the other celestial, in a shop at Lydd that would look well in a drawing-room, and inevitably increase in value. . . . Kipps either did or did not agree to this purchase, he was unable to recollect.

The south-west wind perhaps helped him back; at any rate he found himself through Dymchurch without having noticed the place. There came an odd effect as he drew near Hythe. The hills on the left and the trees on the right seemed to draw together and close in upon him until his way was straight and narrow. He could not turn round on that treacherous half-tamed machine, but he knew that behind him, he knew so well, spread the wide vast flatness of the Marsh shining under the afternoon sky. In some way this was material to his thoughts.

And as he rode through Hythe he came upon the idea that there was a considerable amount of incompatibility between the existence of one who was practically a gentleman and of Ann.

In the neighbourhood of Seabrook he began to think he had, in some subtle way, lowered himself by walking along by the side of Ann. . . . After all, she was only a servant.

Ann!

She called out all the least gentlemanly instincts of his nature. There had been a moment in their conversation when he had quite distinctly thought it would really be an extremely nice thing for some one to kiss her lips. . . . There was something warming about Ann – at least for Kipps. She impressed him as having, somewhen during their vast interval of separation, contrived to make herself in some distinctive way his.

Fancy keeping that half-sixpence all this time!

It was the most flattering thing that ever happened to Kipps.

II

He found himself presently sitting over *The Art of Conversing*, lost in the strangest musings. He got up, walked about, became stagnant at the window for a space, roused himself, and by way of something lighter tried *Sesame and Lilies*. From that too his attention wandered. He sat back. Anon he smiled, anon sighed. He arose, pulled his keys from his pocket, looked at them, decided, and went upstairs. He opened the little yellow box that had been the nucleus of all his possessions in the world, and took out a small 'Escritoire', the very humblest sort of present, and opened it – kneeling. And there in the corner was a little packet of paper, sealed as a last defence against any prying invader with red sealing-wax. It had gone untouched for years. He held this little packet between finger and thumb for a moment, regarding it, and then put down the escritoire and broke the seal. . . .

As he was getting into bed that night he remembered something for the first time!

'Dash it!' he said. 'Deshed if I told 'em *this time*. . . . *Well*!

'I shall 'ave to go over to New Romney again!'

He got into bed, and remained sitting pensively on the pillow for a space.

'Rum world,' he reflected, after a vast interval.

Then he recalled that she had noticed his moustache. He embarked upon a sea of egotistical musing.

He imagined himself telling Ann how rich he was. What a surprise that would be for her!

Finally he sighed profoundly, blew out his candle, and snuggled down, and in a little while he was asleep. . . .

But the next morning, and at intervals afterwards, he found himself thinking of Ann, – Ann the bright, the desirable, the welcoming, and with an extraordinary streakiness he wanted quite badly to go, and then as badly not to go, over to New Romney again.

Sitting on the Leas in the afternoon, he had an idea. 'I ought to 'ave told 'er, I suppose, about my being engaged.

'Ann!'

All sorts of dreams and impressions that had gone clean out of his mental existence came back to him, changed and brought up-to-date to fit her altered presence. He thought of how he had gone back to New Romney for his Christmas holidays, determined to kiss her, and of the awful blankness of the discovery that she had gone away.

It seemed incredible now, and yet not wholly incredible, that he had cried real tears for her, – how many years was it ago?

III

Daily I should thank my Maker that He did not delegate to me the Censorship of the world of men. I should temper a fierce injustice with a spasmodic indecision, that would prolong rather than mitigate the bitterness of the Day. For human dignity, for all conscious human superiority I should lack the beginnings of charity; for bishops, prosperous schoolmasters, judges, and all large respect-pampered souls. And more especially bishops, towards whom I bear an atavistic Viking grudge, dreaming not infrequently and with invariable zest of galleys and landings, and well-known living ornaments of the episcopal bench sprinting inland on twinkling gaiters before my thirsty blade – all these people, I say, I should treat below their deserts; but, on the other hand, for such as Kipps—There the exasperating indecisions would come in. The Judgment would be arrested at Kipps. Every one and everything would wait. The balance would sway and sway, and whenever it heeled towards an adverse decision, my finger would set it swaying again. Kings, warriors, statesmen, brilliant women, 'personalities' panting with indignation, headline humanity in general, would stand undamned, unheeded, or be damned in the most casual manner for their importunity, while my eye went about for anything possible that could be said on behalf of Kipps. . . . Albeit I fear nothing can save him from condemnation upon this present score, that within two days he was talking to Ann again.

One seeks excuses. Overnight there had been an encounter of Chitterlow and young Walshingham in his presence that had certainly warped his standards. They had called within a few minutes of each other, and the two, swayed by virile attentions to Old Methuselah Three Stars, had talked against each other, over and at the hospitable presence of Kipps. Walshingham had seemed to win at the beginning, but finally Chitterlow had made a magnificent display of vociferation and swept him out of existence. At the beginning Chitterlow had opened upon the great profits of playwrights, and young Walshingham had capped him at once with a cynical but impressive display of knowledge of the High Finance. If Chitterlow boasted his thousands, young Walshingham boasted his hundreds of thousands, and was for a space left in sole possession of the stage, juggling with the wealth of nations. He was going on by way of Financial Politics to the Overman, before Chitterlow recovered from his first check, and came back to victory. 'Talking of Women,' said Chitterlow, coming in abruptly upon some things not generally known, beyond Walshingham's more immediate circle, about a recently departed Empire-builder; 'Talking of Women and the way they Get at a man—'

(Though, as a matter of fact, they had been talking of the Corruption of Society by Speculation.)

Upon this new topic Chitterlow was soon manifestly invincible. He knew so much, he had known so many. Young Walshingham did his best with epigrams and reservations, but even to Kipps it was evident that this was a book-learned depravity. One felt Walshingham had never known the inner realities of passion. But Chitterlow convinced and amazed. He had run away with girls, he had been run away with by girls, he

had been in love with several at a time – 'not counting Bessie' –
he had loved and lost, he had loved and refrained, and he had
loved and failed. He threw remarkable lights upon the moral
state of America – in which country he had toured with great
success. He set his talk to the tune of one of Mr Kipling's best-
known songs.* He told an incident of simply romantic passion,
a delirious dream of love and beauty in a Saturday to Monday
steamboat trip up the Hudson, and tagged his end with 'I learnt
about women from 'er!' After that he adopted the refrain, and
then lapsed into the praises of Kipling. 'Little Kipling,' said
Chitterlow, with the familiarity of affection, '*he* knows,' and
broke into quotation –

> I've taken my fun where I've found it;
>   I've rogued and I've ranged in my time;
> I've 'ad my picking of sweet'earts,
>   An' four of the lot was Prime.

(These things, I say, affect the moral standards of the best of
us.)

'*I'd* have liked to have written that,' said Chitterlow. 'That's
Life, that is! but go and put it on the Stage, put even a bit of the
Realities of Life on the Stage and see what they'll do to you!
Only Kipling could venture on a job like that. That Poem
KNOCKED me! I won't say Kipling hasn't knocked me before
and since, but that was a Fair Knock Out. And yet – you know
– there's one thing in it . . . this –

> I've taken my fun where I've found it,
>   And now I must pay for my fun,
> For the more you 'ave known o' the others,
>   The less will you settle to one.

Well. In my case anyhow – I don't know how much that proves,
seeing I'm exceptional in so many things and there's no good
denying it – but so far as I'm concerned – I tell you two, but, of
course, you needn't let it go any farther – I've been perfectly
faithful to Muriel ever since I married her – ever since. . . . Not
once. Not even by accident have I ever said or done anything in
the slightest—' His little brown eye became pensive after this
flattering intimacy, and the gorgeous draperies of his abundant
voice fell into graver folds. '*I learnt about women from 'er,*' he
said impressively.

'Yes,' said Walshingham, getting into the hinder spaces of that splendid pause, 'a man must know about women. And the only sound way of learning is the experimental method.'

'If you want to know about the experimental method, my boy,' said Chitterlow, resuming. . . .

So they talked. *Ex pede Herculem*, as Coote, that cultivated polyglot, would have put it. And in the small hours Kipps went to bed, with his brain whirling with words and whisky, and sat for an unconscionable time upon his bed edge, musing sadly upon the unmanly monogamy that had cast its shadow upon his career, musing with his thoughts pointing round more and more certainly to the possibility of at least duplicity with Ann.

IV

For some days he had been refraining with some insistence from going off to New Romney again. . . .

I do not know if this may count in palliation of his misconduct. Men, real Strong-Souled, Healthy Men, should be, I suppose, impervious to conversational atmospheres, but I have never claimed for Kipps a place at these high levels. The fact remains, that next day he spent the afternoon with Ann, and found no scruple in displaying himself a budding lover.

He had met her in the High Street, had stopped her, and almost on the spur of the moment had boldly proposed a walk, 'for the sake of old times'.

'*I* don't mind,' said Ann.

Her consent almost frightened Kipps. His imagination had not carried him to that. 'It would be a lark,' said Kipps, and looked up the street and down. 'Now?' he said.

'I don't mind a bit, Artie. I was just going for a walk along towards St Mary's.'

'Let's go that way be'ind the church,' said Kipps; and presently they found themselves drifting seaward in a mood of pleasant commonplace. For a while they talked of Sid. It went clean out of Kipps' head, at that early stage even, that Ann was a 'girl' according to the exposition of Chitterlow, and for a time he remembered only that she was Ann. But afterwards, with the reek of that talk in his head, he lapsed a little from that personal

relation. They came out upon the beach and sat down in a
tumbled pebbly place where a meagre grass and patches of sea
poppy were growing, and Kipps reclined on his elbow and
tossed pebbles in his hand, and Ann sat up, sunlit, regarding
him. They talked in fragments. They exhausted Sid, they
exhausted Ann, and Kipps was chary of his riches.

He declined to a faint love-making. 'I got that 'arf-sixpence
still,' he said.

'Reely?'

That changed the key. 'I always kept mine, some'ow,' said
Ann; and there was a pause.

They spoke of how often they had thought of each other
during those intervening years. Kipps may have been untruthful,
but Ann perhaps was not. 'I met people here and there,' said
Ann; 'but I never met any one quite like you, Artie.'

'It's jolly our meeting again, anyhow,' said Kipps. 'Look at
that ship out there. She's pretty close in. . . .'

He had a dull period, became, indeed, almost pensive, and
then he was enterprising for a while. He tossed up his pebbles
so that, as if by accident, they fell on Ann's hand. Then, very
penitently, he stroked the place. That would have led to all sorts
of coquetries on the part of Flo Bates, for example, but it
disconcerted and checked Kipps to find Ann made no objection,
smiled pleasantly down on him, with eyes half shut because of
the sun. She was taking things very much for granted.

He began to talk, and Chitterlow standards resuming possession of him, he said he had never forgotten her.

'I never forgotten you either, Artie,' she said. 'Funny, 'sn't
it?'

It impressed Kipps also as funny.

He became reminiscent, and suddenly a warm summer's
evening came back to him. 'Remember them cockchafers, Ann?'
he said. But the reality of the evening he recalled was not the
chase of cockchafers. The great reality that had suddenly arisen
between them was that he had never kissed Ann in his life. He
looked up, and there were her lips.

He had wanted to very badly, and his memory leaped and
annihilated an interval. That old resolution came back to him,
and all sorts of new resolutions passed out of mind. And he had
learnt something since those boyish days. This time he did not

ask. He went on talking, his nerves began very faintly to quiver, and his mind grew bright.

Presently, having satisfied himself that there was no one to see, he sat up beside her, and remarked upon the clearness of the air, and how close Dungeness seemed to them. Then they came upon a pause again.

'Ann,' he whispered, and put an arm that quivered about her.

She was mute and unresisting, and, as he was to remember, solemn.

He turned her face towards him and kissed her lips, and she kissed him back again – kisses frank and tender as a child's.

§ v

It was curious that in the retrospect he did not find nearly the satisfaction in this infidelity he had imagined was there. It was no doubt desperately doggish, doggish to an almost Chitterlow-esque degree, to recline on the beach at Littlestone with a 'girl', to make love to her and to achieve the triumph of kissing her, when he was engaged to another 'girl' at Folkestone; but somehow these two people were not 'girls', they were Ann and Helen. Particularly Helen declined to be considered as a 'girl'. And there was something in Ann's quietly friendly eyes, in her frank smile, in the naïve pressure of her hand, there was something undefended and welcoming that imparted a flavour to the business upon which he had not counted. He had learnt about women from her. That refrain ran through his mind and deflected his thoughts, but, as a matter of fact, he had learnt about nothing but himself.

He wanted very much to see Ann some more and explain— He did not clearly know what it was he wanted to explain.

He did not clearly know anything. It is the last achievement of the intelligence to get all of one's life into one coherent scheme, and Kipps was only in a measure more aware of himself as a whole than is a tree. His existence was an affair of dissolving and recurring moods. When he thought of Helen or Ann, or any of his friends, he thought sometimes of this aspect and some-times of that – and often one aspect was finally incongruous with another. He loved Helen, he revered Helen. He was also beginning to hate her with some intensity. When he thought of that expedition to Lympne, profound, vague, beautiful emotions flooded his being; when he thought of paying calls with her perforce, or of her latest comment, on his bearing, he found himself rebelliously composing fierce and pungent insults, couched in the vernacular. But Ann, whom he had seen so much less of, was a simpler memory. She was pretty, she was almost softly feminine, and she was possible to his imagination just exactly where Helen was impossible. More than anything else, she carried the charm of respect for him, the slightest glance of her eyes was balm for his perpetually wounded self-conceit.

Chance suggestions it was set the tune of his thoughts, and his state of health and repletion gave the colour. Yet somehow he had this at least almost clear in his mind, that to have gone to see Ann a second time, to have implied that she had been in possession of his thoughts through all this interval, and, above all, to have kissed her, was shabby and wrong. Only unhappily this much of lucidity had come now just a few hours after it was needed.

VI

Four days after this it was that Kipps got up so late. He got up late, cut his chin while shaving, kicked a slipper into his sponge bath, and said 'Dash!'

Perhaps you know these intolerable mornings, dear Reader, when you seem to have neither the heart nor the strength to rise, and your nervous adjustments are all wrong and your fingers thumbs, and you hate the very birds for singing. You feel inadequate to any demand whatever. Often such awakenings follow a poor night's rest, and commonly they mean indiscriminate eating, or those subtle mental influences old Kipps ascribed to 'Foozle Ile' in the system, or worry. And with Kipps – albeit Chitterlow had again been his guest overnight – assuredly worry had played a leading *rôle*. Troubles had been gathering upon him for days, there had been a sort of concentration of these hosts of Midian overnight, and in the grey small hours Kipps had held his review.

The predominating trouble marched under this banner –

MR KIPPS

MRS BINDON BOTTING

At Home,

Thursday, September 16th.

Anagrams, 4 to 6.30.   RSVP

---

a banner that was the facsimile of a card upon his looking-glass in the room below. And in relation to this terribly significant document, things had come to a pass with Helen, that he would only describe in his own expressive idiom as 'words'.

It had long been a smouldering issue between them that Kipps was not availing himself with any energy or freedom of the opportunities he had of social exercises, much less was he seeking additional opportunities. He had, it was evident, a peculiar dread of that universal afternoon enjoyment, the Call, and Helen made it unambiguously evident that this dread was 'silly' and had to be overcome. His first display of this unmanly weakness occurred at the Cootes on the day before he kissed Ann. They were all there, chatting very pleasantly, when the little servant with the big cap announced the younger Miss Wace.

Whereupon Kipps manifested a lively horror and rose partially from his chair. 'O Gum!' he protested. 'Carn't I go upstairs?'

Then he sank back, for it was too late. Very probably the younger Miss Wace had heard him as she came in.

Helen said nothing of that, though her manner may have shown her surprise, but afterwards she told Kipps he must get used to seeing people, and suggested that he should pay a series of calls with Mrs Walshingham and herself. Kipps gave a reclutant assent at the time, and afterwards displayed a talent for evasion that she had not expected in him. At last she did succeed in securing him for a call upon Punchafer of Radnor Park – a particularly easy call, because, Miss Punchafer being so deaf, one could say practically what one liked – and then outside the gate he shirked again. 'I can't go in,' he said, in a faded voice.

'You must,' said Helen, beautiful as ever, but even more than a little hard and forbidding.

'I can't.'

He produced his handkerchief hastily, thrust it to his face, and regarded her over it with rounded hostile eyes.

'Possible,' he said in a hoarse, strange voice out of the handkerchief. 'Nozzez bleedin'.'

But that was the end of his power of resistance, and when the rally for the Anagram Tea occurred, she bore down his feeble protests altogether. She insisted. She said frankly, 'I am going to give you a good talking to about this;' and she did. . . .

From Coote he gathered something of the nature of Anagrams and Anagram parties. An anagram, Coote explained, was a word spelt the same way as another, only differently arranged; as, for instance, TOCOE would be an anagram for his own name Coote.

'TOCOE,' repeated Kipps, very carefully.

'Or TOECO,' said Coote.

'Or TOECO,' said Kipps, assisting his poor head by nodding it at each letter.

'Toe Company like,' he said, in his efforts to comprehend.

When Kipps was clear what an anagram meant, Coote came to the second heading, the Tea. Kipps gathered there might be from thirty to sixty people present, and that each one would have an anagram pinned on. 'They gave you a card to put your guesses on, rather like a dence programme, and then, you know, you go round and guess,' said Coote. 'It's rather good fun.'

'Oo, rather!' said Kipps, with simulated gusto.

'It shakes everybody up together,' said Coote.

Kipps smiled and nodded. . . .

In the small hours all his painful meditations were threaded by the vision of that Anagram Tea; it kept marching to and fro and in and out of his other troubles, from thirty to sixty people, mostly ladies and callers, and a great number of the letters of the alphabet, and more particularly PIKPS and TOECO, and he was trying to make one word out of the whole interminable procession. . . .

This word, as he finally gave it with some emphasis to the silence of the night, was, '*Demn*!'

Then wreathed as it were in this lettered procession was the figure of Helen as she had appeared at the moment of 'words';

her face a little hard, a little irritated, a little disappointed. He imagined himself going round and guessing under her eye. . . .

He tried to think of other things, without lapsing upon a still deeper uneasiness that was decorated with yellow sea-poppies, and the figures of Buggins, Pearce, and Carshot, three murdered friendships, rose reproachfully in the stillness and changed horrible apprehensions into unspeakable remorse. Last night had been their customary night for the banjo, and Kipps, with a certain tremulous uncertainty, had put Old Methuselah amidst a retinue of glasses on the table and opened a box of choice cigars. In vain. They were in no need, it seemed of *his* society. But instead Chitterlow had come, anxious to know if it was all right about that syndicate plan. He had declined anything but a very weak whisky-and-soda, 'just to drink', at least until business was settled, and had then opened the whole affair with an effect of great orderliness to Kipps. Soon he was taking another whisky by sheer inadvertency, and the complex fabric of his conversation was running more easily from the broad loom of his mind. Into that pattern had interwoven a narrative of extensive alterations in the Pestered Butterfly – the neck-and-beetle business was to be restored – the story of a grave indifference of opinion with Mrs Chitterlow, where and how to live after the play had succeeded, the reasons why the Hon. Thomas Norgate had never financed a syndicate, and much matter also about the syndicate now under discussion. But if the current of their conversation had been vortical and crowded, the outcome was perfectly clear. Kipps was to be the chief participator in the syndicate, and his contribution was to be two thousand pounds. Kipps groaned and rolled over, and found Helen again, as it were, on the other side. 'Promise me,' she had said, 'you won't do anything without consulting me.'

Kipps at once rolled back to his former position, and for a space lay quite still. He felt like a very young rabbit in a trap.

Then suddenly, with extraordinary distinctness, his heart cried out for Ann, and he saw her as he had seen her at New Romney, sitting amidst the yellow sea-poppies with the sunlight on her face. His heart called out for her in the darkness as one calls for rescue. He knew, as though he had known it always, that he loved Helen no more. He wanted Ann, he wanted to hold her and be held by her, to kiss her again and again, to turn his back for ever on all these other things. . . .

He rose late, but this terrible discovery was still there, undispelled by cockcrow or the day. He rose in a shattered condition, and he cut himself while shaving, but at last he got into his dining-room, and could pull the bell for the hot constituents of his multifarious breakfast. And then he turned to his letters. There were two real letters in addition to the customary electric-belt advertisement, continental lottery circular, and betting tout's card. One was a slight mourning envelope, and addressed in an unfamiliar hand. This he opened first, and discovered a note –

Mrs Raymond Wace
requests the pleasure of
Mr Kipps'
Company at Dinner
on Tuesday, Sept 21st, at 8 o'clock.

RSVP

With a hasty movement Kipps turned his mind to the second letter. It was an unusually long one from his Uncle, and ran as follows: –

My Dear Nephew,
We are considerably startled by your letter though expecting something of the sort and disposed to hope for the best. If the young lady is a relation to the Earl of Beauprés well and good but take care you are not being imposed upon for there are many who will be glad enough to snap you up now your circumstances are altered. I waited on the old Earl once while in service and he was remarkably close with his tips and suffered from corns. A hasty old gent and hard to please – I daresay he has forgotten me altogether – and anyhow there is no need to rake up bygones. To-morrow is bus day and as you say the young lady is living near by we shall shut up shop for there is really nothing doing now what with all the visitors bringing everything with them down to their very children's pails and say how de do to her and give her a bit of a kiss and encouragement if we think her suitable – she will be pleased to see your old uncle. We wish we could have had a look at her first but still there is not much mischief done and hoping that all will turn out well yet I am

Your affectionate Uncle
Edward George Kipps

My heartburn still very bad. I shall bring over a few bits of rhubub I picked up, a sort you won't get in Folkestone and if possible a good bunch of flowers for the young lady.

'Comin' over to day,' said Kipps, standing helplessly with the letter in his hand.

''Ow the Juice—?'

'I carn't.'

'Kiss 'er!'

A terrible anticipation of that gathering framed itself in his mind, a hideous impossible disaster.

'I carn't even face 'er—!'

His voice went up to a note of despair. 'And it's too late to telegrarf and stop 'em!'

VII

About twenty minutes after this, an out-porter in Castle Hill Avenue was accosted by a young man with a pale, desperate face, an exquisitely rolled umbrella, and a heavy Gladstone bag.

'Carry this to the station, will you?' said the young man. 'I want to ketch the nex' train to London. . . . You'll 'ave to look sharp; I 'even't very much time.'

Chapter Seven

London

I

London was Kipps' third world. There were, no doubt, other worlds, but Kipps knew only these three; firstly, New Romney and the Emporium, constituting his primary world, his world of origin, which also contained Ann; secondly, the world of culture and refinement, the world of which Coote was chaperon, and into which Kipps was presently to marry, a world, it was fast becoming evident, absolutely incompatible with the first; and thirdly, a world still to a large extent unexplored, London. London presented itself as a place of great grey spaces and incredible multitudes of people, centering about Charing Cross station and the Royal Grand Hotel, and containing at unexpected arbitrary points shops of the most amazing sort, statuary, squares, restaurants – where it was possible for clever people like Walshingham to order a lunch item by item to the waiters' evident respect and sympathy – exhibitions of incredible things – the Walshinghams had taken him to the Arts and Crafts and to a Picture Gallery – and theatres. London, moreover, is rendered habitable by hansom cabs. Young Walshingham was a natural cab-taker; he was an all-round, large-minded young man, and he had in the course of their two days' stay taken Kipps into no less than nine, so that Kipps was singularly not afraid of these vehicles. He knew that wherever you were, so soon as you were thoroughly lost, you said 'Hi!' to a cab, and then 'Royal Grend Hotel.' Day and night these trusty conveyances are returning the strayed Londoner back to his point of departure, and were it not for their activity, in a little while the whole population, so vast and incomprehensible is the intricate complexity of this great city, would be hopelessly lost for ever. At any rate, that is how the thing presented itself to Kipps, and I have heard much the same from visitors from America.

His train was composed of corridor carriages, and he forgot his troubles for a time in the wonders of this modern substitute

for railway compartments. He went from the non-smoking to
the smoking carriage, and smoked a cigarette, and strayed from
his second-class carriage to a first and back. But presently Black
Care got aboard the train and came and sat beside him. The
exhilaration of escape had evaporated now, and he was presented with a terrible picture of his Aunt and Uncle arriving at
his lodgings and finding him fled. He had left a hasty message
that he was called away suddenly on busines, 'ver' important
business', and they were to be sumptuously entertained. His
immediate motive had been his passionate dread of an encounter
between these excellent but unrefined old people and the Walshinghams, but now that end was secured, he could see how
thwarted and exasperated they would be.

How to explain to them?

He ought never to have written to tell them!

He ought to have got married, and told them afterwards.

He ought to have consulted Helen.

'Promise me,' she had said.

'Oh, *desh*!' said Kipps, and got up and walked back into the
smoking-car and began to consume cigarettes.

Suppose, after all, they found out the Walshinghams' address
and went there!

At Charing Cross, however, were distractions again. He took
a cab in an entirely Walshingham manner, and was pleased to
note the enhanced respect of the cabman when he mentioned
the Royal Grand. He followed Walshingham's routine on their
previous visit with perfect success. They were very nice in the
office, and gave him an excellent room at fourteen shillings the
night.

He went up and spent a considerable time examining the
furniture of his room, scrutinizing himself in its various mirrors,
and sitting on the edge of the bed whistling. It was a vast and
splendid apartment, and cheap at fourteen shillings. But finding
the figure of Ann inclined to resume possession of his mind, he
roused himself and descended by the staircase, after a momentary hesitation before the lift. He had thought of lunch, but he
drifted into the great drawing-room, and read a guide to the
Hotels of Europe for a space, until a doubt whether he was
entitled to use this palatial apartment without extra charge arose
in his mind. He would have liked something to eat very much
now, but his inbred terror of the table was strong. He did at last

get by a porter in uniform towards the dining-room, but at the sight of a number of waiters and tables with remarkable complications of knives and glasses, terror seized him, and he backed out again with a mumbled remark to the waiter in the doorway about this not being the way.

He hovered in the hall and lounge until he thought the presiding porter regarded him with suspicion, and then went up to his room again by the staircase, got his hat and umbrella, and struck out boldly across the courtyard. He would go a restaurant instead.

He had a moment of elation in the gateway. He felt all the Strand must notice him as he emerged through the great gate of the hotel. 'One of these here rich swells,' they would say. 'Don't they go it just!' A cabman touched his hat. 'No fear,' said Kipps, pleasantly. . . .

Then he remembered he was hungry again.

Yet he decided he was in no great hurry for lunch, in spite of an internal protest, and turned eastward along the Strand in a leisurely manner. He would find a place to suit him soon enough. He tried to remember the sort of things Walshingham had ordered. Before all things he didn't want to go into a place and look like a fool. Some of these places rook you dreadful, besides making fun of you. There was a place near Essex Street where there was a window brightly full of chops, tomatoes, and lettuce. He stopped at this and reflected for a time, and then it occurred to him that you were expected to buy these things raw and cook them at home. Anyhow, there was sufficient doubt in the matter to stop him. He drifted on to a neat window with champagne bottles, a dish of asparagus, and a framed menu of a two-shilling lunch. He was about to enter, when fortunately he perceived two waiters looking at him over the back screen of the window with a most ironical expression, and he sheered off at once. There was a wonderful smell of hot food halfway down Fleet Street, and a nice-looking tavern with several doors, but he could not decide which door. His nerve was going under the strain.

He hesitated at Farringdon Street, and drifted up to St Paul's and round the churchyard, full chiefly of dead bargains in the shop windows, to Cheapside. But now Kipps was getting demoralized, and each house of refreshment seemed to promise still more complicated obstacles to food. He didn't know how

you went in, and what was the correct thing to do with your
hat; he didn't know what you said to the waiter, or what you
called the different things; he was convinced absolutely he would
'fumble', as Shalford would have said, and look like a fool.
Somebody might laugh at him! The hungrier he got, the more
unendurable was the thought that any one should laugh at him.
For a time he considered an extraordinary expedient to account
for his ignorance. He would go in and pretend to be a foreigner,
and not know English. Then they might understand. . . . Presently he had drifted into a part of London where there did not
seem to be any refreshment places at all.

'Oh, *desh*!' said Kipps, in a sort of agony of indecisiveness.
'The very nex' place I see, in I go.'

The next place was a fried-fish shop in a little side street,
where there were also sausages on a gas-lit grill.

He would have gone in, but suddenly a new scruple came to
him, that he was too well dressed for the company he could see
dimly through the steam sitting at the counter and eating with a
sort of nonchalant speed.

II

He was half minded to resort to a hansom and brave the terrors
of the dining-room of the Royal Grand – they wouldn't know
why he had gone out really – when the only person he knew in
London appeared (as the only person one does know will do in
London) and slapped him on the shoulder. Kipps was hovering
at a window at a few yards from the fish shop pretending to
examine some really strikingly cheap pink baby-linen, and trying
to settle finally about those sausages. 'Hullo, Kipps!' cried Sid,
'spending the millions?'

Kipps turned and was glad to perceive no lingering vestige of
the chagrin that had been so painful at New Romney. Sid looked
grave and important, and he wore a quite new silk hat that gave
a commercial touch to a generally socialistic costume. For the
moment the sight of Sid uplifted Kipps wonderfully. He saw
him as a friend and helper, and only presently did it come clearly
into his mind that this was the brother of Ann.

He made amiable noises.

'I've just been up this way,' Sid explained, 'buying in a second-hand 'namelling stove. . . . I'm going to 'namel myself.'

'Lor!' said Kipps.

'Yes. Do me a lot of good. Let the customer choose his colour. See? What brings *you* up?'

Kipps had a momentary vision of his foiled Uncle and Aunt. 'Jest a bit of a change,' he said.

Sid came to a swift decision. 'Come down to my little show. I got some one I'd like to see talking to you.'

Even then Kipps did not think of Ann in this connection.

'Well,' he said, trying to invent an excuse on the spur of the moment. 'Fact is,' he explained, 'I was jest looking round to get a bit of lunch.'

'Dinner we call it,' said Sid. 'But that's all right. You can't get anything to eat hereabout. If you're not too haughty to do a bit of slumming, there's some mutton spoiling for me now—'

The word mutton affected Kipps greatly.

'It won't take us 'arf an hour,' said Sid, and Kipps was carried.

He discovered another means of London locomotion in the Underground Railway, and recovered his self-possession in that interest. 'You don't mind going third?' asked Sid; and Kipps said, 'Nort a *bit* of it.' They were silent in the train for a time, on account of strangers in the carriage, and then Sid began to explain who it was he wanted Kipps to meet. 'It's a chap named Masterman, – do you no end of good.

'He occupies our first-floor front room, you know. It isn't so much of gain I let as company. We don't *want* the whole 'ouse, that's one thing, and another is I knew the man before. Met him at our Sociological, and after a bit he said he wasn't comfortable where he was. That's how it came about. He's a first-class chap – first class. Science! You should see his books!

'Properly he's a sort of journalist. He's written a lot of things, but he's been too ill lately to do very much. Poetry he's written, all sorts. He writes for the *Commonweal* sometimes, and sometimes he reviews books. 'E's got 'eaps of books – 'eaps. Besides selling a lot.

'He knows a regular lot of people, and all sorts of things. He's been a dentist, and he's a qualified chemist, and I seen 'im often reading German and French. Taught 'imself. He was here—'

Sid indicated South Kensington, which had come opportunely outside the carriage windows, with a nod of his head, '—three

years. Studying science. But you'll see 'im. When he really gets
to talking – he *pours* it out.'

'Ah!' said Kipps, nodding sympathetically, with his two hands
on his umbrella knob.

'He'll do big things some day,' said Sid. 'He's written a book
on science already. *Physiography,* it's called. *Elementary Physiography!* Some day he'll write an Advanced – when he gets
time.'

He let this soak into Kipps.

'I can't introduce you to lords and swells,' he went on, 'but I
can show you a Famous Man, that's going to be. I *can* do that.
Leastways—Unless—'

Sid hesitated.

'He's got a frightful cough,' he said.

'He won't care to talk to me,' weighed Kipps.

'That's all right; *he* won't mind. He's fond of talking. He'd
talk to any one,' said Sid, reassuringly, and added a perplexing
bit of Londonized Latin. 'He doesn't *pute* anything, *non
alienum.* You know.'

'*I* know,' said Kipps, intelligently, over his umbrella knob,
though of course that was altogether untrue.

III

Kipps found Sid's shop a practical-looking establishment,
stocked with the most remarkable collection of bicycles and
pieces of bicycle that he had ever beheld. 'My hiring stock,' said
Sid, with a wave to this ironmongery; 'and there's the best
machine at a democratic price in London, The Red Flag, built
by *me*. See?'

He indicated a graceful grey brown framework in the window.
'And there's my stock of accessories – store prices.

'Go in for motors a bit,' added Sid.

'Mutton?' said Kipps, not hearing him distinctly.

'Motors I *said*. . . . 'Owever, Mutton Department 'ere; and he
opened a door that had a curtain-guarded window in its upper
panel, to reveal a little room with red walls and green furniture,
with a white-clothed table and the generous promise of a meal.
'Fanny!' he shouted. 'Here's Art Kipps.'

A bright-eyed young woman of five or six and twenty in a

pink print appeared, a little flushed from cooking, and wiped a hand on an apron and shook hands and smiled and said it would all be ready in a minute. She went on to say she had heard of Kipps and his luck, and meanwhile Sid vanished to draw the beer, and returned with two glasses for himself and Kipps.

'Drink that,' said Sid; and Kipps felt all the better for it.

'I give Mr Masterman '*is* upstairs a hour ago,' said Mrs Sid. 'I didn't think 'e ought to wait.'

A rapid succession of brisk movements on the part of every one and they were all four at dinner – the fourth person being Master Walt Whitman Pornick, a cheerful young gentleman of one and a half, who was given a spoon to hammer on the table with, to keep him quiet, and who got 'Kipps' right at the first effort and kept it all through the meal, combining it first with this previous acquisition and then that. 'Peacock Kipps,' said master Walt, at which there was great laughter, and also 'More Mutton Kipps.'

'He's a regular one,' said Mrs Sid, 'for catching up words. You can't say a word but what 'e's on to it.'

There were no serviettes and less ceremony, and Kipps thought he had never enjoyed a meal so much. Every one was a little excited by the meeting and chatting and disposed to laugh, and things went easily from the very beginning. If there was a pause, Master Walt filled it in. Mrs Sid, who tempered her enormous admiration for Sid's intellect and his socialism and his severe business methods by a motherly sense of her sex and seniority, spoke of them both as 'you boys', and dilated – when she was not urging Kipps to have some more of this or that – on the disparity between herself and her husband.

'Shouldn't ha' thought there was a year between you,' said Kipps; 'you seem jest a match.'

'*I*'m *his* match anyhow,' said Mrs Sid, and no epigram of young Walshingham's was ever better received.

'Match,' said young Walt, coming in on the tail of the joke and getting a round for himself.

Any sense of superior fortune had long vanished from Kipps' mind, and he found himself looking at host and hostess with enormous respect. Really old Sid was a wonderful chap, here in his own house at two and twenty, carving his own mutton and lording it over wife and child. No legacies needed by him! And

Mrs Sid, so kind and bright and hearty! And the child, old Sid's child! Old Sid had jumped round a bit. It needed the sense of his fortune at the back of his mind to keep Kipps from feeling abject. He resolved he'd buy young Walt something tremendous in toys at the very first opportunity.

'Drop more beer, Art?'

'Right you are, old man.'

'Cut Mr Kipps a bit more bread, Sid.'

'Can't I pass *you* a bit? . . .'

Sid was all right, Sid was; there was no mistake about that.

It was growing up in his mind that Sid was the brother of Ann, but he said nothing about her, for excellent reasons. After all, Sid's irritation at her name when they had met in New Romney seemed to show a certain separation. They didn't tell each other much. . . . He didn't know how things might be between Ann and Mrs Sid either.

Still, for all that, Sid was Ann's brother.

The furniture of the room did not assert itself very much above the cheerful business of the table, but Kipps was impressed with the idea that it was pretty. There was a dresser at the end with a number of gay plates and a mug or so, a Labour Day poster by Walter Crane on the wall, and through the glass and over the blind of the shop door one had a glimpse of the bright-colour advertisement cards of bicycle dealers, and a shelfful of boxes labelled The Paragon Bell, The Scarum Bell, and The Patent Omi! Horn. . . .

It seemed incredible that he had been in Folkestone that morning, that even now his Aunt and Uncle—!

B-r-r-r. It didn't do to think of his Aunt and Uncle.

IV

When Sid repeated his invitation to come and see Masterman, Kipps, now flushed with beer and Irish stew, said he didn't mind if he did, and after a preliminary shout from Sid that was answered by a voice and a cough, the two went upstairs.

'Masterman's a rare one,' said Sid over his arm and in an undertone. 'You should hear him speak at a meeting. . . . If he's in form, that is.'

He rapped and went into a large untidy room.

'This is Kipps,' he said. 'You know. The chap I told you of. With twelve 'undred a year.'

Masterman sat gnawing an empty pipe, and as close to the fire as though it was alight and the season midwinter. Kipps concentrated upon him for a space, and only later took in something of the frowsy furniture, the little bed half behind and evidently supposed to be wholly behind a careless screen, the spittoon by the fender, the remains of a dinner on the chest of drawers, and the scattered books and papers. Masterman's face showed him a man of forty or more, with curious hollows at the side of his forehead and about his eyes. His eyes were very bright, there was a spot of red in his cheeks, and the wiry black moustache under his short red nose had been trimmed with scissors into a sort of brush along his upper lip. His teeth were darkened ruins. His jacket collar was turned up about a knitted white neck-wrap, and his sleeves betrayed no cuffs. He did not rise to greet Kipps, but he held out a thin wristed hand and pointed with the other to a bedroom armchair.

'Glad to see you,' he said. 'Sit down and make yourself at home. Will you smoke?'

Kipps said he would, and produced his store. He was about to take one, and then with a civil afterthought handed the packet first to Masterman and Sid. Masterman pretended surprise to find his pipe out before he took one. There was an interlude of matches. Sid pushed the end of the screen out of his way, sat down on the bed thus frankly admitted, and prepared, with a certain quiet satisfaction of manner, to witness Masterman's treatment of Kipps.

'And how does it feel to have twelve hundred a year?' asked Masterman, holding his cigarette to his nose tip in a curious manner.

'It's rum,' confided Kipps, after a reflective interval. 'It feels juiced rum.'

'I've never felt it,' said Masterman.

'It takes a bit of getting into,' said Kipps. 'I can tell you that.'

Masterman smoked and regarded Kipps with curious eyes.

'I expect it does,' he said presently.

'And has it made you perfectly happy?' he asked abruptly.

'I couldn't 'ardly say *that*,' said Kipps.

Masterman smiled. 'No,' he said. 'Has it made you much happier?'

'It did at first.'

'Yes. But you got used to it. How long, for example, did the real delirious excitement last?'

'Oo, *that*! Perhaps a week,' said Kipps.

Masterman nodded his head. 'That's what discourages *me* from amassing wealth,' he said to Sid. 'You adjust yourself. It doesn't last. I've always had an inkling of that, and it's interesting to get it confirmed. I shall go on sponging for a bit longer on *you*, I think.'

'You don't,' said Sid. 'No fear.'

'Twenty-four thousand pounds,' said Masterman, and blew a cloud of smoke. 'Lord! Doesn't it worry you?'

'It's a bit worrying at times. . . . Things 'appen.'

'Going to marry?'

'Yes.'

'H'm. Lady, I guess, of a superior social position?'

'Rather,' said Kipps. 'Cousin to the Earl of Beauprés.'

Masterman readjusted his long body with an air of having accumulated all the facts he needed. He snuggled his shoulder-blades down into the chair and raised his angular knees. 'I doubt,' he said flicking cigarette ash into the atmosphere, 'if any great gain or loss of money does – as things are at present – make more than the slightest difference in one's happiness. It ought to – if money was what it ought to be, the token given for service, one ought to get an increase in power and happiness for every pound one got. But the plain fact is, the times are out of joint, and money – money, like everything else – is a deception and a disappointment.'

He turned his face to Kipps and enforced his next words with the index finger of his lean lank hand. 'If I thought otherwise,' he said, 'I should exert myself to get some. But – if one sees things clearly one is so discourged. So confoundedly discouraged. . . . When you first got your money you thought that it meant you might buy just anything you fancied?'

'It was a bit that way,' said Kipps.

'And you found you couldn't. You found that for all sorts of things it was a question of where to buy and how to buy, and what you didn't know how to buy with your money, straight away this world planted something else upon you.'

'I got rather done over a banjo first day,' said Kipps. 'Leastways, my uncle says so.'

'Exactly,' said Masterman.

Sid began to speak from the bed. 'That's all very well, Masterman,' he said, 'but after all money *is* Power, you know. You can do all sorts of things—'

I'm talking of happiness,' said Masterman. 'You can do all sorts of things with a loaded gun in the Hammersmith Broadway, but nothing – practically – that will make you or any one else very happy. Nothing. Power's a different matter altogether. As for happiness, you want a world in order before money or property or any of those things have any real value, and this world, I tell you, is hopelessly out of joint. Man is a social animal with a mind nowadays that goes round the globe, and a community cannot be happy in one part and unhappy in another. It's all or nothing, no patching any more for ever. It is the standing mistake of the world not to understand that. Consequently people think there is a class or order somewhere just above them or just below them, or a country or place somewhere that is really safe and happy. . . . The fact is, Society is one body, and it is either well or ill. That's the law. This society we live in is ill. It's a fractious, feverish invalid, gouty, greedy, ill-nourished. You can't have a happy left leg with neuralgia, or a happy throat with a broken leg. That's my position, and that's the knowledge you'll come to. I'm so satisfied of it that I sit here and wait for my end quite calmly, sure that I can't better things by bothering – in my time and so far as I am concerned that is. I'm not even greedy any more – my egotism's at the bottom of a pond with a philosophical brick round its neck. The world is ill, my time is short, and my strength is small. I'm as happy here as anywhere.'

He coughed, was silent for a moment, then brought the index finger round to Kipps again. 'You've had the opportunity of sampling two grades of society, and you don't find the new people you're among much better or any happier than the old?'

'No,' said Kipps, reflectively. 'No. I 'aven't see it quite like that before, but—No. They're not.'

'And you might go all up the scale and down the scale and find the same thing. Man's a gregarious beast, a gregarious beast, and no money will buy you out of your own time – any more than out of your own skin. All the way up and all the way down the scale there's the same discontent. No one is quite sure where they stand, and every one's fretting. The herd's uneasy and feverish. All the old tradition goes or has gone, and there's no one to make a new tradition. Where are your nobles now? Where are your gentlemen? They vanished directly the peasant found out he wasn't happy and ceased to be a peasant. There's big men and little men mixed up together, and that's all. None of us know where we are. Your cads in a bank-holiday train, and your cads on a two-thousand-pound motor, except for a difference in scale, there's not a pin to choose between them. Your smart society is as low and vulgar and uncomfortable for a balanced soul as a gin palace, no more and no less; there's no place or level of honour or fine living left in the world, so what's the good of climbing?'

"Ear, 'ear,' said Sid.

'It's true,' said Kipps.

'*I* don't climb,' said Masterman, and accepted Kipps' silent offer of another cigarette.

'No,' he said. 'This world is out of joint. It's broken up, and I doubt if it'll heal. I doubt very much if it'll heal. We're in the beginning of the Sickness of the World.'

He rolled his cigarette in his lean fingers and repeated with satisfaction, 'The Sickness of the World.'

'It's we've got to make it beter,' said Sid, and looked at Kipps.

'Ah, Sid's an optimist,' said Masterman.

'So you are, most times,' said Sid.

Kipps lit another cigarette with an air of intelligent participation.

'Frankly,' said Masterman, recrossing his legs and expelling a jet of smoke luxuriously, 'frankly, I think this civilization of ours is on the topple.'

'There's Socialism,' said Sid.

'There's no imagination to make use of it.'

'We've got to *make* one,' said Sid.

'In a couple of centuries, perhaps,' said Masterman. 'But meanwhile we're going to have a pretty acute attack of universal confusion. Universal confusion. Like one of those crushes when men are killed and maimed for no reason at all, going into a meeting or crowding for a train. Commercial and Industrial Stresses. Political Exploitation. Tariff Wars. Revolutions. All the bloodshed that will come of some fools calling half the white world yellow. These things alter the attitude of everybody to everybody. Everybody's going to feel 'em. Every fool in the world panting and shoving. We're all going to be as happy and comfortable as a household during a removal. What else can we expect?'

Kipps was moved to speak, but not in answer to Masterman's inquiry. 'I've never rightly got the 'eng of this Socialism,' he said. 'What's it going to do, like?'

They had been imagining that he had some elementary idea in the matter, but as soon as he had made it clear that he hadn't, Sid plunged at exposition, and in a little while Masterman, abandoning his pose of the detached man ready to die, joined in. At first he joined in only to correct Sid's version, but afterwards he took control. His manner changed. He sat up and rested his elbow on his knees, and his cheek flushed a little. He expanded his case against property and the property class with such vigour that Kipps was completely carried away, and never thought of asking for a clear vision of the thing that would fill the void this abolition might create. For a time he quite forgot his own private opulence. And it was as if something had been lit in Masterman. His languor passed. He enforced his words by gestures of his long thin hands. And as he passed swiftly from point to point of his argument, it was evident he grew angry.

'To-day,' he said, 'the world is ruled by rich men; they may do almost anything they like with the world. And what are they doing? Laying it waste!'

'Hear, hear!' said Sid, very sternly.

Masterman stood up, gaunt and long, thrust his hands in his pockets, and turned his back to the fireplace.

'Collectively, the rich to-day have neither heart nor imagination. No! They own machinery, they have knowledge and instruments and powers beyond all previous dreaming, and what are they doing with them? Think what they are doing with them, Kipps, and think what they might do. God gives them a power like the motor-car, and all they can do with it is to go careering about the roads in goggled masks, killing children and making machinery hateful to the soul of man! ('True,' said Sid, 'true.') God gives them means of communication, power unparalleled of every sort, time, and absolute liberty! They waste it all in folly! Here under their feet (and Kipps' eyes followed the direction of a lean index finger to the hearthrug), under their accursed wheels, the great mass of men festers and breeds in darkness, darkness those others make by standing in the light.

The darkness breeds and breeds. It knows no better. . . . Unless
you can crawl or pander or rob you must stay in the stew you
are born in. And those rich beasts above claw and clutch as
though they had nothing! They grudge us our schools, they
grudge us a gleam of light and air, they cheat us, and then seek
to forget us. . . . There is no rule, no guidance, only accidents
and happy flukes. . . . Our multitudes of poverty increase, and
this crew of rulers makes no provision, foresees nothing, antici-
pates nothing!'

He paused, and made a step, and stood over Kipps in a white
heat of anger. Kipps nodded in a non-committal manner, and
looked hard and rather gloomily at his host's slipper as he
talked.

'It isn't as though they had something to show for the waste
they make of us, Kipps. They haven't. They are ugly and
cowardly and mean. Look at their women! Painted, dyed, and
drugged, hiding their ugly shapes under a load of dress! There
isn't a woman in the swim of society at the present time who
wouldn't sell herself body and soul, who wouldn't lick the boots
of a Jew or marry a nigger, rather than live decently on a
hundred a year! On what would be wealth for you or me! They
know it. They know we know it. . . . No one believes in them.
No one believes in nobility any more. Nobody believes in
kingship any more. Nobody believes there is justice in the
law. . . . But people have habits, people go on in the old grooves,
as long as there's work, as long as there's weekly money. . . . It
won't last Kipps.'

He coughed and paused. 'Wait for the lean years,' he cried.
'Wait for the lean years.' And suddenly he fell into a struggle
with his cough, and spat a gout of blood. 'It's nothing,' he said
to Kipps' note of startled horror.

He went on talking, and the protests of his cough interlaced
with his words, and Sid beamed in an ecstasy of painful
admiration.

'Look at the fraud they have let life become, the miserable
mockery of the hope of one's youth. What have *I* had? I found
myself at thirteen being forced into a factory like a rabbit into a
chloroformed box. Thirteen! – when *their* children are babies.
But even a child of that age could see what it meant, that Hell
of a factory! Monotony and toil and contempt and dishonour!
And then death. So I fought – at thirteen!'

Minton's 'crawling up a drainpipe till you die' echoed in Kipps' mind, but Masterman, instead of Minton's growl, spoke in a high indignant tenor.

'I got out at last – somehow,' he said quietly, suddenly plumping back in his chair. He went on after a pause. 'For a bit. Some of us get out by luck, some by cunning, and crawl on to the grass, exhausted and crippled, to die. That's a poor man's success, Kipps. Most of us don't get out at all. I worked all day, and studied half the night, and here I am with the common consequences. Beaten! And never once have I had a fair chance, never once!' His lean clenched fist flew out in a gust of tremulous anger. 'These Skunks shut up all the university scholarships at nineteen for fear of men like me. And then – do *nothing*. . . . We're wasted for nothing. By the time I'd learnt something the doors were locked. I thought knowledge would do it – I did think that! I've fought for knowledge as other men fight for bread. I've starved for knowledge. I've turned my back on women; I've done even that. I've burst my accursed lung. . . .' His voice rose with impotent anger. 'I'm a better man than any ten princes alive. And I'm beaten and wasted. I've been crushed, trampled, and defiled by a drove of hogs. I'm no use to myself or the world. I've thrown my life away to make myself too good for use in this hucksters' scramble. If I had gone in for business, if I had gone in for plotting to cheat my fellow-men. . . . Ah, well! It's too late for anything now! And I couldn't have done it. . . . And over in New York now there's a pet of society making a corner in wheat!

'By God!' he cried hoarsely, with a clutch of the lean hand. 'By God! if I had his throat! Even now! I might do something for the world.'

He glared at Kipps, his face flushed deep, his sunken eyes glowing with passion, and then suddenly he changed altogether.

There was a sound of tea-things rattling upon a tray outside the door, and Sid rose to open it.

'All of which amounts to this,' said Masterman, suddenly quiet again and talking against time. 'The world is out of joint, and there isn't a soul alive who isn't half waste or more. You'll find it the same with you in the end, wherever your luck may take you. . . . I suppose you won't mind my having another cigarette?'

He took Kipps' cigarette with a hand that trembled so

violently it almost missed its object, and stood up, with something of guilt in his manner, as Mrs Sid came into the room.

Her eye met his, and marked the flush upon his face.

'Been talking Socialism?' said Mrs Sid, a little severely.

v

Six o'clock that day found Kipps drifting eastward along the southward margin of Rotten Row. You figure him a small respectably attired person going slowly through a sometimes immensely difficult and always immense world. At times he becomes pensive, and whistles softly; at times he looks about him. There are a few riders in the Row; a carriage flashes by every now and then along the roadway, and among the great rhododendrons and laurels and upon the green sward there are a few groups and isolated people dressed – in the style Kipps adopted to call upon the Walshinghams when first he was engaged. Amid the complicated confusion of Kipps' mind was a regret that he had not worn his other things. . . .

Presently he perceived that he would like to sit down; a green chair tempted him. He hesitated at it, took possession of it, and leant back and crossed one leg over the other.

He rubbed his under lip with his umbrella handle, and reflected upon Masterman and his denunciation of the world.

'Bit orf 'is 'ead, poor chap,' said Kipps; and added, 'I wonder—'

He thought intently for a space.

'I wonder what 'e meant by the lean years.' . . .

The world seemed a very solid and prosperous concern just here, and well out of reach of Masterman's dying clutch. And yet—

It was curious he should have been reminded of Minton.

His mind turned to a far more important matter. Just at the end Sid had said to him, 'Seen Ann?' and as he was about to answer, 'You'll see a bit more of her now. She's got a place in Folkestone.'

It had brought him back from any concern about the world being out of joint or anything of that sort.

Ann!

One might run against her any day.

He tugged at his little moustache.

He would like to run against Ann very much. . . .

And it would be juiced awkward if he did!

In Folkestone! It was a jolly sight too close. . . .

Then at the thought that he might run against Ann in his beautiful evening dress on the way to the band, he fluttered into a momentary dream, that jumped abruptly into a nightmare.

Suppose he met her when he was out with Helen! 'Oh, Lor!' said Kipps. Life had developed a new complication that would go on and go on. For some time he wished with the utmost fervour that he had not kissed Ann, that he had not gone to New Romney the second time. He marvelled at his amazing forgetfulness of Helen on that occasion. Helen took possession of his mind. He would have to write to Helen, an easy offhand letter to say he had come to London for a day or so. He tried to imagine her reading it. He would write just such another letter to the old people, and say he had had to come up on business. That might do for *them* all right, but Helen was different. She would insist on explanations.

He wished he could never go back to Folkestone again. That would about settle the whole affair.

A passing group attracted his attention, two faultlessly dressed gentlemen and a radiantly expensive lady. They were talking, no doubt, very brilliantly. His eyes followed them. The lady tapped the arm of the left-hand gentleman with a daintily tinted glove. Swells! No end. . . .

His soul looked out upon life in general as a very small nestling might peep out of its nest. What an extraordinary thing life was to be sure, and what a remarkable variety of people there were in it!

He lit a cigarette, and speculated upon that receding group of three, and blew smoke and watched them. They seemed to do it all right. Probably they all had incomes of very much over twelve hundred a year. Perhaps not. Probably they none of them suspected as they went past that he too was a gentleman of independent means, dressed as he was without distinction. Of course things were easier for them. They were brought up always to dress well and do the right thing from their very earliest years; they started clear of all his perplexities; they had never got mixed up with all sorts of different people who didn't go together. If, for example, that lady there got engaged to that gentleman, she would be quite safe from any encounter with a corpulent, osculatory Uncle, or Chitterlow, or the dangerously significant eye of Pearce.

His thoughts came round to Helen.

When they were married and Cuyps, or Cuyp – Coote had failed to justify his 's' – and in that West-end flat, and shaken free of all these low-class associations, would he and she parade here of an afternoon dressed like that? It would be rather fine to do so. If one's dress was all right.

Helen!

She was difficult to understand at times.

He blew extensive clouds of cigarette smoke.

There would be teas, there would be dinners, there would be calls—Of course he would get into the way of it.

But Anagrams were a bit stiff to begin with!

It was beastly confusing at first to know when to use your fork at dinner, and all that. Still—

He felt an extraordinary doubt whether he would get into the way of it. He was interested for a space by a girl and groom on horseback, and then he came back to his personal preoccupations.

He would have to write to Helen. What could he say to explain his absence from the Anagram Tea? She had been pretty clear she wanted him to come. He recalled her resolute face without any great tenderness. He *knew* he would look like a silly ass at that confounded tea! Suppose he shirked it and went back in time for the dinner! Dinners were beastly difficult too, but not so bad as anagrams. The very first thing that might happen when he got back to Folkestone would be to run against Ann. Suppose, after all, he did meet Ann when he was with Helen!

What queer encounters were possible in the world!

Thank goodness, they were going to live in London!

But that brought him round to Chitterlow. The Chitterlows would be coming to London too. If they didn't get money they'd come after it; they weren't the sort of people to be choked off easily, and if they did, they'd come to London to produce their play. He tried to imagine some seemly social occasion invaded by Chitterlow and his rhetoric, by his torrential thunder of self-assertion, the whole company flattened thereunder like wheat under a hurricane.

Confound and hang Chitterlow! Yet somehow, somewhen, one would have to settle accounts with him! And there was Sid! Sid was Ann's brother. He realized with sudden horror the social indiscretion of accepting Sid's invitation to dinner.

Sid wasn't the short of chap one could snub or cut, and besides – Ann's brother! He didn't want to cut him; it would be worse than cutting Buggins and Pearce – a sight worse. And after that lunch! It would be next thing to cutting Ann herself. And even as to Ann!

Suppose he was with Helen or Coote! . . .

'Oh, Blow!' he said at last, and then viciously, '*Blow*!' and so rose and flung away his cigarette end and pursued his reluctant dubitating way towards the really quite uncongenial splendours of the Royal Grand. . . .

And it is vulgarly imagined that to have money is to have no troubles at all!

VI

Kipps endured splendour at the Royal Grand Hotel for three nights and days, and then he retreated in disorder. The Royal Grand defeated and overcame and routed Kipps not of intention, but by sheer royal grandeur, grandeur combined with an organization for his comfort carried to excess. On his return he came upon a difficulty, he had lost his circular piece of cardboard with the number of his room, and he drifted about the hall and passages in a state of perplexity for some time, until he thought all the porters and officials in gold lace caps must be watching him, and jesting to one another about him. Finally, in a quiet corner down below near the hairdresser's shop, he found a kindly-looking personage in bottle green, to whom he broached his difficulty. 'I say,' he said, with a pleasant smile, 'I can't find my room nohow.' The personage in bottle green, instead of laughing in a nasty way, as he might well have done, became extremely helpful, showed Kipps what to do, got his key, and conducted him by lift and passage to his chamber. Kipps tipped him half a crown.

Safe in his room, Kipps pulled himself together for dinner. He had learnt enough from young Walshingham to bring his dress clothes, and now he began to assume them. Unfortunately in the excitement of his flight from his Aunt and Uncle he had forgotten to put in his other boots, and he was some time deciding between his purple cloth slippers with a golden marigold and the prospect of cleaning the boots he was wearing with the towel, but finally, being a little footsore, he took the slippers.

Afterwards, when he saw the porters and waiters and the other guests catch sight of the slippers, he was sorry he had not chosen the boots. However, to make up for any want of style at that end, he had his crush hat under his arm.

He found the dining-room without excessive trouble. It was a vast and splendidly decorated place, and a number of people, evidently quite *au fait*, with dining there at little tables lit with electric red-shaded candles, gentlemen in evening dress, and ladies with dazzling astonishing necks. Kipps had never seen evening dress in full vigour before, and he doubted his eyes. And there were also people not in evening dress, who no doubt wondered what noble family Kipps represented. There was a band in a decorated recess, and the band looked collectively at the purple slippers, and so lost any chance they may have had of a donation so far as Kipps was concerned. The chief drawback to this magnificent place was the excessive space of floor that had to be crossed before you got your purple slippers hidden under a table.

He selected a little table – not the one where a rather impudent-looking waiter held a chair, but another – sat down, and, finding his gibus in his hand, decided after a moment of thought to rise slightly and sit on it. (It was discovered in his abandoned chair at a late hour by a supper-party and restored to him next day.)

He put the napkin carefully on one side, selected his soup without difficulty, 'Clear please,' but he was rather floored by the presentation of a quite splendidly bound wine-card. He turned it over, discovered a section devoted to whisky, and had a bright idea.

''Ere,' he said to the waiter, with an encouraging movement of the head; and then in a confidential manner, 'You 'aven't any Old Methuselah Three Stars, 'ave you?'

The waiter went away to inquire, and Kipps went on with his soup with an enhanced self-respect. Finally, Old Methuselah being unattainable, he ordered a claret from about the middle of the list. 'Let's 'ave some of this,' he said. He knew claret was a good sort of wine.

'A half bottle?' said the waiter.

'Right you are,' said Kipps.

He felt he was getting on. He leant back after his soup, a man of the world, and then slowly brought his eyes round to the ladies in evening dress on his right. . . .

He couldn't have thought it!

They were scorchers. Jest a bit of black velvet over the shoulders!

He looked again. One of them was laughing with a glass of wine half raised — wicked-looking woman she was; the other, the black velvet one, was eating bits of bread with nervous quickness and talking fast.

He wished old Buggins could see them.

He found a waiter regarding him and blushed deeply. He did not look again for some time, and became confused about his knife and fork over the fish. Presently he remarked a lady in pink to the left of him eating the fish with an entirely different implement.

It was over the *vol au vent* that he began to go to pieces. He took a knife to it; then saw the lady in pink was using a fork only, and hastily put down his knife, with a considerable amount of rich creaminess on the blade, upon the cloth. Then he found that a fork in his inexperienced hand was an instrument of chase rather than capture. His ears became violently red, and then he looked up to discover the lady in pink glancing at him, and then smiling, as she spoke to the man beside her.

He hated the lady in pink very much.

He stabbed a large piece of the *vol au vent* at last, and was too glad of his luck not to make a mouthful of it. But it was an extensive fragment, and pieces escaped him. Shirt-front! 'Desh it!' he said, and had resort to his spoon. His waiter went and spoke to two other waiters, no doubt jeering at him. He became very fierce suddenly. ''Ere!' he said, gesticulating; and then, 'Clear this away!'

The entire dinner-party on his right, the party of the ladies in advanced evening dress, looked at him. . . . He felt that every one was watching him and making fun of him, and the injustice of this angered him. After all, they had had every advantage he hadn't. And then, when they got him there doing his best, what must they do but glance and sneer and nudge one another. He tried to catch them at it, and then took refuge in a second glass of wine.

Suddenly and extraordinarily he found himself a Socialist. He did not care how close it was to the lean years when all these things would end.

Mutton came with peas. He arrested the hand of the waiter. 'No peas,' he said. He knew something of the danger and difficulty of eating peas. Then, when the peas went away, he was embittered again. . . . Echoes of Masterman's burning rhetoric began to reverberate in his mind. Nice lot of people these were to laugh at any one! Women half undressed—It was that made him so beastly uncomfortable. How could one eat one's dinner with people about him like that? Nice lot they were. He was glad he wasn't one of them anyhow. Yes, they might look. He resolved, if they looked at him again, he would ask one of the men who he was staring at. His perturbed and angry face would have concerned any one. The band, by an unfortunate accident, was playing truculent military music. The mental change Kipps underwent was, in its way, what psychologists call a conversion. In a few moments all Kipps' ideals were changed. He who had been 'practically a gentleman', the sedulous pupil of Coote, the punctilious raiser of hats, was instantly a rebel, an outcast, the hater of everything 'stuck up', the foe of Society and the social order of to-day. Here they were among the profits of their robbery, these people who might do anything with the world. . . .

'No thenks,' he said to a dish.

He addressed a scornful eye at the shoulders of the lady to his left.

Presently he was refusing another dish. He didn't like it – fussed-up food! Probably cooked by some foreigner. He finished up his wine and his bread. . . .

'No, thenks.'

'No, thenks.' . . .

He discovered the eye of a diner fixed curiously upon his flushed face. He responded with a glare. Couldn't he go without things if he liked?

'What's this?' said Kipps, to a great green cone.

'Ice,' said the waiter.

'I'll 'ave some,' said Kipps.

He seized fork and spoon and assailed the bombe. It cut rather stiffly. 'Come up!' said Kipps, with concentrated bitterness, and the truncated summit of the bombe flew off suddenly, travelling eastward with remarkable velocity. Flop, it went upon the floor a yard away, and for a while time seemed empty.

At the adjacent table they were laughing altogether.

Shy the rest of the bombe at them?

Flight?

At any rate, a dignified withdrawal.

'No!' said Kipps, 'no more,' arresting the polite attempt of the waiter to serve him with another piece. He had a vague idea he might carry off the affair as though he meant the ice to go on the floor – not liking ice, for example, and being annoyed at the badness of his dinner. He put both hands on the table, thrust back his chair, disengaged a purple slipper from his napkin, and rose. He stepped carefully over the prostrate ice, kicked the napkin under the table, thrust his hands deep into his pockets, and marched out – shaking the dust of the place as it were from his feet. He left behind him a melting fragment of ice upon the floor, his gibus hat, warm and compressed in his chair, and, in addition, every social ambition he had ever entertained in the world.

VII

Kipps went back to Folkestone in time for the Anagram Tea. But you must not imagine that the change of heart that came to him in the dining-room of the Royal Grand Hotel involved any change of attitude towards this promised social and intellectual treat. He went back because the Royal Grand was too much for him.

Outwardly calm, or at most a little flushed and ruffled, inwardly Kipps was a horrible, tormented battleground of scruples, doubts, shames, and self-assertions during that three days of silent, desperate grappling with the big hotel. He did not intend the monstrosity should beat him without a struggle; but at last he had sullenly to admit himself overcome. The odds were terrific. On the one hand himself – with, among other things, only one pair of boots; on the other a vast wilderness of rooms, covering several acres, and with over a thousand people, staff and visitors, all chiefly occupied in looking queerly at Kipps, in laughing at him behind his back, in watching for difficult corners at which to confront and perplex him and inflict humiliations upon him. For example, the hotel scored over its electric light. After the dinner the chambermaid, a hard, unsympathetic young woman with a superior manner, was summoned by a bell Kipps had rung under the impression the button was the electric-light switch. 'Look 'ere,' said Kipps, rubbing a shin that had suffered during his search in the dark, 'why aren't there any candles or matches?' The hotel explained and scored heavily.

'It isn't every one is up to these things,' said Kipps.

'No, it isn't,' said the chambermaid with ill-concealed scorn, and slammed the door at him.

'S'pose I ought to have tipped her,' said Kipps.

After that Kipps cleaned his boots with a pocket-handkerchief and went for a long walk, and got home in a hansom; but the hotel scored again by his not putting out his boots, and so having to clean them again in the morning. The hotel also snubbed him by bringing him hot water when he was fully dressed and looking surprised at his collar, but he got a breakfast, I must admit, with scarcely any difficulty.

After that the hotel scored heavily by the fact that there are twenty-four hours in the day and Kipps had nothing to do in any of them. He was a little footsore from his previous day's pedestrianism, and he could make up his mind for no long excursions. He flitted in and out of the hotel several times, and it was the polite porter who touched his hat every time that first set Kipps tipping.

'What e wants is a tip,' said Kipps.

So at the next opportunity he gave the man an unexpected shilling, and, having once put his hand in his pocket, there was no reason why he should not go on. He bought a newspaper at the bookstall and tipped the boy the rest of the shilling, and then went up by the lift and tipped the man sixpence, leaving his newspaper inadvertently in the lift. He met his chambermaid in the passage and gave her half a crown. He resolved to demonstrate his position to the entire establishment in this way. He didn't like the place; he disapproved of it politically, socially, morally; but he resolved no taint of meanness should disfigure his sojourn in its luxurious halls. He went down by the lift (tipping again), and, being accosted by a waiter with his gibus, tipped the finder half a crown. He had a vague sense that he was making a flank movement upon the hotel and buying over its staff. They would regard him as a 'character'; they would get to like him. He found his stock of small silver diminishing and replenished it at a desk in the hall. He tipped a man in bottle green, who looked like the man who had shown him his room the day before; and then he saw a visitor eyeing him, and doubted whether he was in this instance doing right. Finally he went out and took chance buses to their destinations, and wandered a little in remote wonderful suburbs, and returned. He lunched at a chop-house in Islington, and found himself back in the Royal Grand, now unmistakably footsore and London-weary, about three. He was attracted to the drawing-room by a neat placard about afternoon tea.

It occurred to him that the campaign of tipping upon which he had embarked was, perhaps after all, a mistake. He was confirmed in this by observing that the hotel officials were watching him, not respectfully, but with a sort of amused wonder, as if to see whom he would tip next. However, if he backed out now, they would think him an awful fool. Every one wasn't so rich as he was. It was his way to tip. Still—

He grew more certain the hotel had scored again.

He pretended to be lost in thought, and so drifted by, and, having put hat and umbrella in the cloakroom, went into the drawing-room for afternoon tea.

There he did get what for a time he held to be a point in his favour. The room was large and quiet at first, and he sat back restfully until it occurred to him that his attitude brought his extremely dusty boots too prominently into the light, so instead he sat up, and then people of the upper and upper middle classes began to come and group themselves about him and have tea likewise, and so revive the class animosities of the previous day.

Presently a fluffy fair-haired lady came into prominent existence a few yards away. She was talking to a respectful low-voiced clergyman, whom she was possibly entertaining at tea. 'No,' she said; 'dear Lady Jane wouldn't like that!'

'Mumble, mumble, mumble,' from the clergyman.

'Poor dear Lady Jane was always so sensitive,' the voice of the lady sang out clear and emphatic.

A fat, hairless, important-looking man joined this group, took a chair and planted it firmly with its back in the face of Kipps, a thing that offended Kipps mightily. 'Are you telling him,' gurgled the fat, hairless man,' about dear Lady Jane's affliction?' A young couple, lady brilliantly attired, and the man in a magnificently cut frock-coat, arranged themselves to the right, also with an air of exclusion towards Kipps. 'I've told him,' said the gentleman in a flat abundant voice. 'My!' said the young lady with an American smile. No doubt they all thought Kipps was out of it. A great desire to assert himself in some way surged up in his heart. He felt he would like to cut in on the conversation in some dramatic way. A monologue, something in the manner of Masterman? At any rate, abandoning that as impossible, he would like to appear self-centred and at ease. His eye, wandering over the black surfaces of a noble architectural mass close by, discovered a slot and an enamelled plaque of directions.

It was some sort of musical box!

It occurred to Kipps that he would like some music, that to inaugurate some would show him a man of taste and at his ease at the same time. He rose, read over a list of tunes, selected one haphazard, pressed his sixpence – it was sixpence! – home, and prepared for a confidential refined little melody.

Considering the high social tone of the Royal Grand, it was really a very loud instrument indeed. It gave vent to three deafening brays, and so burst the dam of silence that had long pent it in. It seemed to be chiefly full of the great-uncles of trumpets, megalo-trombones, and railways brakes. It made sounds like shunting trains. It did not so much begin as blow up your counterscarp and rush forward to storm under cover of melodious shrapnel. It had not so much an air as a *ricochette*. The music had in short the inimitable quality of Sousa. It swept down upon the friend of Lady Jane and carried away something socially striking into the eternal night of the unheard; the American girl to the left of it was borne off shrieking. 'HIGH cockalorum Tootletootle tootle loo. High cockalorum tootle lootle loo. BUMP, bump, bump – BUMP,' – Native American music, full of native American notes, full of the spirit of western college yells and election howls, joyous exorbitant music from the gigantic nursery of the Future, bearing the hearer along upon its torrential succession of sounds, as if he was in a cask on

Niagara. Whiroo! Yah, Have at you! the Strenuous Life! Yaha!
Stop! A Reprieve! A Reprieve! No! Bang! Bump!

Everybody looked round, conversation ceased and gave place
to gestures.

The friend of Lady Jane became terribly agitated.

'Can't it be stopped?' she vociferated, pointing a gloved finger
and saying something to the waiter about 'that dreadful young
man'.

'Ought not to be working,' said the clerical friend of Lady
Jane.

The waiter shook his head at the fat, hairless gentleman.

People began to move away. Kipps leant back luxurious, and
then tapped with a half-crown to pay.

He paid, tipped like a gentleman, rose with an easy gesture,
and strolled towards the door. His retreat evidently completed
the indignation of the friend of Lady Jane, and from the door he
could still discern her gestures as asking, 'Can't it be stopped?'
The music followed him into the passage and pursued him to
the lift, and only died away completely in the quiet of his own
room, and afterwards from his window he saw the friend of
Lady Jane and her party having their tea carried out to a little
table in the court.

Certainly that was a point to him. But it was his only score;
all the rest of the game lay in the hands of the upper classes and
the big hotel. And presently he was doubting whether even this
was really a point. It seemed a trifle vulgar, come to think it
over, to interrupt people when they were talking.

He saw a clerk peering at him from the office, and suddenly it
occurred to him that the place might be back at him tremendously over the bill.

They would probably take it out of him by charging pounds
and pounds.

Suppose they charged more than he had!

The clerk had a particularly nasty face, just the face to take
advantage of a vacillating Kipps.

He became aware of a man in a cap touching it, and produced
his shilling automatically, but the strain was beginning to tell. It
was a deuce and all of an expense – this tipping.

If the hotel chose to stick it on to the bill something tremendous, what was Kipps to do? Refuse to pay? Make a row?

If he did he couldn't fight all these men in bottle green. . . .

He went out about seven and walked for a long time, and dined at last upon a chop in the Euston Road; then he walked along to the Edgeware Road and sat and rested in the Metropolitan Music Hall for a time, until a trapeze performance unnerved him, and finally he came back to bed. He tipped the lift-man sixpence and wished him good night. In the silent watches of the night he reviewed the tale of the day's tipping, went over the horrors of the previous night's dinner, and heard again the triumphant bray of the harmonicon* devil released from its long imprisonment. Every one would be told about him to-morrow. He couldn't go on! He admitted his defeat. Never in their whole lives had any of these people seen such a Fool as he! Ugh! . . .

His method of announcing his withdrawal to the clerk was touched with bitterness.

'I'm going to get out of this,' said Kipps, blowing windily. 'Let's see what you got on my bill.'

'One breakfast?' asked the clerk.

'Do I *look* as if I'd ate two?'

At his departure Kipps, with a hot face, convulsive gestures, and an embittered heart, tipped every one who did not promptly and actively resist, including an absent-minded South African diamond merchant who was waiting in the hall for his wife. He paid his cabman a four-shilling piece at Charing Cross, having no smaller change, and wished he could burn him alive. Then in a sudden reaction of economy he refused the proffered help of a porter, and carried his bag quite violently to the train.

Chapter Eight

Kipps Enters Society

I

Submission to Inexorable Fatè took Kipps to the Anagram Tea.

At any rate he would meet Helen there in the presence of other people, and be able to carry off the worst of the difficulty of explaining his little jaunt to London. He had not seen her since his last portentous visit to New Romney. He was engaged to her, he would have to marry her, and the sooner he faced her again the better. Before wild plans of turning socialist, defying the world and repudiating all calling for ever, his heart, on second thoughts, sank. He felt Helen would never permit anything of the sort. As for the Anagrams, he could do no more than his best, and that he was resolved to do. What had happened at the Royal Grand, what had happened at New Romney, he must bury in his memory and begin again at the reconstruction of his social position. Ann, Buggins, Chitterlow – all these, seen in the matter-of-fact light of the Folkestone corridor train, stood just as they stood before – people of an inferior social position, who had to be eliminated from his world. It was a bother about Ann, a bother and a pity. His mind rested so for a space on Ann until the memory of those Anagrams drew him away. If he could see Coote that evening he might, he thought, be able to arrange some sort of connivance about the anagrams, and his mind was chiefly busy sketching proposals for such an arrangement. It would not, of course, be ungentlemanly cheating, but only a little mystification. Coote, very probably, might drop him a hint of the solution of one or two of the things – not enough to win a prize, but enough to cover his shame. Or failing that, he might take a humorous, quizzical line, and pretend he was pretending to be very stupid. There were plenty of ways out of it if one kept a sharp look-out. . . .

The costume Kipps wore to the Anagram Tea was designed as a compromise between the strict letter of high fashion and seaside laxity – a sort of easy semi-state for afternoon. Helen's first reproof had always lingered in his mind. He wore a frock-coat, but mitigated it by a Panama hat of romantic shape with a black band, grey gloves, but, for relaxation, brown button boots. The only other man besides the clergy present – a new doctor with an attractive wife – was in full afternoon dress. Coote was not there.

Kipps was a little pale, but quite self-possessed, as he approached Mrs Bindon Botting's door. He took a turn while some people went in, and then faced it manfully. The door opened and revealed – Ann!

In the background, through a draped doorway, behind a big fern in a great art pot, the elder Miss Botting was visible talking to two guests; the auditory background was a froth of feminine voices. . . .

Our two young people were much too amazed to give one another any formula of greeting, though they had parted warmly enough. Each was already in a state of extreme tension to meet the demands of this great and unprecedented occasion – an Anagram Tea. 'Lor!' said Ann, her sole remark; and then the sense of Miss Botting's eye ruled her straight again. She became very pale, but she took his hat mechanically, and he was already removing his gloves. 'Ann,' he said in a low tone, and then 'Fency!'

The eldest Miss Botting knew Kipps was the sort of guest who requires nursing, and she came forward vocalizing charm. She said it was 'awfully jolly of him to come – awfully jolly. It was awfully difficult to get any good men!'

She handed Kipps forward, mumbling, and in a dazed condition, to the drawing-room, and there he encountered Helen, looking unfamiliar in an unfamiliar hat. It was as if he had not met her for years.

She astonished him. She didn't seem to mind in the least his going to London. She held out a shapely hand, and smiled encouragingly. 'You've faced the anagrams?' she said.

The second Miss Botting accosted them, a number of oblong pieces of paper in her hand, mysteriously inscribed. 'Take an anagram,' and boldly pinned one of these brief documents to Kipp's lapel. The letters were 'Cpyshi', and Kipps from the very beginning suspected this was an anagram for Cuyps. She also left a thing like a long dance programme, from which dangled a little pencil, in his hand. He found himself being introduced to people, and then he was in a corner with the short lady in a big bonnet, who was pelting him with gritty little bits of small talk, that were gone before you could take hold of them and reply.

'Very hot,' said this lady. 'Very hot indeed – hot all the summer – remarkable year – all the years remarkable now – don't know what we're coming to. Don't you think so, Mr Kipps?'

'Oo rather,' said Kipps, and wondered if Ann was still in the hall. Ann!

He ought not to have stared at her like a stuck fish, and pretended not to know her. That couldn't be right. But what *was* right?

The lady in the big bonnet proceeded to a second discharge. 'Hope you're fond of anagrams, Mr Kipps – difficult exercise – still, one most do something to bring people together – better than Ludo, anyhow. Don't you think so, Mr Kipps?'

Ann fluttered past the open door. Her eyes met his in amazed inquiry. Something had got dislocated in the world for both of them. . . .

He ought to have told her he was engaged. He ought to have explained things to her. Perhaps, even now, he might be able to drop her a hint.

'Don't you think so, Mr Kipps?'

'Oo rather,' said Kipps for the third time.

A lady with a tired smile, who was labelled conspicuously 'Wogdelenk,' drifted towards Kipps' interlocutor, and the two fell into conversation. Kipps found himself socially aground. He looked about him. Helen was talking to a curate and laughing. Kipps was overcome by a vague desire to speak to Ann. He was for sidling doorward.

'What are *you* please?' said an extraordinarily bold, tall girl, and arrested him while she took down 'Cypshi.'

'I'm sure I don't know what it means,' she explained. 'I'm Sir Bubh. Don't you think anagrams are something chronic?'

Kipps made stockish noises, and the young lady suddenly became the nucleus of a party of excited friends who were forming a syndicate to guess, and barred his escape. She took no further notice of him. He found himself jammed against an occasional table and listening to the conversation of Mrs 'Wogdelenk' and his lady with the big bonnet.

'She packed her two beauties off together,' said the lady in the big bonnet. 'Time enough, too. Don't think much of this girl she's got as housemaid now. Pretty, of course, but there's no occasion for a housemaid to be pretty – none whatever. And she doesn't look particularly up to her work either. Kind of 'mazed expression.'

'You never can tell,' said the lady labelled 'Wogdelenk'; 'you never can tell. My wretches are big enough, Heaven knows, and do they work? Not a bit of it! . . .'

Kipps felt dreadfully out of it with regard to all these people, and dreadfully in it with Ann.

He scanned the back of the big bonnet, and concluded it was an extremely ugly bonnet indeed. It got jerking forward as each short, dry sentence was snapped off at the end, and a plume of osprey on it jerked excessively. 'She hasn't guessed even one!' followed by a shriek of girlish merriment, came from the group about the tall, bold girl. They'd shriek at him presently, perhaps! Beyond thinking his own anagram might be Cuyps, he hadn't a notion. What a chatter they were all making! It was just like a summer sale! Just the sort of people who'd give a lot of trouble and swap you! And suddenly the smouldering fires of rebellion leapt to flame again. These were a rotten lot of people, and the anagrams were rotten nonsense, and he (Kipps) had been a rotten fool to come. There was Helen away there still laughing with her curate. Pity she couldn't marry a curate, and leave him (Kipps) alone! Then he'd know what to do. He disliked the whole gathering, collectively and in detail. Why were they all trying to make him one of themselves? He perceived unexpected ugliness everywhere about him. There were two great pins jabbed through the tall girl's hat, and the swirls of her hair below the brim, with the minutest piece of tape tie-up showing, did not repay close examination. Mrs 'Wogdelenk' wore a sort of mumps bandage of lace, and there was another lady perfectly dazzling with beads and jewels and bits of trimming. They were all flaps and angles and flounces, these women. Not one of them looked as neat and decent a shape as Ann's clean, trim little figure. Echoes of Masterman woke up in him again. Ladies indeed! Here were all these chattering people, with money, with leisure, with every chance in the world, and all they could do was to crowd like this into a couple of rooms and jabber nonsense about anagrams.

'Could Cypshi really mean Cuyps?' floated like a dissolving wreath of mist across his mind.

Abruptly resolution stood armed in his heart. He was going to get out of this!

''Scuse me,' he said, and began to wade neck-deep through the bubbling tea-party.

He was going to get out of it all!

He found himself close by Helen. 'I'm orf,' he said, but she gave him the briefest glance. She did not appear to hear him. 'Still, Mr Spratlingdown, you *must* admit there's a limit even to conformity,' she was saying. . . .

He was in a curtained archway, and Ann was before him, carrying a tray supporting several small sugar-bowls.

He was moved to speech. '*What* a Lot!' he said, and then mysteriously, 'I'm engaged to *her*.' He indicated Helen's new hat, and became aware of a skirt he had stepped upon.

Ann stared at him helplessly, borne past in the grip of incomprehensible imperatives.

Why shouldn't they talk together?

He was in a small room, and then at the foot of the staircase in the hall. He heard the rustle of a dress, and what was conceivably his hostess was upon him.

'But you're not going, Mr Kipps?' she said.

'I must,' he said. 'I got to.'

'But, Mr Kipps!'

'I must,' he said. 'I'm not well.'

'But before the guessing! Without any tea!'

Ann appeared and hovered behind him.

'I got to go,' said Kipps.

If he parleyed with her Helen might awake to his desperate attempt.

'Of course, if you *must* go.'

'It's something I've forgotten,' said Kipps, beginning to feel regrets. 'Reely I must.'

Mrs Botting turned with a certain offended dignity, and Ann, in a state of flushed calm that evidently concealed much, came forward to open the door.

'I'm very sorry,' he said, 'I'm very sorry,' half to his hostess and half to her, and was swept past her by superior social forces – like a drowning man in a mill-race – and into the Upper

Sandgate Road. He half turned upon the step, and then slam went the door. . . .

He retreated along the Leas, a thing of shame and perplexity, Mrs Botting's aggrieved astonishment uppermost in his mind. . . .

Something – reinforced by the glances of the people he was passing – pressed its way to his attention through the tumultuous disorder of his mind.

He became aware that he was still wearing his little placard with the letters 'Cypshi'.

'Desh it!' he said, clutching off this abomination. In another moment its several letters, their task accomplished, were scattering gleefully before the breeze down the front of the Leas.

II

Kipps was dressed for Mrs Wace's dinner half an hour before it was time to start, and he sat waiting until Coote should come to take him round. *Manners and Rules of Good Society* lay beside him neglected. He had read the polished prose of the Member of the Aristocracy on page 96 as far as –

> 'the acceptance of an invitation is in the eyes of diners out, a binding obligation which only ill-health, family bereavement, or some all-important reason justifies its being set on one side or other-wise evaded' –

and then he had lapsed into gloomy thoughts.

That afternoon he had had a serious talk with Helen.

He had tried to express something of the change of heart that had happened to him. But to broach the real state of the matter had been altogether too terrible for him. He had sought a minor issue. 'I don't like all this Seciety,' he had said.

'But you must *see* people,' said Helen.

'Yes, but—It's the short of people you see.' He nerved himself. 'I didn't think much of that lot at the Enegram Tea.'

'You have to see all sorts of people if you want to see the world,' said Helen.

Kipps was silent for a space, and a little short of breath.

'My dear Arthur,' she began almost kindly, 'I shouldn't ask

you to go to these affairs if I didn't think it good for you, should I?'

Kipps acquiesced in silence.

'You will find the benefit of it all when we get to London. You learn to swim in a tank before you go out into the sea. These people here are good enough to learn upon. They're stiff and rather silly, and dreadfully narrow, and not an idea in a dozen of them, but it really doesn't matter at all. You'll soon get Savoir Faire.'

He made to speak again, and found his powers of verbal expression lacking. Instead he blew a sigh.

'You'll get used to it all very soon,' said Helen, helpfully. . . .

As he sat meditating over that interview, and over the vistas of London that opened before him, on the little flat and teas and occasions, and the constant presence of Brudderkins and all the bright prospect of his new and better life, and how he would never see Ann any more, the housemaid entered with a little package, a small, square envelope for 'Arthur Kipps, Esquire'.

'A young woman left this Sir,' said the housemaid, a little severely.

'Eh?' said Kipps. 'What young woman?' and then suddenly began to understand.

'She looked an ordinary young woman,' said the housemaid, coldly.

'Ah!' said Kipps. *That's* orlright.'

He waited till the door had closed behind the girl, staring at the envelope in his hand, and then, with a curious feeling of increasing tension, tore it open. As he did so, some quicker sense than sight or touch told him its contents. It was Ann's half-sixpence. And besides, not a word!

Then she must have heard him—'

He was standing with the envelope in his hand when Coote became audible without.

Coote appeared in evening dress, a clean and radiant Coote, with large greenish white gloves, and a particularly large white tie edged with black. 'For a third cousin,' he presently explained. 'Nace, isn't it?' He could see Kipps was pale and disturbed, and put this down to the approaching social trial. 'You keep your nerve up, Kipps, my dear chap, and you'll be all right,' said Coote, with a big brotherly glove on Kipps' sleeve.

III

The dinner came to a crisis so far as Kipps' emotions were concerned with Mrs Bindon Botting's talk about servants, but before that there had been several things of greater or smaller magnitude to perturb and disarrange his social front. One little matter that was mildly insurgent throughout the entire meal was, if I may be permitted to mention so intimate a matter, the behaviour of his left brace. The webbing – which was of a cheerful scarlet silk – had slipped away from its buckle, fastened, no doubt, in agitation, and had developed a strong tendency to place itself obliquely, in the manner rather of an official decoration, athwart his spotless front. It first asserted itself before they went in to dinner. He replaced this ornament by a dexterous thrust when no one was looking, and thereafter the suppression of this novel innovation upon the stereotyped sombreness of evening dress became a standing preoccupation. On the whole he was inclined to think his first horror excessive; at any rate, no one remarked upon it. However, you imagine him constantly throughout the evening with one eye and one hand, whatever the rest of him might be doing, predominantly concerned with the weak corner.

But this, I say, was a little matter. What exercised him much more was to discover Helen, quite terribly in evening dress.

The young lady had let her imagination rove Londonward, and this costume was perhaps an anticipation of that clever little flat, not too far west, which was to become the centre of so delightful a literary and artistic set. It was, of all the feminine costumes present, most distinctly an evening dress. One was advised Miss Walshingham had arms and shoulders of a type by no means despicable; one was advised Miss Walshingham was capable not only of dignity but charm, even a certain glow of charm. It was, you know, her first evening dress, a tribute paid by Walshingham finance to her brightening future. Had she wanted keeping in countenance, she would have had to have fallen back upon her hostess, who was resplendent in black and steel. The other ladies had to a certain extent compromised. Mrs Walshingham had dressed with just a refined little V, and Mrs Bindon Botting, except for her dear mottled arms, confided scarcely more of her plump charm to the world. The elder Miss Botting stopped short of shoulder, and so did Miss Wace. But

Helen didn't. She was – had Kipps had eyes to see it – a quite beautiful human figure; she knew it, and she met him with a radiant smile that had forgotten all the little difference of the afternoon. But to Kipps her appearance was the last release. With that she had become as remote, as foreign, as incredible as a wife and mate, as though the Cnidian Venus herself, in all her simple elegance, was, before witnesses, declared to be his. If, indeed, she had ever been credible as a wife and mate!

She ascribed his confusion to modest reverence, and, having blazed smiling upon him for a moment, turned a shapely shoulder towards him and exchanged a remark with Mrs Bindon Botting. Ann's poor little half-sixpence came against Kipps' fingers in his pocket, and he clutched at it suddenly as though it was a talisman. Then he abandoned it to suppress his Order of the Brace. He was affected by a cough. 'Miss Wace tells me Mr Revel is coming,' Mrs Botting was saying.

'Isn't it delightful?' said Helen. 'We saw him last night. He's stopped on his way to Paris. He's going to meet his wife there.'

Kipps' eyes rested for a moment on Helen's dazzling deltoid, and then went inquiringly, accusingly, almost, to Coote's face. Where in the presence of this terrible emergence was the gospel of suppression now? that Furtive treatment of Religion and Politics, and Birth and Death, and Bathing and Babies and 'all those things', which constitute your True Gentleman? He had been too modest even to discuss this question with his Mentor, but surely, surely this quintessence of all that is good and nice could regard these unsolicited confidences only in one way. With something between relief and confirmation of his worst fears he perceived, by a sort of twitching of the exceptionally abundant muscles about Coote's lower jaw, in a certain deliberate avoidance of one particular direction by those pale but resolute grey eyes, by the almost convulsive grip of the ample, greenish-white gloves behind him, a grip broken at times for controlling pats at the black-bordered tie and the back of that spacious head, and by a slight but increasing disposition to cough, that *Coote did not approve*!

To Kipps Helen had once supplied a delicately beautiful dream, a thing of romance and unsubstantial mystery. But this was her final materialization, and the last thin wreath of glamour about her was dispelled. In some way (he had forgotten how, and it was perfectly incomprehensible) he was bound to this dark, solid and determined young person, whose shadow and suggestion he had once loved. He had to go through with the thing as a gentleman should. Still—

And when he was sacrificing Ann!

He wouldn't stand this sort of thing, whatever else he stood. . . . Should he say something about her dress to her – to-morrow?

He could put his foot down firmly. He could say, 'Look 'ere. I don't care. I ain't going to stand it. See?'

She'd say something unexpected of course. She always did say something unexpected.

Suppose for once he overrode what she said, and simply repeated his point.

He found these thoughts battling with certain conversational aggressions from Mrs Wace, and then Revel arrived and took the centre of the stage.

The author of that brilliant romance, *Red Hearts a-Beating*, was a less imposing man than Kipps had anticipated, but he speedily effaced that disappointment by his predominating manners. Although he lived habitually in the vivid world of London, his collar and tie were in no way remarkable, and he was neither brilliantly handsome, nor curly, nor long-haired. His personal appearance suggested armchairs rather than the equestrian exercises and amorous toyings and passionate intensities of his masterpiece; he was inclined to be fat, with whitish flesh, muddy-coloured straight hair; he had a rather shapeless and truncated nose, and his chin was asymmetrical. One eye was more inclined to stare than the other. He might have been esteemed a little undistinguished-looking were it not for his beeswaxed moustache, which came amidst his features with a pleasing note of incongruity, and the whimsical wrinkles above and about his greater eye. His regard sought and found Helen's as he entered the room, and they shook hands presently with an air of intimacy Kipps, for no clear reason, found objectionable. He saw them clasp their hands, heard Coote's characteristic cough – a sound rather more like a very, very old sheep a quarter of a mile away being blown to pieces by a small charge of gunpowder than anything else in the world – did some confused beginnings of a thought, and then they were all going in to dinner, and Helen's shining bare arm lay along his sleeve. Kipps was in no state for conversation. She glanced at him, and, though he did not know it, very slightly pressed his elbow. He struggled with strange respiratory dislocations. Before them went Coote, discoursing in amiable reverberations to Mrs Walshingham, and at the head of the procession was Mrs Bindon Botting, talking fast and brightly beside the erect military figure of little Mr Wace. (He was not a soldier really, but he had caught a martinet bearing by living so close to Shorncliffe.) Revel came last, in charge of Mrs Wace's queenly black and steel, politely admiring in a flute-like cultivated voice the mellow wall-paper of the staircase. Kipps marvelled at everybody's self-possession.

From the earliest spoonful of soup it became evident that Revel considered himself responsible for table-talk. And before the soup was over it was almost as manifest that Mrs Bindon Botting inclined to consider his sense of responsibility excessive. In her circle Mrs Bindon Botting was esteemed an agreeable rattle, her manner and appearance were conspicuously vivacious for one so plump, and she had an almost Irish facility for humorous description. She would keep people amused all through an afternoon call with the story of how her jobbing gardener had got himself married and what his home was like, or how her favourite butt, Mrs Stigson Warder, had all his unfortunate children taught almost every conceivable instrument because they had the phrenological bump of music abnormally large. The family itself was also abnormally large. 'They got to trombones, my dear!' she would say, with her voice coming to a climax. Usually her friends conspired to draw her out, but on this occasion they neglected to do so, a thing that militated against her keen desire to shine in Revel's eyes. After a time she perceived that the only thing for her to do was to cut in on the talk, on her own account, and this she began to do. She made several ineffectual snatches at the general attention, and then Revel drifted towards a topic she regarded as particularly her own – the ordering of households.

They came to the thing through talk about localities. 'We are leaving our house in The Boltons,' said Revel, 'and taking a little place at Wimbledon, and I think of having rooms in Dane's Inn. It will be more convenient in many ways. My wife is furiously addicted to golf and exercise of all sorts, and I like to sit about in clubs – I haven't the strength necessary for these hygienic proceedings – and the old arrangement suited neither of us. And besides, no one could imagine the demoralization the domestics of West London have undergone during the last three years.'

'It's the same everywhere,' said Mrs Bindon Botting.

'Very possibly it is. A friend of mine calls it the servile tradition in decay, and regards it all as a most hopeful phenomenon—'

'He ought to have had my last two criminals,' said Mrs Bindon Botting.

She turned to Mrs Wace, while Revel came again a little too late with a 'Possibly—'

'And I haven't told you, my dear,' she said, speaking with voluble rapidity, 'I'm in trouble again.'

'That last girl?'

'The last girl. Before I can get a cook, my hard-won housemaid' – she paused – 'chucks it.'

'Panic?' asked young Walshingham.

'Mysterious grief! Everything merry as a marriage-bell until my Anagram Tea! Then in the evening a portentous rigour of bearing, a word or so from my Aunt and immediately – Floods of Tears and Notice!' For a moment her eye rested thoughtfully on Kipps as she said, 'Is there anything heart-rending about Anagrams?'

'I find them so,' said Revel. 'I—'

But Mrs Bindon Botting got away again. 'For a time it made me quite uneasy—'

Kipps jabbed his lip with his fork rather painfully, and was recalled from a fascinated glare at Mrs Botting to the immediate facts of dinner.

'—whether anagrams might not have offended the good domestic's Moral Code – you never can tell. We made inquiries. No. No. She *must* go, and that's all!'

'One perceives,' said Revel, 'in these disorders, dimly and distantly, the last dying glow of the age of Romance. Let us suppose, Mrs Botting, let us at least try to suppose – it is Love.'

Kipps clattered with his knife and fork.

'It's love,' said Mrs Botting; 'what else can it be? Beneath the orderly humdrum of our lives these romances are going on, until at last they bust up and give Notice and upset our humdrum altogether. Some fatal, wonderful soldier—'

'The passions of the common or house-domestic – ' began Revel, and recovered possession of the table.

Upon the troubled disorder of Kipps' table manners there had supervened a quietness, an unusual calm. For once in his life he had distinctly made up his mind on his own account. He listened no more to Revel. He put down his knife and fork and refused everything that followed. Coote regarded him with tactful concern, and Helen flushed a little.

IV

About half-past nine that night there came a violent pull at the bell of Mrs Bindon Botting, and a young man in a dress-suit and a gibus and other marks of exalted social position stood without. Athwart his white expanse of breast lay a ruddy bar of patterned silk that gave him a singular distinction and minimized the glow of a few small stains of Burgundy. His gibus was thrust back, and exposed a disorder of hair that suggested a reckless desperation. He had, in fact, burnt his boats and refused to join the ladies. Coote, in the subsequent conversation, had protested quietly, 'You're going on all right, you know,' to which Kipps had answered he didn't care a 'Eng' about that, and so, after a brief tussle with Walshingham's detaining arm, had got away. 'I got something to do,' he said. ''Ome.' And here he was – panting an extraordinary resolve. The door opened, revealing the pleasantly furnished hall of Mrs Bindon Botting, lit by rose-tinted lights, and in the centre of the picture, neat and pretty in black and white, stood Ann. At the sight of Kipps her colour vanished.

'Ann,' said Kipps, 'I want to speak to you. I got something to say to you right away. See? I'm—'

'This ain't the door to speak to me at,' said Ann.

'But, Ann! It's something special.'

'You spoke enough,' said Ann.

'Ann!'

'Besides, that's my door, down there. Basement. If I was caught talking at *this* door—!'

'But, Ann, *I'm*—'

'Basement after nine. Them's my hours. I'm a servant, and likely to keep one. If you're calling here, what name, please? but you got your friends and I got mine, and you mustn't go talking to *me*.'

'But, Ann, I want to ask you—'

Some one appeared in the hall behind Ann. 'Not here,' said Ann. 'Don't know any one of that name,' and incontinently slammed the door in his face.

'What was that, Ann?' said Mrs Bindon Botting's invalid Aunt.

'Ge'm a little intoxicated, Ma'am – asking for the wrong name, Ma'am.'

'What name did he want?' asked the lady, doubtfully.

'No name that *we* know, Ma'am,' said Ann, hustling along the hall towards the kitchen stairs.

'I hope you weren't too short with him, Ann.'

'No shorter than he deserved, considering 'ow he be'aved,' said Ann, with her bosom heaving.

And Mrs Bindon Botting's invalid Aunt, perceiving suddenly that this call had some relation to Ann's private and sentimental trouble, turned, after one moment of hesitating scrutiny, away.

She was an extremely sympathetic lady was Mrs Bindon Botting's invalid Aunt; she took an interest in the servants, imposed piety, extorted confessions and followed human nature, blushing and lying defensively to its reluctantly revealed recesses; but Ann's sense of privacy was strong, and her manner, under drawing-out and encouragement, sometimes even alarming. . . .

So the poor lady went upstairs again.

v

The basement door opened, and Kipps came into the kitchen. He was flushed and panting.

He struggled for speech.

''Ere,' he said, and held out two half-sixpences.

Ann stood behind the kitchen table – face pale and eyes round, and now – and it simplified Kipps very much – he could see she had indeed been crying.

'Well?' she said.

'Don't you see?'

Ann moved her head slightly.

'I kep' it all these years.'

'You kep' it too long.'

His mouth closed and his flush died away. He looked at her. The amulet, it seemed, had failed to work.

'Ann!' he said.

'Well?'

'Ann.'

The conversation still hung fire.

'Ann,' he said; made a movement with his hands that suggested appeal and advanced a step.

Ann shook her head more definitely, and became defensive.

'Look here, Ann,' said Kipps. 'I been a fool.'

They stared into each other's miserable eyes.

'Ann,' he said. 'I want to marry you.'

Ann clutched the table edge. 'You can't, she said faintly.

He made as if to approach her round the table, and she took a step that restored their distance.

'I must,' he said.

'You can't.'

'I must. You *got* to marry me, Ann.'

'You can't go marrying everybody. You got to marry *'er.*'

'I shan't.'

Ann shook her head. 'You're engaged to that girl. Lady, rather. You can't be engaged to me.'

'I don't want to be engaged to you. I *been* engaged. I want to be married to you. See? Right away.'

Ann turned a shade paler. 'But what d'you mean?' she asked.

'Come right off to London and marry me. Now.'

'What d'you mean?'

Kipps became extremely lucid and earnest.

'I mean, come right off and marry me now before any one else can. See?'

'In London?'

'In London.'

They stared at one another again. They took things for granted in the most amazing way.

'I couldn't,' said Ann. 'For one thing, my month's not up for mor'n free weeks yet.'

They hung before that for a moment as though it was insurmountable.

'Look 'ere, Ann! Arst to go. Arst to go!'

'*She* wouldn't,' said Ann.

'Then come without arsting,' said Kipps.

'She'd keep my box—'

'She won't.'

'She will.'

'She won't.'

'You don't know 'er.'

'Well, desh 'er – let 'er! LET 'ER! Who cares? I'll buy you a 'undred boxes if you'll come.'

'It wouldn't be right towards Her.'

'It isn't Her you got to think about, Ann. It's me.'

'And you 'aven't treated me properly,' she said. 'You 'aven't treated me properly, Artie. You didn't ought to 'ave—'

'I didn't say I 'ad,' he interrupted, 'did I? Ann,' he appealed, 'I didn't come to arguefy. I'm all wrong. I never said I wasn't. It's yes or no. Me or not. . . . I been a fool. There! See? I been a fool. Ain't that enough? I got myself all tied up with every one and made a fool of myself all round. . . .'

He pleaded, 'It isn't as if we didn't care for one another, Ann.'

She seemed impassive, and he resumed his discourse.

'I thought I wasn't likely ever to see you again, Ann. I reely did. It isn't as though I was seein' you all the time. I didn't know what I wanted, and I went and be'aved like a fool – jest as any one might. I know what I want, and I know what I don't want now.

'Ann!'

'Well?'

'Will you come? . . . Will you come? . . .'

Silence.

'If you don't answer me, Ann – I'm despirt – if you don't answer me now, if you don't say you'll come, I'll go right out now—'

He turned doorward passionately as he spoke, with his threat incomplete.

'I'll go,' he said. I 'aven't a friend in the world!' I been and throwed everything away. I don't know why I done things and why I 'aven't. All I know is I can't stand nothing in the world any more,' He choked. 'The pier,' he said.

He fumbled with the door-latch, grumbling some inarticulate self-pity, as if he sought a handle, and then he had it open.

Clearly he was going.

'Artie!' said Ann, sharply.

He turned about, and the two hung white and tense.

'I'll do it,' said Ann.

His face began to work, he shut the door and came a step back to her, staring; his face became pitiful, and then suddenly they moved together. 'Artie!' she cried, 'don't go!' and held out her arms, weeping.

They clung close to one another. . . .

'Oh, I *been* so mis'bel!' cried Kipps, clinging to this lifebuoy; and suddenly his emotion, having no further serious work in hand, burst its way to a loud *boohoo*! His fashionable and expensive gibus flopped off, and fell and rolled and lay neglected on the floor.

'I been so mis'bel,' said Kipps, giving himself vent. 'Oh, I *been* so mis'bel, Ann!'

'Be quiet,' said Ann, holding his poor blubbering head tightly to her heaving shoulder, herself all aquiver; 'be quiet. She's there! Listenin'. She'll 'ear you, Artie, on the stairs. . . .'

VI

Ann's last words when, an hour later, they parted – Mrs and Miss Bindon Botting having returned very audibly upstairs – deserve a section to themselves.

'I wouldn't do this for every one, mind you,' whispered Ann.

Chapter Nine

The Labyrinthodon

I

You imagine them fleeing through our complex and difficult social system as it were for life, first on foot and severally to the Folkestone Central Station, then in a first-class carriage, with Kipps' bag as sole chaperon to Charing Cross, and then in a four-wheeler, a long, rumbling, palpitating, slow flight through the multitudinous swarming London streets to Sid. Kipps kept peeping out of the window. 'It's the next corner after this, I believe,' he would say. For he had a sort of feeling that at Sid's he would be immune from the hottest pursuit. He paid the cabman in a manner adequate to the occasion, and turned to his prospective brother-in-law. 'Me and Ann,' he said, 'we're going to marry.'

'But I thought—' began Sid.

Kipps motioned him towards explanations in the shop. . . .

'It's no good my arguing with you,' said Sid, smiling delightedly as the case unfolded. 'You done it now.' And Masterman, being apprised of the nature of the affair, descended slowly in a state of flushed congratulation.

'I thought you might find the Higher Life a bit difficult,' said Masterman, projecting a bony hand. 'But I never thought you'd have the originality to clear out. . . . Won't the young lady of the superior classes swear! Never mind – it doesn't matter anyhow.

'You were starting to climb,' he said at dinner, 'that doesn't lead anywhere. You would have clambered from one refinement of vulgarity to another, and never got to any satisfactory top. There isn't a top. It's a squirrel's cage. Things are out of joint, and the only top there is is a lot of blazing card-playing women and betting men, seasoned with archbishops and officials and all that sort of glossy pandering Tosh. . . . You'd have hung on, a disconsolate, dismal little figure, somewhere up the ladder, far below even the motor-car class, while your wife larked about, or fretted because she wasn't a bit higher than she was. . . . I found it all out long ago. I've seen women of that sort. And I don't climb any more.'

'I often thought about what you said last time I saw you,' said Kipps.

'I wonder what I said,' said Masterman, in parenthesis. 'Anyhow, you're doing the right and sane thing, and that's a rare spectacle. You're going to marry your equal, and you're going to take your own line, quite independently of what people up there, or people down there, think you ought or ought not to do. That's about the only course one can take nowadays, with everything getting more muddled and upside down every day. Make your own little world and your own house first of all; keep that right side up whatever you do, and marry your mate. . . . That, I suppose is what *I* should do – if *I* had a mate. . . . But people of my sort, luckily for the world, don't get made in pairs. No!

'Besides—However—' And abruptly taking advantage of an interruption by Master Walt, he lapsed into thought.

Presently he came out of his musings.

'After all,' he said, 'there's Hope.'

'What about?' said Sid.

'Everything,' said Masterman.

'Where there's life there's hope,' said Mrs Sid. 'But none of you aren't eating anything like you ought to.'

Masterman lifted his glass.

'Here's to Hope!' he said, 'the Light of the World!'

Sid beamed at Kipps, as who should say, 'You don't meet a character like *this* every dinner-time.'

'Here's to Hope!' repeated Masterman. 'The best thing one can have. Hope of life—Yes.'

He imposed his moment of magnificent self-pity on them all. Even young Walt was impressed.

II

They spent the days before their marriage in a number of agreeable excursions together. One day they went to Kew by steamboat, and admired the house full of paintings of flowers extremely; and one day they went early to have a good long day at the Crystal Palace, and enjoyed themselves very much indeed. They got there so early that nothing was open inside; all the stalls were wrapped up, and all the minor exhibitions locked and barred. They seemed the minutest creatures even to themselves in that enormous empty aisle, and their echoing footsteps indecently loud. They contemplated realistic groups of plaster savages, and Ann thought they'd be queer people to have about. She was glad there were none in this country. They meditated upon replicas of classical statuary without excessive comment. Kipps said, at large, it must have been a queer world then; but Ann very properly doubted if they really went about like that. But the place at that early hour was really lonely. One began to fancy things. So they went out into the October sunshine of the mighty terraces, and wandered amidst miles of stucco tanks, and about those quiet Gargantuan grounds. A great grey emptiness it was, and it seemed marvellous to them, but not nearly so marvellous as it might have seemed. 'I never see a finer place, never,' said Kipps, turning to survey the entirety of the enormous glass front with Paxton's vast image in the centre.

'What it must 'ave cost to build!' said Ann, and left her sentence eloquently incomplete.

Presently they came to a region of caves and waterways, and amidst these waterways strange reminders of the possibilities of the Creator. They passed under an arch made of whale's jaws, and discovered amidst herbage, browsing or standing unoccupied and staring as if amazed at themselves, huge effigies of iguanodons,* and deinotheria, and mastodons and such-like cattle gloriously done in green and gold.

'They got everything,' said Kipps. 'Earl's Court isn't a patch on it.'

His mind was very greatly exercised by these monsters, and he hovered about them and returned to them. 'You'd wonder 'ow they ever got enough to eat,' he said several times.

III

It was later in the day, and upon a seat in the presence of the green and gold Labyrinthodon that looms so splendidly above the lake, that the Kippses fell into talk about their future. They had made a sufficient lunch in the palace, they had seen pictures and no end of remarkable things, and that and the amber sunlight made a mood for them, quiet and philosophical – a haven mood. Kipps broke a contemplative silence with an abrupt allusion to one principle preoccupation. 'I shall offer an 'pology, and I shall offer 'er brother damages. If she likes to bring an action for Breach after that, well, – I done all I can. . . . They can't get much out of reading my letters in court, because I didn't write none. I dessay a thousan' or two'll settle all that, anyhow. I ain't much worried about that. That don't worry me very much, Ann – No.'

And then, 'It's a lark our marrying.

'It's curious 'ow things come about. If I 'adn't run against you, where should I 'ave been now – eh? . . . Even after we met I didn't seem to see it like – not marrying you, I mean – until that night I came. I didn't – reely.'

'I didn't neither,' said Ann, with thoughtful eyes on the water.

For a time Kipps' mind was occupied by the prettiness of her thinking face. A faint tremulous network of lights, reflected from the ripples of a passing duck, played subtly over her cheek and faded away.

Ann reflected. 'I s'ppose things 'ad to be,' she said.

Kipps mused. 'It's curious 'ow ever I got on to be engaged to 'er.'

'She wasn't suited to you,' said Ann.

'Suited? No fear! That's jest it. 'Ow did it come about?'

'I expect she led you on,' said Ann.

Kipps was half minded to assent. Then he had a twinge of conscience. 'It wasn't that, Ann,' he said. 'It's curious. I don't know what it was, but I wasn't that. I don't recollect. . . . No. . . . Life's jolly rum; that's one thing, any'ow. And I suppose I'm a rum sort of feller. I get excited sometimes, and then I don't seem to care what I do. That's about what it was, reely. Still—'

They meditated, Kipps with his arms folded and pulling at his scanty moustache. Presently a faint smile came over his face.

'We'll get a nice little 'ouse out Ithe way.'

'It's 'omelier than Folkestone,' said Ann.

'Jest a nice little 'ouse,' said Kipps. 'There's Hughenden, of course. But that's let. Besides being miles too big. And I wouldn't live in Folkestone again some'ow – not for anything.'

'I'd like to 'ave a 'ouse of my own,' said Ann. 'I've often

thought, being in service, 'ow much I'd like to manage a 'ouse of my own.'

'You'd know all about what the servants was up to, anyhow,' said Kipps, amused.

'Servants! We don't want no servants,' said Ann, startled.

'You'll 'ave to 'ave a servant,' said Kipps. 'If it's only to do the 'eavy work of the 'ouse.'

'What! and not be able 'ardly to go into my own kitchen?' said Ann.

'You ought to 'ave a servant,' said Kipps.

'One could easy 'ave a woman in for anything that's 'eavy,' said Ann. 'Besides—If I 'ad some of the girls one sees about nowadays, I should want to be taking the broom out of 'er 'and and do it all over myself. I'd manage better without 'er.'

'We ought to 'ave one servant, anyhow,' said Kipps, 'else 'ow should we manage if we wanted to go out together or anything like that?'

'I might get a *young* girl,' said Ann, 'and bring 'er up in my own way.'

Kipps left the matter at that and came back to the house.

'There's little 'ouses going into Hythe just the sort we want, not too big and not too small. We'll 'ave a kitching and a dining-room and a little room to sit in of a night.'

'It mustn't be a 'ouse with a basement,' said Ann.

'What's a basement?'

'It's a downstairs, where there's not 'arf enough light and everything got to be carried – up and down, up and down, all day – coals and everything. And it's got to 'ave a water-tap and sink and things upstairs. You'd 'ardly believe, Artie, if you 'adn't been in service, 'ow cruel and silly some 'ouses are built – you'd think they 'ad a spite against servants the way the stairs are made.'

'We won't 'ave one of that sort,' said Kipps. . . . 'We'll 'ave a quiet little life. Now go out a bit – now come 'ome again. Read a book, perhaps, if we got nothing else to do. 'Ave old Buggins in for an evening at times. 'Ave Sid down. There's bicycles—.'

'I don't fancy myself on a bicycle,' said Ann.

''Ave a trailer,' said Kipps, 'and sit like a lady. I'd take you out to New Romney easy as anything, just to see the old people.'

'I wouldn't mind that,' said Ann.

'We'll jest 'ave a sensible little 'ouse, and sensible things. No art or anything of that sort, nothing stuck-up or anything, but jest sensible. We'll be as right as anything, Ann.'

'No socialism,' said Ann, starting a lurking doubt.

'No socialism,' said Kipps, 'just sensible – that's all.'

'I dessay it's all right for them that understand it, Artie, but I don't agree with this socialism.'

'I don't neither, reely,' said Kipps. 'I can't argue about it, but it don't seem real like to me. All the same, Masterman's a clever fellow, Ann.'

'I didn't like 'im at first, Artie, but I do now – in a way. You don't understand 'im all at once.'

''E's so clever,' said Kipps. ''Arf the time I can't make out what 'e's up to. 'E's the cleverest chap I ever met. I never 'eard such talking. 'E ought to write a book. . . . It's a rum world, Ann, when a chap like that isn't 'ardly able to earn a living.'

'It's 'is 'ealth,' said Ann.

'I expect it is,' said Kipps, and ceased to talk for a little while.

'We shall be 'appy in that little 'ouse, Ann, don't y' think?'

She met his eyes and nodded.

'I seem to see it,' said Kipps, 'sort of cosy like. 'Bout teatime and muffins, kettle on the 'ob, cat on the 'earth-rug – we must get a cat, Ann – and *you* there. Eh?'

They regarded each other with appreciative eyes, and Kipps became irrelevant.

'I don't believe, Ann,' he said, 'I 'aven't kissed you not for 'arf an hour. Leastways, not since we was in those caves.'

For kissing had already ceased to be a matter of thrilling adventure for them.

Ann shook her head. 'You be sensible and go on talking about Mr Masterman,' she said. . . .

But Kipps had wandered to something else. 'I like the way your 'air turns back jest there,' he said, with an indicative finger. 'It was like that, I remember, when you was a girl. Sort of wavy. I've often thought of it. . . . Member when we raced that time – out be'ind the church?'

Then for a time they sat idly, each following out agreeable meditations.

'It's rum,' said Kipps.

'What's rum?'

''Ow everything's 'appened,' said Kipps. 'Who'd 'ave thought of our being 'ere like this six weeks ago? . . . Who'd 'ave thought of my ever 'aving any money?'

His eyes went to the big Labyrinthodon. He looked first carelessly and then suddenly with a growing interest in its vast face. 'I'm deshed,' he murmured. Ann became interested. He laid a hand on her arm and pointed. Ann scrutinized the Labyrinthodon, and then came round to Kipps' face in mute interrogation.

'Don't you see it?' said Kipps.

'See what?'

''E's *jest* like old Coote.'

'It's extinct,' said Ann, not clearly apprehending.

'I dessay 'e is. But 'e's jest like old Coote, all the same for that.'

Kipps meditated on the monstrous shapes in sight. 'I wonder 'ow all these old antediluvium animals *got* extinct,' he said. 'No one couldn't possibly 'ave killed 'em.'

'Why, *I* know that!' said Ann. 'They was overtook by the Flood. . . .'

Kipps meditated for a while. 'But I thought they had to take two of everything there was—'

'Within reason they 'ad,' said Ann. . . .

The Kippses left it at that.

The great green and gold Labyrinthodon took no notice of their conversation. It gazed with its wonderful eyes over their heads into the infinite – inflexibly calm. It might indeed have been Coote himself there, Coote the unassuming, cutting them dead.

There was something about its serenity that suggested patience, suggested the indifference of a power that waits. In the end this quality, dimly apprehended, made the Kippses uneasy, and after a while they got up and, glancing backward, went their way.

IV

And in due course these two simple souls married, and Venus Urania, the Goddess of Wedded Love, who is indeed a very great and noble and kindly goddess, bent down and blessed their union.

Book Three
Kippses

Chapter One

The Housing Problem

Honeymoons and all things come to an end, and you see at last Mr and Mrs Arthur Kipps descending upon the Hythe platform – coming to Hythe to find that nice *little* house, to realize that bright dream of a home they had first talked about in the grounds of the Crystal Palace. They are a valiant couple, you perceive, but small, and the world is a large, incongruous system of complex and difficult things. Kipps wears a grey suit, with a wing poke collar and a neat, smart tie. Mrs Kipps is the same bright and healthy little girl-woman you saw in the marsh, not an inch has been added to her stature in all my voluminous narrative. Only now she wears a hat.

It is a hat very unlike the hats she used to wear on her Sundays out – a flourishing hat, with feathers and a buckle and bows and things. The price of that hat would take many people's breath away – it cost two guineas! Kipps chose it. Kipps paid for it. They left the shop with flushed cheeks and smarting eyes, glad to be out of range of the condescending saleswoman.

'Artie,' said Ann, 'you didn't ought to 'ave—'

That was all. And, you know, the hat didn't suit Ann a bit. Her clothes did not suit her at all. The simple, cheap, clean brightness of her former style had given place not only to this hat, but to several other things in the same key. And out from among these things looked her pretty face, the face of a wise little child – an artless wonder struggling through a preposterous dignity.

They had bought that hat one day when they had gone to see the shops in Bond Street. Kipps had looked at the passers-by, and it had suddenly occurred to him that Ann was dowdy. He had noted the hat of a very proud-looking lady passing in an electric brougham, and had resolved to get Ann the nearest thing to that.

The railway porters perceived some subtle incongruity in Ann, so did the knot of cabmen in the station doorway, the two golfers, and the lady with daughters, who had also got out of the train. And Kipps, a little pale, blowing a little, not in complete possession of himself, knew that they noticed her and him. And Ann—It is hard to say just what Ann observed of these things.

"Ere!' said Kipps to a cabman, and regretted too late a vanished 'H'.

'I got a trunk up there,' he said to a ticket-inspector, 'marked A. K.'

'Ask a porter,' said the inspector, turning his back.

'Demn!' said Kipps, not altogether inaudibly.

II

It is all very well to sit in the sunshine and talk of the house you will have, and another altogether to achieve it. We English – all the world indeed to-day – live in a strange atmosphere of neglected great issues, of insistent, triumphant petty things; we are given up to the fine littlenesses of intercourse; table manners and small correctitudes are the substance of our lives. You do not escape these things for long, even by so catastrophic a proceeding as flying to London with a young lady of no wealth and inferior social position. The mists of noble emotion swirl and pass, and there you are, divorced from all your deities, and grazing in the meadows under the Argus eyes of the social system, the innumerable mean judgments you feel raining upon you, upon your clothes and bearing, upon your pretensions and movements.

Our world to-day is a meanly conceived one – it is only an added meanness to conceal that fact. For one consequence, it has very few nice little houses. Such things do not come for the asking; they are not to be bought with money during ignoble times. Its houses are built on the ground of monstrously rich, shabbily extortionate landowners, by poor, parsimonious, greedy people in a mood of elbowing competition. What can you expect from such ridiculous conditions? To go house-hunting is to spy out the nakedness of this pretentious world, to see what our civilization amounts to when you take away curtains and flounces and carpets, and all the fluster and distraction of people and fittings. It is to see mean plans meanly executed for mean ends, the conventions torn aside, the secrets stripped, the substance underlying all such Chester Cootery, soiled and worn and left.

So you see our poor dear Kippses going to and fro, in Hythe, in Sandgate, in Ashford, and Canterbury and Deal and Dover – at last even in Folkestone – with 'orders to view', pink and green and white and yellow orders to view, and labelled keys in Kipps' hand, and frowns and perplexity upon their faces. . . .

They did not clearly know what they wanted, but whatever it was they saw, they knew they did not want that. Always they found a confusing multitude of houses they could not take, and none they could. Their dreams began to turn mainly on empty, abandoned-looking rooms, with unfaded patches of paper to mark the place of vanished pictures, and doors that had lost their keys. They saw rooms floored with boards that yawned apart and were splintered, skirtings eloquent of the industrious mouse, kitchens with a dead black-beetle in the empty cupboard, and a hideous variety of coal-holes and dark cupboards under the stairs. They stuck their little heads through roof trap-doors, and gazed at disorganized ball-taps, at the black filthiness of unstopped roofs. There were occasions when it seemed to them that they must be the victims of an elaborate conspiracy of house agents, so bleak and cheerless is a second-hand empty house in comparison with the humblest of inhabited dwellings.

Commonly the houses were too big. They had huge windows that demanded vast curtains in mitigation, countless bedrooms, acreage of stone steps to be cleaned, kitchens that made Ann protest. She had come so far towards a proper conception of Kipps' social position as to admit the prospect of one servant. 'But lor!' she would say, 'you'd want a man-servant in this 'ouse.' When the houses were not too big, then they were almost always the product of speculative building, of that multitudinous hasty building for the extravagant swarm of new births that was the essential disaster of the nineteenth century. The new houses Ann refused as damp, and even the youngest of those that had been in use showed remarkable signs of a sickly constitution – the plaster flaked away, the floors gaped, the paper moulded and peeled, the doors dropped, the bricks were scaled, and the railings rusted; Nature, in the form of spiders, earwigs, cockroaches, mice, rats, fungi, and remarkable smells, was already fighting her way back. . . .

And the plan was invariably invonvenient, invariably. All the houses they saw had a common quality for which she could find no word, but for which the proper word is 'incivility'. 'They build these 'ouses,' she said, 'as though girls wasn't 'uman beings.' Sid's social democracy had got into her blood, perhaps, and anyhow they went about discovering the most remarkable inconsiderateness in the contemporary house. 'There's kitching stairs to go up, Artie!' Ann would say. 'Some poor girl's got to go up and down, up and down, and be tired out, jest because they haven't the sense to leave enough space to give their steps a proper rise – and no water upstairs anywhere – every drop got to be carried! It's 'ouses like this wear girls out.

'It's 'aving 'ouses built by men, I believe, makes all the work and trouble,' said Ann. . . .

The Kippses, you see, thought they were looking for a reasonably simple little contemporary house, but indeed they were looking either for dreamland or 1975 A.D., or thereabouts, and it hadn't come.

III

But it was a foolish thing of Kipps to begin building a house.

He did that out of an extraordinary animosity for house-agents he had conceived.

Everybody hates house-agents, just as everybody loves sailors. It is, no doubt, a very wicked and unjust hatred, but the business of a novelist is not ethical principle, but facts. Everybody hates house-agents because they have everybody at a disadvantage. All other callings have a certain amount of give and take, the house-agent simply takes. All other callings want you; your solicitor is afraid you may change him, your doctor cannot go too far, your novelist – if only you knew it – is mutely abject towards your unspoken wishes; and as for your tradespeople, milkmen will fight outside your front door for you, and green-grocers call in tears if you discard them suddenly; but who ever heard of a house-agent struggling to serve any one? You want a house; you go to him; you, dishevelled and angry from travel, anxious, inquiring; he calm, clean, inactive, reticent, quietly doing nothing. You beg him to reduce rents, whitewash ceilings, produce other houses, combine the summer-house of No. 6 with the conservatory of No.4 – much he cares! You want to dispose of a house; then he is just the same – serene, indifferent. On one occasion I remember he was picking his teeth all the time he answered me. Competition is a mockery among house-agents; they are all alike; you cannot wound them by going to the opposite office, you cannot dismiss them, you can at most dismiss yourself. They are invulnerably placed behind mahogany and brass, too far usually even for a sudden swift lunge with an umbrella; to throw away the keys they lend you instead of returning them is larceny, and punishable as such. . . .

It was a house-agent in Dover who finally decided Kipps to build. Kipps, with a certain faltering in his voice, had delivered his ultimatum – no basement, not more than eight rooms, hot and cold water upstairs, coal-cellar in the house, but with intervening doors to keep dust from the scullery and so forth. He stood blowing. 'You'll have to build a house,' said the house-agent, sighing wearily, 'if you want all that.' It was rather for the sake of effective answer than with any intention at the time that Kipps mumbled, 'That's about what I shall do – this goes on.'

Whereupon the house-agent smiled. He smiled!

When Kipps came to turn the thing over in his mind, he was surprised to find quite a considerable intention had germinated and was growing up in him. After all, lots of people *have* built houses. How could there be so many if they hadn't? Suppose he 'reely' did! Then he would go to the house-agent and say, ''Ere, while you been getting me a sootable 'ouse, blowed if I 'aven't built one!' Go round to all of them – all the house-agents in Folkestone, in Dover, Ashford, Canterbury, Margate, Ramsgate, saying that—! Perhaps then they might be sorry. It was in the small hours that he awoke to a realization that he had made up his mind in the matter.

'Ann,' he said, 'Ann,' and also used the sharp of his elbow.

Ann was at last awakened to the pitch of an indistinct inquiry what was the matter.

'I'm going to build a house, Ann.'

'Eh?' said Ann, suddenly, as if awake.

'Build a house.'

Ann said something incoherent about he'd better wait until

the morning before he did anything of the sort, and immediately with a fine trustfulness went fast asleep again.

But Kipps lay awake for a long while building his house, and in the morning at breakfast he made his meaning clear. He had smarted under the indignities of house-agents long enough, and this seemed to promise revenge – a fine revenge. 'And, you know, we might reely make rather a nice little 'ouse out of it – like we want.'

So resolved, it became possible for them to take a house for a year, with a basement, no service lift, blackleading to do everywhere, no water upstairs, no bathroom, vast sash windows to be cleaned from the sill, stone steps with a twist and open to the rain, into the coal-cellar, insufficient cupboards, unpaved path to the dustbin, no fireplace to the servant's bedroom, no end of splintery wood to scrub – in fact, a very typical English middle-class house. And having added to this house some furniture, and a languid young person with unauthentic golden hair named Gwendolen, who was engaged to a sergeant-major and had formerly been in an hotel, having 'moved in' and spent some sleepless nights, varied by nocturnal explorations in search of burglars, because of the strangeness of being in a house for which they were personally responsible, Kipps settled down for a time and turned himself with considerable resolution to the project of building a home.

IV

At first Kipps gathered advice, finding an initial difficulty in how to begin. He went into a builder's shop at Seabrook one day and told the lady in charge that he wanted a house built. He was breathless, but quite determined, and he was prepared to give his order there and then; but she temporized with him, and said her husband was out, and he left without giving his name. Also he went and talked to a man in a cart, who was pointed out to him by a workman as the builder of a new house near Saltwood, but he found him first sceptical, and then overpoweringly sarcastic. 'I suppose you build a 'ouse every 'oliday,' he said, and turned from Kipps with every symptom of contempt.

Afterwards Carshot told alarming stories about builders, and shook Kipps' expressed resolution a good deal, and then Pearce raised the question whether one ought to go in the first instance to a builder at all, and not rather to an architect. Pearce knew a man at Ashford whose brother was an architect, and as it is always better in these matters to get some one you know, the Kippses decided, before Pearce had gone, and Carshot's warnings had resumed their sway, to apply to him. They did so – rather dubiously.

The architect, who was brother of Pearce's friend, appeared as a small, alert individual with a black bag and a cylindrical silk hat, and he sat at the dining-room table, with his hat and his bag exactly equidistant right and left of him, and maintained a demeanour of impressive woodenness, while Kipps, on the hearthrug, with a quaking sense of gigantic enterprise, vacillated answers to his inquiries. Ann held a watching brief for herself, in a position she had chosen as suitable to the occasion, beside the corner of the carved oak sideboard. They felt, in a sense, at bay.

The architect began by asking for the site, and seemed a little discomposed to discover this had still to be found. 'I thought of building just anywhere,' said Kipps. 'I 'aven't made up my mind about that yet.' The architect remarked that he would have preferred to see the site in order to know where to put what he called his 'ugly side', but it was quite possible, of course, to plan a house 'in the air', on the level, 'simply with back and front assumed' – if they would like to do that. Kipps flushed slightly, and secretly hoping it would make no great difference in the fees, said a little doubtfully that he thought that would be all right.

The architect then marked off, as it were, the first section of his subject, with a single dry cough, opened his bag, took out a spring tape measure, some hard biscuits, a metal flask, a new pair of dogskin gloves, a clockwork motor-car partially wrapped in paper, a bunch of violets, a paper of small brass screws, and finally a large distended notebook; he replaced the other objects carefully, opened his notebook, put a pencil to his lips and said, 'And what accommodation will you require?' To which Ann, who had followed his every movement with the closest attention and a deepening dread, replied with the violent suddenness of one who has lain in wait, 'Cubbuds!'

'Anyhow,' she added, catching her husband's eye.

The architect wrote it down.

'And how many rooms?' he said, coming to secondary matters.

The young people regarded one another. It was dreadfully like giving an order.

'How many bedrooms, for example?' asked the architect.

'One?' suggested Kipps, inclined now to minimize at any cost.

'There's Gwendolen!' said Ann.

'Visitors, perhaps,' said the architect; and temperately, 'You never know.'

'Two p'r'aps?' said Kipps. 'We don't want no more than a *little* 'ouse, you know.'

'But the merest shooting-box—' said the architect. . . .

They got to six, he beat them steadily from bedroom to bedroom, the word 'nursery' played across their imaginative skies – he mentioned it as the remotest possibility – and then six being reluctantly conceded, Ann came forward to the table, sat down, and delivered herself of one of her prepared conditions. ''Ot and cold water,' she said, 'laid on to each room – any'ow.'

It was an idea long since acquired from Sid.

'Yes,' said Kipps, on the hearthrug, ''ot and cold water laid on to each bedroom – we've settled on that.'

It was the first intimation to the architect that he had to deal with a couple of exceptional originality, and as he had spent the previous afternoon in finding three large houses in *The Builder*, which he intended to combine into an original and copyright design of his own, he naturally struggled against these novel requirements. He enlarged on the extreme expensiveness of plumbing, on the extreme expensiveness of everything not already arranged for in his scheme, and only when Ann declared she'd as soon not have the house as not have her requirements, and Kipps, blenching the while, had said he didn't mind what a thing cost him so long as he got what he wanted, did he allow a kindred originality of his own to appear beneath the acquired professionalism of his methods. He dismissed their previous talk with his paragraphic cough. 'Of course,' he said, 'if you don't mind being unconventional—'

He explained that he had been thinking of a Queen Anne style of architecture (Ann, directly she heard her name, shook her head at Kipps in an aside) so far as the exterior went. For his own part, he said, he liked to have the exterior of a house in a style, not priggishly in a style, but mixed, with one style uppermost, and the gables and dormers and casements of the Queen Anne style, with a littke roughcast and sham timbering here and there, and perhaps a bit of an overhang, diversified a house and made it interesting. The advantages of what he called a Queen Annde style was that it had such a variety of features. . . . Still, if they were prepared to be unconventional, it could be done. A number of houses were now built in the unconventional style, and were often very pretty. In the unconventional style one frequently had what perhaps he might call Internal Features – for example, an old English oak staircase and gallery. White roughcast and green paint were a good deal favoured in houses of this type.

He indicated that this excursus on style was finished by a momentary use of his cough, and reopened his notebook, which he had closed to wave about in a moment of descriptive enthusiasm while expatiating on the unbridled wealth of External Features associated with Queen Anne. 'Six bedrooms,' he said, moistening his pencil. 'One with barred windows, suitable for a nursery if required.'

Kipps endorsed this huskily and reluctantly.

There followed a most interesting discussion upon house-building, in which Kipps played a minor part. They passed from bedrooms to the kitchen and scullery, and there Ann displayed an intelligent exactingness that won the expressed admiration of the architect. They were particularly novel upon the position of the coal-cellar, which Ann held to be altogether too low in the ordinary house, necessitating much heavy carrying. They dismissed as impracticable the idea of having coal-cellar and kitchen at the top of the house, because that would involve carrying all the coal through the house, and therewith much subsequent cleaning, and for a time they dealt with a conception of a coal-cellar on the ground floor with a light staircase running up outside to an exterior shoot. 'It might be made a Feature,' said the architect a little doubtfully, jotting down a note of it. 'It would be apt to get black, you know.'

Thence they passed to the alternative of service lifts, and then, by an inspiration of the architect's, to the possibilities of gas-heating. Kipps did a complicated verbal fugue on the theme, 'gas-heating heats the air', with variable aspirates; he became very red, and was lost to the discussion altogether for a time, though his lips kept silently moving.

Subsequently the architect wrote to say that he found in his notebook very full and explicit directions for bow windows to all rooms, for bedrooms, for water supply, lift, height of stairs and absence of twists therein, for a well-ventilated kitchen twenty feet square, with two dressers and a large box window-seat, for scullery and outhouses and offices, but nothing whatever about drawing-room, dining-room, library, or study, or approximate cost, and he awaited further instructions. He presumed there would be a breakfast-room, dining-room, drawing-room, and study for Mr Kipps – at least that was his conception – and the young couple discussed this matter long and ardently.

Ann was distinctly restrictive in this direction. 'I don't see what you want a drawin'-room and a dinin' *and* a kitchin for. If we was going to let in summer – well and good. But we're not going to let. Consequently we don't want so many rooms. Then there's a 'all. What use is a 'all? It only makes work. And a study!'

Kipps had been humming and stroking his moustache since he had read the architect's letter. 'I think I'd like a little bit of a study – not a big one, of course, but one with a desk and bookshelves, like there was in Hughenden. I'd like that.'

It was only after they had talked to the architect again, and seen how scandalized he was at the idea of not having a drawing-room, that they consented to that Internal Feature. They consented to please him. 'But we shan't never use it,' said Ann.

Kipps had his way about a study. 'When I get that study,' said Kipps, 'I shall do a bit of reading I've long wanted to do. I shall make a nabit of going in there and reading something an hour every day. There's Shakespeare and a lot of things a man like me ought to read. Besides, we got to 'ave *somewhere* to put the Encyclopaedia. I've always thought a study was about what I've wanted all along. You can't 'elp reading if you got a study. If you 'aven't, there's nothing for it, so far's *I* can see, but treshy novels.'

He looked down at Ann, and was surprised to see a joyless thoughtfulness upon her face.

'Fency, Ann!' he said not too buoyantly, ''aving a little 'ouse of our own!'

It won't be a little 'ouse,' said Ann, 'not with all them rooms.'

V

Any lingering doubt in that matter was dispelled when it came to plans.

The architect drew three sets of plans on a transparent bluish sort of paper that smelt abominably. He painted them very nicely; brick-red and ginger, and arsenic green and a leaden sort of blue, and brought them over to show our young people. The first set were very simple, with practically no External Features – 'a plain style', he said it was – but it looked a big sort of house, nevertheless; the second had such extras as a conservatory, bow windows of various sorts, one roughcast gable and one half-timbered ditto in plaster, and a sort of overhung verandah, and was much more imposing; and the third was quite fungoid with External Features, and honeycombed with Internal ones; it was, he said, 'practically a mansion', and altogether a very noble fruit of the creative mind of man. It was, he admitted, perhaps almost too good for Hythe; his art had run away with him and produced a modern mansion in the 'best Folkestone style'; it had a central hall with a staircase, a Moorish gallery, and a Tudor stained-glass window, crenelated battlements to the leading over the portico, an octagonal bulge with octagonal bay windows, surmounted by an Oriental dome of metal, lines of yellow bricks to break up the red and many other richnesses and attractions. It was the sort of house, ornate and in its dignified way voluptuous, that a city magnate might build, but it seemed excessive to the Kippses. The first plan had seven bedrooms, the second eight, the third eleven; they had, the architect explained, 'worked in' as if they were pebbles in a mountaineer's boot.

'They're big 'ouses,' said Ann, directly the elevations were unrolled.

Kipps listened to the architect, with round eyes and an exuberant caution in his manner, anxious not to commit himself further than he had done to the enterprise, and the architect pointed out the Features and other objects of interest with the scalpel belonging to a pocket manicure set that he carried. Ann watched Kipps' face, and communicated with him furtively over the architect's head. '*Not so big*,' said Ann's lips.

'It's a bit big for what I meant,' said Kipps, with a reassuring eye on Ann.

'You won't think it big when you see it up,' said the architect; 'you take my word for that.'

'We don't want no more than six bedrooms,' said Kipps.

'Make this one a box-room, then,' said the architect.

A feeling of impotence silenced Kipps for a time.

'Now which,' said the architect, spreading them out, 'is it to be?'

He flattened down the plans of the most ornate mansion to show it to better effect.

Kipps wanted to know how much each would cost 'at the outside,' which led to much alarmed signalling from Ann. But the architect could estimate only in the most general way.

They were not really committed to anything when the architect went away; Kipps had promised to think it over – that was all.

'We can't 'ave that 'ouse,' said Ann.

'They're miles too big – all of them,' agreed Kipps.

'You'd want—Four servants wouldn't be 'ardly enough,' said Ann.

Kipps went to the hearthrug and spread himself. His tone was almost offhand. 'Nex' time 'e comes,' said Kipps, 'I'll 'splain to him. It isn't at all the sort of thing we want. It's – it's a misunderstanding. You got no occasion to be anxious 'bout it, Ann.'

'I don't see much good reely in building an 'ouse at all,' said Ann.

'Oo, we *got* to build a 'ouse now we begun,' said Kipps. 'But now supposin' we 'ad—'

He spread out the most modest of the three plans and scratched his cheek.

VI

It was unfortunate that old Kipps came over the next day.

Old Kipps always produced peculiar states of mind in his nephew – a rash assertiveness, a disposition towards display unlike his usual self. There had been great difficulty in reconciling both these old people to the Pornick *mésalliance*, and at times the controversy echoed in old Kipps' expressed thoughts. This perhaps it was, and no ignoble vanity, that set the note of florid successfulness going in Kipps' conversation whenever his uncle appeared. Mrs Kipps was, as a matter of fact, not reconciled at all; she had declined all invitations to come over on the bus, and was a taciturn hostess on the one occasion when the young people called at the toy-shop *en route* for Mrs Pornick. She displayed a tendency to sniff that was clearly due to pride rather than catarrh, and, except for telling Ann she hoped she would not feel too 'stuck up' about her marriage, confined her conversation to her nephew or the infinite. The call was a brief one, and made up chiefly of pauses, no refreshment was offered or asked for, and Ann departed with a singularly high colour. For some reason she would not call at the toy-shop a second time when they found themselves again in New Romney.

But old Kipps, having adventured over and tried the table of the new *ménage* and found it to his tast, showed many signs of softening towards Ann. He came again, and then again. He would come over by the bus, and, except when his mouth was absolutely full, he would give his nephew one solid and continuous mass of advice of the most subtle and disturbing description until it was time to toddle back to the High Street for the afternoon bus. He would walk with him to the sea front, and commence *pourparlers* with boatmen for the purchase of one of their boats – 'You ought to keep a boat of your own,' he said – though Kipps was a singularly poor sailor – or he would pursue a plan that was forming in his mind in which he should own and manage what he called 'weekly' property in the less conspicuous streets of Hythe. The cream of that was to be a weekly collection of rents in person, the nearest approach to feudal splendour left in this democratized country. He gave no hint of the source of the capital he designed for this investment, and at times it would appear he intended it as an occupation for his nephew rather than himself.

But there remained something in his manner towards Ann – in the glances of scrutiny he gave her unawares, that kept Kipps alertly expansive whenever he was about; and in all sorts of ways. It was on account of old Kipps, for example, that our Kipps plunged one day – a golden plunge – and brought home a box of cummerbundy ninepenny cigars, and substituted blue label old Methusaleh Four Stars for the common and generally satifactory white brand.

'Some of this is whisky, my boy,' said old Kipps, when he tasted it, smacking critical lips. . . .

'Saw a lot of young officery fellers coming along,' said old Kipps. 'You ought to join the volunteers, my boy, and get to know a few.'

'I dessay I shall,' said Kipps. 'Later.'

'They'd make you an officer, you know, 'n no time. They want officers,' said old Kipps. 'It isn't every one can afford it. They'd be regular glad to 'ave you. . . . Ain't bort a dog yet?'

'Not yet, Uncle. 'Ave a segar?'

'Nor a moty car?'

'Not yet, Uncle.'

'There's no 'urry about that. And don't get one of these 'ere trashy cheap ones when you do get it, my boy. Get one as'll last a lifetime. . . . I'm surprised you don't 'ire a bit more.'

'Ann don't seem to fency a moty car,' said Kipps.

'Ah,' said old Kipps, 'I expect not,' and glanced a comment at the door. 'She ain't used to going out,' he said. 'More at 'ome indoors.'

'Fact is,' said Kipps, hastily, 'we're thinking of building a 'ouse.'

'I wouldn't do that, my boy,' began old Kipps; but his nephew was routing in the cheffonier drawer amidst the plans. He got them in time to check some further comment on Ann. 'Um,' said the old gentleman, a little impressed by the extraordinary odour and the unusual transparency of the tracing-paper Kipps put into his hands. 'Thinking of building a 'ouse, are you?'

Kipps began with the most modest of the three projects.

Old Kipps read slowly through his silver-rimmed spectacles, 'Plan of a 'ouse for Arthur Kipps, Esquire. Um.'

He didn't warm to the project all at once, and Ann drifted into the room to find him still scrutinizing the architect's proposals a little doubtfully.

'We couldn't find a decent 'ouse anywhere,' said Kipps, leaning against the table and assuming an offhand note. 'I didn't see why we shouldn't run up one for ourselve.' Old Kipps could not help liking the tone of that.

'We thought we might see—' said Ann.

'It's a spekerlation, of course,' said old Kipps, and held the plan at a distance of two feet or more from his glasses and frowned. 'This isn't exactly the 'ouse I should expect you to 'ave thought of though,' he said. 'Practically it's a villa. It's the sort of 'ouse a bank clerk might 'ave. 'Tisn't what I should call a gentleman's 'ouse, Artie.'

'It's plain, of course,' said Kipps, standing beside his Uncle and looking down at this plan, which certainly did seem a little less magnificent now than it had at the first encounter.

'You mustn't 'ave it too plain,' said old Kipps.

'If it's comfortable—' Ann hazarded.

Old Kipps glanced at her over his spectacles. 'You ain't comfortable, my gel, in this world, not if you don't live up to your position,' – so putting compactly into contemporary English that fine old phrase *noblesse oblige*. 'A 'ouse of this sort is what a retired tradesman might 'ave, or some little whippersnapper of a s'licitor. But *you*—'

'Course that isn't the o'ny plan,' said Kipps, and tried the middle one.

But it was the third one won over old Kipps. 'Now that's a *'ouse*, my boy,' he said at the sight of it.

Ann came and stood just behind her husband's shoulder, while old Kipps expanded upon the desirability of the larger scheme. 'You ought to 'ave a billiard-room,' he said; 'I don't see that, but all the rest's about right! A lot of these 'ere officers 'ere 'ud be glad of a game of billiards. . . .

'What's all these dots?' said old Kipps.

'S'rubbery,' said Kipps. 'Flow'ing s'rubs.'

'There's eleven bedrooms in that 'ouse,' said Ann. 'It's a bit of a lot, ain't it, Uncle?'

'You'll want 'em, my girl. As you get on you'll be 'aving visitors. Friends of your 'usband's, p'r'aps, from the School of Musketry – what you want 'im to get on with. You can't never tell.'

'If we 'ave a great s'rubbery,' Ann ventured, 'we shall 'ave to keep a gardener.'

'If you don't 'ave a s'rubbery,' said old Kipps, with a note of patient reasoning, ''ow are you to prevent every jackanapes that goes by starin' into your drorin'-room winder – p'r'aps when you get some one a bit special to entertain?'

'We ain't *used* to a s'rubbery,' said Ann, mulishly; 'we get on very well 'ere.'

'It isn't what you're used to,' said old Kipps, 'it's what you ought to 'ave *now*.' And with that Ann dropped out of the discussion.

'Study and lib'ry,' old Kipps read. 'That's right. I see a Tantalus* the other day over Brookland, the very thing for a gentleman's study. I'll try and get over and bid for it. . . .'

By bus time old Kipps was quite enthusiastic about the house-building, and it seemed to be definitely settled that the largest plan was the one decided upon.

But Ann had said nothing further in the matter.

VII

When Kipps returned from seeing his Uncle into the bus – there always seemed a certain doubt whether that portly figure would go into the little red 'Tip-top' box – he found Ann still standing by the table, looking with an expression of comprehensive disapproval at the three plans.

'There don't seem much the matter with Uncle,' said Kipps, assuming the hearthrug, 'spite of 'is 'eartburn. 'E 'opped up them steps like a bird.'

Ann remained staring at the plans.

'You don't like them plans?' hazarded Kipps.

'No; I don't, Artie.'

'We got to build somethin' now.'

'But—It's a gentleman's 'ouse, Artie!'

'It's – it's a decent size, o' course.'

Kipps took a flirting look at the drawing and went to the window.

'Look at the cleanin'. Free servants'll be lost in that 'ouse, Artie.'

'We must 'ave servants,' said Kipps.

Ann looked despondently at her future residence.

'We got to keep up our position any'ow,' said Kipps, turning towards her. 'It stands to reason, Ann, we got a position. Very well! I can't 'ave you scrubbin' floors. You got to 'ave a servant, and you got to manage a 'ouse. You wouldn't 'ave me ashamed—'

Ann opened her lips and did not speak.

'What?' asked Kipps.

'Nothing,' said Ann, 'only I did want it to be a *little* 'ouse, Artie. I wanted it to be a 'andy little 'ouse, jest for us.'

Kipps' face was suddenly flushed and obstinate. He took up

the curiously smelling tracings again. 'I'm not a-going to be looked down upon,' he said. 'It's not only Uncle I'm thinking of!'

Ann stared at him.

Kipps went on. 'I won't 'ave that young Walshingham, f'r instance, sneering and sniffing at me. Making out as if we was all wrong. I see 'im yesterday. . . . Nor Coote neether. I'm as good – we're as good – whatever's 'appened.'

Silence, and the rustle of plans.

He looked up and saw Ann's eyes bright with tears. For a moment the two stared at one another.

'We'll 'ave the big 'ouse,' said Ann, with a gulp. 'I didn't think of that, Artie.'

Her aspect was fierce and resolute, and she struggled with emotion. 'We'll 'ave the big 'ouse,' she repeated. 'They shan't say I dragged you down wiv me – none of them shan't say that. I've thought—I've always been afraid of that.'

Kipps looked again at the plan, and suddenly the grand house had become very grand indeed. He blew.

'No, Artie. None of them shan't say that,' and, with something blind in her motions, Ann tried to turn the plan round to her. . . .

After all, Kipps thought, there might be something to say for the milder project. . . . But he had gone so far that now he did not know how to say it.

And so the plans went out to the builders, and in a little while Kipps was committed to two thousand five hundred pounds' worth of building. But then, you know, he had an income of twelve hundred a year.

VIII

It is extraordinary what minor difficulties cluster about house-building.

'I say, Ann,' remarked Kipps one day. 'We shall 'ave to call this little 'ouse by a name. I was thinking of Ome Cottage. But I dunno whether Ome Cottage is quite the thing like. All these little fisherman's places are called Cottages.'

'I like "Cottage",' said Ann.

'It's got eleven bedrooms, y' see,' said Kipps. 'I don't see 'ow you call it a cottage with more bedrooms than four. Prop'ly speaking, it's a Large Villa. Prop'ly it's almost a Big 'Ouse. Leastways a 'Ouse.'

'Well,' said Ann, 'if you must call it Villa – Home Villa. . . . I wish it wasn't.'

Kipps meditated.

''Ow about Eureka Villa?' he said, raising his voice.

'What's Eureka?'

'It's a name,' he said. 'There used to be Eureka Dress Fasteners. There's lots of names, come to think of it, to be got out of a shop. There's Pyjama Villa. I remember that in the hosiery. No, come to think, that wouldn't do. But Maraposa – sort of oatmeal cloth, that was. . . . No! Eureka's better.'

Ann meditated. 'It seems silly like to 'ave a name that don't mean much.'

'Perhaps it does,' said Kipps. 'Though it's what people 'ave to do.'

He became meditative. 'I got it!' he cried.

'Not Oreeka!' said Ann.

'No! There used to be a 'ouse at Hastings opposite our school – quite a big 'ouse it was – St Ann's. Now *that*—'

'No,' said Mrs Kipps, with decision. 'Thanking you kindly, but I don't have no butcher-boys making game of me. . . .'

They consulted Carshot, who suggested, after some days of reflection, Waddycombe, as a graceful reminder of Kipps' grandfather; old Kipps, who was for 'Upton Manor House', where he had once been second footman; Buggins, who favoured either a stern, simple number, 'Number One' – if there were no other houses there, or something patriotic, as 'Empire Villa'; and Pearce, who inclined to 'Sandringham'; but in spite of all this help they were still undecided, when admidst violent perturbations of the soul, and after the most complex and difficult hagglings, wranglings, fears, muddles, and goings to and fro, Kipps became the joyless owner of a freehold plot of three-eighths of an acre, and saw the turf being wheeled away from the site that should one day be his home.

Chapter Two

The Callers

The Kippses sat at their midday dinner-table amidst the vestiges of rhubarb pie, and discussed two postcards the one o'clock post had brought. It was a rare bright moment of sunshine in a wet and windy day in the March that followed their marriage. Kipps was attired in a suit of brown, with a tie of fashionable green, while Ann wore one of those picturesque loose robes that are usually associated with sandals and advanced ideas. But there weren't any sandals on Ann or any advanced ideas, and the robe had come quite recently through the counsels of Mrs Sid Pornick. 'It's Art-like,' said Kipps, but giving way. 'It's more comfortable,' said Ann. The room looked out by French windows upon a little patch of green and the Hythe parade. The parade was all shiny wet with rain, and the green-grey sea tumbled and tumbled between parade and sky.

The Kipps' furniture, except for certain chromolithographs of Kipps' incidental choice, that struck a quiet note amidst the wall-paper, had been tactfully forced by an expert salesman, and it was in a style of mediocre elegance. There was a sideboard of carved oak that had only one fault – it reminded Kipps at times of woodcarving, and its panel of bevelled glass now reflected the back of his head. On its shelf were two books from Parsons' Library, each with a 'place' marked by a slip of paper; neither of the Kippses could have told you the title of either book they read, much less the author's name. There was an ebonized overmantel set with phials and pots of brilliant colour, each duplicated by looking-glass, and bearing also a pair of Chinese jars made in Birmingham, a wedding-present from Mr and Mrs Sidney Pornick, and several sumptuous Japanese fans. And there was a Turkey carpet of great richness. In addition to these modern exploits of Messrs Bunt and Bubble, there were two inactive tall clocks, whose extreme dilapidation appealed to the connoisseur; a terrestrial and a celestial globe, the latter deeply indented; a number of good old iron-moulded and dusty books; and a stuffed owl, wanting one (easily replaceable) glass eye, obtained by the exertions of Uncle Kipps. The table equipage was as much as possible like Mrs Bindon Botting's, only more costly, and in addition there were green and crimson wine-glasses – though the Kippses never drank wine. . . .

Kipps turned to the more legible of his two postcards again.

'"Unavoidably prevented from seein' me to-day," 'e says. I like 'is cheek. After I give 'im 'is start and everything.'

He blew.

''E certainly treats you a bit orf'and,' said Ann.

Kipps gave vent to his dislike of young Walshingham. 'He's getting too big for 'is britches,' he said. 'I'm beginning to wish she *'ad* brought an action for breach. Ever since 'e said she wouldn't, 'e's seemed to think I've got no right to spend my own money.'

''E's never liked your building the 'ouse,' said Ann.

Kipps displayed wrath. 'What the goodness 'as it got to do wiv 'im?'

'Overman, indeed!' he added; 'Overmantel!. . . . 'E trys that on with me – I'll tell 'im something 'e won't like.'

He took up the second card. 'Dashed if I can read a word of it. I can jest make out Chit'low at the end, and that's all.'

He scrutinized it. 'It's like some one in a fit writing. This here might be W-H-A-T – *what*. P-R-I-C-E – *I* got it! What price Harry now? It was a sort of saying of 'is. I expect 'e's either done something or not done something towards starting that play, Ann.'

'I expect that's about it,' said Ann.

Kipps grunted with effort. 'I can't read the rest,' he said at last, 'nohow.'

A thoroughly annoying post. He pitched the card on the table, stood up and went to the window, where Ann, after a momentary reconnaissance at Chitterlow's hieroglyphics, came to join him.

'Wonder what I shall do this afternoon,' said Kipps, with his hands deep in his pockets.

He produced and lit a cigarette.

'Go for a walk, I s'pose,' said Ann.

'I *been* for a walk this morning.

'S'pose I must go for another,' he added, after an interval.

They regarded the windy waste of sea for a space.

'Wonder why it is 'e won't see me,' said Kipps, returning to the problem of young Walshingham. 'It's all lies about 'is being too busy.'

Ann offered no solution.

'Rain again!' said Kipps – as the lash of the little drops stung the window.

'Oo, bother!' said Kipps, 'you got to do something. Look 'ere, Ann! I'll go orf for a reg'lar tramp through the rain, up by Saltwood, round by Newington, over the camp, and so round and back, and see 'ow they're getting on about the 'ouse. See? And look 'ere! – you get Gwendolen to go out a bit before I come back. If it's still rainy, she can easy go round and see 'er sister. Then we'll 'ave a bit of tea, with teacake – all buttery – see? Toce it ourselves p'r'aps. Eh?'

'I dessay I can find something to do in the 'ouse,' said Ann, considering. 'You'll take your mackintosh and leggings, I s'pose? You'll get wet without your mackintosh over those roads.'

'Right-O,' said Kipps; and went to ask Gwendolen for his brown leggings and his other pair of boots.

II

Things conspired to demoralize Kipps that afternoon.

When he got outside the house everything looked so wet under the drive of the south-wester that he abandoned the prospect of the clay lanes towards Newington altogether, and turned east to Folkestone along the Seabrook digue. His mackintosh flapped about him, the rain stung his cheek; for a time he felt a hardy man. And then as abruptly the rain ceased and the wind fell, and before he was through Sandgate High Street it was a bright spring day. And there was Kipps in his mackintosh and squeaky leggings, looking like a fool!

Inertia carried him another mile to the Leas, and there the whole world was pretending there had never been such a thing as rain – ever. There wasn't a cloud in the sky; except for an occasional puddle, the asphalte paths looked as dry as a bone. A smartly dressed man, in one of those overcoats that look like ordinary cloth, and are really most deceitfully and unfairly waterproof, passed him and glanced at the stiff folds of his mackintosh. 'Demn!' said Kipps. His mackintosh swished against his leggings, his leggings piped and whistled over his boot-tops.

'Why do I never get anything right?' Kipps asked of a bright implacable universe.

Nice old ladies passed him, refined people with tidy umbrellas, bright, beautiful, supercilious-looking children. Of course, the right thing for such a day as this was a light overcoat and an umbrella. A child might have known that. He had them at home, but how could one explain that? He decided to turn down by the Harvey monument and escape through Clifton Gardens towards the hills. And thereby he came upon Coote.

He already felt the most abject and propitiatory of social outcasts when he came upon Coote, and Coote finished him. He passed within a yard of Coote. Coote was coming along towards the Leas, and when Kipps saw him his legs hesitated about their office, and he seemed to himself to stagger about all over the footpath. At the sight of him Coote started visibly. Then a sort of *rigor vitae* passed through his frame, his jaw protruded, and errant bubbles of air seemed to escape and run about beneath his loose skin. (Seemed, I say, – I am perfectly well aware that there is really connective tissue in Coote, as in all of us, to prevent anything of the sort.) His eyes fixed themselves on the horizon and glazed. As he went by Kipps could hear his even, resolute breathing. He went by, and Kipps staggered on into a universe of dead cats and dust-heaps, rind and ashes – *cut*!

It was part of the inexorable decrees of Providence that almost immediately afterwards the residuum of Kipps had to pass a very, very long and observant-looking girls' school.

Kipps recovered consciousness again on the road between Shorncliffe station and Cheriton, though he cannot remember, indeed to this day he has never attempted to remember, how he got there. And he was back at certain thoughts suggested by his last night's novel-reading, that linked up directly with the pariah-like emotions of these last encounters. The novel lay at home upon the cheffonier; it was one about society and politics – there is no need whatever to give the title or name the author – written with a heavy-handed thoroughness that overrode any possibility of resistance on the part of the Kipps' mind. It had crushed all his poor edifice of ideals, his dreams of a sensible, unassuming existence, of snugness, of not caring what people said and all the rest of it, to dust; it had reinstated, squarely and strongly again, the only proper conception of English social life. There was a character in the book who trifled with Art, who was addicted to reading French novels, who dressed in a loose careless way, who was a sorrow to his dignified, silvery haired, politico-religious mother, and met the admonitions of bishops with a front of brass. He treated a 'nice girl', to whom they had got him engaged, badly; he married beneath him – some low thing or other. And sank. . . .

Kipps could not escape the application of the case. He was enabled to see how this sort of thing looked to decent people; he was enabled to gauge the measure of the penalties due. His mind went from that to the frozen marble of Coote's visage.

He deserved it! . . .

That day of remorse! Later it found him upon the site of his building operations and surveying the disorder of preparation in a mood near to despair, his mackintosh over his arm.

Hardly any one was at work that day – no doubt the builders were having him in some obscure manner – and the whole place seemed a dismal and depressing litter. The builder's shed, black-lettered WILKINS, BUILDER, HYTHE, looked like a stranded thing amidst a cast-up disorder of wheelbarrows and wheeling planks, and earth, and sand, and bricks. The foundations of the walls were trenches full of damp concrete, drying in patches; the rooms – it was incredible they could ever be rooms – were shaped out as squares and oblongs of coarse wet grass and sorrel. They looked absurdly small – dishonestly small. What could you expect? Of course the builders were having him, building too small, building all wrong, using bad materials! Old Kipps had told him a wrinkle or two. The builders were having him, young Walshingham was having him, everybody was having him! They were having him and laughing at him because they didn't respect him. They didn't respect him because he couldn't do things right. Who could respect him? . . .

He was an outcast, he had no place in the society of mankind. He had had his chance in the world and turned his back on it. He had 'behaved badly' – that was the phrase. . . .

Here a great house was presently to arise – a house to be paid for, a house neither he nor Ann could manage – with eleven bedrooms, and four disrespectful servants having them all the time!

How had it all happened exactly?

This was the end of his great fortune! What a chance he had had! If he had really carried out his first intentions and stuck to things, how much better everything might have been! If he had got a tutor – that had been in his mind originally – a special sort of tutor, to show him everything right. A tutor for gentlemen of neglected education. If he had read more and attended better to what Coote had said. . . .

Coote, who had just cut him! . . .

Eleven bedrooms! What had possessed him? No one would ever come to see them; no one would ever have anything to do with them. Even his Aunt cut him! His Uncle treated him with a half-contemptuous sufferance. He had not a friend worth counting in the world! Buggins, Carshot, Pearce – shop assistants! The Pornicks – a low socialist lot! He stood among his foundations like a lonely figure among ruins; he stood among the ruins of his future, and owned himself a foolish and mistaken man. He saw himself and Ann living out their shameful lives in this great crazy place – as it would be – with everybody laughing secretly at them, and the eleven bedrooms and nobody approaching them – nobody nice and right that is – for ever. And Ann!

What was the matter with Ann? She'd given up going for walks lately, got touchy and tearful, been fitful with her food. Just when she didn't ought to. It was all a part of the judgment upon wrong-doing; it was all part of the social penalties that Juggernaut of a novel had brought home to his mind.

III

He let himself in with his latch-key. He went moodily into the dining-room and got out the plans to look at them. He had a vague hope that there would prove to be only ten bedrooms. But he found there were still eleven. He became aware of Ann standing over him. 'Look 'ere, Artie!' said Ann.

He looked up and found her holding a number of white oblongs.

His eyebrows rose.

'It's Callers,' said Ann.

He put his plans aside slowly, and took and read the cards in silence, with a sort of solemnity. Callers! Then perhaps he wasn't to be left out of the world after all. Mrs G. Porrett Smith; Miss Porrett Smith; Miss Mabel Porrett Smith; and two smaller cards of the Rev. G. Porrett Smith. 'Lor!' he said. '*Clergy*!'

'There was a lady,' said Ann, 'and two growed-up gels – all dressed up!'

'And 'im?'

'There wasn't no 'im.'

'Not—?' He held out the little card.

'No. There was a lady and two young ladies.'

'But – these cards! Whad they go and leave these two little cards with the Rev. G. Smith on for? Not if 'e wasn't with 'em.'

''E wasn't with 'em.'

'Not a little chap – dodgin' about be'ind the others? And didn't come in?'

'I didn't see no gentleman with them at all,' said Ann.

'Rum!' said Kipps. A half-forgotten experience came back to him. 'I know,' he said, waving the reverend gentleman's card, ''e give 'em the slip; that's what he'd done. Gone off while they was rapping before you let 'em in. It's a fair call any'ow.' He felt a momentary base satisfaction at his absence. 'What did they talk about, Ann?'

There was a pause. 'I didn't let 'em in,' said Ann.

He looked up suddenly and perceived that something unusual was the matter with Ann. Her face was flushed, her eyes were red and hard.

'Didn't let 'em in?'

'No! They didn't come in at all.'

He was too astonished for words.

'I answered the door,' said Ann. 'I'd been upstairs, 'namelling the floor. 'Ow was I to think about Callers, Artie? We ain't never 'ad Callers, all the time we been 'ere. I'd sent Gwendolen out for a bref of fresh air, and there I was upstairs, 'namelling that floor she done so bad, so's to get it done before she came back. I thought I'd 'namel that floor and then get tea, and 'ave it quiet with you, toce and all, before she came back. 'Ow was I to think about Callers?'

She paused. 'Well,' said Kipps, 'what then?'

'They came and rapped. 'Ow was I to know? I thought it was a tradesman or something. Never took my apron off, never wiped the 'namel off my 'ands – nothing. There they was!'

She paused again. She was getting to the disagreeable part.

'Wad they say?' said Kipps.

'She says, "Is Mrs Kipps at home?" See? To me.'

'Yes.'

'And me all painty and no cap on and nothing, neither missis nor servant like. There, Artie, I could 'a sunk through the floor with shame, I really could. I could 'ardly get my voice. I couldn't think of nothing to say but just "Not at 'Ome," and out of 'abit like I 'eld the tray. And they give me the cards and went, and 'ow I shall ever look that lady in the face again I don't know. . . . And that's all about it, Artie! They looked me up and down, they did, and then I shut the door on 'em.'

'Goo!' said Kipps.

Ann went and poked the fire needlessly with a passion-quivering hand.

'I wouldn't 'ave 'ad that 'appen for five pounds,' said Kipps. 'Clergyman and all!'

Ann dropped the poker into the fender with some *éclat*, and stood up and looked at her hot face in the glass. Kipps' disappointment grew. 'You did ought to 'ave known better than that, Ann! You reely did.'

He sat forward, cards in hand, with a deepening sense of social disaster. The plates were laid upon the table, toast sheltered under a cover at mid-fender, the teapot warmed beside it, and the kettle, just lifted from the hob, sang amidst the coals. Ann glanced at him for a moment, then stooped with the kettle-holder to wet the tea.

'Tcha!' said Kipps, with his mental state developing.

'I don't see it's any use getting in a state about it now,' said Ann.

'Don't you! I do. See? 'Ere's these people, good people, want to 'ssociate with us, and 'ere you go and slap 'em in the face!'

'I didn't slap 'em in the face.'

'You do – practically. You slams the door in their face, and that's all we see of 'em ever! I wouldn't 'ave 'ad this 'appen not for a ten-pound note.'

He rounded his regrets with a grunt. For a while there was silence, save for the little stir of Ann's few movements preparing tea.

'Tea, Artie,' said Ann, handing him a cup.

Kipps took it.

'I put sugar *once*,' said Ann.

'Oo, dash it! Oo cares?' said Kipps, taking an extraordinarily large additional lump with fury-quivering fingers, and putting his cup, with a slight excess of force, on the recess cupboard. 'Oo cares?'

'I wouldn't 'ave 'ad that 'appen,' he said, bidding steadily against accomplished things, 'for twenty pounds.'

He gloomed in silence through a long minute or so.

Then Ann said the fatal thing that exploded him. 'Artie!' she said.

'What?'

'There's But-tud Toce down there! By your foot!'

There was a pause, husband and wife regarded one another.

'Buttud Toce indeed!' he said. 'You go and mess up them callers, and then you try and stuff me up with Buttud Toce! Buttud Toce indeed! 'Ere's our first chance of knowing any one that's at all fit to 'sociate with—Look 'ere, Ann! Tell you what it is – you got to return that call.'

'Return that call!'

'Yes – you got to return that call. That's what you got to do! I know—' He waved his arm vaguely towards the miscellany of books in the recess. 'It's in "Manners and Rools of Good S'ity". You got to find jest 'ow many cards to leave, and you got to go and leave 'em. See?'

Ann's face expressed terror. 'But, Artie! 'Ow *can* I?'

''Ow *can* you? 'Ow *could* you? You got to do it, any'ow. They won't know you – not in your Bond Street 'At! If they do, they won't say nothing.'

His voice assumed a note of entreaty. 'You mus', Ann.'

'I can't.'

'You mus'.'

'I can't, and I won't. Anything in reason I'll do, but face those people again I can't – after what 'as 'appened.'

'You won't?'

'*No!*'

'So there they go – orf! And we never see them again! And so it goes on! So it goes on! We don't know nobody, and we *shan't* know anybody! And you won't put yourself out not a little bit, or take the trouble to find out anything 'ow it ought to be done.'

Terrible pause.

'I never ought to 'ave married you, Artie, that's the troof.'

'Oh, *don't* go into that!'

'I never ought to 'ave married you, Artie. I'm not equal to the position. If you 'adn't said you'd drown yourself—' She choked.

'I don' see why you shouldn't *try*, Ann—*I've* improved. Why don't you? 'Stead of which you go sending out the servant and 'namelling floors, and then when visitors come—'

''Ow was *I* to know about y'r old visitors?' cried Ann in a wail, and suddenly got up and fled from amidst their ruined tea, the tea of which 'toce, all buttery', was to be the crown and glory.

Kipps watched her with a momentary consternation. Then he hardened his heart. 'Ought to 'ave known better,' he said, 'goin' on like that!' He remained for a space rubbing his knees and muttering. He emitted scornfully, 'I carn't, an' I won't.' He saw her as the source of all his shames.

Presently, quite mechanically, he stooped down and lifted the flowery china cover. 'Ter dash 'er Buttud Toce!' he shouted at the sight of it, and clapped the cover down again hard. . . .

When Gwendolen came back she perceived things were in a slightly unusual poise. Kipps sat by the fire in a rigid attitude, reading a casually selected volume of the *Encyclopaedia Britannica*, and Ann was upstairs and inaccessible – to reappear at a later stage with reddened eyes. Before the fire, and still in a perfectly assimilable condition, was what was evidently an untouched supply of richly buttered toast under a cracked cover.

'They've 'ad a bit of a tiff,' said Gwendolen, attending to her duties in the kitchen with her outdoor hat still on, and her mouth full. 'They're rummuns – if ever! My eye!'

And she took another piece of Ann's generously buttered toast.

IV

The Kippses spoke no more that day to one another.

The squabble about cards and buttered toast was as serious to them as the most rational of differences. It was all rational to them. Their sense of wrong burnt within them; their sense of what was owing to themselves, the duty of implacability, the obstinacy of pride. In the small hours Kipps lay awake at the nadir of unhappiness, and came near groaning. He saw life as an extraordinarily desolating muddle; his futile house, his social

discredit, his bad behaviour to Helen, his low marriage with
Ann. . . .

He became aware of something irregular in Ann's
breathing. . . .

He listened. She was awake, and quietly and privately
sobbing! . . .

He hardened his heart, resolutely he hardened his heart. And
presently Ann lay still.

V

The stupid little tragedies of these clipped and limited lives!

As I think of them lying unhappily there in the darkness, my
vision pierces the night. See what I can see! Above them,
brooding over them, I tell you there is a monster, a lumpish
monster, like some great clumsy griffin thing, like the Crystal
Palace labyrinthodon, like Coote, like the leaden goddess of the
Dunciad,* like some fat, proud flunkey, like pride, like indol-
ence, like all that is darkening and heavy and obstructive in life.
It is matter and darkness, it is the anti-soul, it is the ruling power
of this land, Stupidity. My Kippses live in its shadow. Shalford
and his apprenticeship system, the Hastings Academy, the ideas
of Coote, the ideas of the old Kippses, all the ideas that have
made Kipps what he is, – all these are a part of its shadow. But
for that monster they might not be groping among false ideas to
hurt one another so sorely; but for that, the glowing promise of
childhood and youth might have had a happier fruition; thought
might have awakened in them to meet the thought of the world,
the quickening sunshine of literature pierced to the substance of
their souls; their lives might not have been divorced, as now
they are divorced, from the apprehension of beauty that we
favoured ones are given, – the vision of the Grail that makes life
fine for ever. I have laughed, and I laugh at these two people; I
have sought to make you laugh. . . .

But I see through the darkness the souls of my Kippses as they
are, as little pink strips of quivering living stuff, as things like
the bodies of little, ill-nourished, ailing, ignorant children –
children who feel pain, who are naughty and muddled and
suffer, and do not understand why. And the claw of this Beast
rests upon them!

Chapter Three

Terminations

I

Next morning came a remarkable telegram from Folkestone. 'Please come at once, – urgent, – Walshingham,' said the telegram, and Kipps, after an agitated but still ample breakfast, departed. . . .

When he returned his face was very white, and his countenance disordered. He let himself in with his latch-key and came into the dining-room, where Ann sat, affecting to work at a little thing she called a bib. She heard his hat fall in the hall before he entered, as though he had missed the peg. 'I got something to tell you, Ann,' he said, disregarding their overnight quarrel, and went to the hearthrug and took hold of the mantel and stared at Ann as though the sight of her was novel.

'Well?' said Ann, not looking up, and working a little faster.

'' 'E's gone!'

Ann looked up sharply, and her hands stopped, '*Who's* gone?' For the first time she perceived Kipps' pallor.

'Young Walshingham – I saw 'er, and she tole me,'

'Gone! What d'you mean?'

'Cleared out! Gone off for good!'

'What for?'

'For 'is 'ealth,' said Kipps, with sudden bitterness, ''E's been speckylating. He's speckylated our money, and 'e's speckylated their money, and now 'e's took 'is 'ook. That's all about it, Ann.'

'You mean—?'

'I mean 'e's orf, and our twenty-four fousand's orf too! And 'ere we are! Smashed up! That's all about it, Ann.' He panted.

Ann had no vocabulary for such an occasion. 'Oh, Lor!' she said, and sat still.

Kipps came about and stuck his hands deeply in his trouser pockets. 'Speckylated every penny – lorst it all – and gorn. . . .'

Even his lips were white.

'You mean we ain't got nothin' left, Artie?'

'Not a penny! Not a bloomin' penny, Ann. No!'

A gust of passion whirled across the soul of Kipps. He flung out a knuckly fist. 'If I 'ad 'im 'ere,' he said, 'I'd – I'd – I'd wring 'is neck for 'im. I'd – I'd—' His voice rose to a shout. He thought of Gwendolen in the kitchen, and fell to, 'Ugh!'

'But, Artie,' said Ann, trying to grasp it, 'd'you mean to say he's took our money?'

'Speckylated it!' said Kipps, with an illustrative flourish of the arm that failed to illustrate. 'Bort things dear and sold 'em cheap, and played the 'ankey-pankey jackass with everything we got. That's what I mean 'e's done, Ann.' He repeated this last sentence with the addition of violent adverbs.

'D'you mean to say our money's *gone*, Artie?'

'Ter-dash it, *Yes*, Ann!' swore Kipps, exploding in a shout. 'Ain't I tellin' you?'

He was immediately sorry. 'I didn't mean to 'oller at you, Ann,' he said, 'but I'm all shook up. I don't 'ardly know what I'm sayin'. Ev'ry penny. . . .'

'But, Artie—'

Kipps grunted. He went to the window and stared for a moment at a sunlit sea. 'Gord!' he swore.

'I mean,' he said, coming back to Ann, and with an air of exasperation, 'that he's 'bezzled and 'ooked it. That's what I mean, Ann.'

Ann put down the bib. 'But wot are we going to *do*, Artie?'

Kipps indicated ignorance, wrath, and despair with one comprehensive gesture of his hands. He caught an ornament from the mantel and replaced it. 'I'm going to bang about,' he said, 'if I ain't precious careful.'

'You saw '*er*, you say?'

'Yes.'

'What did she say 'xactly?' said Ann.

'Told me to see a s'licitor – tole me to get some one to 'elp me at once. She was there in black – like she used to be, and speaking cool and careful like. 'Elen! . . . She's precious 'ard, is 'Elen. She looked at me straight. "It's my fault," she said. "I ought to 'ave warned you. . . . Only under the circumstances it was a little difficult." Straight as anything. I didn't 'ardly say anything to 'er. I didn't seem to begin to take it in until she was showing me out. I 'adn't anything to say. Jest as well, perhaps.

She talked – like a Call a'most. She said – what *was* it she said about her mother? – "My mother's overcome with grief," she said, "so naturally everything comes on me." '

'And she told you to get some one to 'elp you?'

'Yes. I been to old Bean.'

'O' Bean?'

'Yes. What I took my business away from!'

'What did he say?'

'He was a bit off 'and at first, but then 'e come round. He couldn't tell me anything till 'e knew the facts. What I know of young Walshingham, there won't be much 'elp in the facts. No!'

He reflected for a space. 'It's a Smash-up, Ann. More likely than not, Ann – 'e's left us over'ead in debt. We got to get out of it just 'ow we can. . . .

'We got to begin again,' he went on. '*Ow*, I don't know. All the way 'ome – my 'ead's been going. We got to get a living some'ow or other. 'Aving time to ourselves, and a bit of money to spend, and no hurry and worry; it's all over for ever, Ann. We was fools, Ann. We didn't know our benefits. We been caught. Gord! . . . Gord!'

He was on the verge of 'banging about' again.

They heard a jingle in the passage, the large, soft impact of a servant's indoor boots. As if she were a part, a mitigatory part of Fate, came Gwendolen to lay the midday meal. Kipps displayed self-control forthwith. Ann picked up the bib again and bent over it, and the Kippses bore themselves gloomily perhaps, but not despairfully, while their dependant was in the room. She spread the cloth and put out the cutlery with a slow inaccuracy, and Kipps, after a whisper to himself, went again to the window. Ann got up and put away her work methodically in the cheffonier.

'When I think,' said Kipps, as soon as the door closed again behind Gwendolen – 'when I think of the 'ole people, and 'aving to tell 'em of it all, I want to smesh my 'ead against the nearest wall. Smesh my silly brains out! And Buggins – Buggins, what I'd 'arf promised to start in a lill' outfitting shop in Rendezvous Street. . . .'

Gwendolen returned and restored dignity.

The midday meal spread itself slowly before them. Gwendolen, after her custom, left the door open, and Kipps closed it carefully before sitting down.

He stood for a moment, regarding the meal doubtfully.

'I don't feel as if I could swaller a mouffful,' he said.

'You got to eat,' said Ann. . . .

For a time they said little, and once swallowing was achieved, ate on with a sort of melancholy appetite. Each was now busy thinking.

'After all,' said Kipps, presently, 'whatever 'appens, they can' turn us out or sell us up before nex' quarter day. I'm pretty sure about that.'

'Sell us up!' said Ann.

'I dessay we're bankrup',' said Kipps, trying to say it easily, and helping himself with a trembling hand to unnecessary potatoes.

Then a long silence. Ann ceased to eat, and there were silent tears.

'More potatoes, Artie?' choked Ann.

'I couldn't,' said Kipps. 'No.'

He pushed back his plate, which was indeed replete with potatoes, got up and walked about the room. Even the dinner-table looked distraught and unusual.

'What to do, I *don't* know,' he said.

'Oh, *Lord*!' he ejaculated, and picked up and slapped down a book.

Then his eye fell upon another postcard that had come from Chitterlow by the morning's post, and which now lay by him on the mantelshelf. He took it up, glanced at its imperfectly legible message, and put it down.

'Delayed!' he said scornfully. 'Not prodooced in the smalls. Or is it smells 'e says? 'Ow can one understand that? Any'ow, 'e's 'umbugging again. Somefing about the Strand. No! . . . Well, 'e's 'ad all the money 'e'll ever get out of me! . . . I'm done.'

He seemed to find a momentary relief in the dramatic effect of his announcement. He came near to a swagger of despair upon the hearthrug, and then suddenly came and sat down next to Ann, and rested his chin on the knuckles of his two clenched hands.

'I been a fool, Ann,' he said in a gloomy monotone. 'I been a brasted fool. But it's 'ard on us, all the same. It's 'ard.'

''Ow was you to know?' said Ann.

'I ought to 'ave known. I did in a sort of way know. And 'ere we are! I wouldn't care so much if it was myself, but it's *you*, Ann! 'Ere we are! Regular smashed up! And you—' He checked at an unspeakable aggravation of their disaster. 'I knew 'e wasn't to be depended upon, and there I left it! And you got to pay. . . . What's to 'appen to us all, I don't know.'

He thrust out his chin and glared at fate.

''Ow do you know 'e's speckylated everything?' said Ann, after a silent survey of him.

''E 'as,' said Kipps, irritably, holding firm to disaster.

'She say so?'

'She don't know, of course; but you depend upon it, that's it. She told me she knew something was on, and when she found 'im gone and a note lef' for her, she knew it was up with 'im. 'E went by the night boat. She wrote that telegrarf off to me straight away.'

Ann surveyed his features with tender perplexed eyes; she had never seen him so white and drawn before, and her hand rested an inch or so away from his arm. The actual loss was still, as it were, afar from her. The immediate thing was his enormous distress.

''Ow do you know—?' she said, and stopped. It would irritate him too much.

Kipps' imagination was going headlong.

'Sold up!' he emitted presently, and Ann flinched.

'Going back to work, day after day. I can't stand it, Ann, I can't. And you—'

'It don't do to think of it,' said Ann.

Presently he came upon a resolve. 'I keep on thinking of it, and thinking of it, and what's to be done, and what's to be done. I shan't be any good 'ome s'arfernoon. It keeps on going round and round in my 'ead, and round and round. I better go for a walk or something. I'd be no comfort to you, Ann. I should want to 'owl and 'ammer things if I 'ung about 'ome. My fingers 'r all atwitch. I shall keep on thinking 'ow I might 'ave stopped it, and callin' myself a fool. . . .'

He looked at her between pleading and shame. It seemed like deserting her.

Ann regarded him with tear-dimmed eyes.

'You'd better do what's good for you, Artie,' she said. . . . 'I'll be best cleaning. It's no use sending off Gwendolen before her month, and the top room wants turning out.' She added with a sort of grim humour, 'May as well turn it out now while I got it.'

'I *better* go for a walk,' said Kipps. . . .

And presently our poor exploded Kipps was marching out to bear his sudden misery. Habit turned him up the road towards his growing house, and then suddenly he perceived his direction – 'Oh, Lor!' – and turned aside and went up the steep way to the hill-crest and the Sandling Road, and over the line by that tree-embowered Junction, and athwart the wide fields towards Postling – a little black marching figure – and so up the Downs and over the hills, whither he had never gone before. . . .

II

He came back long after dark, and Ann met him in the passage.

'Where you been, Artie?' she asked, with a strained note in her voice.

'I been walking and walking – trying to tire myself out. All the time I been thinking, what shall I do? Trying to fix something up, all out of nothing.'

'I didn't know you meant to be out all this time.'

Kipps was gripped by compunction. . . .

'I can't think what we ought to do,' he said presently.

'You can't do anything much, Artie, not till you hear from Mr Bean.'

'No. I can't do anything much. That's jest it. And all this time I keep feelin' if I don't do something the top of my 'ead'll bust. . . . Been trying to make up advertisements 'arf the time I been out – 'bout finding a place; good salesman and stockkeeper, good Manchester dresses, window-dressing – Lor! Fancy that all beginning again!' . . . If you went to stay with Sid a bit— If I sent every penny I got to you—I dunno! I dunno!'

When they had gone to bed there was an elaborate attempt to get to sleep. . . . In one of their great waking pauses Kipps remarked in a muffled tone, 'I didn't mean to frighten you, Ann, being out so late. I kep' on walking and walking, and some'ow it seemed to do me good. I went out to the 'ill-top ever so far beyond Stanford, and sat there ever so long, and it seemed to make me better. Jest looking over the marsh like, and seeing the sun set. . . .'

'Very likely,' said Ann, after a long interval, 'it isn't so bad as you think it is, Artie.'

'It's bad,' said Kipps.

'Very likely, after all, it isn't quite so bad. If there's only a little—'

There came another long silence.

'Ann,' said Kipps, in the quiet darkness.

'Yes,' said Ann.

'Ann,' said Kipps, and stopped as though he had hastily shut a door upon speech.

'I kep' thinking,' he said, trying again – 'I kep' thinking, after all, I been cross to you and a fool about things – about them cards, Ann – but' – his voice shook to pieces – 'we 'ave been 'appy, Ann . . . some'ow . . . togever.'

And with that he and then she fell into a passion of weeping.

They clung very tightly together – closer than they had been since ever the first brightness of their married days turned to the grey of common life again. . . .

All the disaster in the world could not prevent their going to sleep at last, with their poor little troubled heads close together on one pillow. There was nothing more to be done; there was nothing more to be thought. Time might go on with his mischiefs, but for a little while at least they still had one another.

III

Kipps returned from his second interview with Mr Bean in a state of strange excitement. He let himself in with his latch-key and slammed the door. 'Ann!' he shouted, in an unusual note; 'Ann!'

Ann replied distantly.

'Something to tell you,' said Kipps; 'something noo!'

Ann appeared apprehensive from the kitchen.

'Ann,' he said, going before her into the little dining-room, for his news was too dignified for the passage, 'very likely, Ann, o' Bean says, we shall 'ave—' He decided to prolong the suspense, 'Guess!'

'I can't, Artie.'

'Think of a lot of money!'

'A 'undred pounds p'r'aps?'

He spoke with immense deliberation. 'Over a fousand pounds!'

Ann stared and said nothing, only went a shade whiter.

'Over,' he said. 'A'most certainly over.'

He shut the dining-room door and came forward hastily, for Ann, it was clear, meant to take this mitigation of their disaster with a complete abandonment of her self-control. She came near flopping; she fell into his arms.

'Artie,' she got to at last, and began to weep, clinging tightly to him.

'Pretty near certain,' said Kipps, holding her. 'A fousand pounds!'

'I *said*, Artie,' she wailed on his shoulder with the note of accumulated wrongs, 'very likely it wasn't so bad. . . .'

'There's things,' he said, when presently he came to particulars, ''e couldn't touch. The noo place! It's freehold and paid for, and with the bit of building of it, there's five or six 'undred pounds p'r'aps – say worf free 'undred for safety. We can't be sold up to finish it, like we thought. O' Bean says we can very likely sell it and get money. 'E says you often get a chance to sell a 'ouse lessen 'arf done, specially free'old. *Very* likely 'e says. Then there's Hughenden. Hughenden 'asn't been mortgaged not for more than 'arf its value. There's a 'undred or so to be got on that, and the furniture, and the rent for the summer still coming in. 'E says there's very likely other things. A fousand pounds; that's what '*e* said. 'E said it might even be more. . . .'

They were sitting now at the table.

'It alters everything,' said Ann.

'I been thinking that, Ann, all the way 'ome. I came in the motor-car. First ride I've had since the Smash. We needn't send off Gwendolen; leastways, not till *after*. You know. We needn't turn out of 'ere – not for a long time. What we been doing for the o'people we can go on doing a'most as much. And your mother! . . . I wanted to 'oller, coming along. I pretty near run coming down the road by the Hotel.'

'Oh, I *am* glad we can stop 'ere and be comfortable a bit,' said Ann. 'I *am* glad for that.'

'I pretty near told the driver on the motor – only 'e was the sort won't talk. . . . You see, Ann, we'll be able to start a shop, we'll be able to get *into* something like. All about our 'aving to go back to places and that – all that doesn't matter any more.'

For a while they abandoned themselves to ejaculating transports. Then they fell talking to shape an idea to themselves of the new prospect that opened before them.

'We must start a sort of shop,' said Kipps, whose imagination had been working. 'It'll 'ave to be a shop.'

'Drapery?' said Ann.

'You want such a lot of capital for the drapery; mor'n a thousand pounds you want by a long way – to start it anything like proper.'

'Well, outfitting. Like Buggins was going to do.'

Kipps glanced at that for a moment, because the idea had not occurred to him. Then he came back to his prepossession.

'Well, I thought of something else, Ann,' he said. 'You see, I've always thought a little bookshop—It isn't like the drapery – 'aving to be learnt. I thought, even before this Smash Up, 'ow I'd like to 'ave something to do, instead of always 'aving 'olidays always like we 'ave been 'aving.'

She reflected.

'You don't know *much* about books, do you, Artie?'

'You don't want to.' He illustrated. 'I noticed when we used to go to the Lib'ry at Folkestone, ladies weren't anything like what they was in a draper's – if you 'aven't got *just* what they want, its "Oh no!" and out they go. But in a bookshop it's different. One book's very like another – after all, what is it? Something to read and done with. It's not a thing that matters like print dresses or serviettes – where you either like 'em or don't, and people judge you by. They take what you give 'em in books and lib'ries, and glad to be told *what* to. See 'ow we was – up at that lib'ry. . . .'

He paused. 'You see, Ann—

'Well, I read 'n 'dvertisement the other day—I been asking Mr Bean. It said – five 'undred pounds.'

'What did?'

'Branches,' said Kipps.

Ann failed to understand. 'It's a sort of thing that gets up bookshops all over the country,' said Kipps. 'I didn't tell you, but I arst about it a bit. On'y I dropped it again. Before this Smash I mean. I'd thought I'd like to keep a shop for a lark, on'y then I thought it silly. Besides, it 'ud 'ave been beneath me.'

He blushed vividly. 'It was a sort of projek of mine, Ann.

'On'y it wouldn't 'ave done,' he added.

It was a tortuous journey when the Kippses set out to explain anything to each other. But through a maze of fragmentary elucidations and questions, their minds did presently begin to approximate to a picture of a compact, bright little shop, as a framework for themselves.

'I thought of it one day when I was in Folkestone. I thought of it one day when I was looking in at a window. I see a chap dressin' a window, and he was whistlin', reg'lar light-hearted. . . .I thought – I'd like to keep a bookshop any'ow, jest for something to do. And when people weren't about, then you could sit and read the books. See? It wouldn't be 'arf bad. . . .'

They mused, each with elbows on table and knuckles to lips, looking with speculative eyes at each other.

'Very likely we'll be 'appier than we should 'ave been with more money,' said Kipps, presently.

'We wasn't 'ardly suited—' reflected Ann, and left her sentence incomplete.

'Fish out of water like,' said Kipps. . . .

'You won't 'ave to return that call now,' said Kipps, opening a new branch of the question. 'That's one good thing.'

'Lor!' said Ann, 'no more I shan't!'

'I don't s'pose they'd want you to even if you did – with things as they are.'

A certain added brightness came into Ann's face. 'Nobody won't be able to come leaving cards on us, Artie, now, any more. We are out of *that*!'

'There isn't no necessity for us to be Stuck Up,' said Kipps, 'any more for ever! 'Ere we are, Ann, common people, with jest no position at all, as you might say, to keep up. No se'v'nts not if you don't like. No dressin' better than other people. If it wasn't we been robbed – dashed if I'd care a rap about losing that money. I b'lieve' – his face shone with the rare pleasure of paradox – 'I reely b'lieve, Ann, it'll prove a savin' in the end.'

IV

The remarkable advertisement which had fired Kipps' imagination with this dream of a bookshop opened out in the most alluring way. It was one little facet in a comprehensive scheme of transatlantic origin, which was to make our old-world methods of bookselling 'sit up,' and it displayed an imaginative briskness, a lucidity and promise that aroused the profoundest scepticism in the mind of Mr Bean. To Kipps' renewed investigations it presented itself in an expository illustrated pamphlet (far too well printed, Mr Bean thought, for a reputable undertaking) of the most convincing sort. Mr Bean would not let him sink his capital in shares in its projected company that was to make all things new in the world of books, but he could not prevent Kipps becoming one of their associated booksellers. And so, when presently it became apparent that an Epoch was not to be made, and the 'Associated Booksellers' Trading Union (Limited)' receded and dissolved and liquidated (a few drops) and vanished and went away to talk about something else, Kipps remained floating undamaged in this interestingly uncertain universe as an independent bookseller.

Except that it failed, the Associated Booksellers' Trading Union had all the stigmata of success. Its fault, perhaps, was that it had them all instead of only one or two. It was to buy wholesale for all its members and associates and exchange stock, having a common books-in-stock list and a common lending library, and it was to provide a uniform registered shop-front to signify all these things to the intelligent passer-by. Except that it was controlled by buoyant young Overmen, with a touch of genius in their arithmetic, it was, I say, a most plausible and hopeful project. Kipps went several times to London, and an agent came to Hythe, Mr Bean made some timely interventions, and then behind a veil of planks and an announcement in the High Street, the uniform registered shop-front came rapidly into being. 'Associated Booksellers' Trading Union', said this shop-front, in a refined artistic lettering that bookbuyers were going to value, as wise men over forty value the proper label for Berncasteler Doctor, and then, 'Arthur Kipps'.

Next to starting a haberdasher's shop, I doubt if Kipps could have been more truly happy than during those weeks of preparation.

There is, of course, nothing on earth, and I doubt at times if there is a joy in heaven, like starting a small haberdasher's shop. Imagine, for example, having a drawerful of tapes (one whole piece most exquisitely blocked of every possible width of tape), or again, an army of neat, large packages, each displaying one sample of hooks and eyes. Think of your cottons, your drawer of coloured silks, the little, less, least of the compartments and thin packets of your needle-drawer! Poor princes and wretched gentlefolk, mysteriously above retail trade, may taste only the faint unsatisfactory shadow of these delights with trays of stamps or butterflies. I write, of course, for those to whom these things appeal; there are clods alive who see nothing, or next to nothing, in spools of mercerized cotton and endless bands of paper-set pins. I write for the wise, and as I write I wonder that Kipps resisted haberdashery. He did. Yet even starting a bookshop is at least twenty times as interesting as building your own house to your own design in unlimited space and time, or any possible thing people with indisputable social position and sound securities can possibly find to do. Upon that I rest.

You figure Kipps 'going to have a look to see how the little shop is getting on', the shop that is not to be a loss and a spending of money, but a gain. He does not walk too fast towards it; as he comes into view of it his paces slacken and his head goes to one side. He crosses to the pavement opposite in order to inspect the fascia better, already his name is adumbrated in faint white lines; stops in the middle of the road and scrutinizes imaginary details, for the benefit of his future next-door neighbour, the curiosity-shop man, and so at last, in. . . . A smell of paint and of the shavings of imperfectly seasoned pinewood! The shop is already glazed, and a carpenter is busy over the fittings for adjustable shelves in the side windows. A painter is busy on the fixtures round about (shelving above and drawers below), which are to accommodate most of the stock, and the counter – the counter and desk are done. Kipps goes inside the desk, the desk which is to be the strategic centre of the shop, brushes away some sawdust, and draws out the marvellous till; here gold is to be, here silver, here copper – notes locked up in a cash-box in the well below. Then he leans his elbows on the desk, rests his chin on his fist and fills the shelves with imaginary stock; books beyond reading. Every day a man who cares to wash his hands and read uncut pages artfully may have his cake and eat it, among that stock. Under the counter to the right paper and string are to lurk, ready to leap up and embrace goods sold; on the table to the left, art publications – whatever they may prove to be. He maps it out, serves an imaginary customer, receives a dream seven-and-sixpence, packs, bows out. He wonders how it was he ever came to fancy a shop a disagreeable place.

'It's different,' he says at last, after musing on that difficulty, 'being your own.'

It *is* different. . . .

Or, again, you figure Kipps with something of the air of a young sacristan, handling his brightly virginal account books, and looking and looking again, and then still looking, at an unparalleled specimen of copperplate engraving, ruled money below, and above bearing the words, 'In Account with ARTHUR KIPPS (loud flourishes), The Booksellers' Trade Union' (temperate decoration). You figure Ann sitting and stitching at one point of the circumference of the light of the lamp, stitching queer little garments for some unknown stranger, and over against her sits Kipps. Before him is one of those engraved memorandum forms, a moist pad, wet with some thick and greasy, greenish purple ink, that is also spreading quietly but steadily over his fingers, a cross-nibbed pen for first-aid surgical assistance to the patient in his hand, a dating rubber stamp. At intervals he brings down this latter with great care and emphasis upon the paper, and when he lifts it there appears a beautiful oval design, of which 'Paid, Arthur Kipps, The Associated Booksellers' Trading Union', and a date, are the essential ingredients, stamped in purple ink.

Anon he turns his attention to a box of small, round yellow labels, declaring 'This book was bought from the Associated Booksellers' Trading Union.' He licks one with deliberate care, sticks it on the paper before him and defaces it with great solemnity. 'I can do it, Ann,' he says, looking up brightly. For the Associated Booksellers' Trading Union, among other brilliant notions and inspirations, devised an ingenious system of taking back its books again in part payment for new ones within a specified period. When it failed all sorts of people were left with these unredeemed pledges in hand.

v

Amidst all this bustle and interest, all this going to and fro before they 'moved in' to the High Street, came the great crisis that hung over the Kippses, and one morning in the small hours Ann's child was born. . . .

Kipps was coming to manhood swiftly now. The once rabbit-like soul that had been so amazed by the discovery of 'chubes' in the human interior and so shocked by the sight of a woman's

shoulder-blades, that had found shame and anguish in a mislaid
Gibus and terror in an Anagram Tea, was at last facing the
greater realities. He came suddenly upon the master thing in life
– birth. He passed through hours of listening, hours of impotent
fear in the night and in the dawn, and then there was put into
his arms something most wonderful, a weak and wailing creature, incredibly, heart-stirringly soft and pitiful, with minute
appealing hands that it wrung his heart to see. He held it in his
arms and touched its tender cheek as if he feared his lips might
injure it. And this marvel was his Son!

And there was Ann, with a greater strangeness and a greater
familiarity in her quality than he had ever found before. There
were little beads of perspiration on her temples and her lips, and
her face was flushed, not pale, as he had feared to see it. She had
the look of one who emerges from some strenuous and invigor-
ating act. He bent down and kissed her, and he had no words to
say. She wasn't to speak much yet, but she stroked his arm with
her hand and had to tell him one thing.

'He's over nine pounds, Artie,' she whispered. 'Bessie's—
Bessie's wasn't no more than eight.'

To have given Kipps a pound of triumph over Sid seemed to
her almost to justify Nunc Dimittis. She watched his face for a
moment, then closed her eyes in a kind of blissful exhaustion as
the nurse, with something motherly in her manner, pushed
Kipps out of the room.

VI

Kipps was far too much preoccupied with his own life to worry
about the further exploits of Chitterlow. The man had got his
two thousand; on the whole Kipps was glad he had had it rather
than young Walshingham, and there was an end to the matter.
As for the complicated transactions he achieved and proclaimed
by mainly illegible and always incomprehensible postcards, they
were like passing voices heard in the street as one goes about
one's urgent concerns. Kipps put them aside, and they got in
between the pages of the stock and were lost for ever, and sold
in with the goods to customers, who puzzled over them mightily.

Then one morning as our bookseller was dusting round before

breakfast, Chitterlow returned, appeared suddenly in the shop doorway.

It was the most unexpected thing in the world. The man was in evening dress, evening dress in that singularly crumpled state it assumes after the hour of dawn, and above his dishevelled red hair a smallish Gibus hat tilted remarkably forward. He opened the door and stood tall and spread, with one vast white glove flung out, as if to display how burst a glove might be, his eyes bright, such wrinkling of brow and mouth as only an experienced actor can produce, and a singular radiance of emotion upon his whole being – an altogether astonishing spectacle.

The bell jangled for a bit, and then gave it up and was silent. For a long long second everything was quietly attentive. Kipps was amazed to his uttermost; had he had ten times the capacity, he would still have been fully amazed. 'It's Chit'low!' he said at last, standing duster in hand.

But he doubted whether it was not a dream.

'Tzit!' gasped that most extraordinary person, still in an incredibly expanded attitude, and then with a slight forward jerk of the starry split glove, 'Bif!'

He could say no more. The tremendous speech he had had ready vanished from his mind. Kipps stared at his facial changes, vaguely conscious of the truth of the teachings of Nisbet and Lombroso concerning men of genius.

Then suddenly Chitterlow's features were convulsed, the histrionic fell from him like a garment, and he was weeping. He said something indistinct about 'Old Kipps! *Good* old Kipps! Oh, old Kipps!' and somehow he managed to mix a chuckle and a sob in the most remarkable way. He emerged from somewhere near the middle of his original attitude, a merely life-size creature. 'My play, boohoo!' he sobbed, clutching at his friend's arm. 'My play, Kipps! (sob). You know?'

'Well?' cried Kipps, with his heart sinking in sympathy. 'It ain't—?'

'No,' howled Chitterlow. 'No. It's a Success! My dear chap! my dear boy! Oh! It's a – Bu – boohoo! – a Big Success!' He turned away and wiped streaming tears with the back of his hand. He walked a pace or so and turned. He sat down on one of the specially designed artistic chairs of the Associated Booksellers' Trading Union and produced an exiguous lady's handkerchief, extraordinarily belaced. He choked. '*My* play,' and covered his face here and there.

He made an unsuccessful effort to control himself, and shrank for a space to the dimensions of a small and pathetic creature. His great nose suddenly came through a careless place in the handkerchief.

'I'm knocked,' he said in a muffled voice, and so remained for a space – wonderful – veiled.

He made a gallant effort to wipe his tears away. 'I had to tell you,' he said gulping.

'Be all right in a minute,' he added, 'Calm!' and sat still. . . .

Kipps stared in commiseration of such success. Then he heard footsteps, and went quickly to the house doorway. 'Jest a minute,' he said. 'Don't go in the shop, Ann, for a minute. It's Chitterlow. He's a bit essited. But he'll be better in a minute. It's knocked him over a bit. You see' – his voice sank to a hushed note as one who announces death – "e's made a success with his play.'

He pushed her back, lest she should see the scandal of another male's tears. . . .

Soon Chitterlow felt better, but for a little while his manner was even alarmingly subdued. 'I *had* to come and tell you,' he said. 'I *had* to astonish some one. Muriel – she'll be first-rate, of course. But she's over at Dymchurch.' He blew his nose with enormous noise, and emerged instantly, a merely garrulous optimist.

'I expect she'll be precious glad.'

'She doesn't know yet, my dear boy. She's at Dymchurch – with a friend. She's seen some of my first nights before. . . . Better out of it. . . . I'm going to her now. I've been up all night – talking to the Boys and all that. I'm a bit off it just for a bit. But – it Knocked 'em. It Knocked everybody.'

He stared at the floor and went on in a monotone. 'They laughed a bit at the beginning – but nothing like a settled laugh – not until the second act – you know – the chap with the beetle down his neck. Little Chisholme did that bit to rights. Then they began – *to* rights.' His voice warmed and increased. 'Laughing! It made *me* laugh! We jumped 'em into the third act before they had time to cool. Everybody was on it. I never saw a first night go so fast. Laugh, laugh, laugh, LAUGH, LAUGH, LAUGH' (he howled the last repetition with stupendous violence). 'Everything they laughed at. They laughed at things that we hadn't meant to be funny – not for one moment. Bif! Bizz! Curtain. A Fair Knock Out! . . . I went on – but I didn't say a word. Chisholme did the patter. Shouting! It was like walking under Niagara – going across that stage. It was like never having seen an audience before. . . .

'Then afterwards – the Boys!'

His emotion held him for a space. 'Dear old Boys!' he murmured.

His word multiplied, his importance increased. In a little while he was restored to something of his old self. He was enormously excited. He seemed unable to sit down anywhere. He came into the breakfast-room so soon as Kipps was sure of him, shook hands with Mrs Kipps parenthetically, sat down and immediately got up again. He went to the bassinet in the corner and looked absent-mindedly at Kipps junior, and said he was glad if only for the youngster's sake. He immediately resumed the thread of his discourse. . . . He drank a cup of coffee noisily and walked up and down the room talking, while they attempted breakfast amidst the gale of his excitement. The infant slept marvellously through it all.

'You won't mind my not sitting down, Mrs Kipps – I couldn't sit down for any one, or I'd do it for you. It's you I'm thinking of more than any one, you and Muriel, and all Old Pals and Good Friends. It means wealth, it means money – hundreds and thousands. . . . If you'd heard 'em, *you'd know*.'

He was silent through a portentous moment, while topics battled for him, and finally he burst and talked of them all together. It was like the rush of water when a dam bursts and washes out a fair-sized provincial town; all sorts of things floated along on the swirl. For example, he was discussing his future behaviour. 'I'm glad it's come now. Not before. I've had my lesson. I shall be very discreet now, trust me. We've learnt the value of money.' He discussed the possibility of a country house, of taking a Martello tower as a swimming-box (as one might say a shooting-box), of living in Venice because of its artistic associations and scenic possibilities, of a flat in Westminster or a house in the West End. He also raised the question of giving up smoking and drinking, and what classes of drink were especially noxious to a man of his constitution. But discourses on all this did not prevent a parenthetical computation of the probable profits on the supposition of a thousand nights here and in America, nor did it ignore the share Kipps was to have, nor the gladness with which Chitterlow would pay that share, nor the surprise and regret with which he had learnt, through an indirect source which awakened many associations, of the turpitude of young Walshingham, nor the distaste Chitterlow had always felt for young Walshingham, and men of his type. An excursus upon Napoleon had got into the torrent somehow, and kept bobbing up and down. The whole thing was thrown into the form of a single complex sentence, with parenthetical and subordinate clauses fitting one into the other like Chinese boxes, and from first to last it never even had an air of approaching anything in the remotest degree partaking of the nature of a full stop.

Into this deluge came the *Daily News*, like the gleam of light in Watts' picture, the waters were assuaged while its sheet was opened, and it had a column, a whole column, of praise. Chitterlow held the paper, and Kipps read over his left hand, and Ann under his right. It made the affair more real to Kipps; it seemed even to confirm Chitterlow against lurking doubts he had been concealing. But it took him away. He departed in a whirl, to secure a copy of every morning paper, every blessed rag there is, and take them all to Dymchurch and Muriel forthwith. It had been the send-off the Boys had given him that had prevented his doing as much at Charing Cross — let alone that he only caught it by the skin of his teeth. . . . Besides which, the bookstall wasn't open. His white face, lit by a vast excitement, bid them a tremendous farewell, and he departed through the sunlight, with his buoyant walk, buoyant almost to the tottering pitch. His hair, as one got it sunlit in the street, seemed to have grown in the night.

They saw him stop a newsboy.

'Every blessed rag,' floated to them on the notes of that gorgeous voice.

The newsboy too had happened on luck. Something like a faint cheer from the newsboy came down the air to terminate that transaction.

Chitterlow went on his way swinging a great budget of papers, a figure of merited success. The newsboy recovered from his emotion with a jerk, examined something in his hand again, transferred it to his pocket, watched Chitterlow for a space, and then in a sort of hushed silence resumed his daily routine. . . .

Ann and Kipps regarded that receding happiness in silence, until it vanished round the bend of the road.

'I *am* glad,' said Ann at last, speaking with a little sigh.

'So'm I,' said Kipps, with emphasis. 'For if ever a feller 'as worked and waited – it's 'im. . . .'

They went back through the shop rather thoughtfully, and, after a peep at the sleeping baby, resumed their interrupted breakfast. 'If ever a feller 'as worked and waited, it's 'im,' said Kipps, cutting bread.

'Very likely it's true,' said Ann, a little wistfully.

'What's true?'

'About all that money coming.'

Kipps meditated. 'I don't see why it shouldn't be,' he decided, and handed Ann a piece of bread on the tip of his knife.

'But we'll keep on the shop,' he said, after an interval for further reflection, 'all the same. . . . I 'aven't much trust in money after the things we've seen.'

VII

That was two years ago, and, as the whole world knows, the 'Pestered Butterfly' is running still. It *was* true. It has made the fortune of a once declining little theatre in the Strand; night after night the great beetle scene draws happy tears from a house packed to repletion, and Kipps – for all that Chitterlow is not what one might call a business man – is almost as rich as he was in the beginning. People in Australia, people in Lancashire, Scotland, Ireland, in New Orleans, in Jamaica, in New York and Montreal, have crowded through doorways to Kipps' enrichment, lured by the hitherto unsuspected humours of the entomological drama. Wealth rises like an exhalation all over our little planet, and condenses, or at least some of it does, in the pockets of Kipps.

'It's rum,' said Kipps.

He sat in the little kitchen out behind the bookshop and philosophized and smiled while Ann gave Arthur Waddy Kipps his evening tub before the fire. Kipps was always present at this ceremony, unless customers prevented; there was something in the mixture of the odours of tobacco, soap, and domesticity that charmed him unspeakably.

'Chuckerdee, o' man,' he said affably, wagging his pipe at his son, and thought incidentally, after the manner of all parents, that very few children could have so straight and clean a body.

'Dadda's got a cheque,' said Arthur Waddy Kipps, emerging for a moment from the towel.

''E gets 'old of everything,' said Ann. 'You can't say a word—'

'Dadda got a cheque,' this marvellous child repeated.

'Yes, o' man, I got a cheque. And it's got to go into a bank for you, against when you got to go to school. See? So's you'll grow up knowing your way about a bit.'

'Dadda's got a cheque,' said the wonder son, and then gave his mind to making mighty splashes with his foot. Every time he splashed, laughter overcame him, and he had to be held up for fear he should tumble out of the tub in his merriment. Finally he was towelled to his toe-tips, wrapped up in warm flannel, and kissed and carried off to bed by Ann's cousin and lady help, Emma. And then after Ann hd carried away the bath into the scullery, she returned to find her husband with his pipe extinct and the cheque still in his hand.

'Two fousand pounds,' he said. 'It's dashed rum. Wot 'ave *I* done to get two fousand pounds, Ann?'

'What 'aven't you – not to?' said Ann.

He reflected upon this view of the case.

'I shan't never give up this shop,' he said at last.

'We're very 'appy 'ere,' said Ann.

'Not if I 'ad *fifty* fousand pounds.'

'No fear,' said Ann.

'You got a shop,' said Kipps, 'and you come along in a year's time and there it is. But money—look 'ow it comes and goes! There's no sense in money. You may kill yourself trying to get it, then it comes when you aren't looking. There's my 'riginal money! Where is it now? Gone! And it's took young Walshingham with it, and 'e's gone too. It's like playing skittles. Long comes the ball, right and left you fly, and there it is rolling away and not changed a bit. No sense in it. 'E's gone, and she's gone – gone off with that chap Revel, that sat with me at dinner. Merried man! And Chit'low rich! Lor! – what a fine place that Gerrik Club is to be sure, where I 'ad lunch wiv' 'im! Better'n *any* 'otel. Footmen in powder they got – not waiters, Ann, – footmen! 'E's rich and me rich – in a sort of way. . . . Don't seem much sense in it, Ann – 'owever you look at it.' He shook his head.

'I know one thing,' said Kipps.

'What?'

'I'm going to put it in jest as many different banks as I can. See? Fifty 'ere, fifty there. 'Posit. I'm not going to 'nvest it – no fear.'

'It's only frowing money away,' said Ann.

'I'm 'arf a mind to bury some of it under the shop. Only I expect one 'ud always be coming down at nights to make sure it was there. . . . I don't seem to trust any one – not with money.' He put the cheque on the table corner and smiled and tapped his pipe on the grate, with his eyes on that wonderful document. 'S'pose old Bean started orf,' he reflected. . . . 'One thing, – 'e *is* a bit lame.'

''E wouldn't,' said Ann; 'not 'im.'

'I was only joking like.' He stood up, put his pipe among the candlesticks on the mantel, took up the cheque and began folding it carefully to put it back in his pocket-book.

A little bell jangled.

'Shop!' said Kipps. 'That's right. Keep a shop and the shop'll keep you. That's 'ow I look at it, Ann.'

He drove his pocket-book securely into his breast-pocket before he opened the living-room door. . . .

But whether indeed it is the bookshop that keeps Kipps, or whether it is Kipps who keeps the bookshop, is just one of those commercial mysteries people of my unarithmetical temperament are never able to solve. They do very well, the dears, anyhow, thank Heaven!

The bookshop of Kipps is on the left-hand side of the Hythe High Street coming from Folkestone, between the yard of the livery-stable and the shop window full of old silver and such-like things – it is quite easy to find – and there you may see him for yourself and speak to him and buy this book of him if you like. He has it in stock I know. Very delicately I've seen to that. His name is not Kipps, of course, you must understand that; but everything else is exactly as I have told you. You can talk to him about books, about politics, about going to Boulogne, about life, and the ups and downs of life. Perhaps he will quote you

Buggins – from whom, by-the-by, one can now buy everything a gentleman's warbrobe should contain at the little shop in Rendezvous Street, Folkestone. If you are fortunate to find Kipps in a good mood, he may even let you know how he inherited a fortune 'once'. 'Run froo it,' he'll say with a not unhappy smile. 'Got another afterwards – speckylating in plays. Needn't keep this shop if I didn't like. But it's something to do. . . .'

Or he may be even more intimate. 'I seen some things,' he said to me once. 'Raver! Life! Why, once I – I *loped*! I did – reely!'

(Of course you will not tell Kipps that he *is* 'Kipps', or that I have put him in this book. He hasn't the remotest suspicion of that. And, you know, you never can tell how people are going to take that sort of thing. I am an old and trusted customer now, and for many amiable reasons I should prefer that things remained exactly on their present footing.)

VIII

One early-closing evening in July they left the baby to the servant cousin, and Kipps took Ann for a row on the Hythe canal. The sun set in a mighty blaze, and left a world warm, and very still. The twilight came. And there was the water, shining bright, and the sky a deepening blue, and the great trees that dipped their boughs towards the water, exactly as it had been when he paddled home with Helen, when her eyes had seemed to him like dusky stars. He had ceased from rowing and rested on his oars, and suddenly he was touched by the wonder of life – the strangeness that is a presence stood again by his side.

Out of the darknesses beneath the shallow weedy stream of his being rose a question, a question that looked up dimly and never reached the surface. It was the question of the wonder of the beauty, the purposeless, inconsecutive beauty, that falls so strangely among the happenings and memories of life. It never reached the surface of his mind, it never took to itself substance or form; it looked up merely as the phantom of a face might look, out of deep waters, and sank again into nothingness.

'Artie,' said Ann.

He woke up and pulled a stroke. 'What?' he said.

'Penny for your thoughts, Artie.'

He considered.

'I reely don't think I was thinking of anything,' he said at last, with a smile. 'No.'

He still rested on his oars.

'I expect,' he said, 'I was thinking jest what a Rum Go everything is. I expect it was something like that.'

'Queer old Artie!'

'Ain't I? I don't suppose there ever was chap quite like me before.'

He reflected for just another minute.

'Oo! – I dunno,' he said at last, and roused himself to pull.

EXPLANATORY NOTES

p. 3 **Dolly Varden hat**. A large-brimmed hat trimmed with flowers, from the name of a character in Charles Dickens' *Barnaby Rudge* (1841).

p. 5 **Colic for the Day**. The Anglican Prayer Book apportions a special prayer, a Collect, for particular days of worship.

p. 12 **Hurons**. A Canadian Indian tribe around Lake Huron, Ontario. They were skilled farmers and fisherman as well as fierce warriors, of the Iroquois people.

p. 19 **Tit Bits**. A popular magazine founded in 1881 by George Newnes, dispensing much miscellaneous, trivial, information, together with jokes, articles, quizzes, stories. In its early days, it featured such writers as Conrad, Bennett and Wells himself. It was one of many such periodicals catering for a new, expanding reading public avid for easy information about science, history, politics and the world at large.

p. 39 **Daughter of Uranus and the sea**. Hesiod relates that the love goddess, Aphrodite, born of the seed of Uranus, castrated by Cronos, rose fully formed from the sea.

p. 64 **Behemoth**. A giant beast mentioned in the biblical 'Book of Job.'

p. 67 **William Archer** (1856–1924). Translator of Ibsen, writer on drama. His play *The Green Goddess* was produced in 1921. He had begun collaborating with Shaw on another play, an unlikely partnership which soon collapsed, but Shaw eventually rediscovered and finished the work, his first play, *Widowers' Houses*.

p. 70 **Clement Scott** (1841–1904). Powerful drama critic for the *Sunday Times* and, best remembered, on the *Daily Telegraph*.

p. 90 **Hughenden**. Hughenden Manor. Disraeli's Buckinghamshire mansion.

p. 96 **Marie Correlli** (1855–1924). Popular romantic novelist, of extravagant prose, much admired by Queen Victoria, author of such best-sellers as *The Sorrows of Satan*.

p. 115 **Overman**. Often translated 'Superman' with later and misleading associations with brute strength and supernatural abilities.

Nietzsche was upholding the necessity for human beings to transcend by will and energy their normal personalities, weakened by stale and sentimental beliefs, squeamishness, negation, thus reaching a higher self, a superior consciousness, and anticipating a culture liberated from the enervating qualities of meekness, tolerance, indiscriminate benevolence, more suited to slaves than to the 'overman'.

p.130 Samuel **Smiles** (1812–1905). Biographer and journalist. His *Self Help* (1859), enthusing about the rewards of personal industry, determination, morality, won huge acclaim, and appeared in seventeen languages.

p.131 **Sartor Resartus**. An allegorical satire by Thomas Carlyle (1795–1881). Together with much else it discusses the symbolism and motivation of clothes.

p.131 Frederick William **Farrar** (1831–1903). Master of Marlborough, Dean of Canterbury, author of lives of Jesus and St Paul, historical romances, and moral tales of youth, including *Eric, or Little by Little*.

p.133 **Sesame and Lilies**. Published 1865. One of Ruskin's collections of lectures outlining the moral and practical responsibilities of men and women. It was unlikely to appeal greatly to Kipps.

p.157 George **Morland** (1763–1804). British painter, mostly of landscapes, country lives and livelihoods.

p.168 **Lacoon**. A Trojan priest of Apollo, overwhelmed with his two sons by sea serpents sent by gods angered by his warnings against the wooden horse.

p.177 **Christian** ... Anglican hymn, adapted by J. M. Neale from a Greek original, beginning 'Christian, dost thou see them/On the holy ground,/How the troops of Midian/ Prowl and prowl around.'

p.187 ... **Mr Kipling's best-known songs**. See his *Barrack Room Ballads* for *The Ladies*, beginning 'I've taken my fun where I've found it', and ending with the famous 'The Colonel's Lady and Judy O'Grady/ Are sisters under their skins.'

p.224 **Harmonicon**. An ancestor of the juke box.

p.244 **Iguanodon** ... giant monsters of the pre-human Mezozoic age vividly described in *The Outline of History*.

p.266 **Tantalus**. A stand containing wines or spirits, protected from guests' hands by being kept behind glass. Named from the Greek son of Zeus, condemned for treachery to stand in Hades surrounded by food and drink, which receded when he attempted to reach them.

p.279 **The Dunciad**. Alexander Pope's satirical poem (1728), mocking the lesser poets of his day for mediocrity, pretentiousness, dullness.

H. G. WELLS AND HIS CRITICS

The best novel in the last forty years.
>   Henry James to a Cambridge University literary group, 1909

Dear Wells . . . *Kipps* is not so much a masterpiece as a mere born gem – you having, I know not how, taken a header straight down into mysterious depths and observation, and knowledge . . . it is of such a brilliancy of *true* truth.
>   Henry James, 1905

An infernally good book . . . I refuse absolutely to be modest about it.
>   H. G. Wells to Frederick Macmillan, 1905

Dear Wells . . . this is a great work . . .
>   Joseph Conrad, 1905

This book, with its rich comic detail, its comedy springing, as all fine comedy must, from strong feeling, was something more than a promise of genius wider, and more profuse, if not so nearly perfect, than anything to be seen from the earlier books.
>   Edward Shanks, Introduction to a 1928 edition

Impatient of detail, mysteriously reticent about the immediate practical steps we must take to ensure any of his policies, Wells believes – like Kipps, in magic: a magic induced by impudence and rebellion.
>   V. S. Pritchett, *Collected Essays*, 1991

When that comic genius has free play, as it has in *Kipps* there may be – there is – the air of improvization to which Henry James objected in *The New Machiavelli*. But although *Kipps* may stumble, it stumbles from point to point, from one comic invention to another, and is a feast of character.
>   Frank Swinnerton, *The Georgian Literary Scene*, 1935

Of all his books, *Kipps* meant most to him. It was the first long novel of character he had embarked on, and it was about himself and the things he knew of . . .
Kipps and *Mr Polly* are wonderful examples of character, sharp

observation, humour and insight, essentially new and 'modern' because they looked at life and contemporary society from the standpoint of a very large and neglected class, the struggling and confused lower-middle class of clerks and shop assistants.

Lovat Dickson, *H.G. Wells*, 1969

Kipps and *Mr Polly* are in the end . . . frankly fairy tales or escapades. They celebrate individual oddities and imperfections, the wild fantasies lurking behind the average human façade. They renew a tradition which since Dickens has been running downhill into the wastes of facetious journalism.

John Gross, *The New Statesman*, 1969

When he began *Kipps*, Wells let his comic genius have free play, and the first two of its three parts show a sureness of touch he never surpassed. They brilliantly describe the origins of Artie Kipps, the servitude of his apprenticeship and his schooling in gentility.

Norman and Jeanne Mackenzie, *The Time Traveller*, 1973

Wells is an important writer for the cultural historian, because he was himself always a historian – of the immediate present, or of the moment that has just past, or on occasion of the future. His ideas were always up to date, or a bit beyond, and so were his feelings.

Samuel Hynes *A War Imagined*, 1991

BIBLIOGRAPHY AND
SUGGESTIONS FOR FURTHER READING

Arnold Bennett, *Journals* (Harmondsworth: Penguin, 1953)
Bernard Bergonzi, *The Early H. G. Wells* (Manchester, 1961)
Michael Coren, *The Invisible Man* (London:Bloomsbury, 1992)
Lovat Dickson, *H. G. Wells 1969* (London:Macmillan, 1969)
John Gross, *The Road to Utopia* (London:*The New Statesman*, 1969)
Samuel Hynes, *A War Imagined* (New York: Atheneum, 1991)
Christopher Isherwood, *Exhumations* (London: Methuen, 1966)
Norman and Jeanne Mackenzie, *The Time Traveller* (Weidenfeld & Nicholson, 1973)
George Orwell, 'Wells, Hitler and the World State', in *Critical Essays* (London:Secker & Warburg, 1946)
V. S. Pritchett, *Collected Essays* (London: Chatto & Windus, 1991)
Frank Swinnerton, *The Georgian Literary Scene* (London:Hutchinson, 1935)
Peter Vansittart, *Voices 1870–1914* (London:Jonathan Cape, 1984)
Virginia Woolf, *The Common Reader* (London:The Hogarth Press, 1923)

TEXT SUMMARY

BOOK ONE THE MAKING OF KIPPS

Chapter 1 The Little Shop at New Romney

Arthur Kipps, an orphan, is raised by his deeply respectable uncle and aunt; he loathes school; he and his friend's sister, Ann Pornick, pledge themselves to each other.

Chapter 2 The Emporium

Kipps goes to Folkestone to work for Mr Shalford, the draper. On returning home at Christmas, he finds Ann gone.

Chapter 3 The Woodcarving Class

Kipps goes to evening woodcarving classes, where he falls in love with his teacher, the goddess-like Helen Walshingham.

Chapter 4 Chitterlow

Chitterlow, a minor playwright, knocks Kipps down with his bicycle, an encounter which leads to a drunken night out.

Chapter 5 Swapped!

Failing to return to Shalford's before curfew because of his meeting with Chitterlow, Kipps is dismissed.

Chapter 6 The Unexpected

Kipps' predicament is resolved by a large and unexpected legacy.

BOOK TWO MR COOTE THE CHAPERON

Chapter 1 The New Conditions

With money, a large house and servants, Kipps enters the 'higher culture' and is taken in hand by the snobbish Chester Coote.

Chapter 2 The Walshinghams

Kipps meets Helen Walshingham while at Mr Coote's; he then goes to the Walshinghams' for tea.

Chapter 3 Engaged

Helen Walshingham and Kipps become engaged; she promises to educate him in the ways of a gentleman.

Chapter 4 The Bicycle Manufacturer

While on a visit to his uncle and aunt, Kipps meets Sid Pornick, now a bicycle manufacturer in London, and a socialist.

Chapter 5 The Pupil Lover

Aided by Coote and Helen, Kipps learns how to be a gentleman; in so doing he loses his former friends.

Chapter 6 Discords

Kipps meets Ann Pornick and remembers their pledge; he is nagged by Helen and starts to dread social gatherings. His aunt and uncle announce they are coming to see him.

Chapter 7 London

Kipps flees to London where he meets Sid Pornick and the socialist journalist Masterman. Out of his depth at the lavish Grand Hotel, he returns to Folkestone.

Chapter 8 Kipps Enters Society

Back in Folkestone, Kipps puts up money to finance Chitterlow's play. Attending Mrs Bindon Botting's tea, he meets Ann Pornick, the lady's maid, and hastily leaves in confusion. Later, he excuses himself from a dinner party, finds Ann and proposes to her.

Chapter 9 The Labyrinthodon

Kipps and Ann go to London where they are made welcome by Sid and Masterman; they plan their future and get married.

BOOK THREE KIPPSES

Chapter 1 The Housing Problem

The couple look for a house but fail to find one they like. Kipps commissions an architect to design one, but the plans are grander than either of them had in mind.

Chapter 2 The Callers

Kipps feels unsettled and his mood is made worse when Ann tells him she turned away visitors from the house.

Chapter 3 Terminations

Helen Walshingham's brother has embezzled Kipps' fortune and they face ruin. But Chitterlow's play is a great success, its royalties rescue them and they are left happily with a home, a child and a small bookshop.

CLASSIC NOVELS
IN EVERYMAN

A SELECTION

The Way of All Flesh
SAMUEL BUTLER
A savagely funny odyssey from joy-less duty to unbridled liberalism **£4.99**

Born in Exile
GEORGE GISSING
A rationalist's progress towards love and compromise in class-ridden Victorian England **£4.99**

David Copperfield
CHARLES DICKENS
One of Dickens' best-loved novels, brimming with humour **£3.99**

The Last Chronicle of Barset
ANTHONY TROLLOPE
Trollope's magnificent conclusion to his Barsetshire novels **£4.99**

He Knew He Was Right
ANTHONY TROLLOPE
Sexual jealousy, money and women's rights within marriage – a novel ahead of its time **£6.99**

Tess of the D'Urbervilles
THOMAS HARDY
The powerful, poetic classic of wronged innocence **£3.99**

Wuthering Heights and Poems
EMILY BRONTE
A powerful work of genius – one of the great masterpieces of literature **£3.50**

Tom Jones
HENRY FIELDING
The wayward adventures of one of literatures most likable heroes **£5.99**

The Master of Ballantrae and Weir of Hermiston
R. L. STEVENSON
Together in one volume, two great novels of high adventure and family conflict **£4.99**

£3.99

£2.99

£3.99

AVAILABILITY

All books are available from your local bookshop or direct from
Littlehampton Book Services Cash Sales, 14 Eldon Way, LinesideEstate, Littlehampton, West Sussex BN17 7HE. PRICES ARE SUBJECT TO CHANGE.

To order any of the books, please enclose a cheque (in £ sterling) made payable to Littlehampton Book Services, or phone your order through with credit card details (Access, Visa or Mastercard) on 0903 721596 (24 hour answering service) stating card number and expiry date. Please add £1.25 for package and postage to the total value of your order.

CLASSIC FICTION
IN EVERYMAN

A SELECTION

Frankenstein

MARY SHELLEY
A masterpiece of Gothic terror in its
original 1818 version **£3.99**

Dracula

BRAM STOKER
One of the best known horror stories
in the world **£3.99**

The Diary of A Nobody

GEORGE AND WEEDON
GROSSMITH
A hilarious account of suburban life
in Edwardian London **£4.99**

Some Experiences
and Further Experiences
of an Irish R. M.

SOMERVILLE AND ROSS
Gems of comic exuberance and
improvisation **£4.50**

Three Men in a Boat

JEROME K. JEROME
English humour at its best **£2.99**

Twenty Thousand Leagues
under the Sea

JULES VERNE
Scientific fact combines with
fantasy in this prophetic tale of
underwater adventure **£4.99**

The Best of Father Brown

G. K. CHESTERTON
An irresistible selection of crime
stories – unique to Everyman **£3.99**

The Collected Raffles

E. W. HORNUNG
Dashing exploits from the most glam-
orous figure in crime fiction **£4.99**

£2.99

£5.99

£5.99

AVAILABILITY

All books are available from your local bookshop or direct from
Littlehampton Book Services Cash Sales, 14 Eldon Way, LinesideEstate,
Littlehampton, West Sussex BN17 7HE. PRICES ARE SUBJECT TO CHANGE.

To order any of the books, please enclose a cheque (in £ sterling) made payable to
Littlehampton Book Services, or phone your order through with credit card details (Access,
Visa or Mastercard) on 0903 721596 (24 hour answering service) stating card number and
expiry date. Please add £1.25 for package and postage to the total value of your order.